ラグーンエンジン
LAGOON ENGINE

YUKIRU SUGISAKI

VOLUME 1

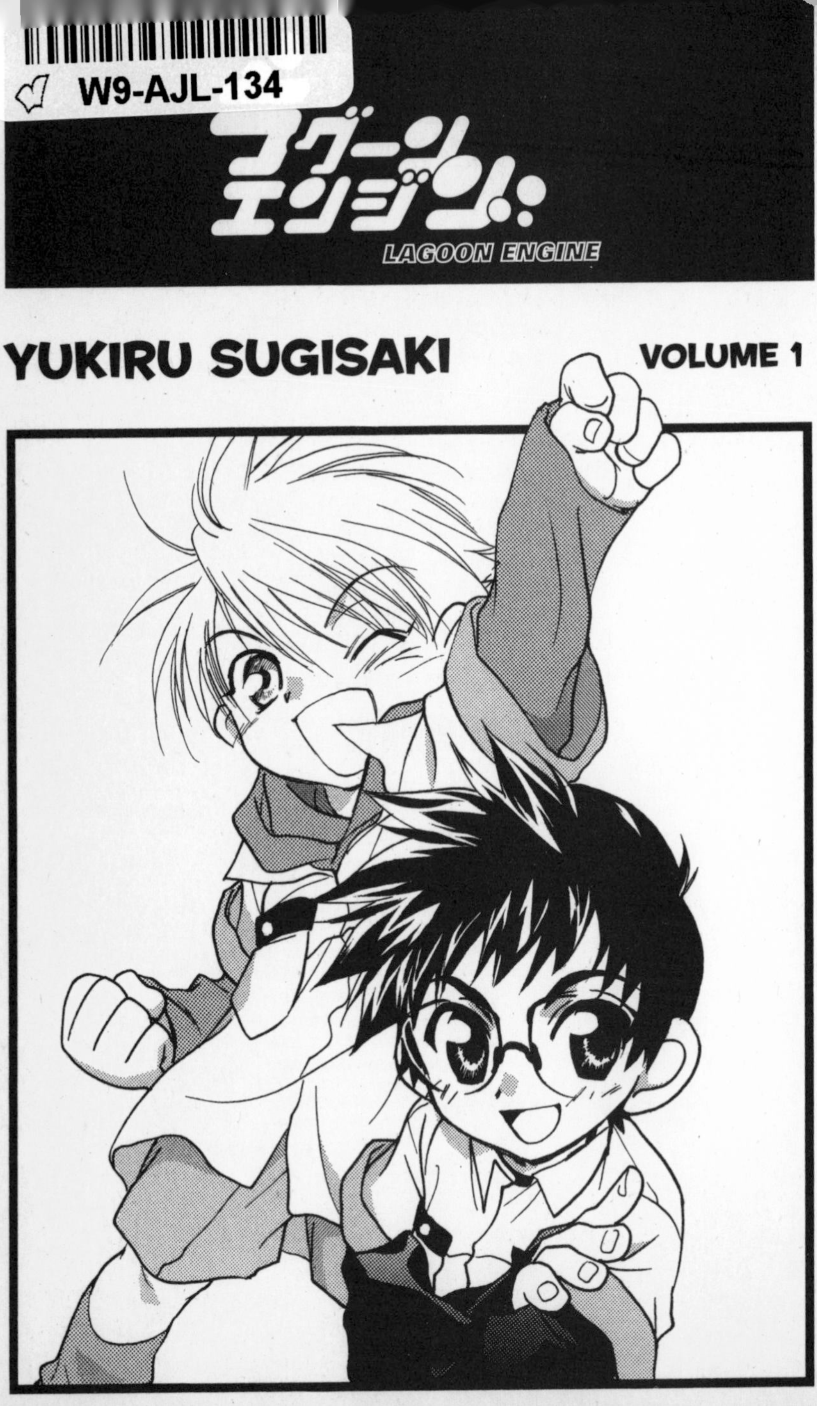

Lagoon Engine Vol. 1
Created by Yukiru Sugisaki

Translation - Alethea and Athena Nibley
Associate Editor - Peter Ahlstrom
Retouch and Lettering - Eva Han
Production Artist - James Lee
Cover Design - Gary Shum

Editor - Paul Morrissey
Digital Imaging Manager - Chris Buford
Pre-Press Manager - Antonio DePietro
Production Managers - Jennifer Miller and Mutsumi Miyazaki
Art Director - Matt Alford
Managing Editor - Jill Freshney
VP of Production - Ron Klamert
Editor-in-Chief - Mike Kiley
President and C.O.O. - John Parker
Publisher and C.E.O. - Stuart Levy

A  Manga

TOKYOPOP Inc.
5900 Wilshire Blvd. Suite 2000
Los Angeles, CA 90036

E-mail: info@TOKYOPOP.com
Come visit us online at www.TOKYOPOP.com

ISBN: 1-59532-359-7

First TOKYOPOP printing: January 2005
10 9 8 7 6 5 4 3 2 1
Printed in the USA

ラグーンエンジン

LAGOON ENGINE

VOLUME 1

BY
YUKIRU SUGISAKI

HAMBURG // LONDON // LOS ANGELES // TOKYO

CONTENTS

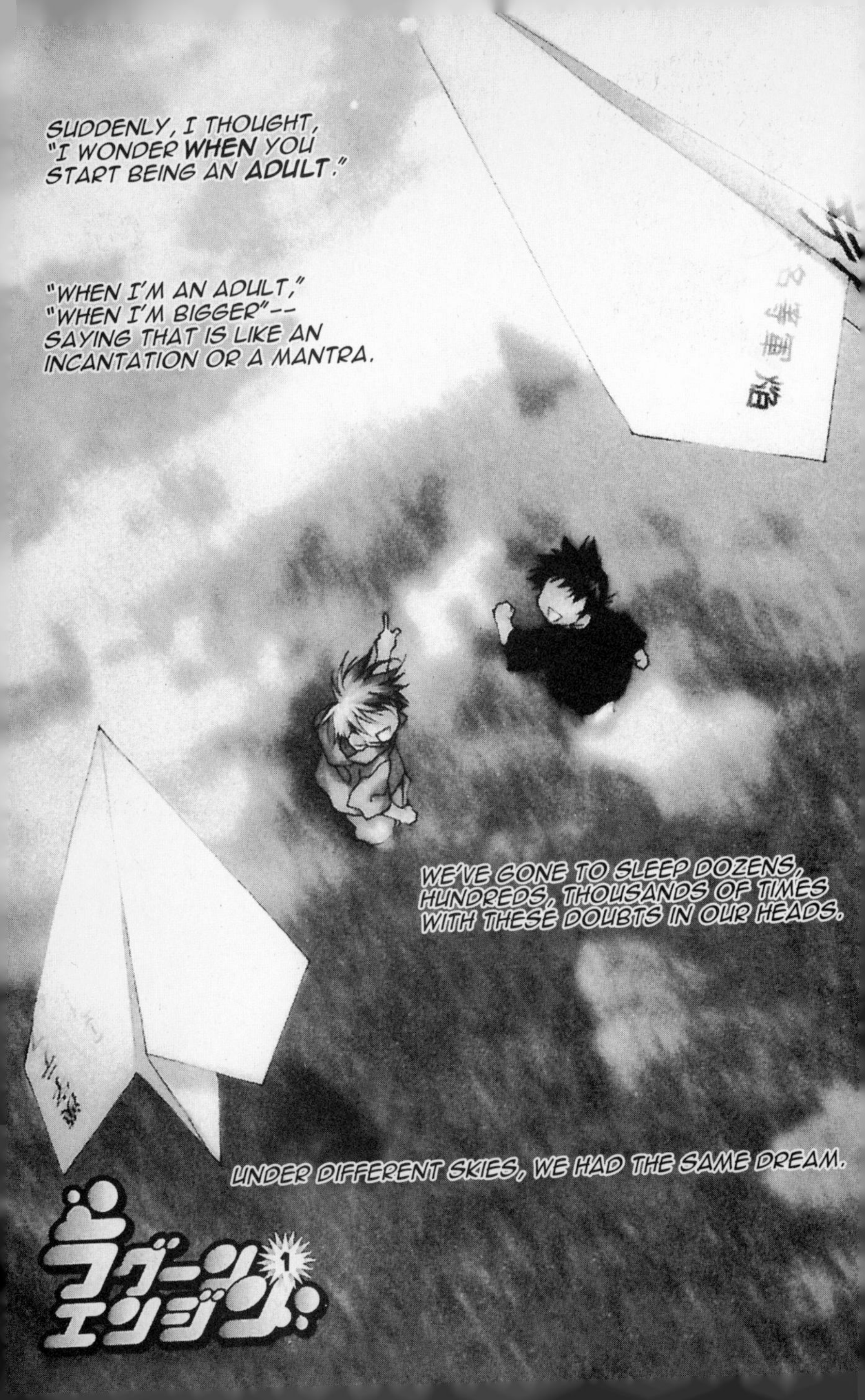
SUDDENLY, I THOUGHT, "I WONDER WHEN YOU START BEING AN ADULT."
"WHEN I'M AN ADULT," "WHEN I'M BIGGER"-- SAYING THAT IS LIKE AN INCANTATION OR A MANTRA.
WE'VE GONE TO SLEEP DOZENS, HUNDREDS, THOUSANDS OF TIMES WITH THESE DOUBTS IN OUR HEADS.
UNDER DIFFERENT SKIES, WE HAD THE SAME DREAM.
ラグーンエンジン
1

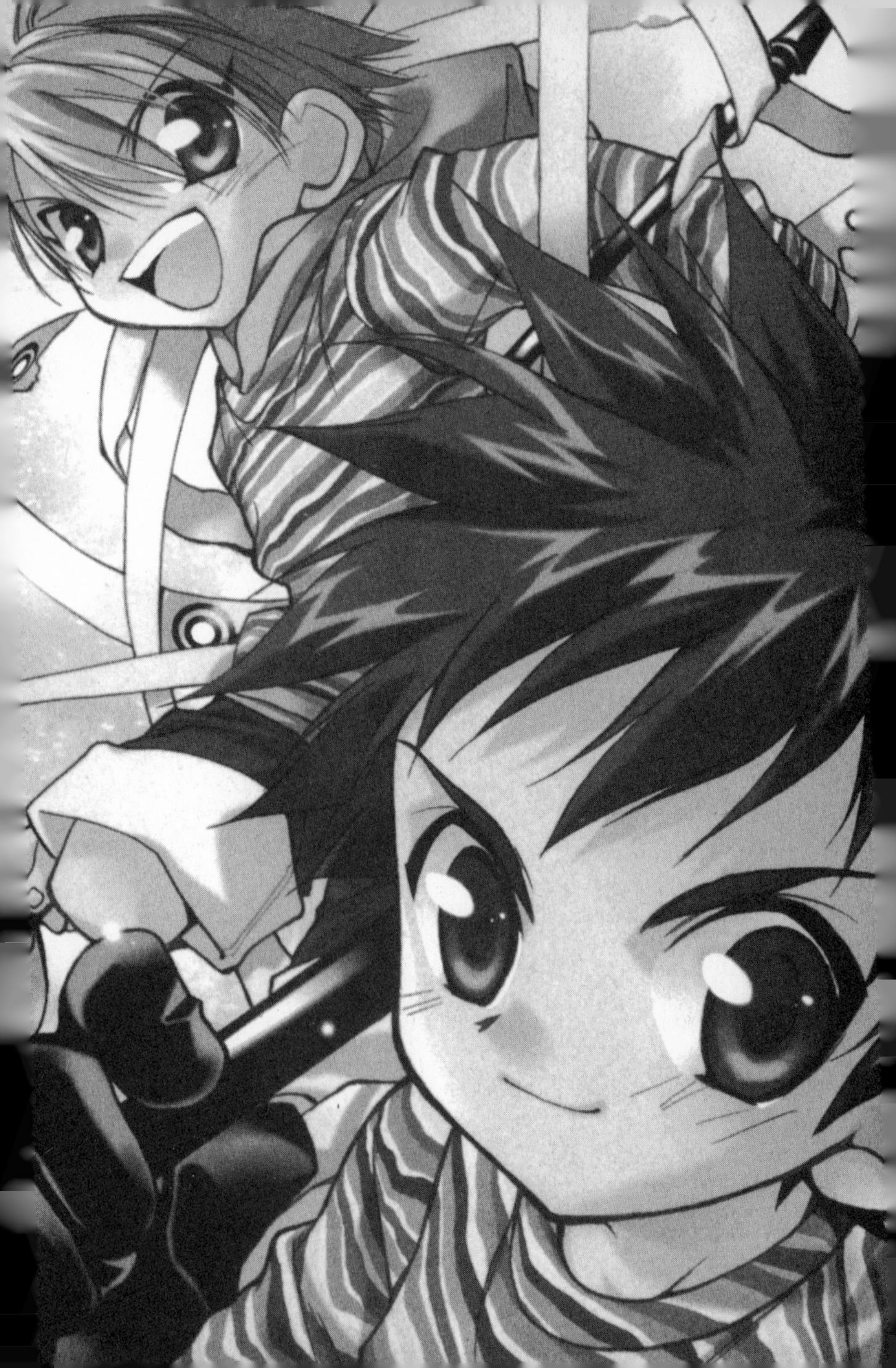

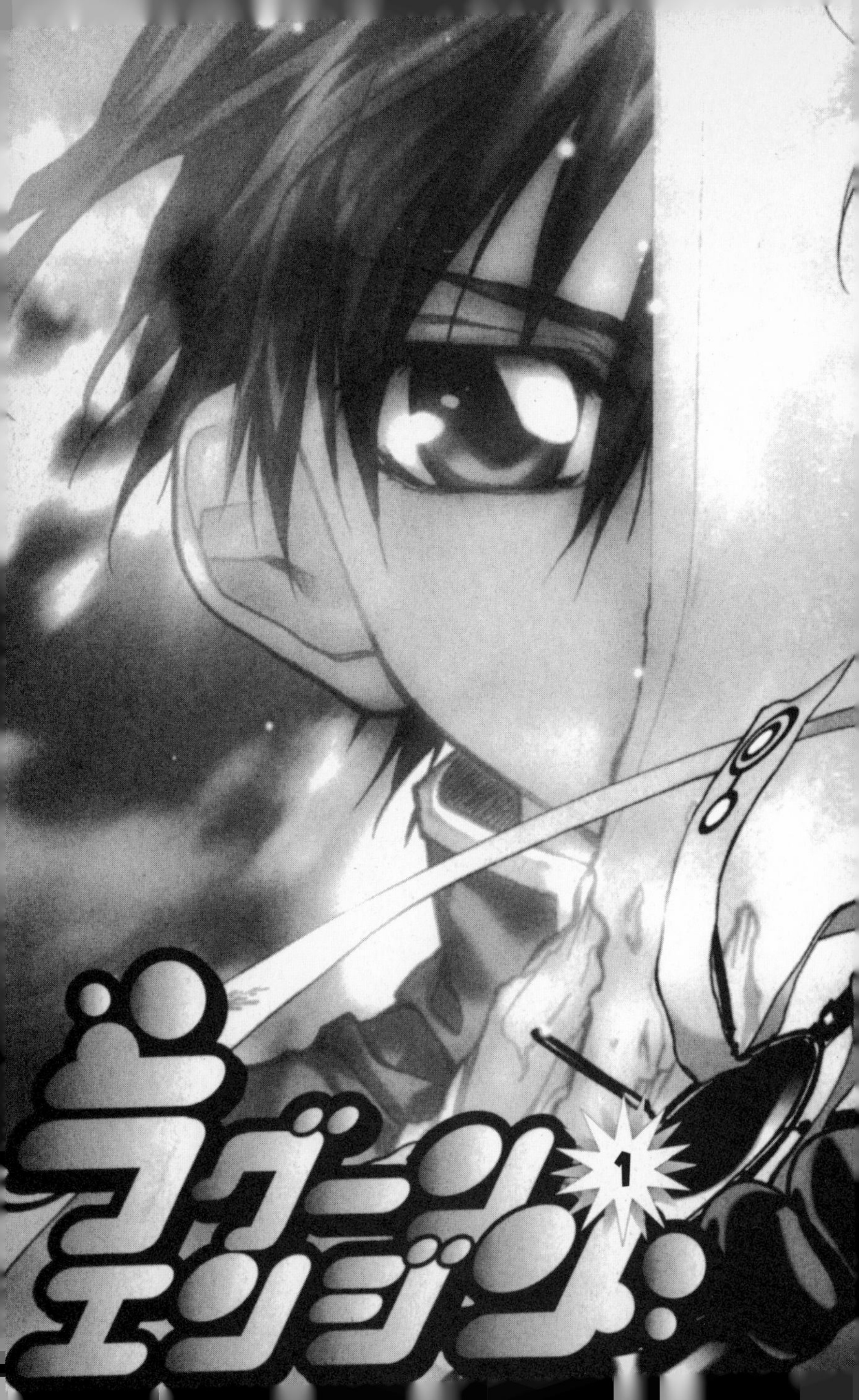
ラグーンエンジン
1

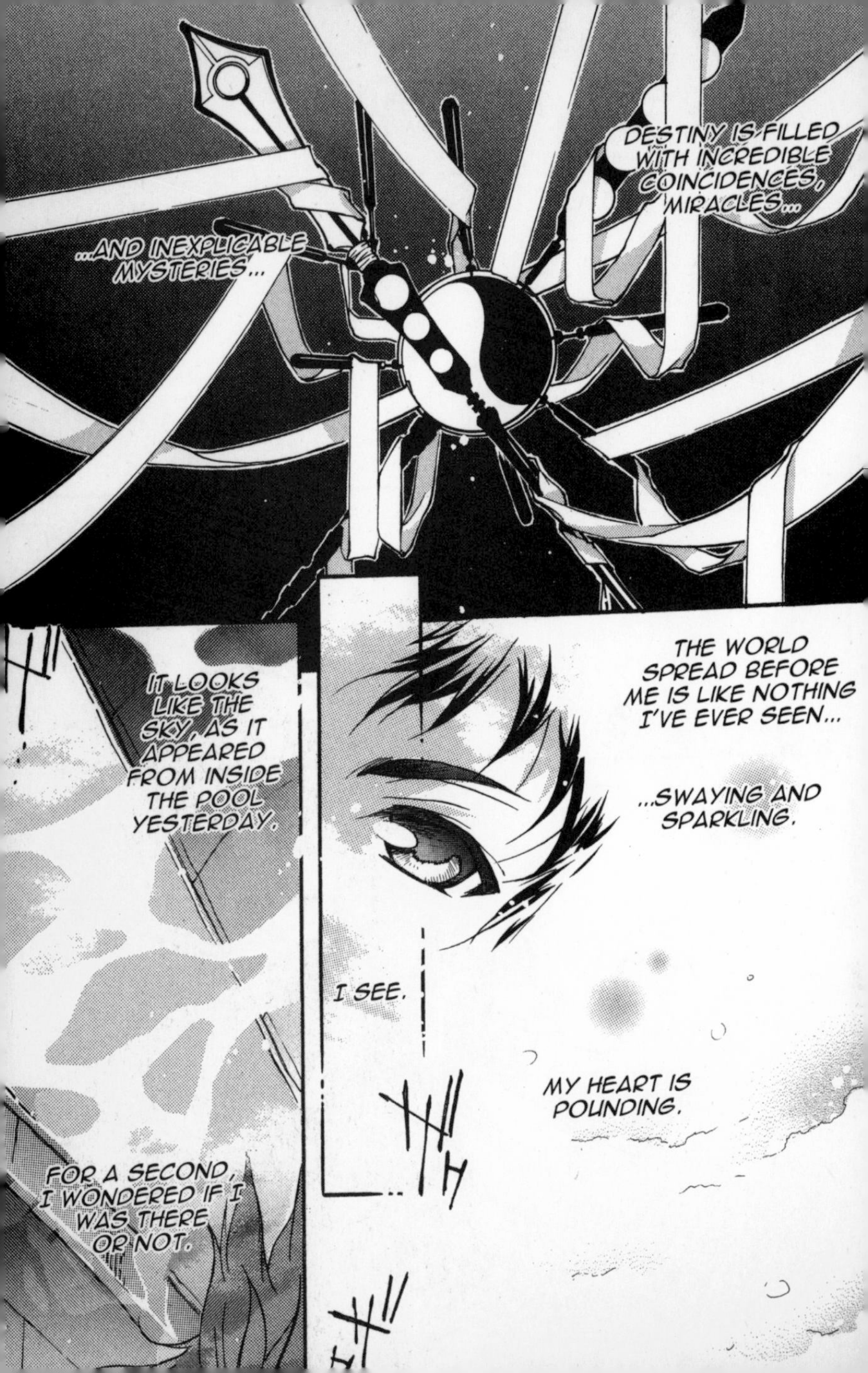
DESTINY IS FILLED WITH INCREDIBLE COINCIDENCES, MIRACLES...
...AND INEXPLICABLE MYSTERIES...
THE WORLD SPREAD BEFORE ME IS LIKE NOTHING I'VE EVER SEEN...
...SWAYING AND SPARKLING.
I SEE.
MY HEART IS POUNDING.
IT LOOKS LIKE THE SKY, AS IT APPEARED FROM INSIDE THE POOL YESTERDAY.
FOR A SECOND, I WONDERED IF I WAS THERE OR NOT.

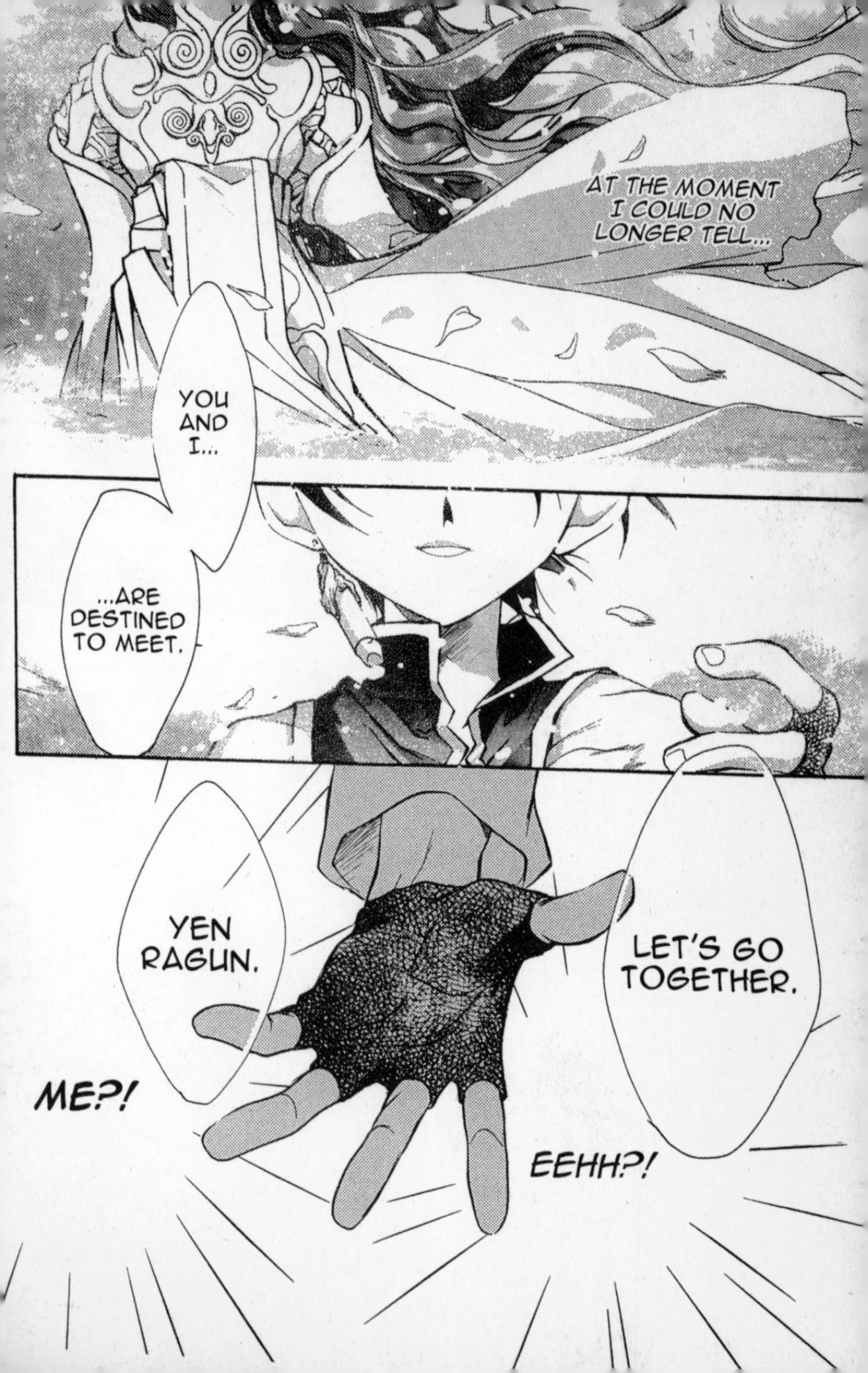
AT THE MOMENT I COULD NO LONGER TELL...
YOU AND I...
...ARE DESTINED TO MEET.
LET'S GO TOGETHER.
YEN RAGUN.
EEHH?!
ME?!

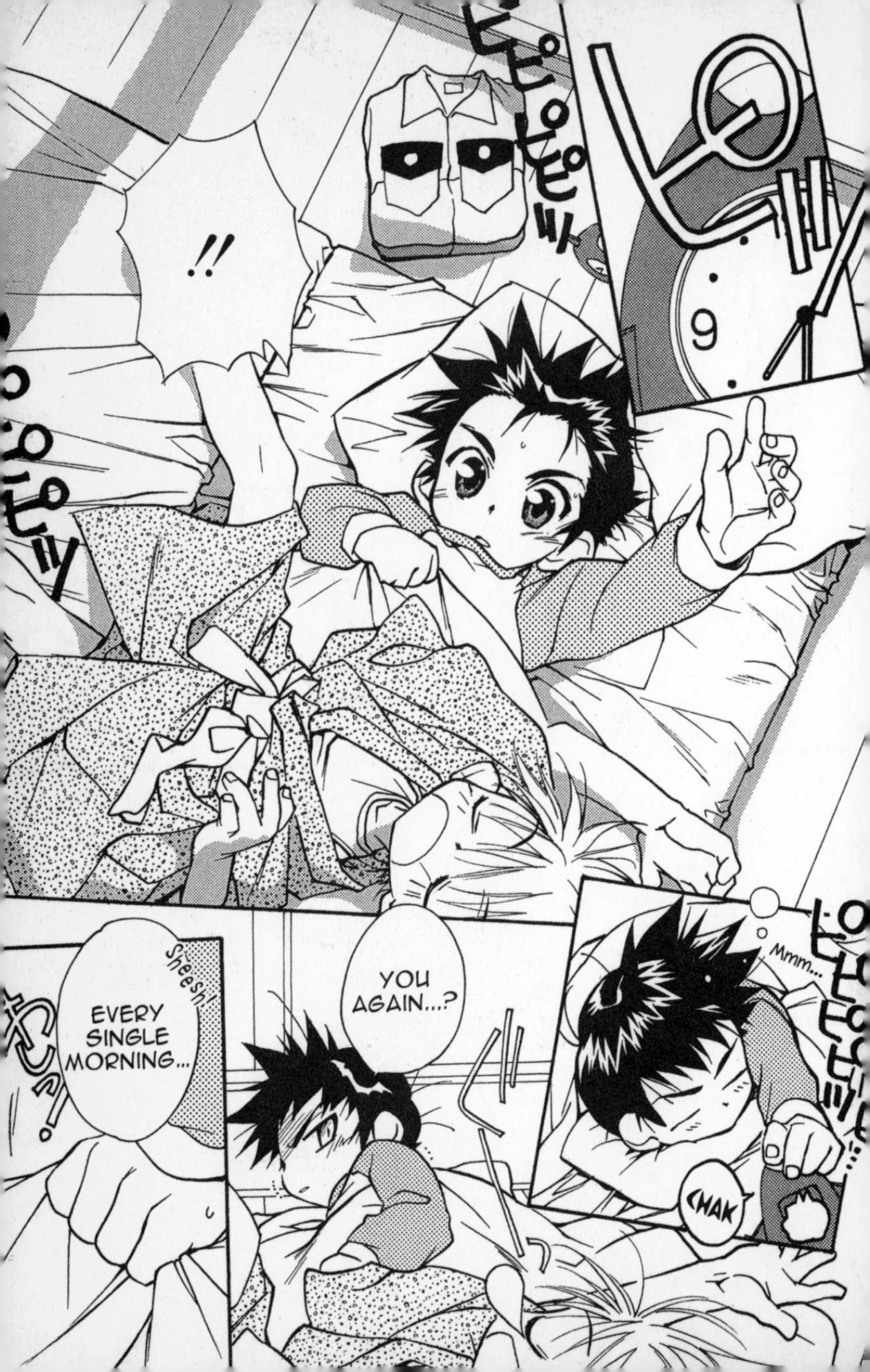
!!
Mmm...
CHAK
YOU AGAIN...?
Sheesh!
EVERY SINGLE MORNING...

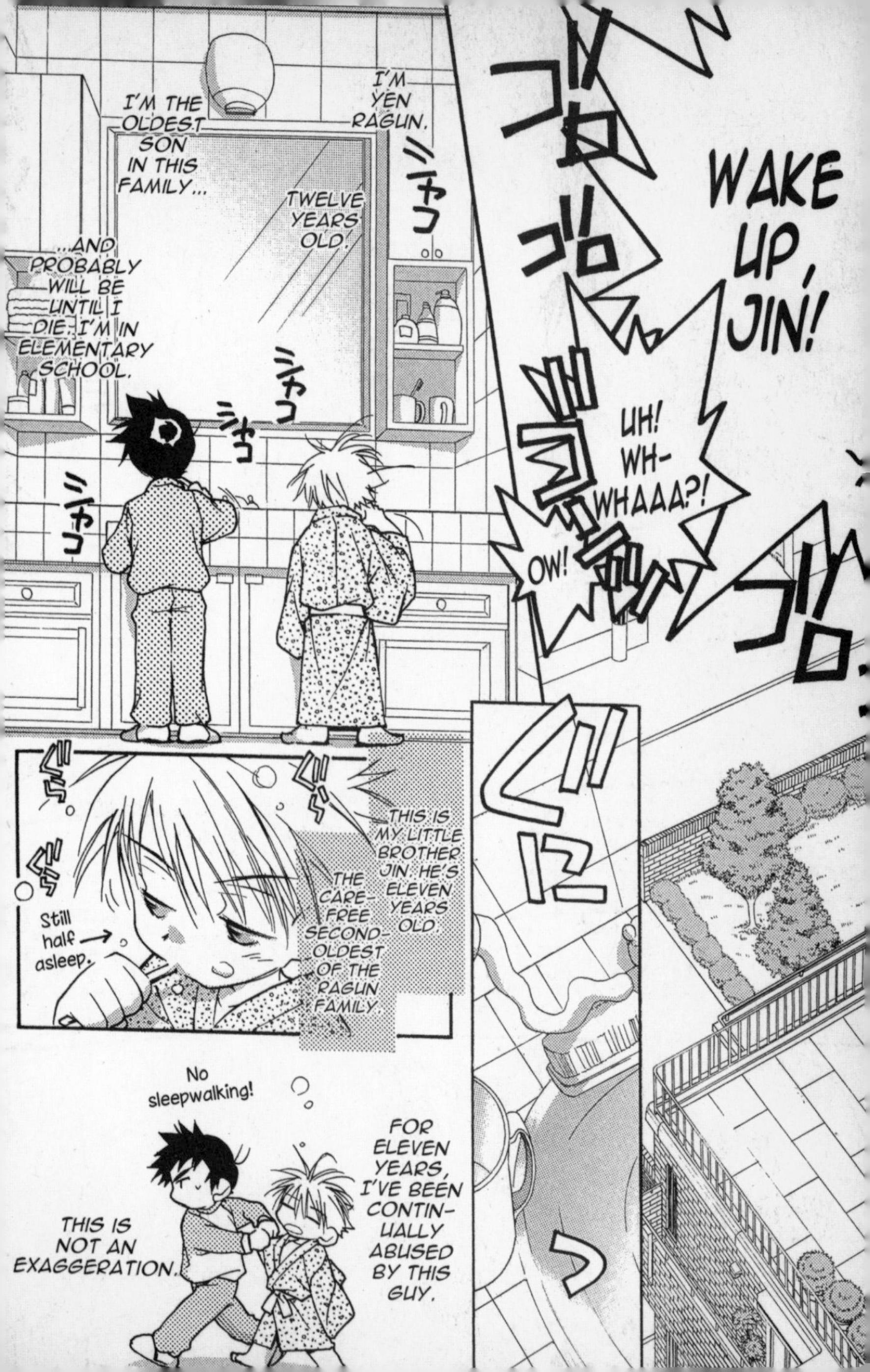
ゴロ
ゴロ
WAKE UP, JIN!
UH! WH-WHAAA?!
OW!
ゴロ
ぐに
つ
I'M YEN RAGUN.
TWELVE YEARS OLD.
I'M THE OLDEST SON IN THIS FAMILY...
...AND PROBABLY WILL BE UNTIL I DIE. I'M IN ELEMENTARY SCHOOL.
シャコ
シャコ
シャコ
シャコ
ぐら
ぐら
ぐら
THIS IS MY LITTLE BROTHER JIN. HE'S ELEVEN YEARS OLD.
THE CAREFREE SECOND-OLDEST OF THE RAGUN FAMILY.
Still half asleep.
FOR ELEVEN YEARS, I'VE BEEN CONTINUALLY ABUSED BY THIS GUY.
No sleepwalking!
THIS IS NOT AN EXAGGERATION.

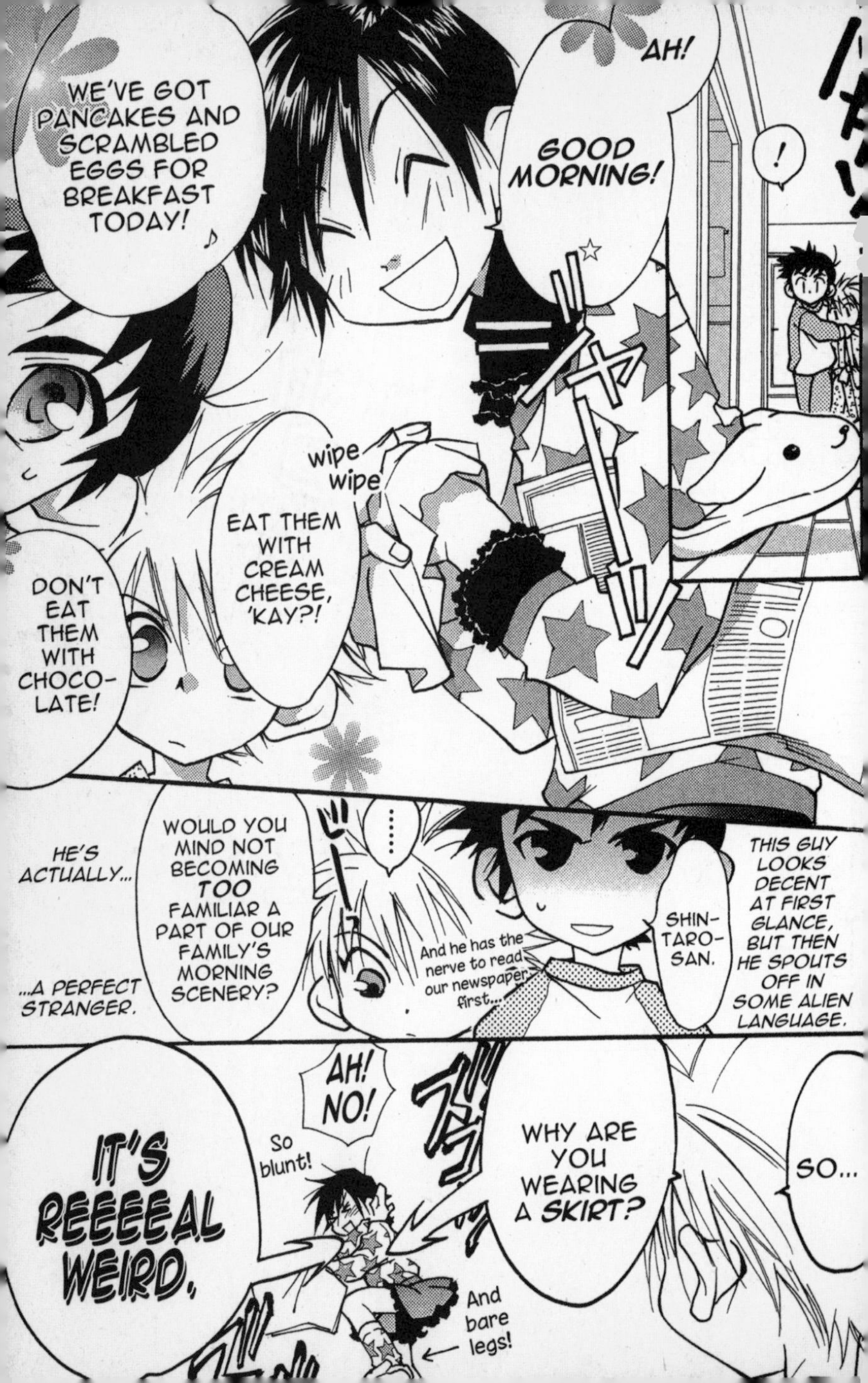
!
AH! GOOD MORNING!
WE'VE GOT PANCAKES AND SCRAMBLED EGGS FOR BREAKFAST TODAY! ♪
wipe wipe
EAT THEM WITH CREAM CHEESE, 'KAY?!
DON'T EAT THEM WITH CHOCOLATE!
THIS GUY LOOKS DECENT AT FIRST GLANCE, BUT THEN HE SPOUTS OFF IN SOME ALIEN LANGUAGE.
SHINTARO-SAN.
And he has the nerve to read our newspaper first...
......
WOULD YOU MIND NOT BECOMING TOO FAMILIAR A PART OF OUR FAMILY'S MORNING SCENERY?
HE'S ACTUALLY...
...A PERFECT STRANGER.
SO...
WHY ARE YOU WEARING A SKIRT?
AH! NO!
So blunt!
And bare legs!
IT'S REEEEEAL WEIRD.

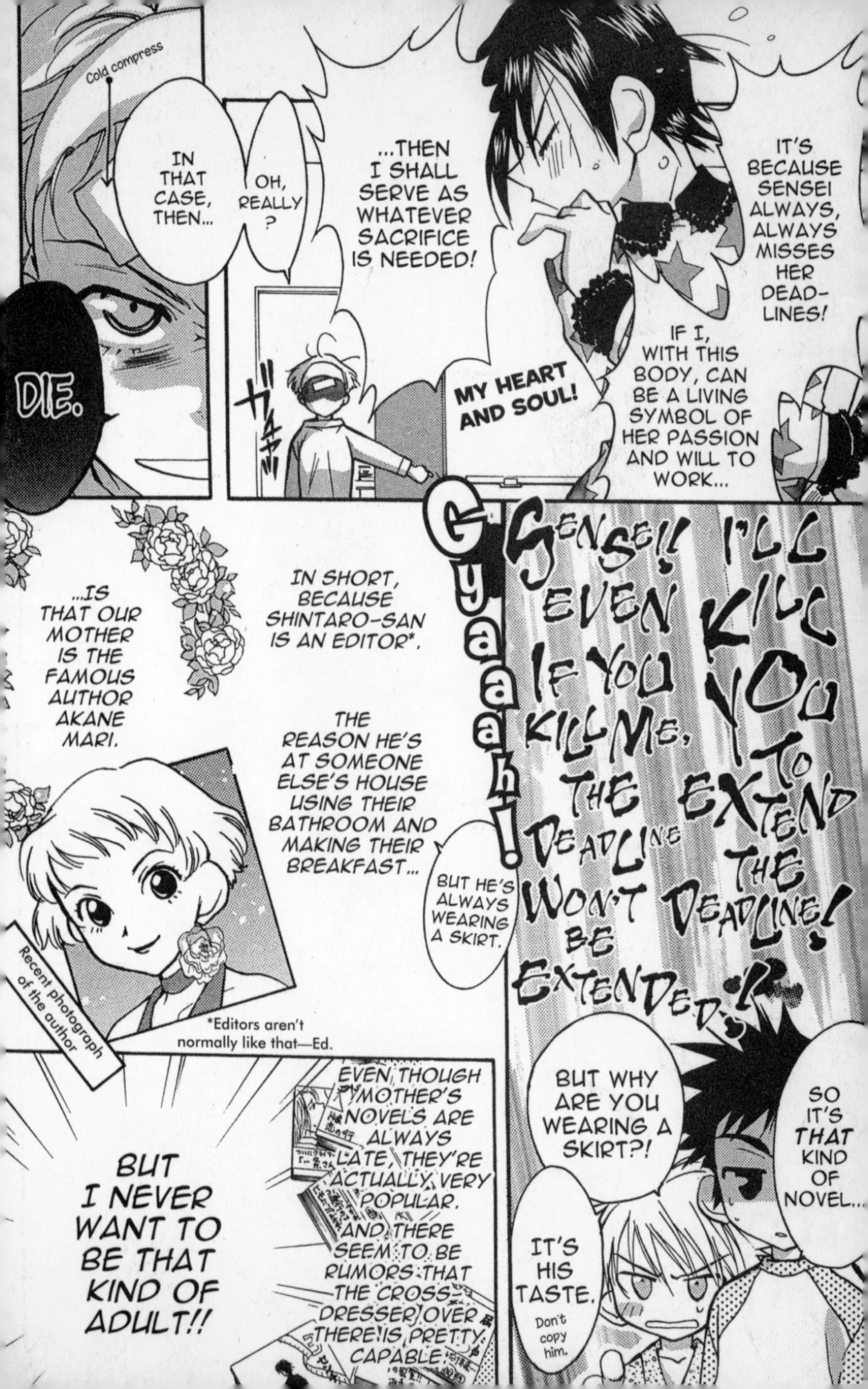
IT'S BECAUSE SENSEI ALWAYS, ALWAYS MISSES HER DEADLINES!
IF I, WITH THIS BODY, CAN BE A LIVING SYMBOL OF HER PASSION AND WILL TO WORK...
...THEN I SHALL SERVE AS WHATEVER SACRIFICE IS NEEDED!
MY HEART AND SOUL!
OH, REALLY?
Cold compress
IN THAT CASE, THEN...
DIE.
Gyaaah!
SENSEI!! EVEN IF YOU KILL ME, THE DEADLINE WON'T BE EXTENDED!?
I'LL KILL YOU TO EXTEND THE DEADLINE!
IN SHORT, BECAUSE SHINTARO-SAN IS AN EDITOR*.
THE REASON HE'S AT SOMEONE ELSE'S HOUSE USING THEIR BATHROOM AND MAKING THEIR BREAKFAST...
...IS THAT OUR MOTHER IS THE FAMOUS AUTHOR AKANE MARI.
BUT HE'S ALWAYS WEARING A SKIRT.
Recent photograph of the author
*Editors aren't normally like that—Ed.
SO IT'S THAT KIND OF NOVEL...
BUT WHY ARE YOU WEARING A SKIRT?!
IT'S HIS TASTE.
Don't copy him.
EVEN THOUGH MOTHER'S NOVELS ARE ALWAYS LATE, THEY'RE ACTUALLY VERY POPULAR. AND THERE SEEM TO BE RUMORS THAT THE CROSS-DRESSER OVER THERE IS PRETTY CAPABLE.
BUT I NEVER WANT TO BE THAT KIND OF ADULT!!

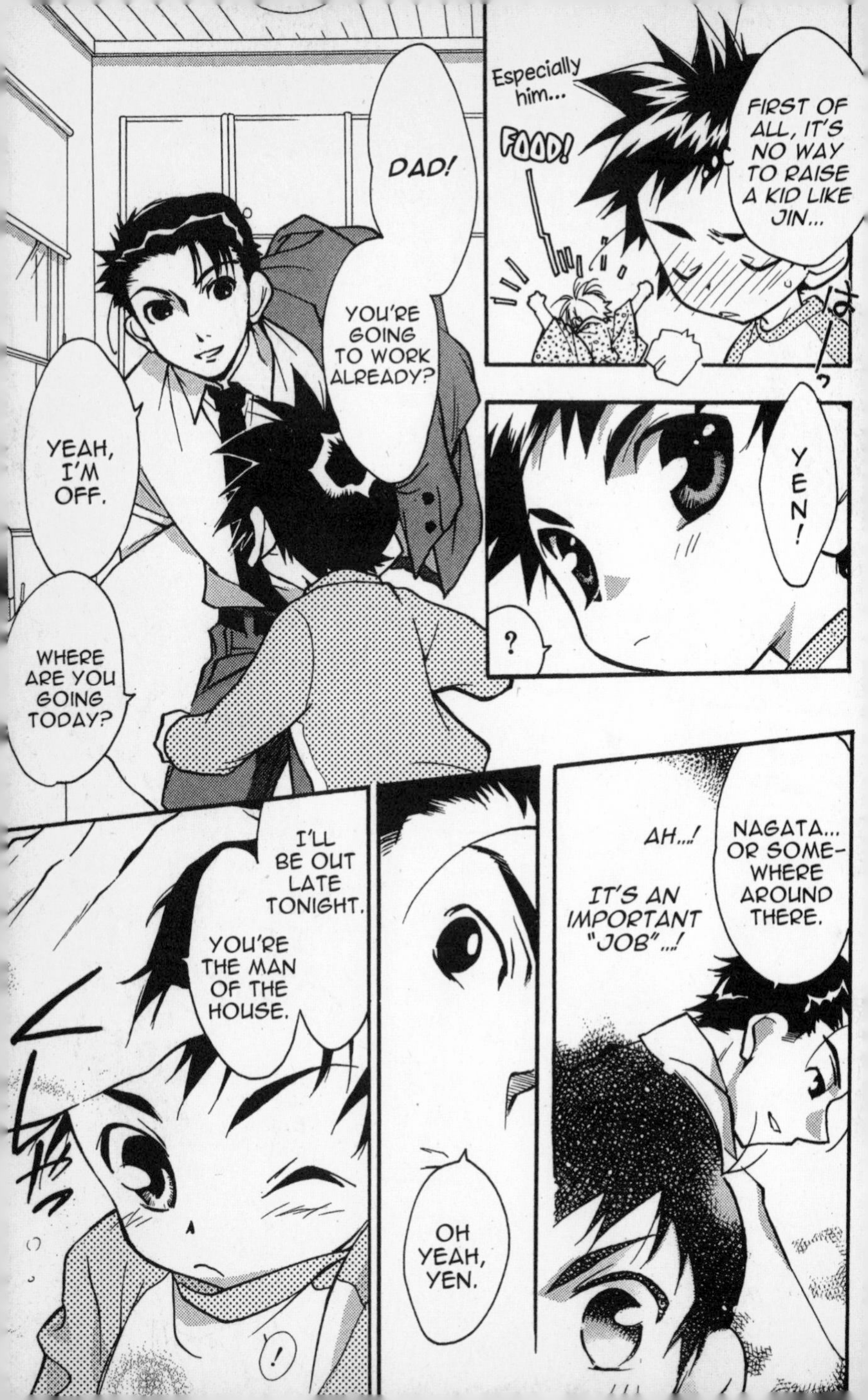
FIRST OF ALL, IT'S NO WAY TO RAISE A KID LIKE JIN...
Especially him...
FOOD!
YEN!
?
DAD!
YOU'RE GOING TO WORK ALREADY?
YEAH, I'M OFF.
WHERE ARE YOU GOING TODAY?
NAGATA... OR SOMEWHERE AROUND THERE.
AH...!
IT'S AN IMPORTANT "JOB"...!
OH YEAH, YEN.
I'LL BE OUT LATE TONIGHT.
YOU'RE THE MAN OF THE HOUSE.
!

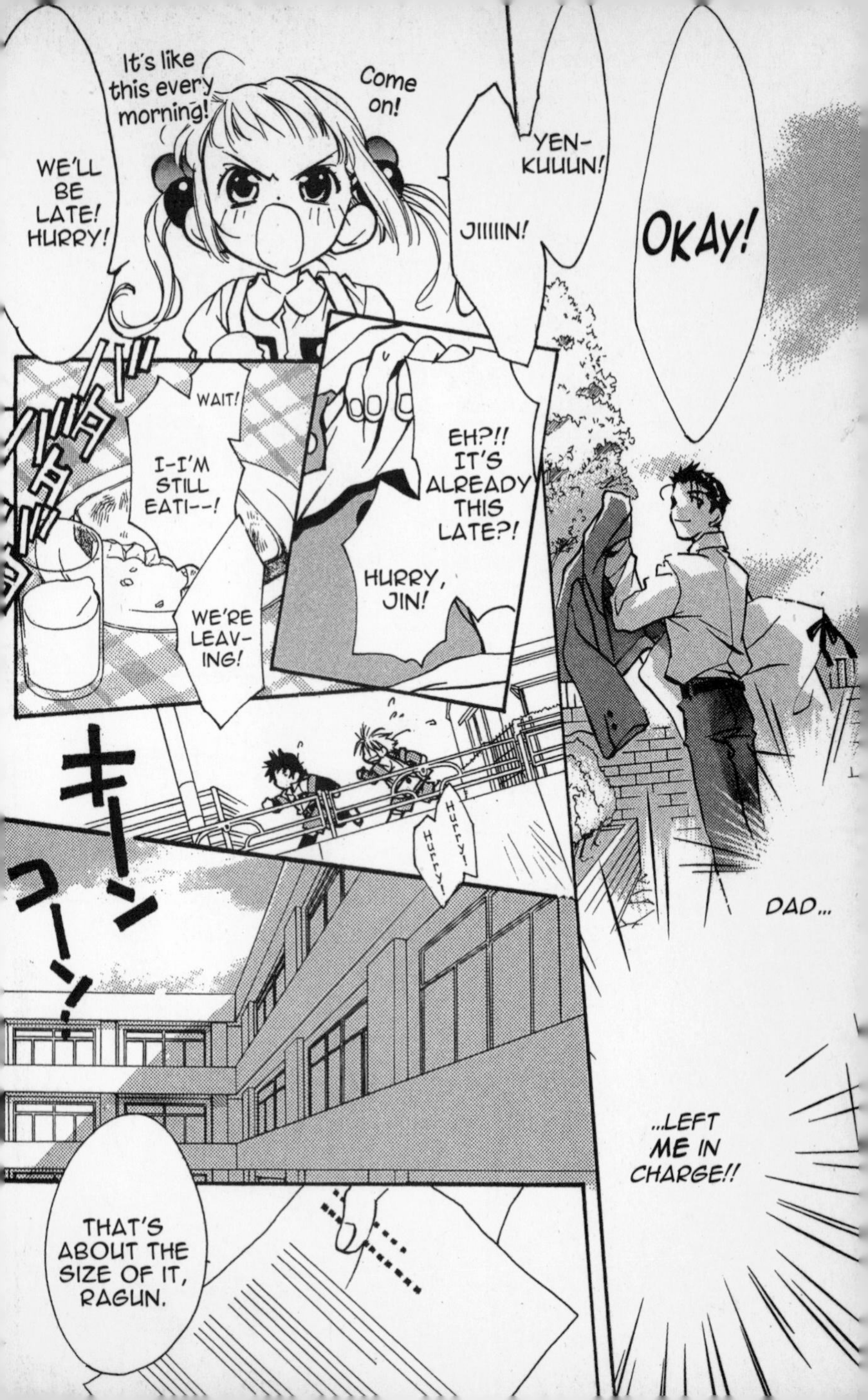
YEN-KUUUN!
JIIIIN!
Come on!
It's like this every morning!
WE'LL BE LATE! HURRY!
OKAY!
EH?!! IT'S ALREADY THIS LATE?!
HURRY, JIN!
WAIT!
I-I'M STILL EATI--!
WE'RE LEAVING!
Hurry!
Hurry!
キーン
コーン
DAD...
...LEFT ME IN CHARGE!!
THAT'S ABOUT THE SIZE OF IT, RAGUN.

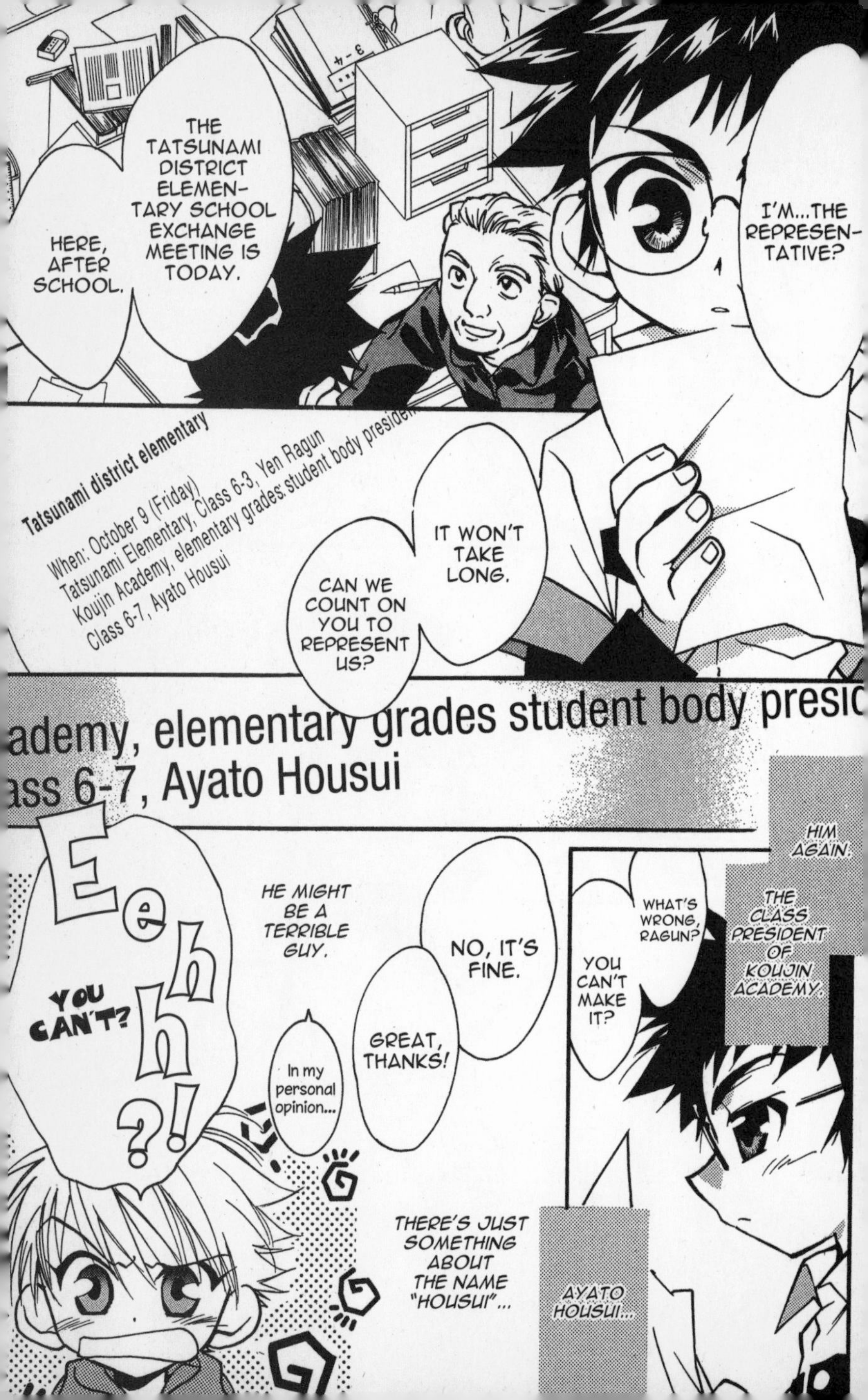
I'M...THE REPRESENTATIVE?
THE TATSUNAMI DISTRICT ELEMENTARY SCHOOL EXCHANGE MEETING IS TODAY.
HERE, AFTER SCHOOL.
Tatsunami district elementary
When: October 9 (Friday)
Tatsunami Elementary, Class 6-3, Yen Ragun
Koujin Academy, elementary grades: student body presid
Class 6-7, Ayato Housui
IT WON'T TAKE LONG.
CAN WE COUNT ON YOU TO REPRESENT US?
ademy, elementary grades student body presic
ass 6-7, Ayato Housui
HIM AGAIN.
THE CLASS PRESIDENT OF KOUJIN ACADEMY.
WHAT'S WRONG, RAGUN?
YOU CAN'T MAKE IT?
AYATO HOUSUI...
NO, IT'S FINE.
GREAT, THANKS!
HE MIGHT BE A TERRIBLE GUY.
THERE'S JUST SOMETHING ABOUT THE NAME "HOUSUI"...
In my personal opinion...
Eehh?!
YOU CAN'T?

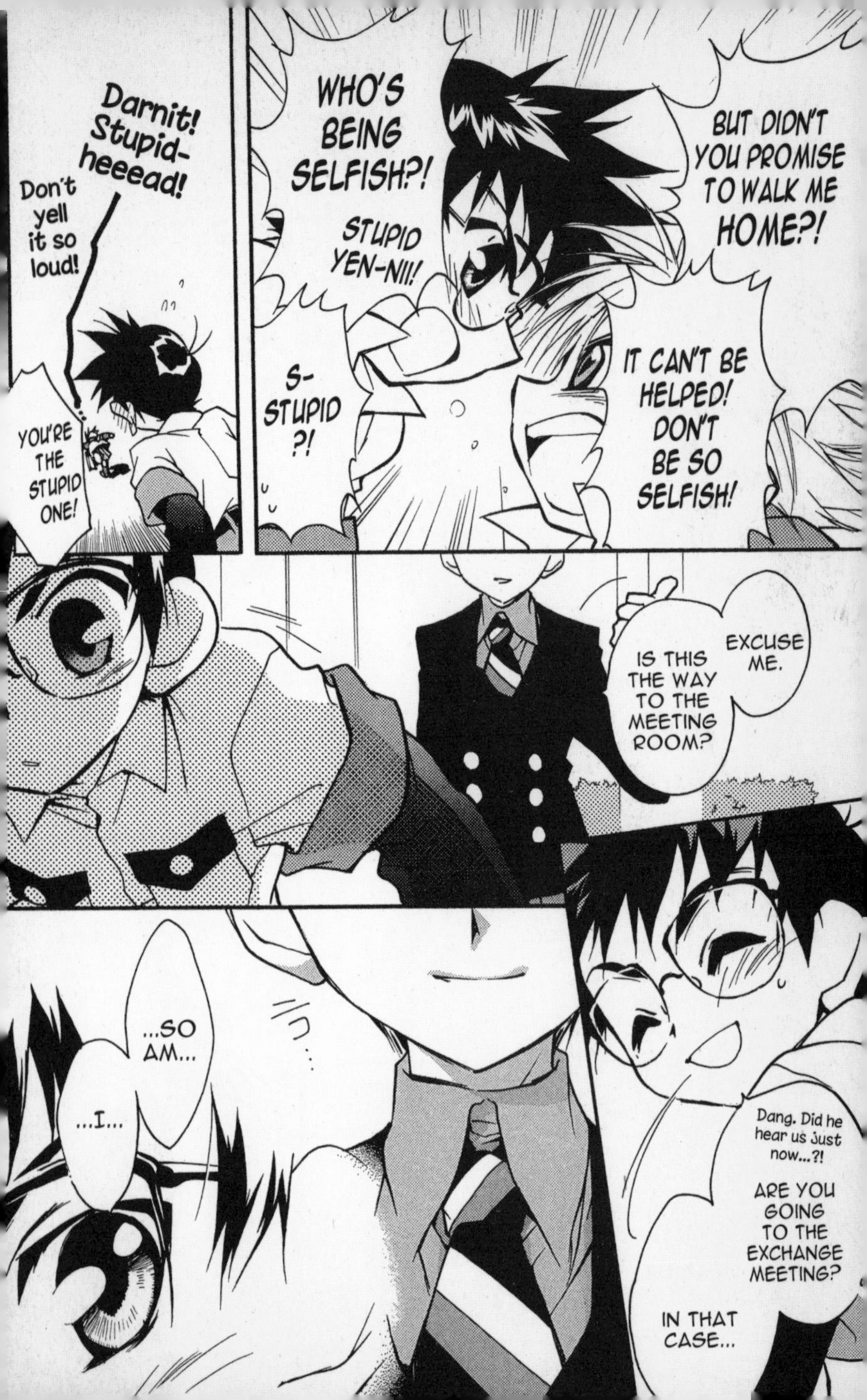
BUT DIDN'T YOU PROMISE TO WALK ME HOME?!
IT CAN'T BE HELPED! DON'T BE SO SELFISH!
WHO'S BEING SELFISH?!
STUPID YEN-NII!
S-STUPID ?!
Darnit! Stupid-heeeead!
Don't yell it so loud!
YOU'RE THE STUPID ONE!
EXCUSE ME.
IS THIS THE WAY TO THE MEETING ROOM?
Dang. Did he hear us just now...?!
ARE YOU GOING TO THE EXCHANGE MEETING?
IN THAT CASE...
...SO AM...
...I...

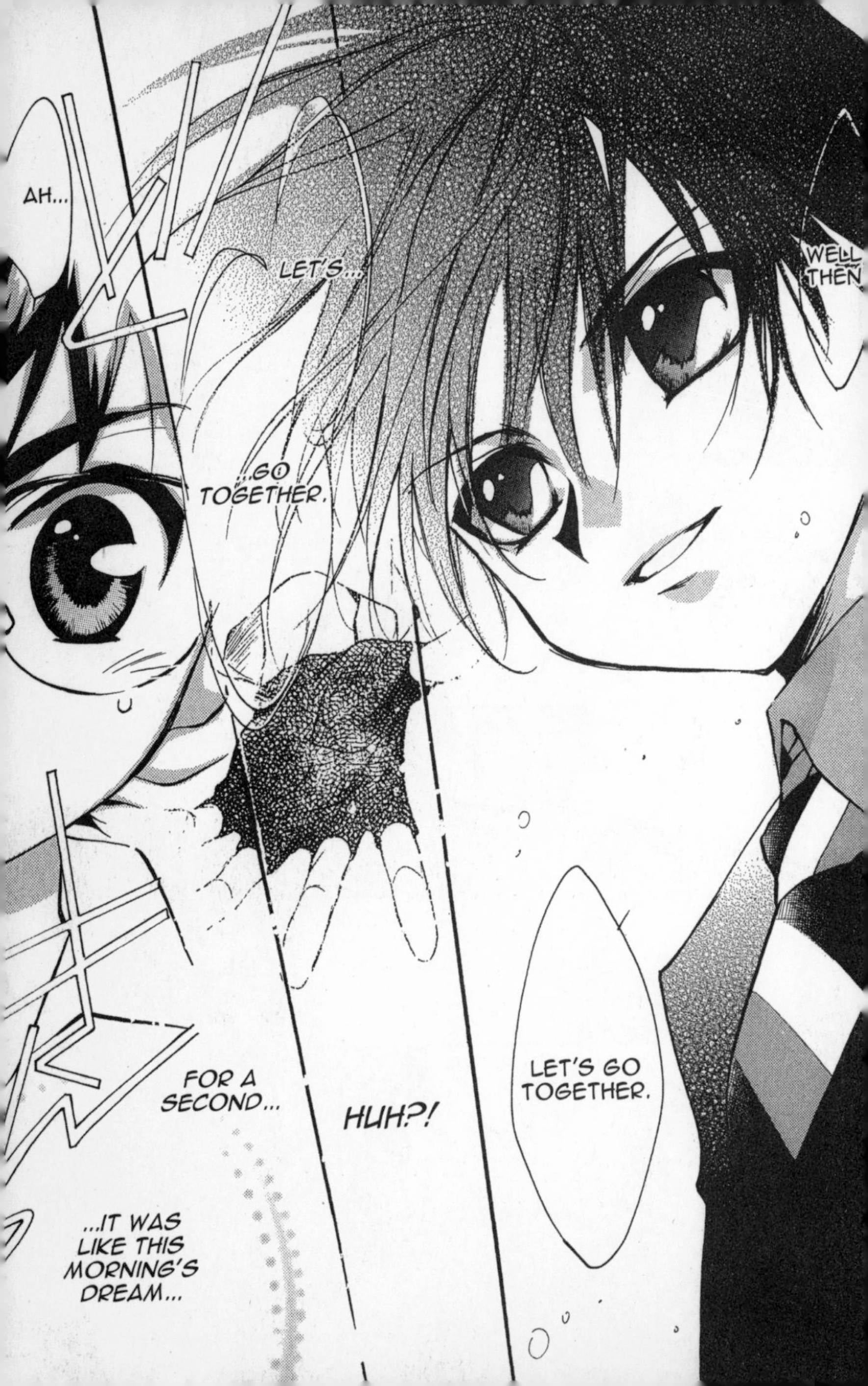
WELL THEN
LET'S GO TOGETHER.
LET'S...
...GO TOGETHER.
HUH?!
AH...
FOR A SECOND...
...IT WAS LIKE THIS MORNING'S DREAM...

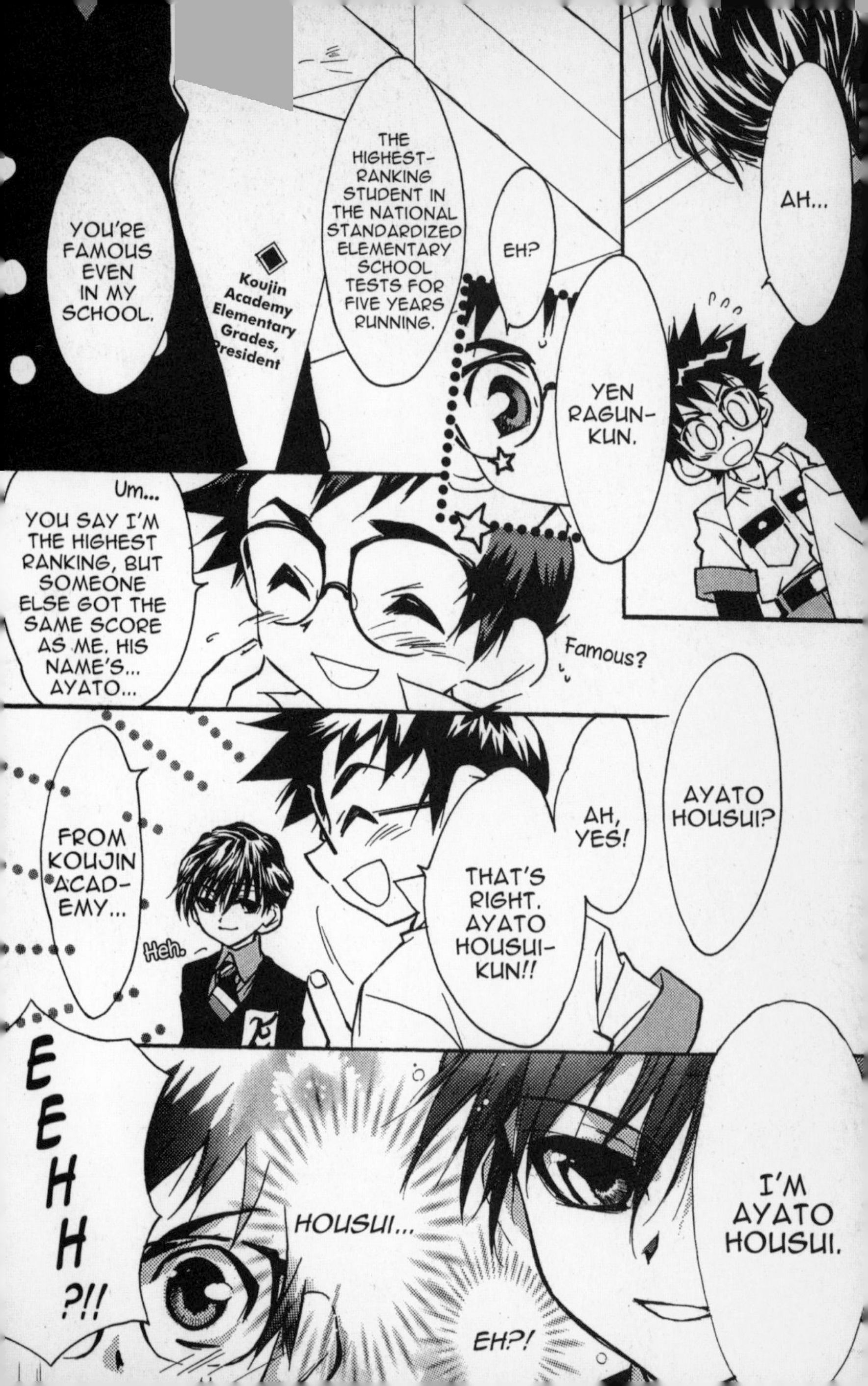
AH...
YEN RAGUN-KUN.
EH?
THE HIGHEST-RANKING STUDENT IN THE NATIONAL STANDARDIZED ELEMENTARY SCHOOL TESTS FOR FIVE YEARS RUNNING.
Koujin Academy Elementary Grades, President
YOU'RE FAMOUS EVEN IN MY SCHOOL.
Famous?
Um... YOU SAY I'M THE HIGHEST RANKING, BUT SOMEONE ELSE GOT THE SAME SCORE AS ME. HIS NAME'S... AYATO...
AYATO HOUSUI?
AH, YES!
THAT'S RIGHT. AYATO HOUSUI-KUN!!
FROM KOUJIN ACADEMY...
Heh.
I'M AYATO HOUSUI.
EH?!
HOUSUI...
EEHH?!!

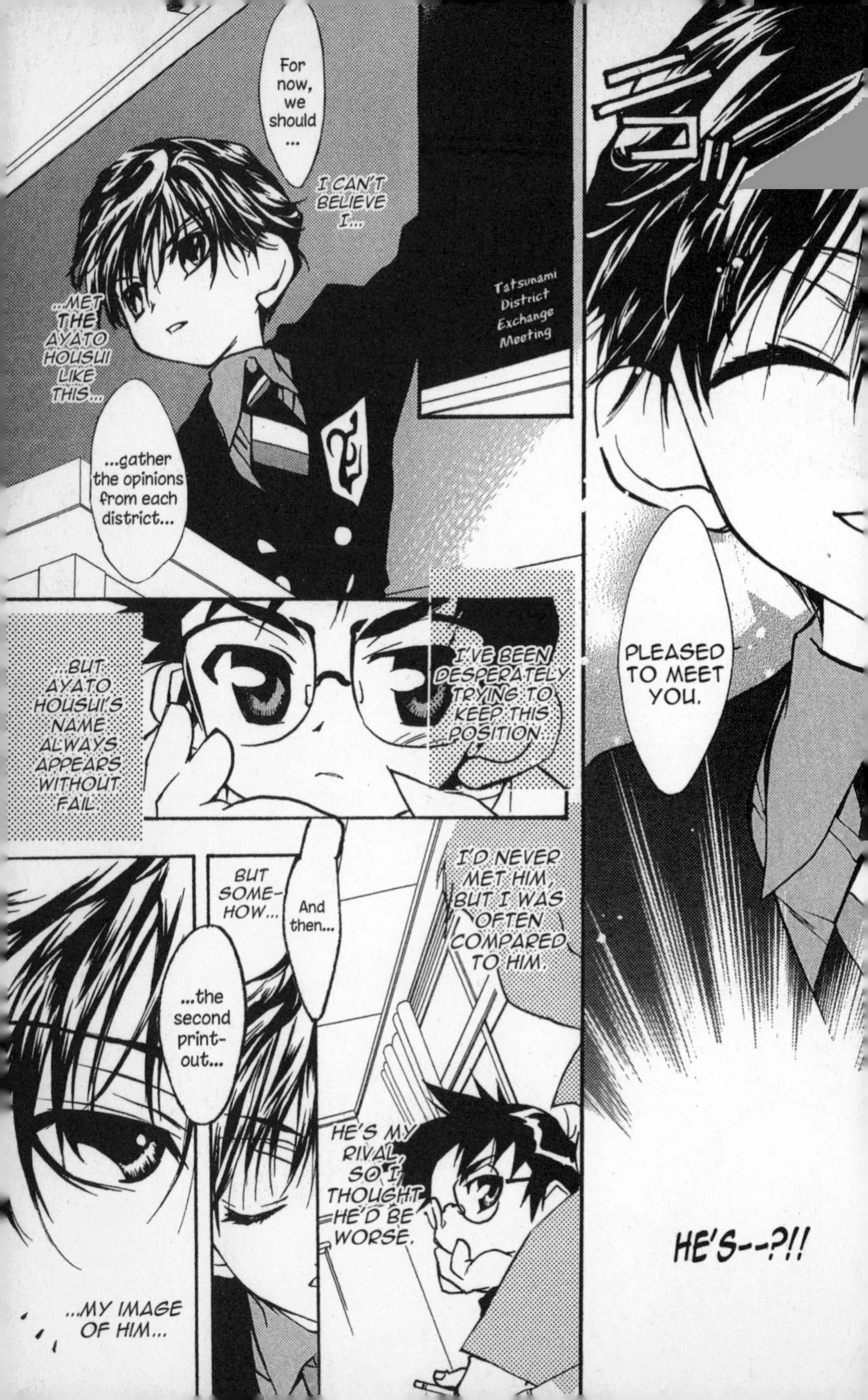
PLEASED TO MEET YOU.
HE'S--?!!
For now, we should...
I CAN'T BELIEVE I...
Tatsunami District Exchange Meeting
...MET THE AYATO HOUSUI LIKE THIS...
...gather the opinions from each district...
I'VE BEEN DESPERATELY TRYING TO KEEP THIS POSITION.
...BUT AYATO HOUSUI'S NAME ALWAYS APPEARS WITHOUT FAIL.
I'D NEVER MET HIM, BUT I WAS OFTEN COMPARED TO HIM.
And then...
HE'S MY RIVAL, SO I THOUGHT HE'D BE WORSE.
BUT SOME-HOW...
...the second print-out...
...MY IMAGE OF HIM...

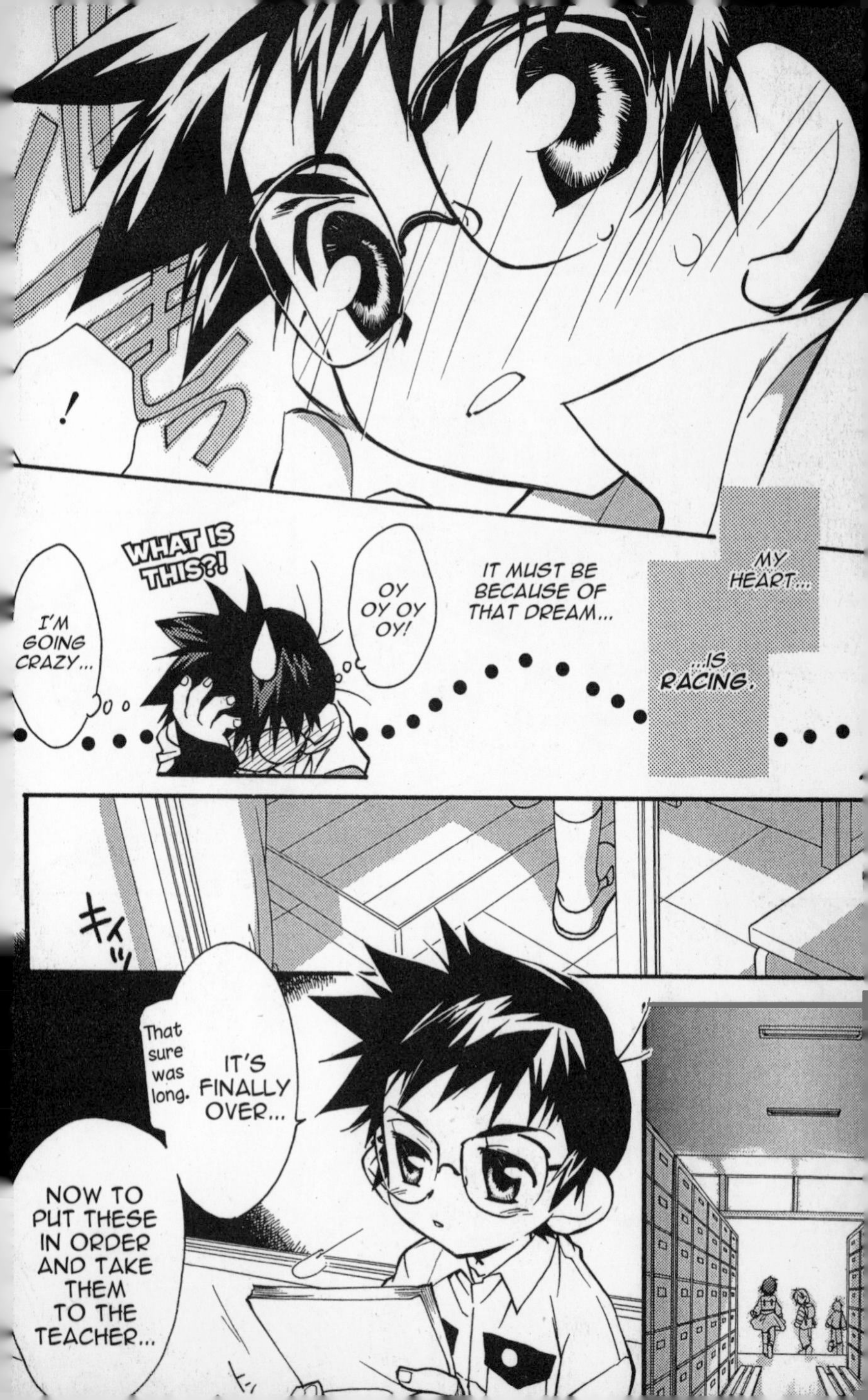
!
MY HEART...
...IS RACING.
IT MUST BE BECAUSE OF THAT DREAM...
OY OY OY OY!
WHAT IS THIS?!
I'M GOING CRAZY...
キィッ
IT'S FINALLY OVER...
That sure was long.
NOW TO PUT THESE IN ORDER AND TAKE THEM TO THE TEACHER...

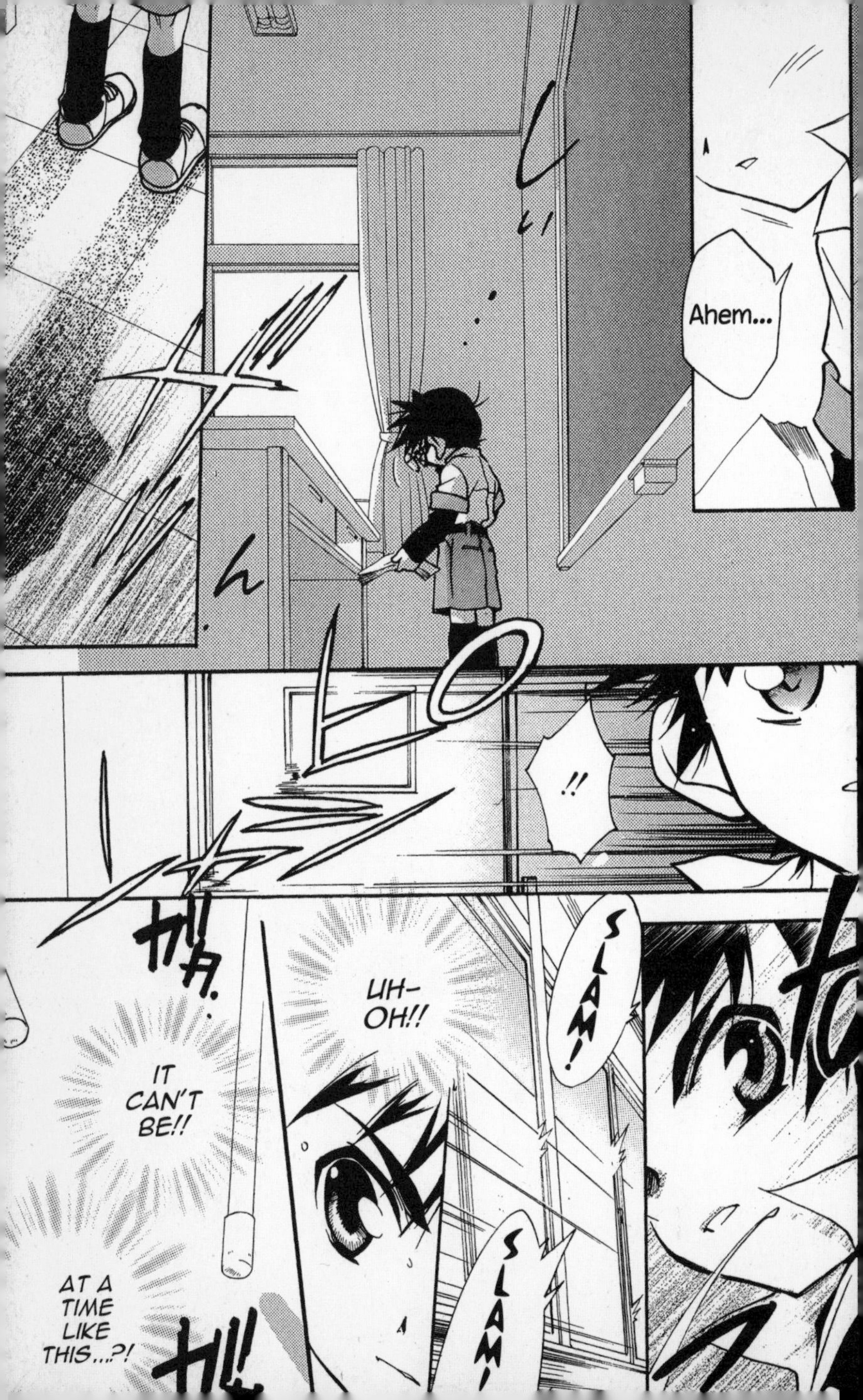
Ahem...
!!
SLAM!
SLAM!
UH-OH!!
IT CAN'T BE!!
AT A TIME LIKE THIS...?!

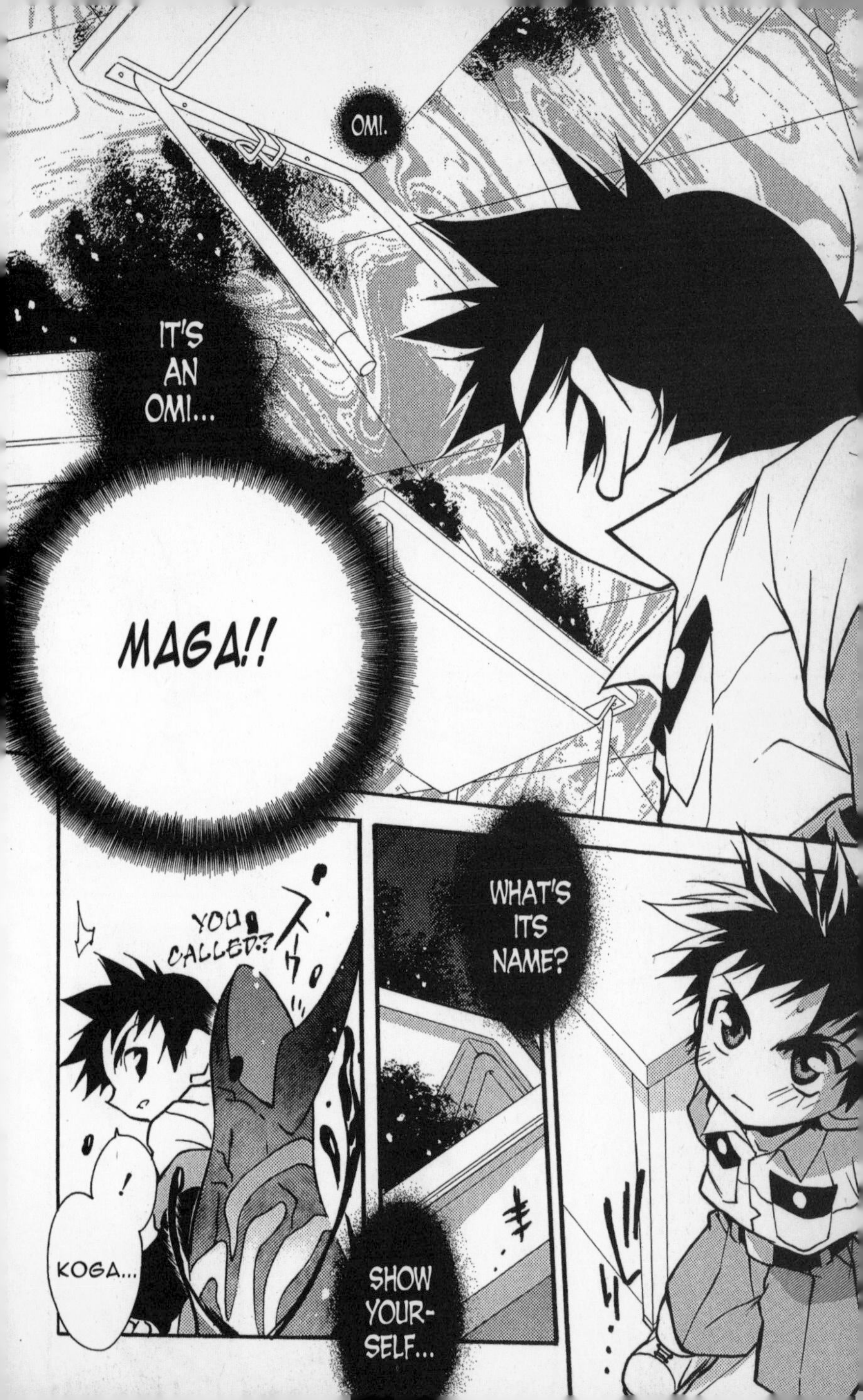
OMI.
IT'S AN OMI...
MAGA!!
WHAT'S ITS NAME?
SHOW YOURSELF...
YOU CALLED?!
!
KOGA...

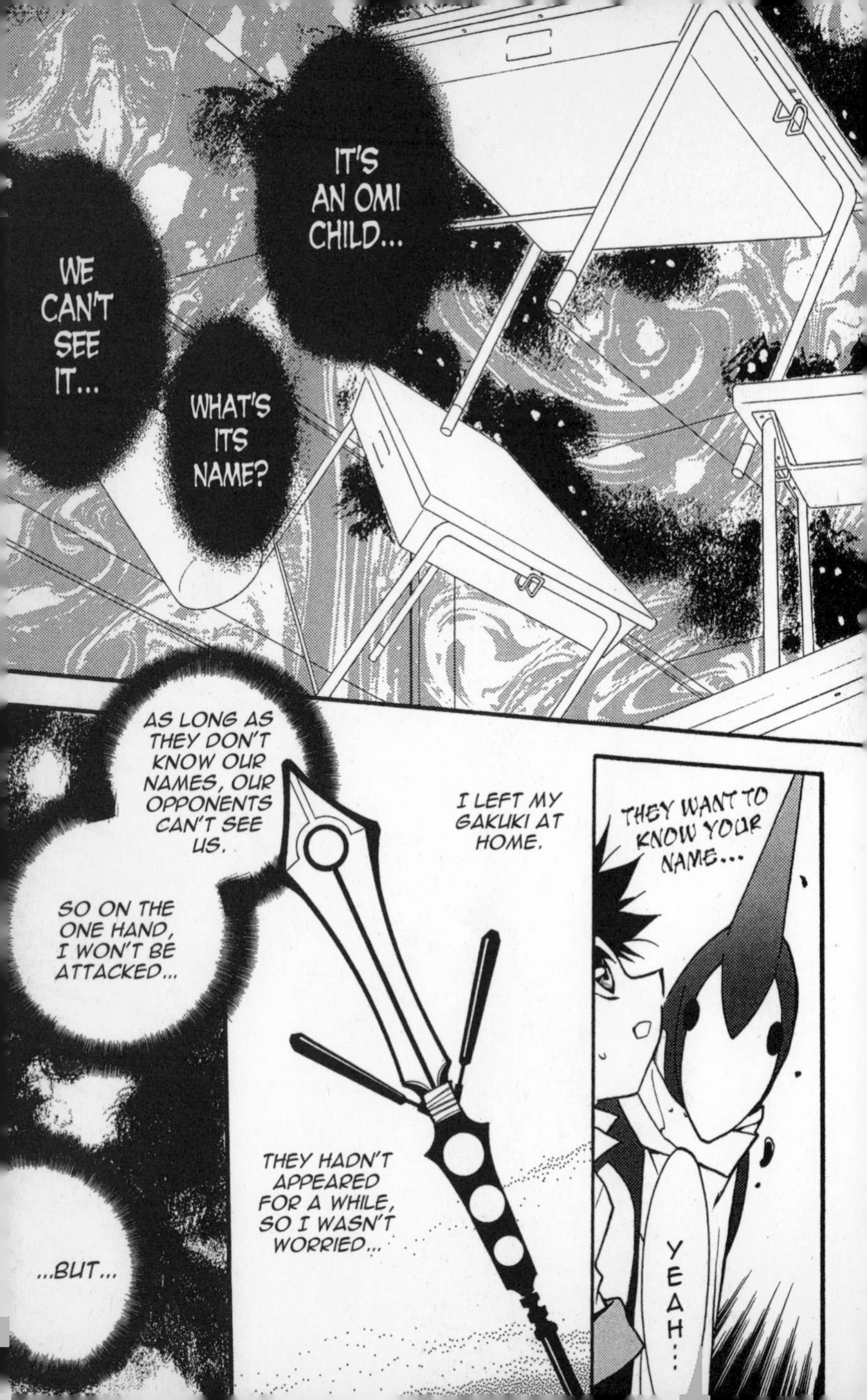
IT'S AN OMI CHILD...
WHAT'S ITS NAME?
WE CAN'T SEE IT...
THEY WANT TO KNOW YOUR NAME...
YEAH...
I LEFT MY GAKUKI AT HOME.
THEY HADN'T APPEARED FOR A WHILE, SO I WASN'T WORRIED...
AS LONG AS THEY DON'T KNOW OUR NAMES, OUR OPPONENTS CAN'T SEE US.
SO ON THE ONE HAND, I WON'T BE ATTACKED...
...BUT...

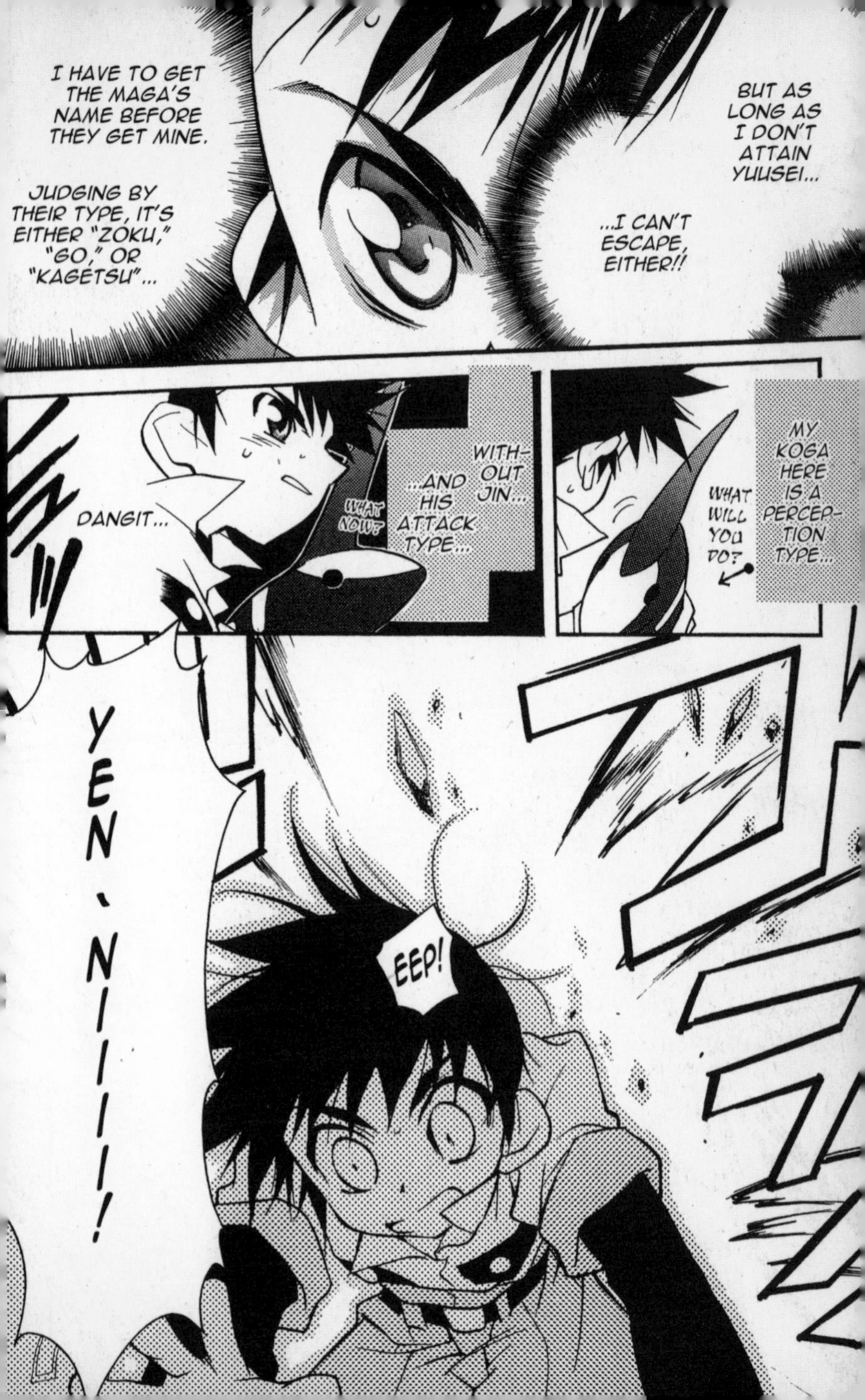
BUT AS LONG AS I DON'T ATTAIN YUUSEI...
...I CAN'T ESCAPE, EITHER!!
I HAVE TO GET THE MAGA'S NAME BEFORE THEY GET MINE.
JUDGING BY THEIR TYPE, IT'S EITHER "ZOKU," "GO," OR "KAGETSU"...
MY KOGA HERE IS A PERCEPTION TYPE...
WHAT WILL YOU DO?
WITHOUT JIN...
...AND HIS ATTACK TYPE...
WHAT NOW?
DANGIT...
EEP!
YEN, NIIIIII!

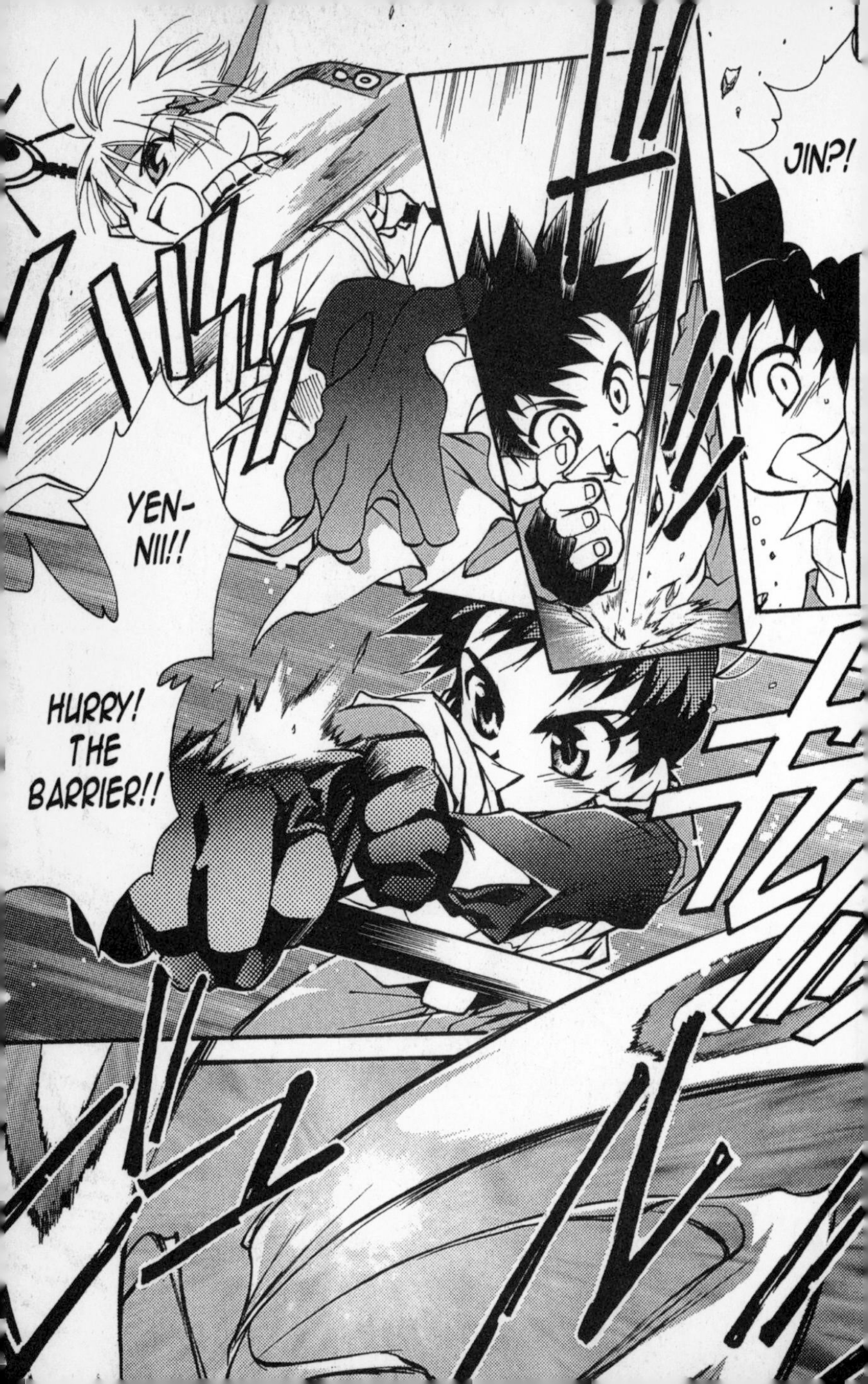
JIN?!
YEN-NII!!
HURRY! THE BARRIER!!

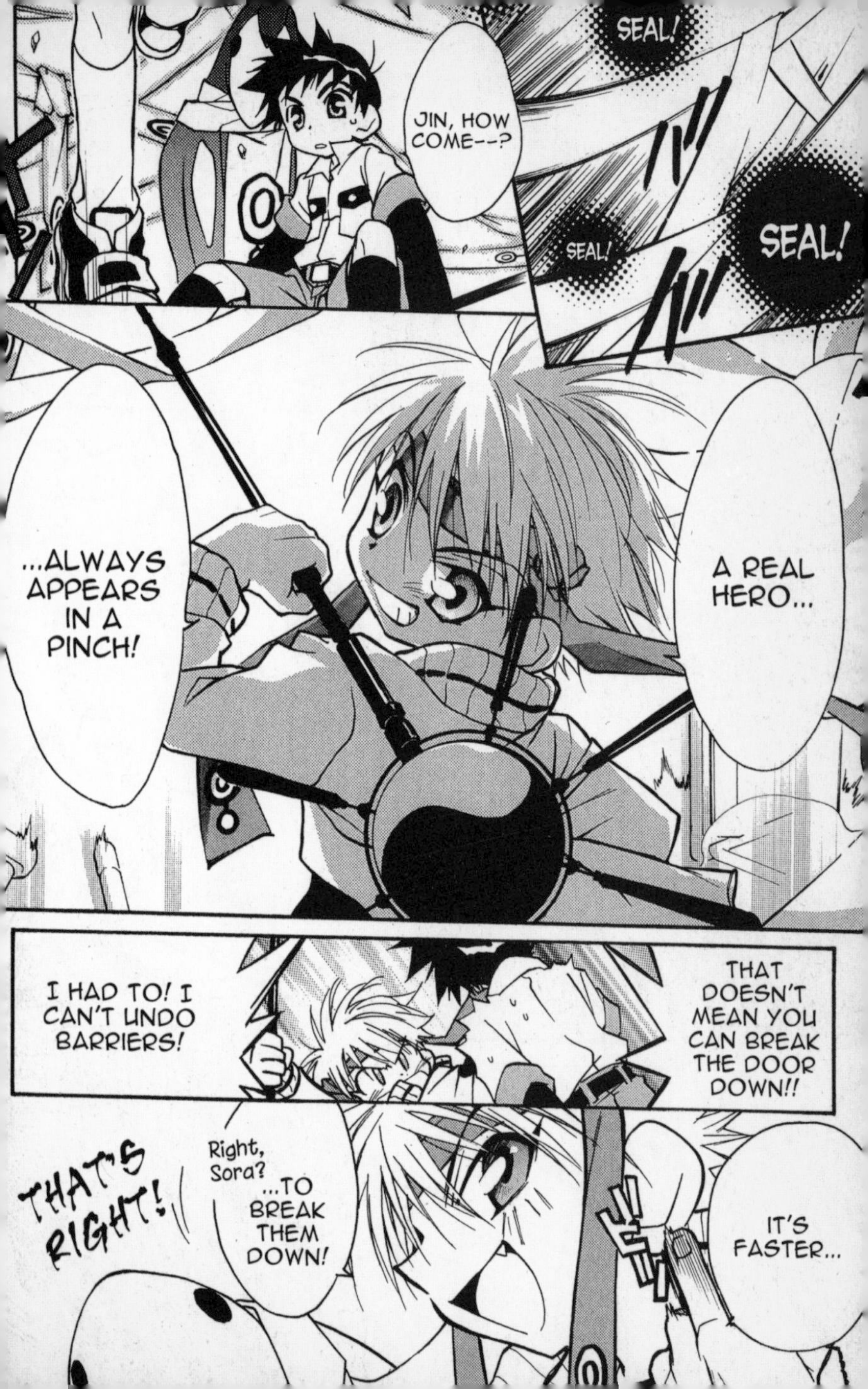
SEAL!
SEAL!
SEAL!
JIN, HOW COME--?
A REAL HERO...
...ALWAYS APPEARS IN A PINCH!
THAT DOESN'T MEAN YOU CAN BREAK THE DOOR DOWN!!
I HAD TO! I CAN'T UNDO BARRIERS!
IT'S FASTER...
...TO BREAK THEM DOWN!
Right, Sora?
THAT'S RIGHT!

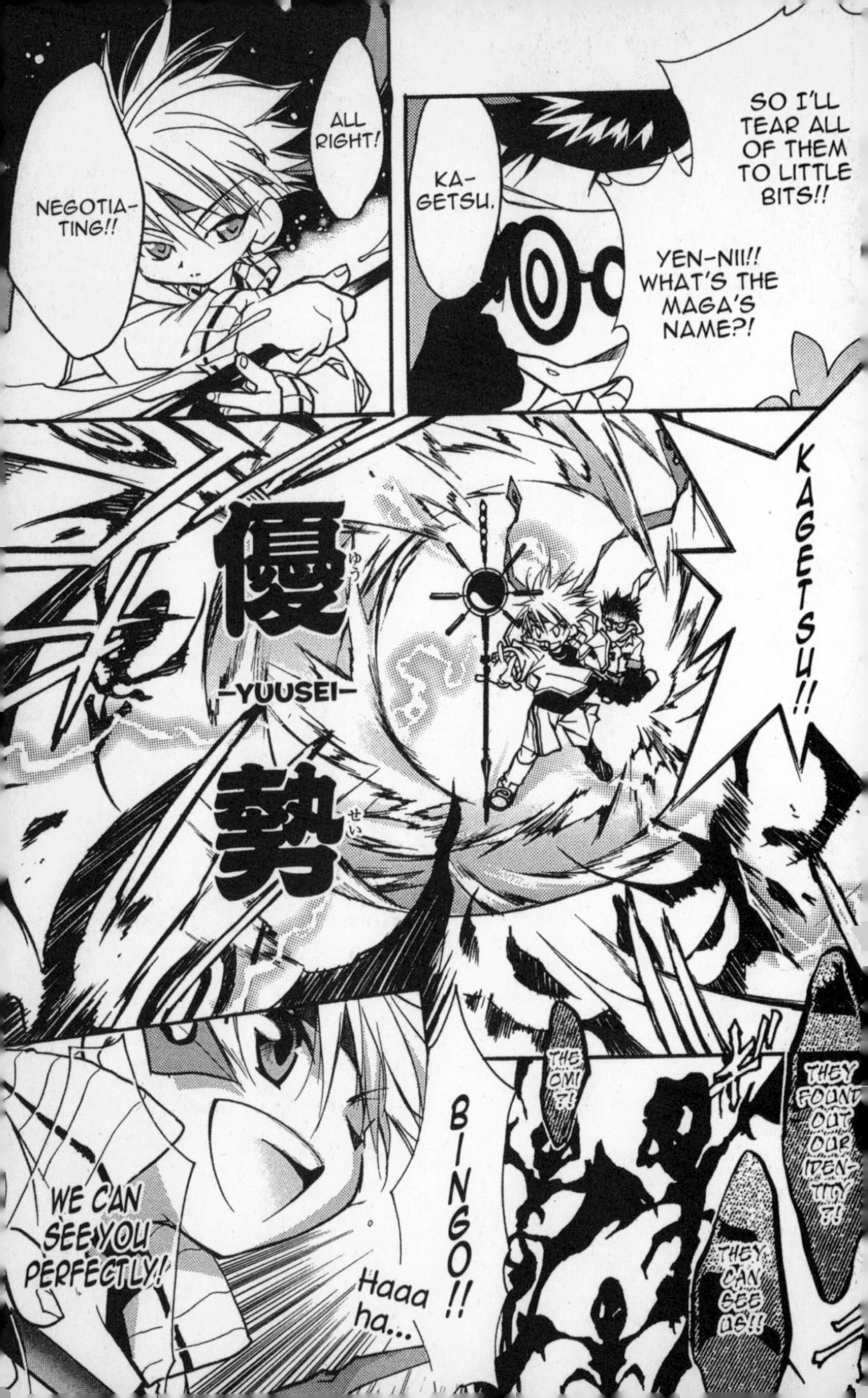
SO I'LL TEAR ALL OF THEM TO LITTLE BITS!!
YEN-NII!! WHAT'S THE MAGA'S NAME?!
KA-GETSU.
ALL RIGHT!
NEGOTIA-TING!!
KAGETSU!!
優勢
ゆう せい
-YUUSEI-
THEY FOUND OUT OUR IDEN-TITY?!
THEY CAN SEE US!!
THE OMI?!
BINGO!!
Haaa ha...
WE CAN SEE YOU PERFECTLY!

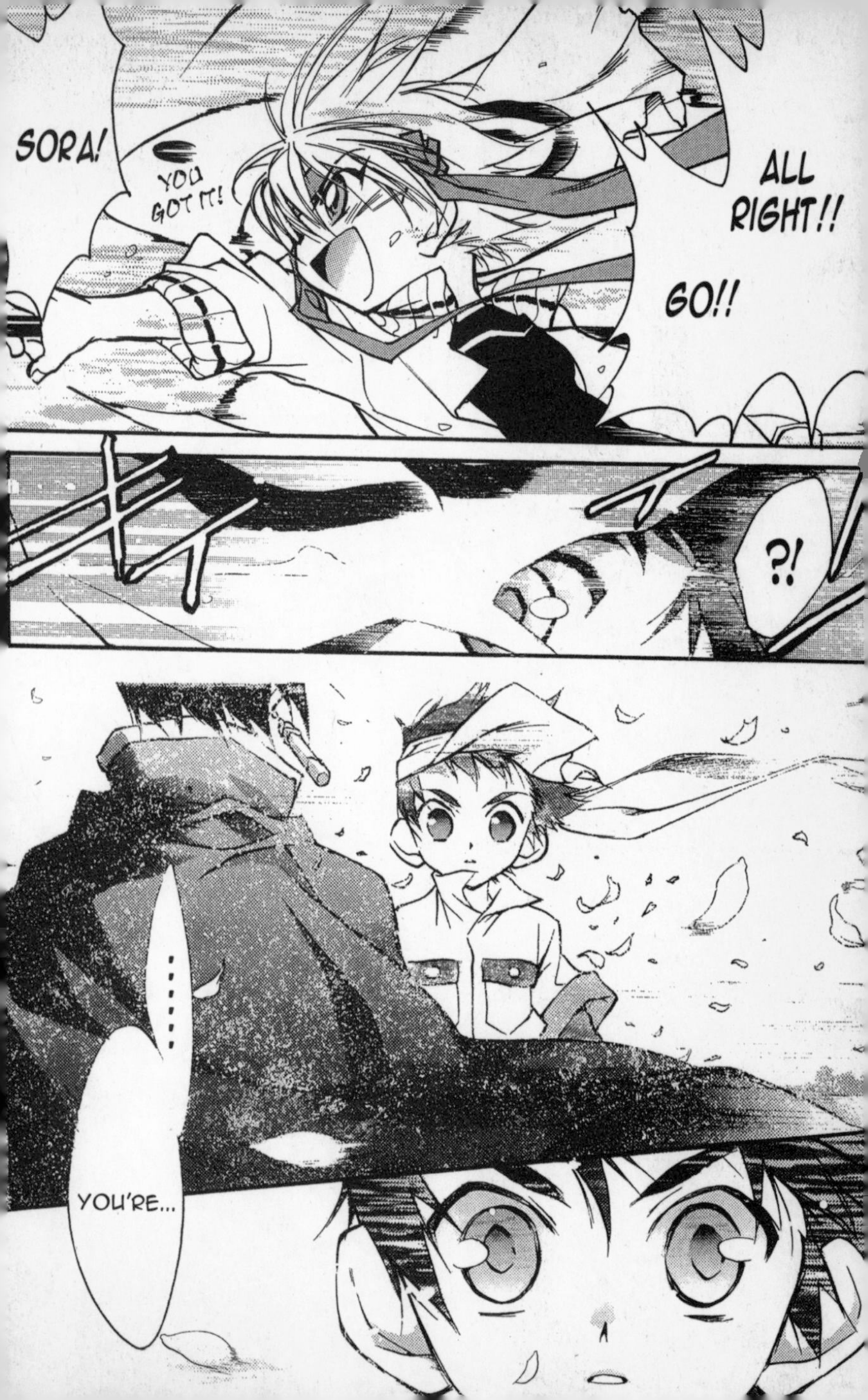
ALL RIGHT!!
GO!!
SORA!
YOU GOT IT!
?!
......
YOU'RE...

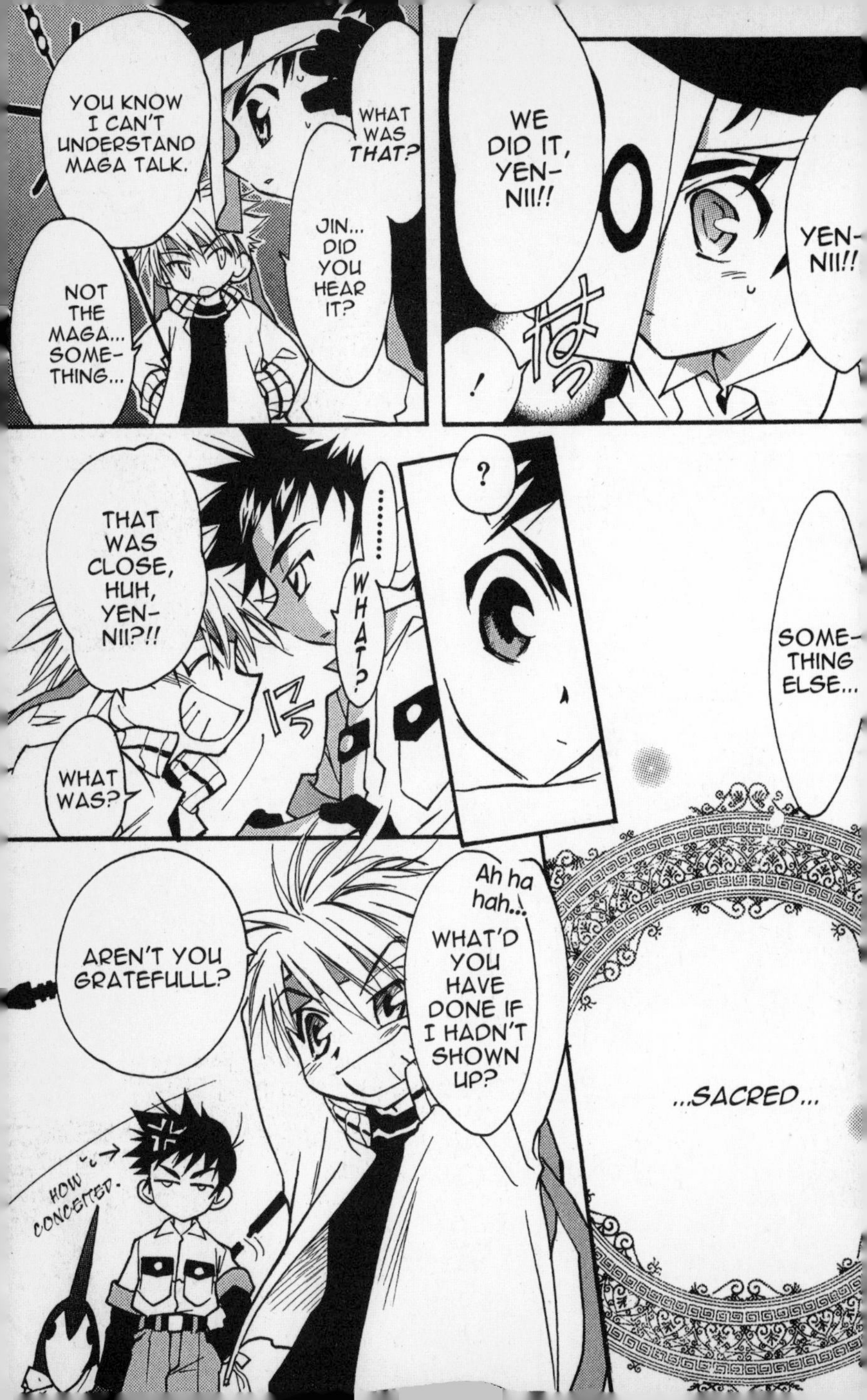
YEN-NII!!
WE DID IT, YEN-NII!!
!
はっ
WHAT WAS THAT?
JIN... DID YOU HEAR IT?
YOU KNOW I CAN'T UNDERSTAND MAGA TALK.
NOT THE MAGA... SOMETHING...
SOMETHING ELSE...
?
......
WHAT?
THAT WAS CLOSE, HUH, YEN-NII?!!
にっ
WHAT WAS?
...SACRED...
Ah ha hah...
WHAT'D YOU HAVE DONE IF I HADN'T SHOWN UP?
AREN'T YOU GRATEFULLL?
HOW CONCEITED.

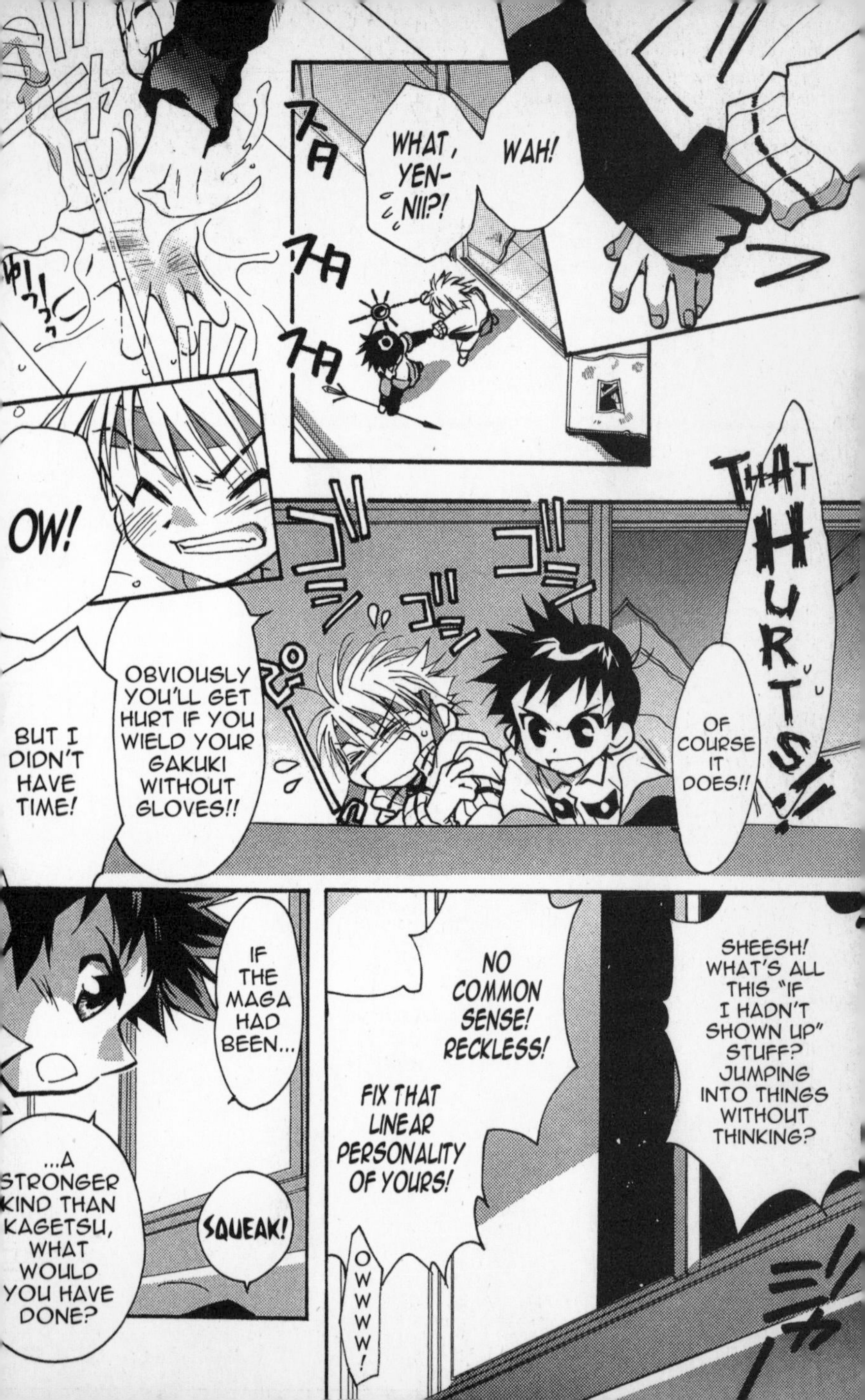
WAH!
WHAT, YEN-NII?!
OW!
THAT HURTS!!
OF COURSE IT DOES!!
OBVIOUSLY YOU'LL GET HURT IF YOU WIELD YOUR GAKUKI WITHOUT GLOVES!!
BUT I DIDN'T HAVE TIME!
SHEESH! WHAT'S ALL THIS "IF I HADN'T SHOWN UP" STUFF? JUMPING INTO THINGS WITHOUT THINKING?
NO COMMON SENSE! RECKLESS!
FIX THAT LINEAR PERSONALITY OF YOURS!
OWWWWW!
IF THE MAGA HAD BEEN...
...A STRONGER KIND THAN KAGETSU, WHAT WOULD YOU HAVE DONE?
SQUEAK!

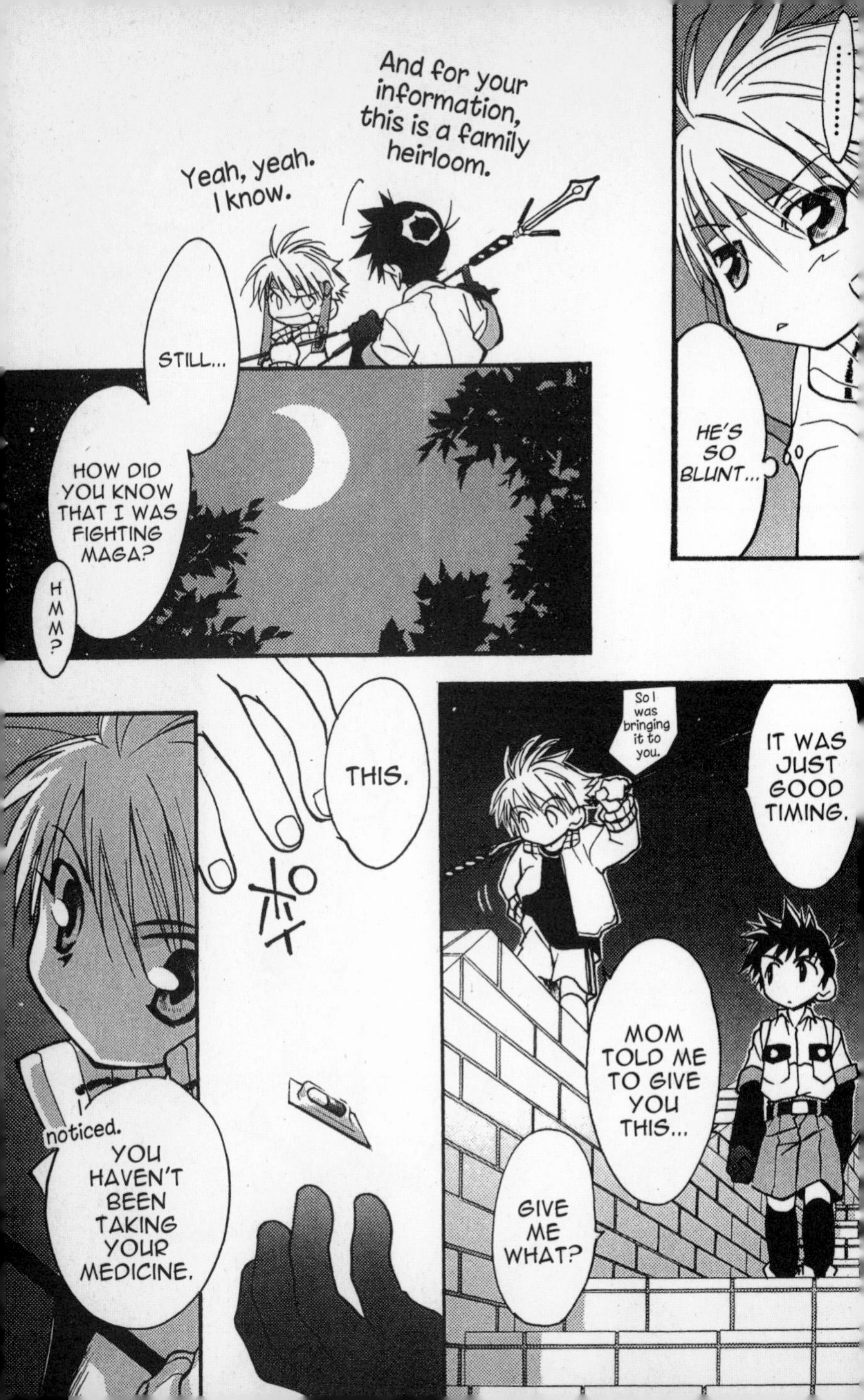
......
HE'S SO BLUNT...
And for your information, this is a family heirloom.
Yeah, yeah. I know.
STILL...
HOW DID YOU KNOW THAT I WAS FIGHTING MAGA?
HMM?
IT WAS JUST GOOD TIMING.
So I was bringing it to you.
MOM TOLD ME TO GIVE YOU THIS...
GIVE ME WHAT?
THIS.
ポイ
I noticed.
YOU HAVEN'T BEEN TAKING YOUR MEDICINE.

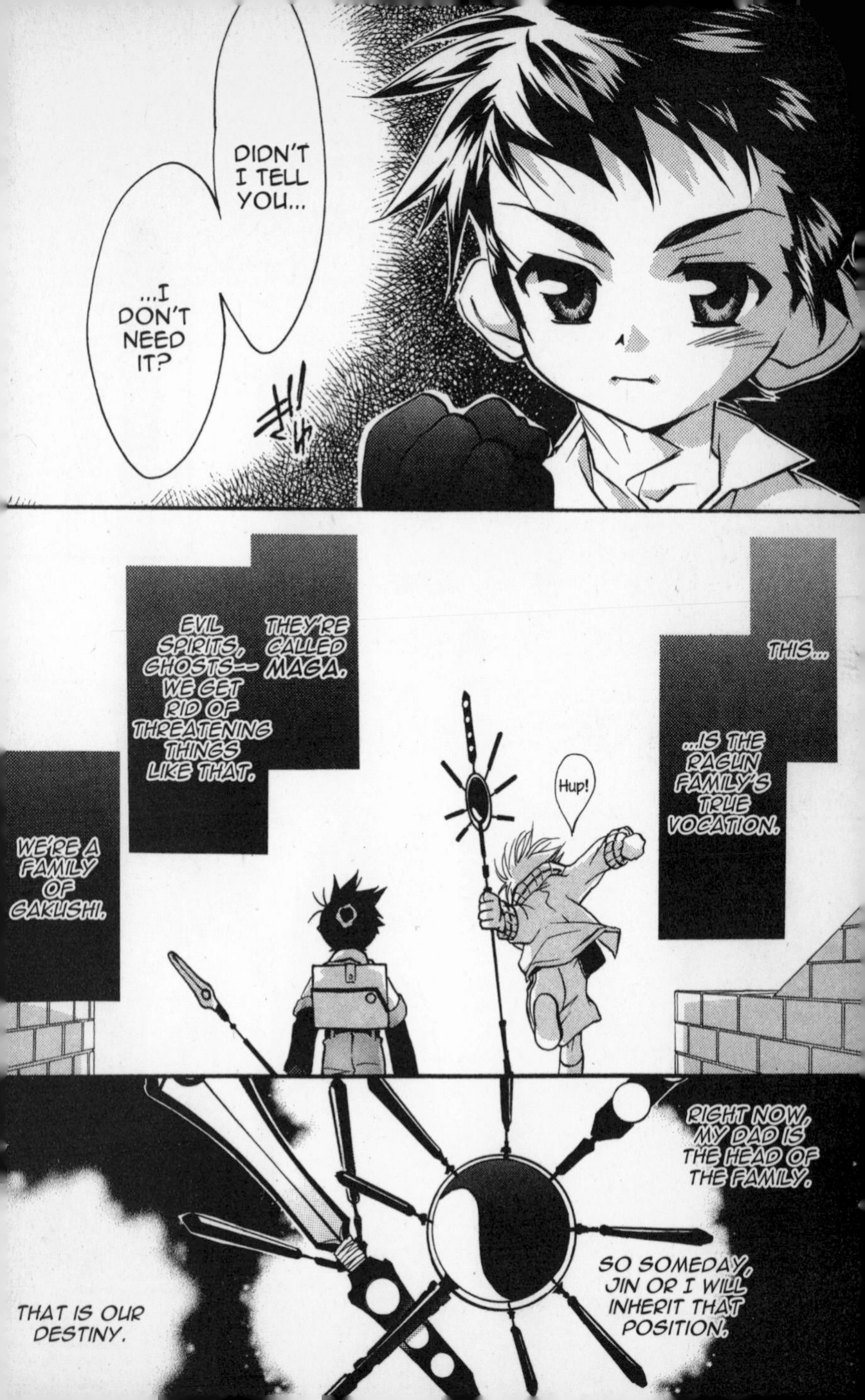
DIDN'T I TELL YOU...
...I DON'T NEED IT?
THIS...
...IS THE RAGUN FAMILY'S TRUE VOCATION.
Hup!
THEY'RE CALLED MAGA.
EVIL SPIRITS, GHOSTS--WE GET RID OF THREATENING THINGS LIKE THAT.
WE'RE A FAMILY OF GAKUSHI.
RIGHT NOW, MY DAD IS THE HEAD OF THE FAMILY.
SO SOMEDAY, JIN OR I WILL INHERIT THAT POSITION.
THAT IS OUR DESTINY.

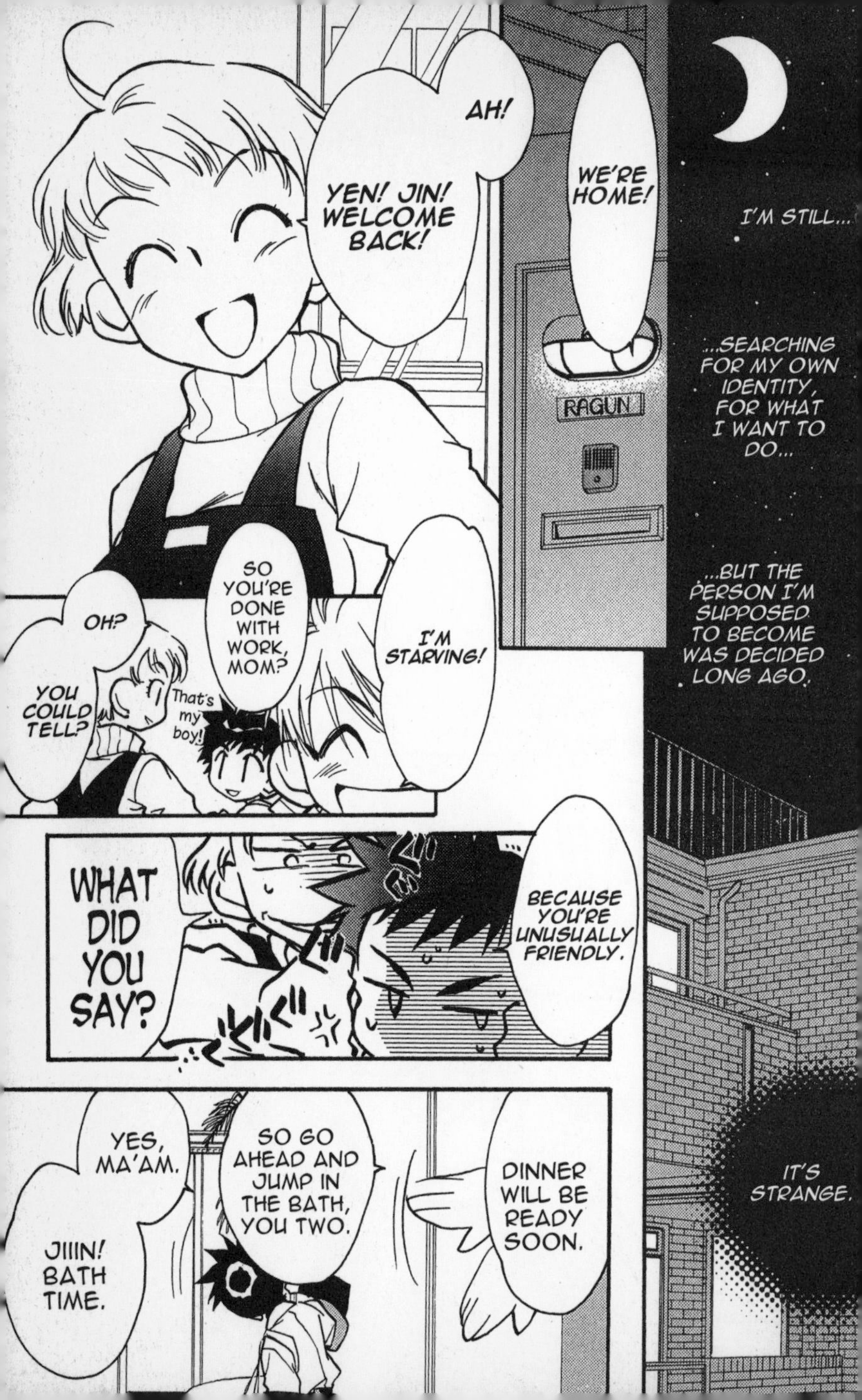
I'M STILL...
...SEARCHING FOR MY OWN IDENTITY, FOR WHAT I WANT TO DO...
...BUT THE PERSON I'M SUPPOSED TO BECOME WAS DECIDED LONG AGO.
IT'S STRANGE.
WE'RE HOME!
AH!
YEN! JIN! WELCOME BACK!
RAGUN
I'M STARVING!
SO YOU'RE DONE WITH WORK, MOM?
OH?
YOU COULD TELL?
That's my boy!
BECAUSE YOU'RE UNUSUALLY FRIENDLY.
WHAT DID YOU SAY?
DINNER WILL BE READY SOON.
SO GO AHEAD AND JUMP IN THE BATH, YOU TWO.
YES, MA'AM.
JIIIN! BATH TIME.

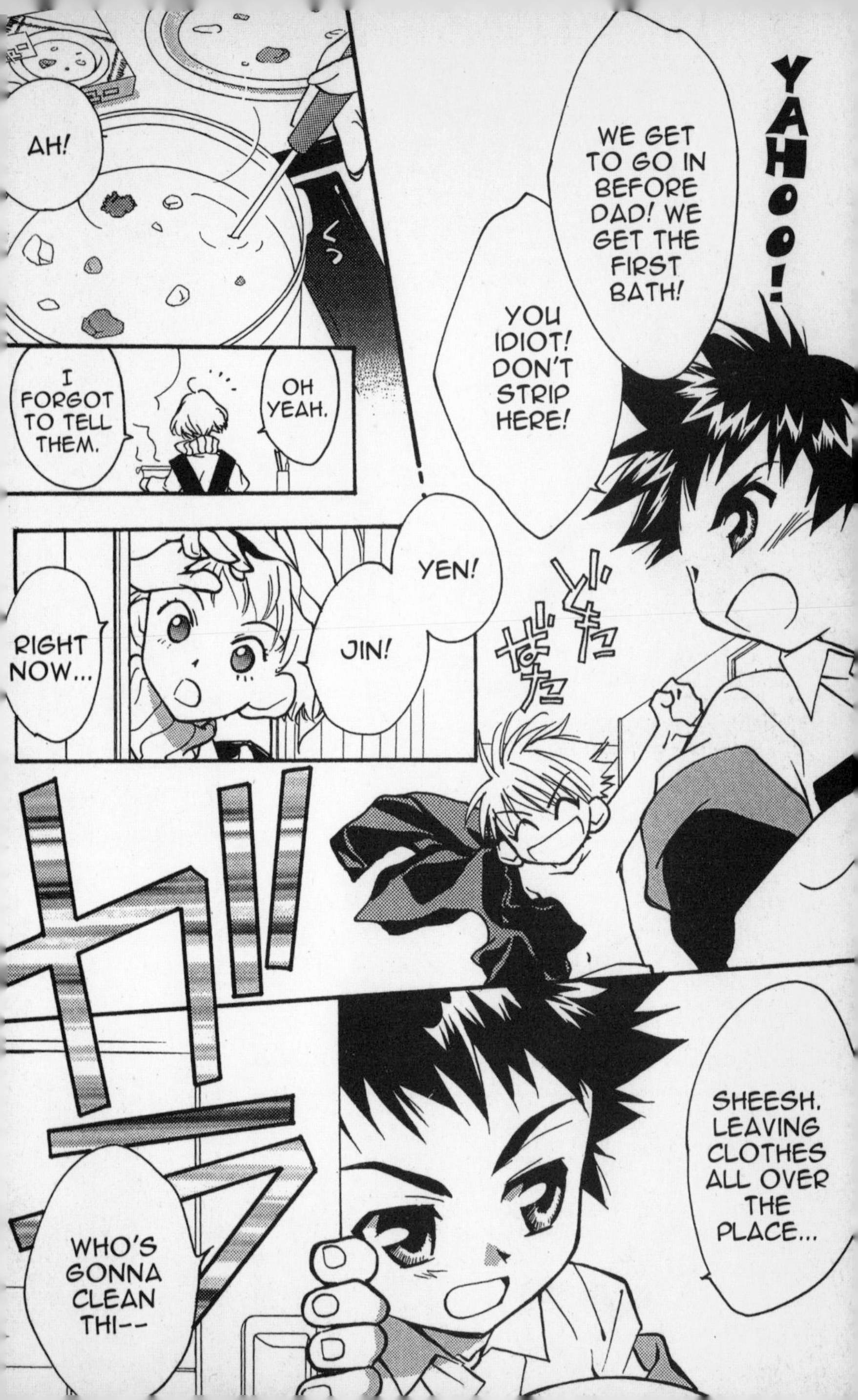
YAHOO!!
WE GET TO GO IN BEFORE DAD! WE GET THE FIRST BATH!
YOU IDIOT! DON'T STRIP HERE!
AH!
OH YEAH.
I FORGOT TO TELL THEM.
YEN!
JIN!
RIGHT NOW...
SHEESH. LEAVING CLOTHES ALL OVER THE PLACE...
WHO'S GONNA CLEAN THI--

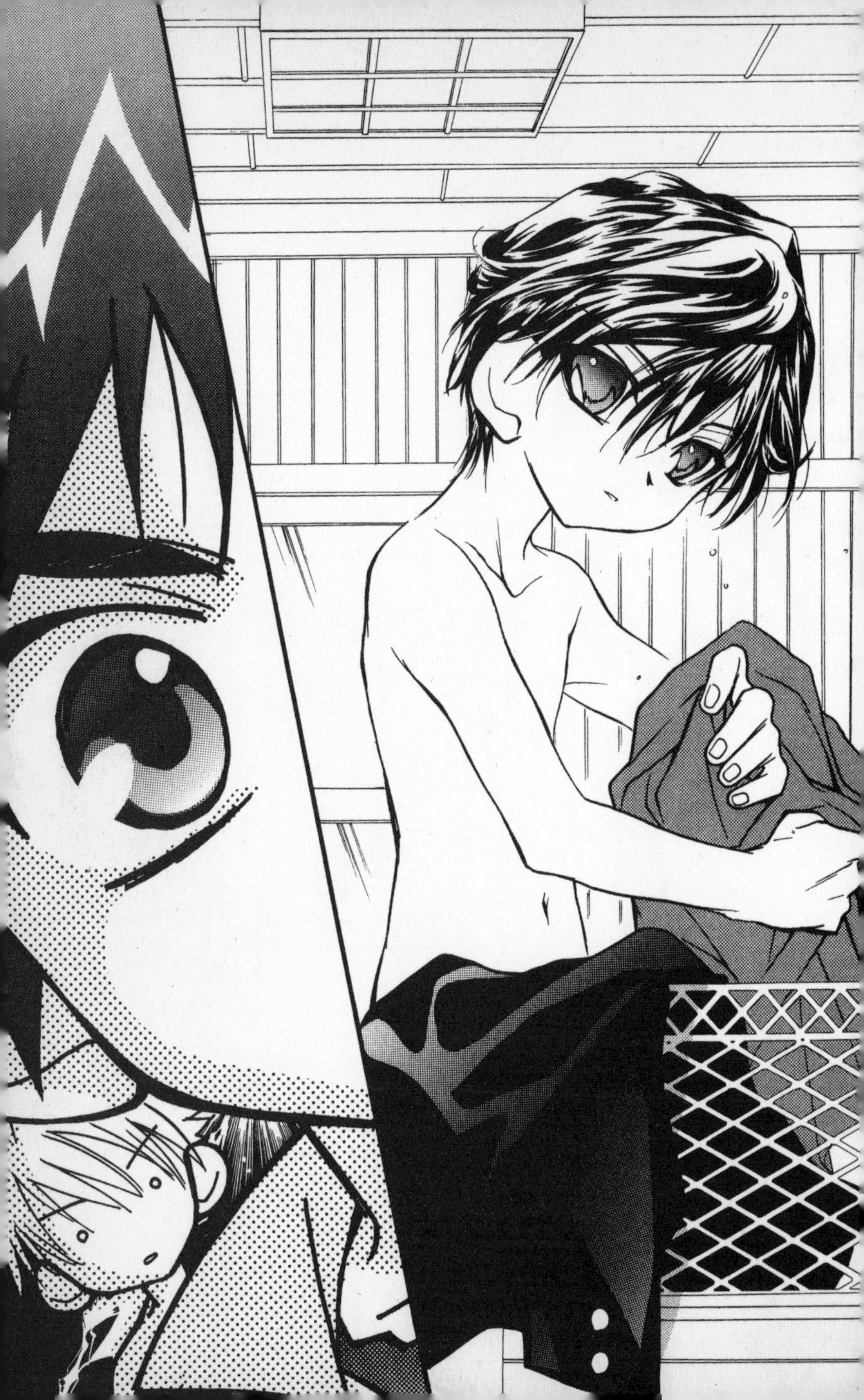

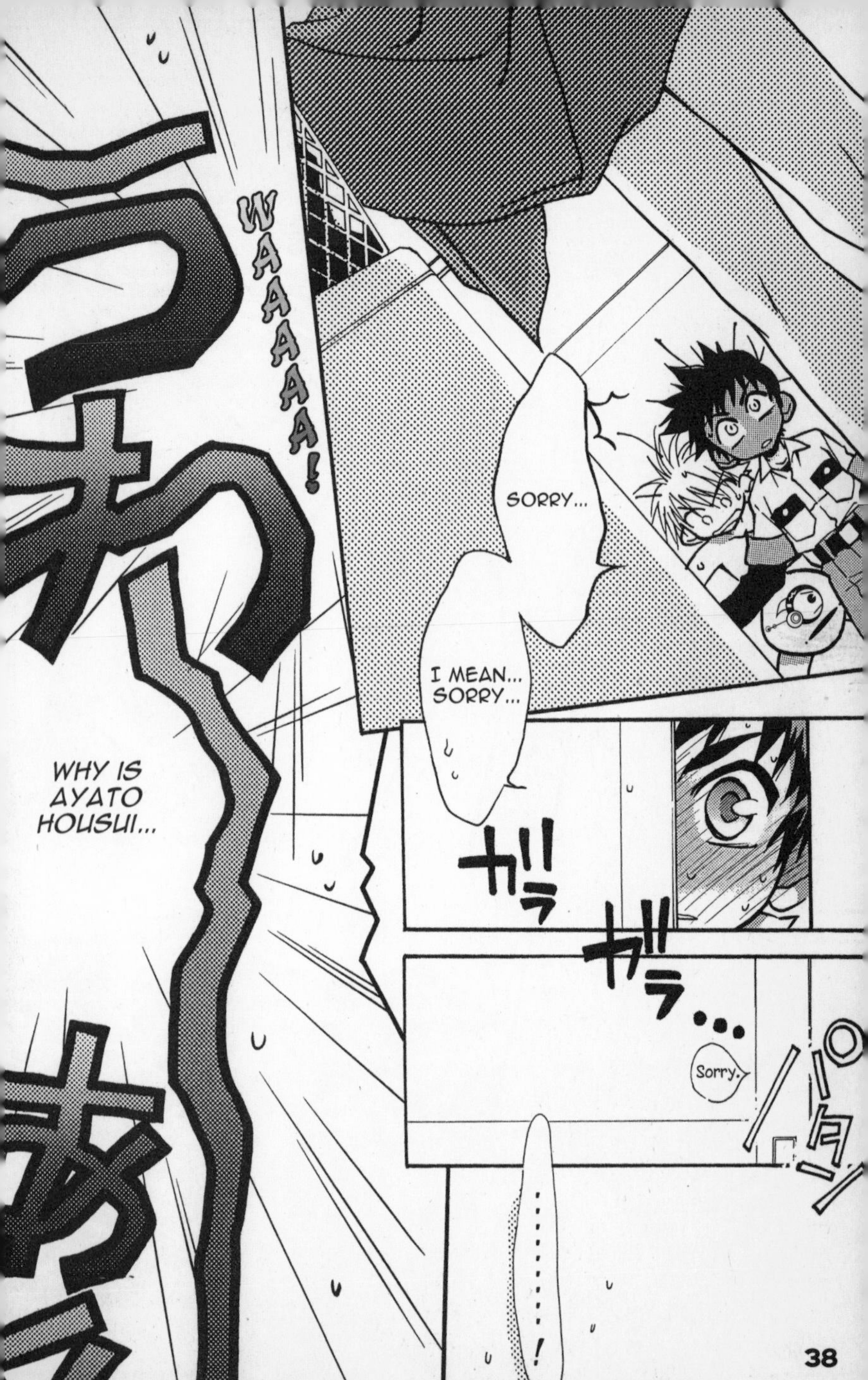
SORRY...
I MEAN... SORRY...
ガラ
ガラ...
Sorry.
パタン
......!
WAAAAAA!
WHY IS AYATO HOUSUI...

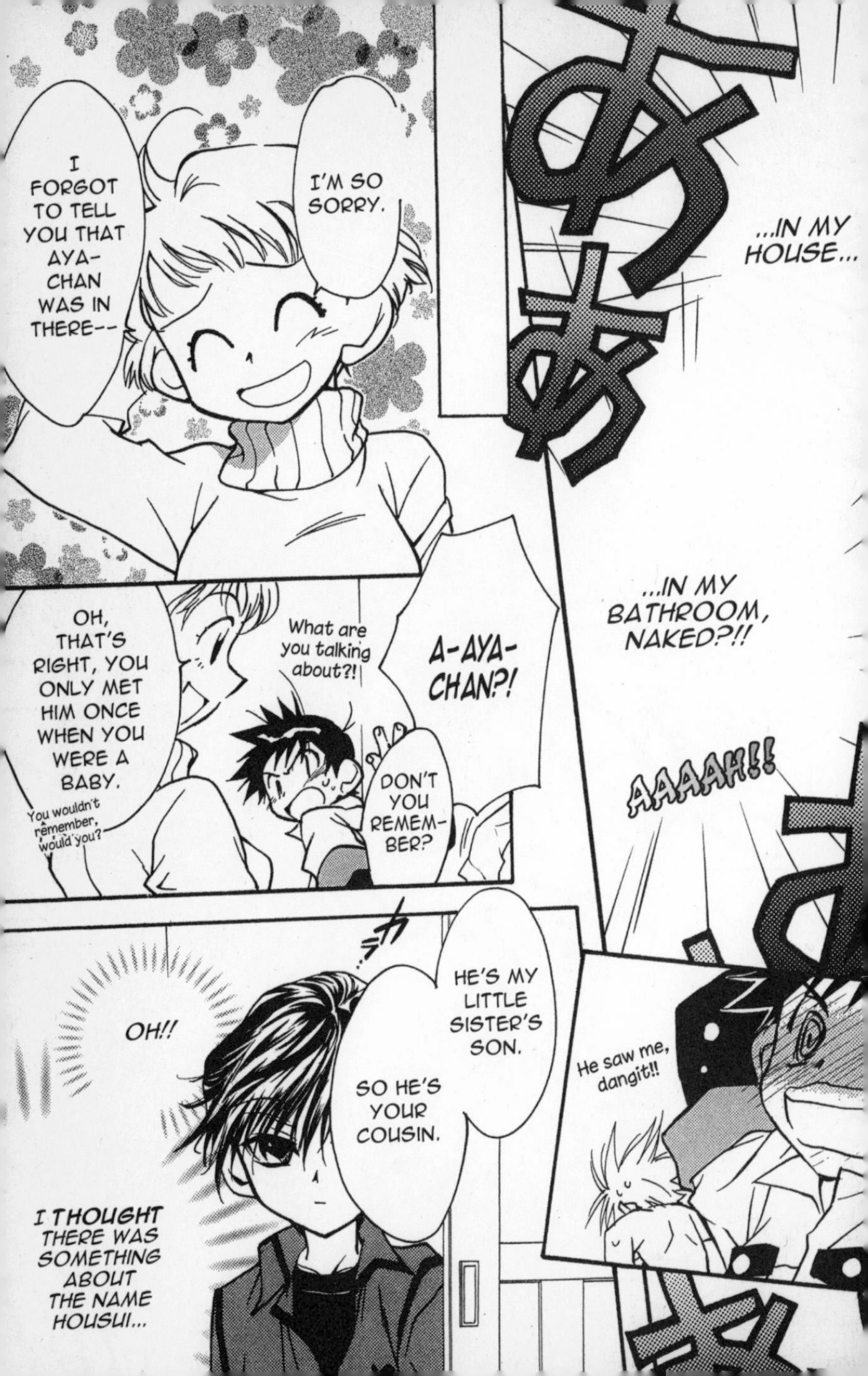
...IN MY HOUSE...
...IN MY BATHROOM, NAKED?!!
AAAAH!!
He saw me, dangit!!
I'M SO SORRY.
I FORGOT TO TELL YOU THAT AYA-CHAN WAS IN THERE--
A-AYA-CHAN?!
What are you talking about?!
DON'T YOU REMEMBER?
OH, THAT'S RIGHT, YOU ONLY MET HIM ONCE WHEN YOU WERE A BABY.
You wouldn't remember, would you?
HE'S MY LITTLE SISTER'S SON.
SO HE'S YOUR COUSIN.
OH!!
I THOUGHT THERE WAS SOMETHING ABOUT THE NAME HOUSUI...

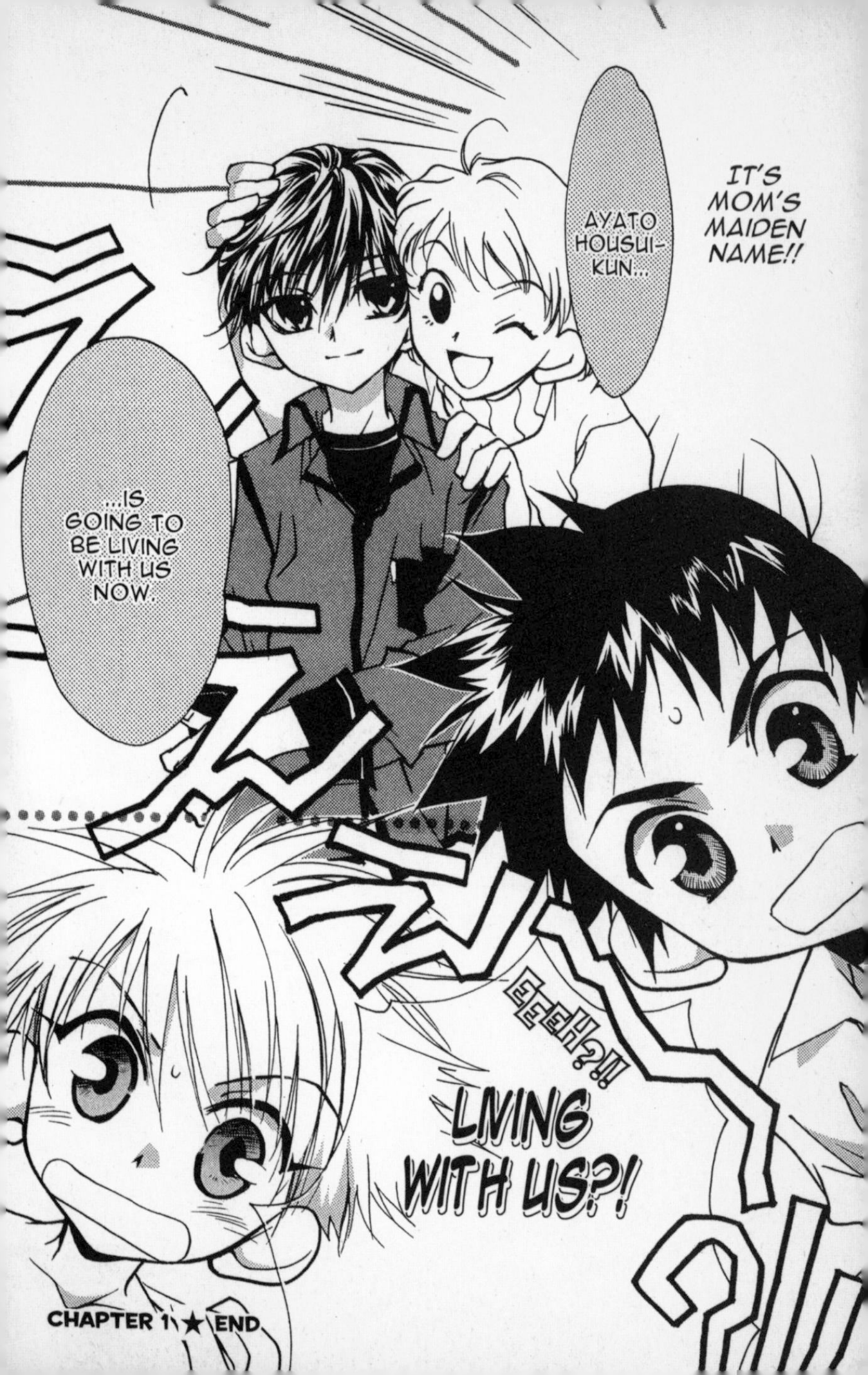
IT'S MOM'S MAIDEN NAME!!
AYATO HOUSUI-KUN...
...IS GOING TO BE LIVING WITH US NOW.
EEEH?!!
LIVING WITH US?!
CHAPTER 1 ★ END

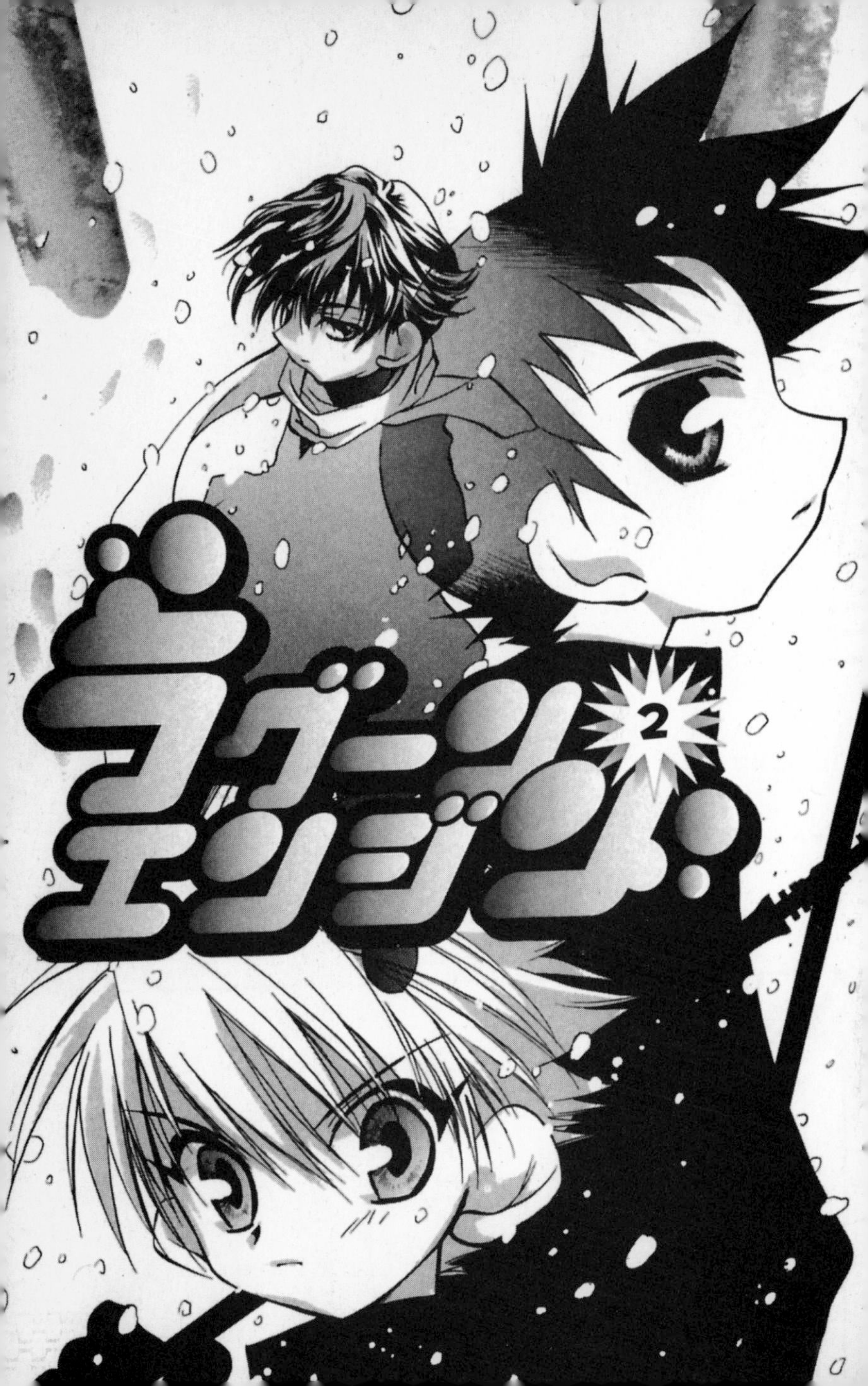
ラグーン
エンジン
2

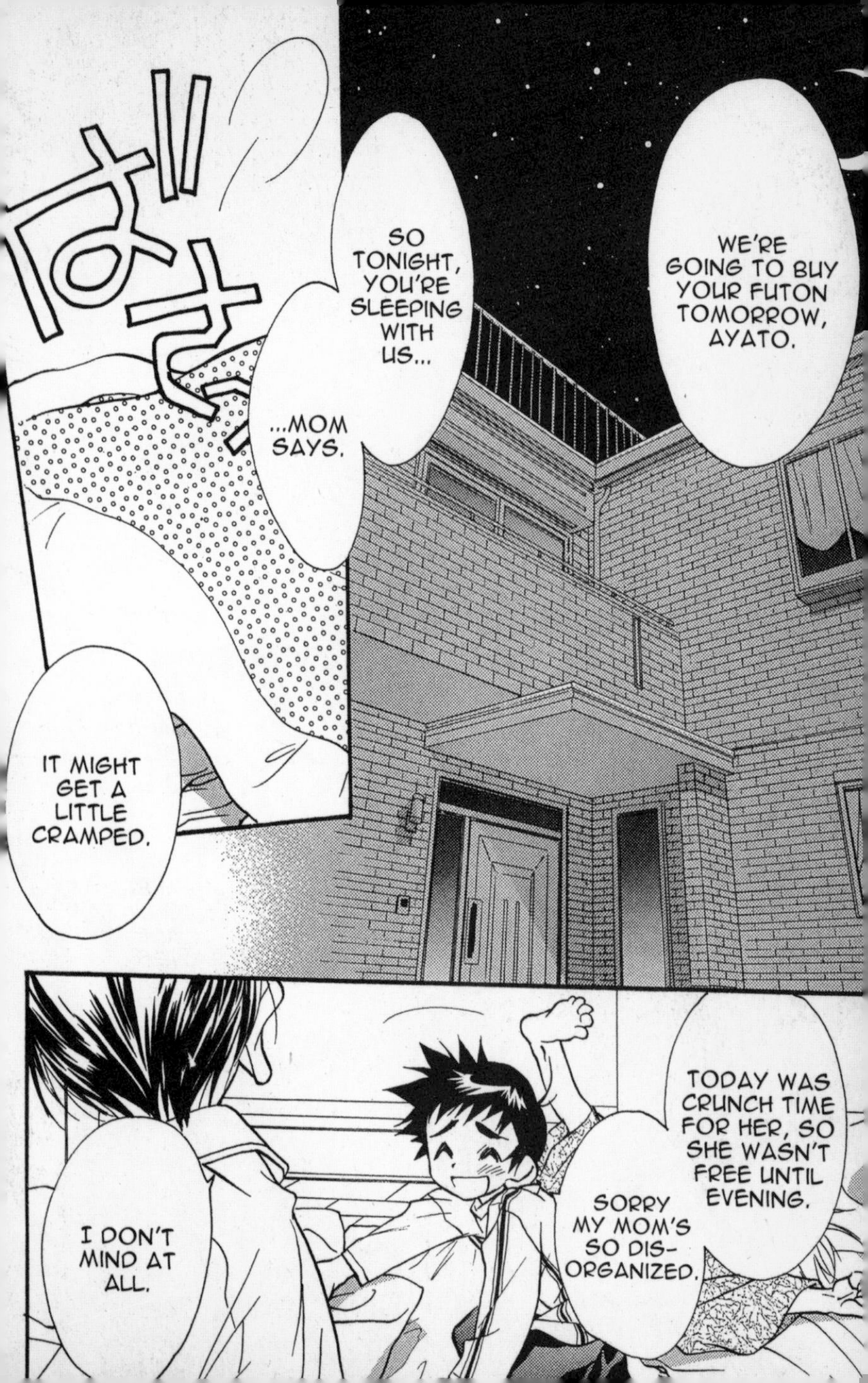
WE'RE GOING TO BUY YOUR FUTON TOMORROW, AYATO.
SO TONIGHT, YOU'RE SLEEPING WITH US...
...MOM SAYS.
ばさ
IT MIGHT GET A LITTLE CRAMPED.
TODAY WAS CRUNCH TIME FOR HER, SO SHE WASN'T FREE UNTIL EVENING.
SORRY MY MOM'S SO DIS-ORGANIZED.
I DON'T MIND AT ALL.

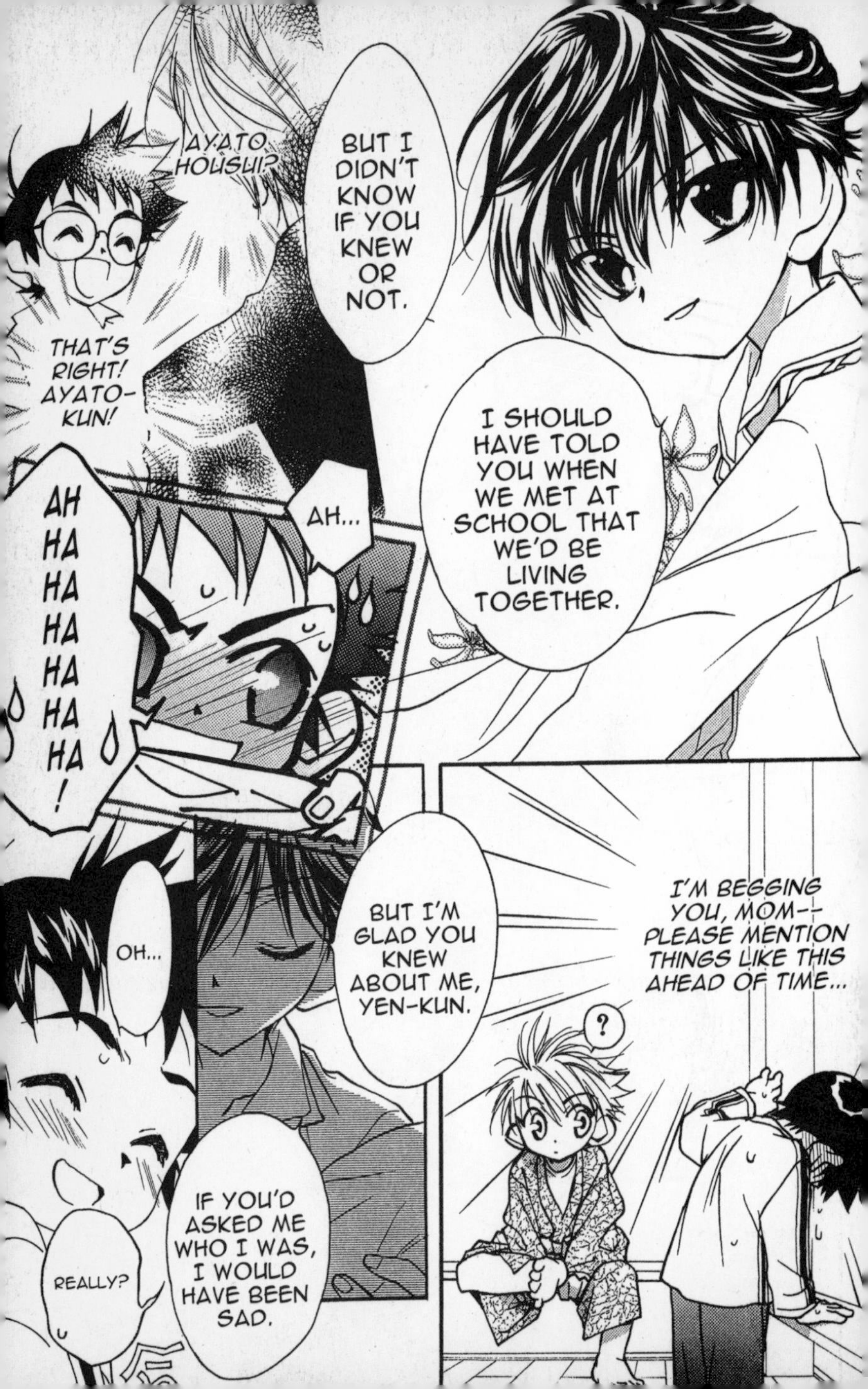
BUT I DIDN'T KNOW IF YOU KNEW OR NOT.
I SHOULD HAVE TOLD YOU WHEN WE MET AT SCHOOL THAT WE'D BE LIVING TOGETHER.
AYATO HOUSUI?
THAT'S RIGHT! AYATO-KUN!
AH...
AH HA HA HA HA HA HA HA!
I'M BEGGING YOU, MOM-- PLEASE MENTION THINGS LIKE THIS AHEAD OF TIME...
?
BUT I'M GLAD YOU KNEW ABOUT ME, YEN-KUN.
OH...
IF YOU'D ASKED ME WHO I WAS, I WOULD HAVE BEEN SAD.
REALLY?

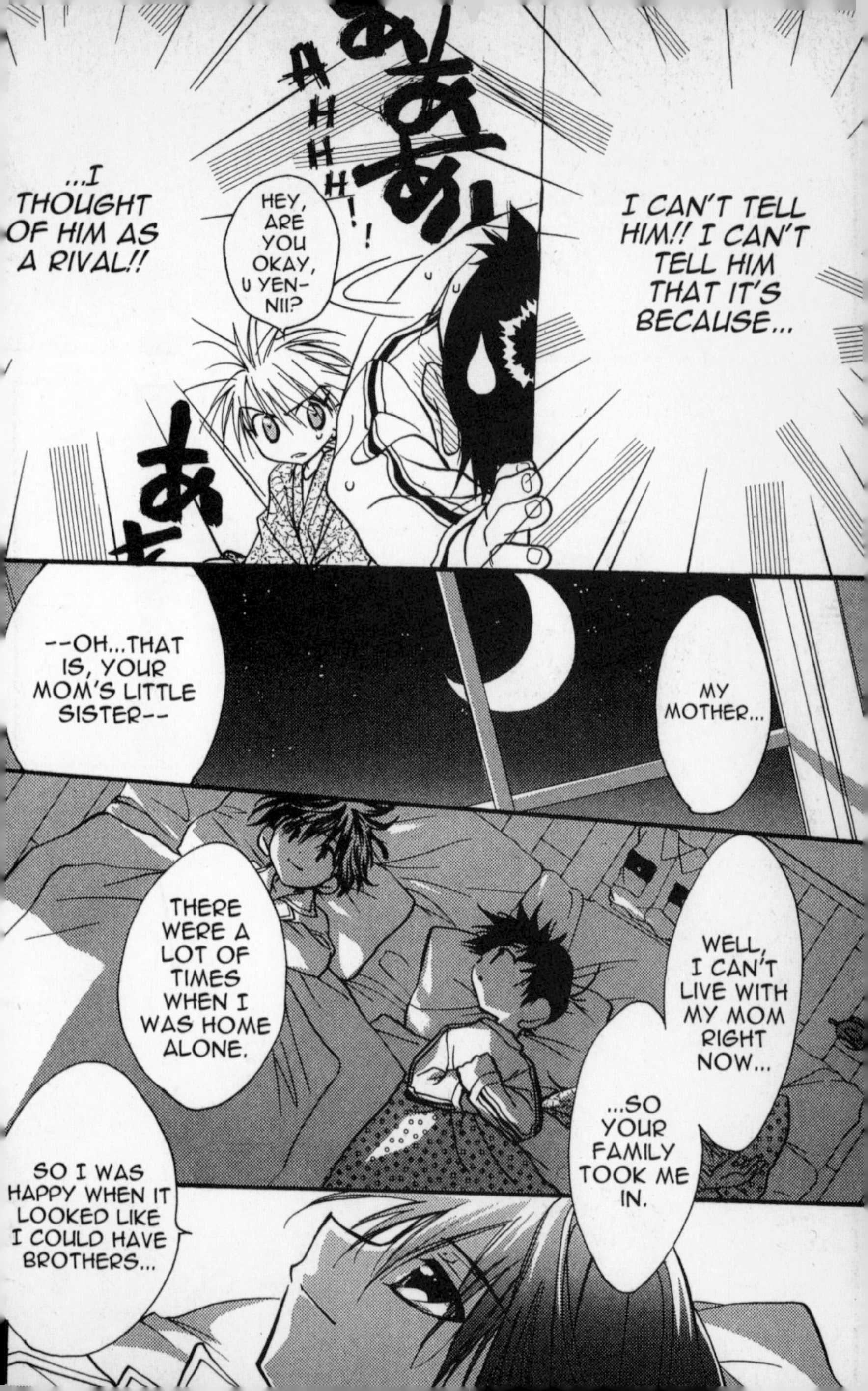
I CAN'T TELL HIM!! I CAN'T TELL HIM THAT IT'S BECAUSE...
AHHHH!!
HEY, ARE YOU OKAY, U YEN-NII?
...I THOUGHT OF HIM AS A RIVAL!!
MY MOTHER...
--OH...THAT IS, YOUR MOM'S LITTLE SISTER--
WELL, I CAN'T LIVE WITH MY MOM RIGHT NOW...
...SO YOUR FAMILY TOOK ME IN.
THERE WERE A LOT OF TIMES WHEN I WAS HOME ALONE.
SO I WAS HAPPY WHEN IT LOOKED LIKE I COULD HAVE BROTHERS...

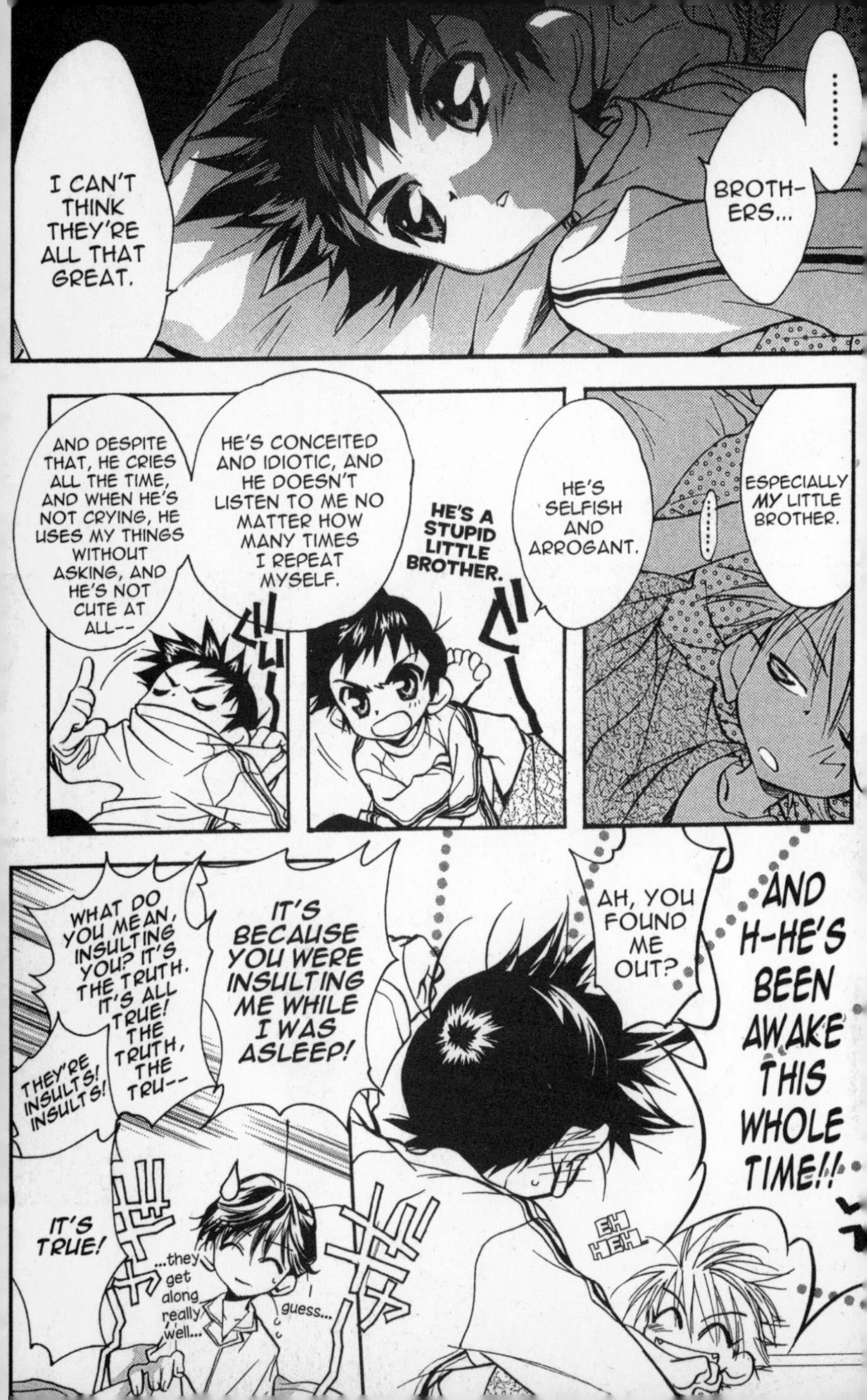
......
BROTH-ERS...
I CAN'T THINK THEY'RE ALL THAT GREAT.
ESPECIALLY MY LITTLE BROTHER.
......
HE'S SELFISH AND ARROGANT.
HE'S A STUPID LITTLE BROTHER.
HE'S CONCEITED AND IDIOTIC, AND HE DOESN'T LISTEN TO ME NO MATTER HOW MANY TIMES I REPEAT MYSELF.
AND DESPITE THAT, HE CRIES ALL THE TIME, AND WHEN HE'S NOT CRYING, HE USES MY THINGS WITHOUT ASKING, AND HE'S NOT CUTE AT ALL--
AND H-HE'S BEEN AWAKE THIS WHOLE TIME!!
AH, YOU FOUND ME OUT?
EH HEH
IT'S BECAUSE YOU WERE INSULTING ME WHILE I WAS ASLEEP!
WHAT DO YOU MEAN, INSULTING YOU? IT'S THE TRUTH. IT'S ALL TRUE! THE TRUTH, THE TRU--
THEY'RE INSULTS! INSULTS!
IT'S TRUE!
...they get along really well...
I guess...

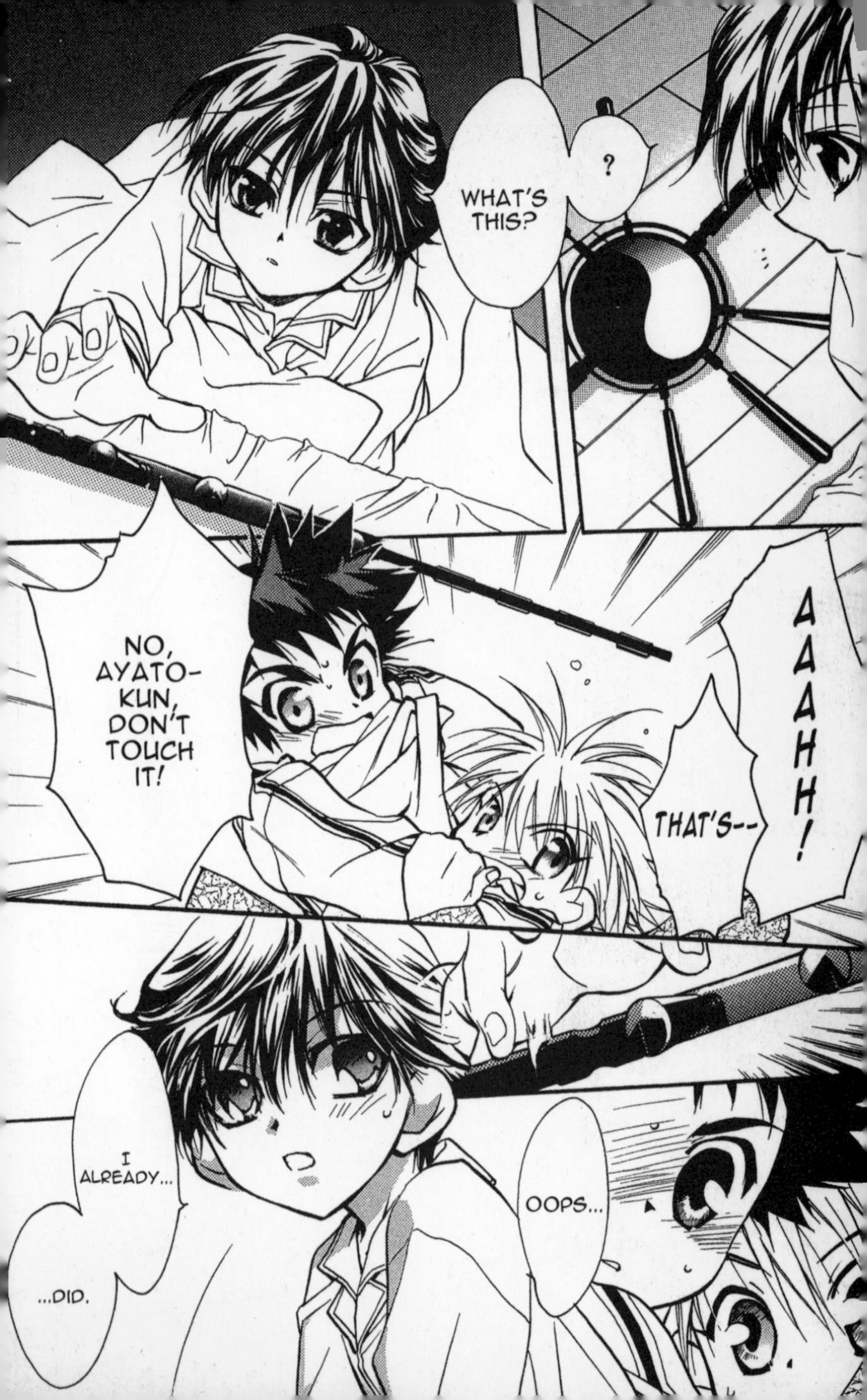
?
WHAT'S THIS?
AAAHH!
THAT'S--
NO, AYATO-KUN, DON'T TOUCH IT!
OOPS...
I ALREADY...
...DID.

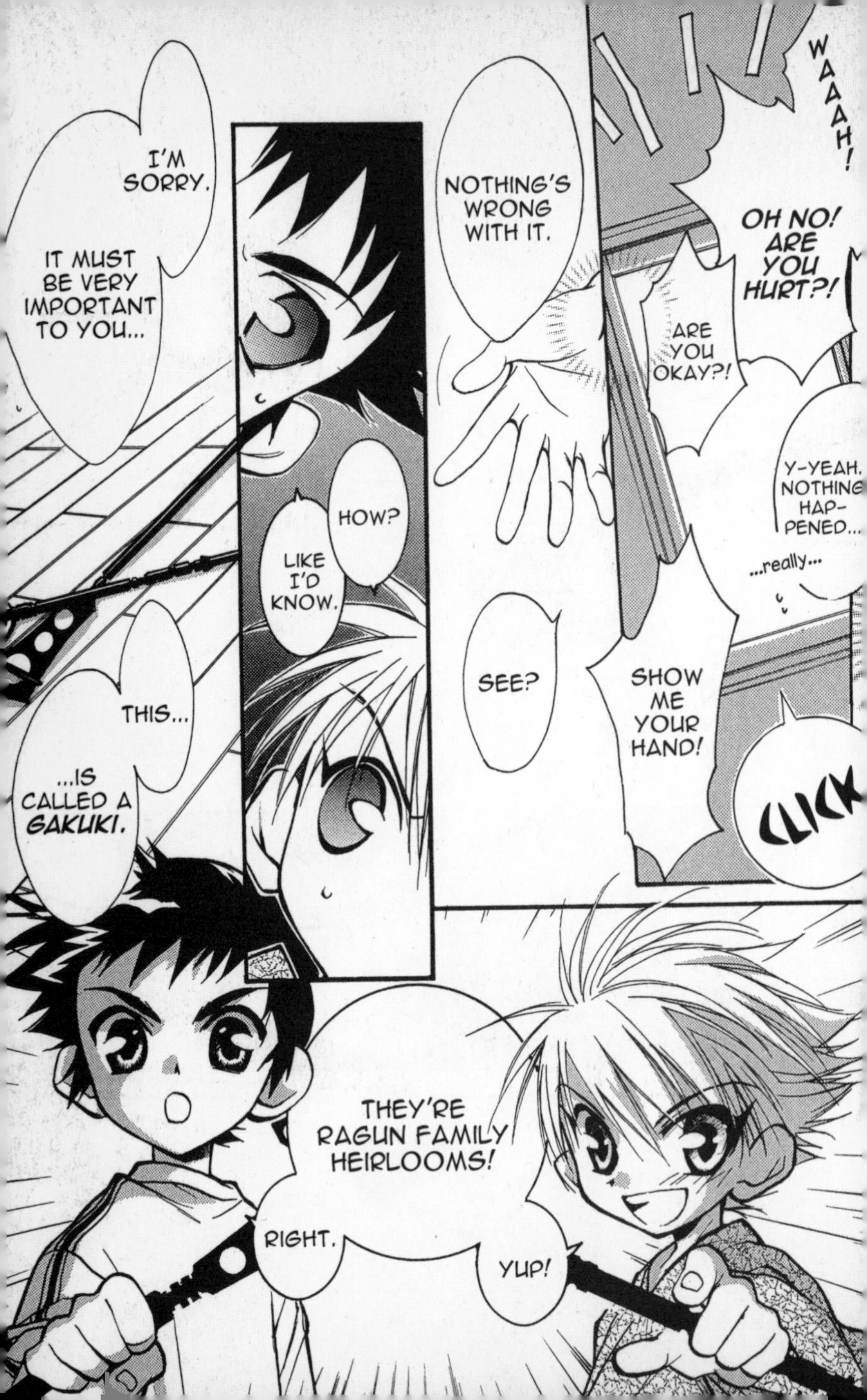

WAAAH!
OH NO! ARE YOU HURT?!
ARE YOU OKAY?!
Y-YEAH. NOTHING HAP-PENED...
...really...
CLICK
SHOW ME YOUR HAND!
NOTHING'S WRONG WITH IT.
SEE?
HOW?
LIKE I'D KNOW.
I'M SORRY.
IT MUST BE VERY IMPORTANT TO YOU...
THIS...
...IS CALLED A **GAKUKI**.
THEY'RE RAGUN FAMILY HEIRLOOMS!
YUP!
RIGHT.

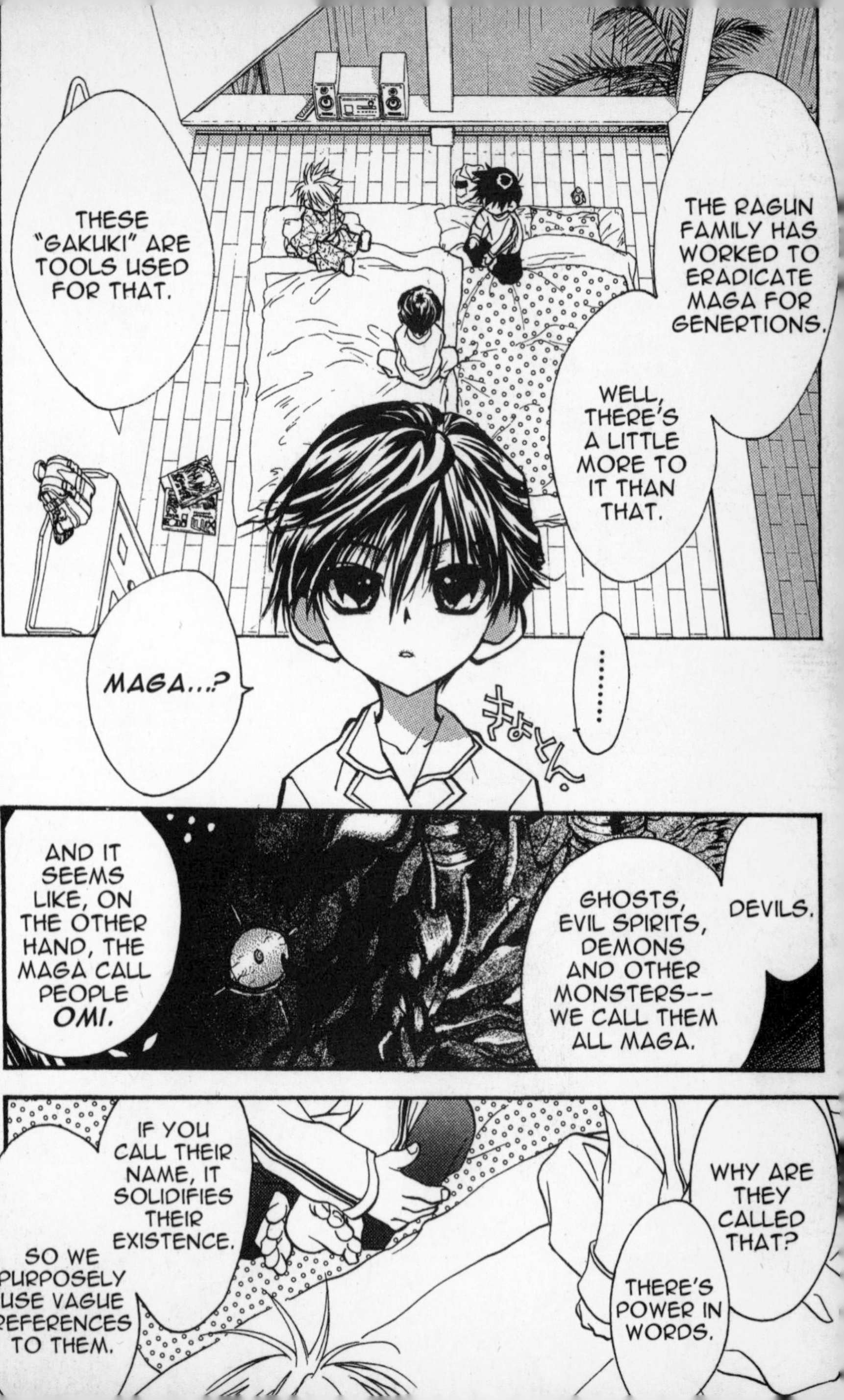
THE RAGUN FAMILY HAS WORKED TO ERADICATE MAGA FOR GENERTIONS.
WELL, THERE'S A LITTLE MORE TO IT THAN THAT.
THESE "GAKUKI" ARE TOOLS USED FOR THAT.
......
きょとん
MAGA...?
DEVILS.
GHOSTS, EVIL SPIRITS, DEMONS AND OTHER MONSTERS-- WE CALL THEM ALL MAGA.
AND IT SEEMS LIKE, ON THE OTHER HAND, THE MAGA CALL PEOPLE OMI.
WHY ARE THEY CALLED THAT?
THERE'S POWER IN WORDS.
IF YOU CALL THEIR NAME, IT SOLIDIFIES THEIR EXISTENCE.
SO WE PURPOSELY USE VAGUE REFERENCES TO THEM.

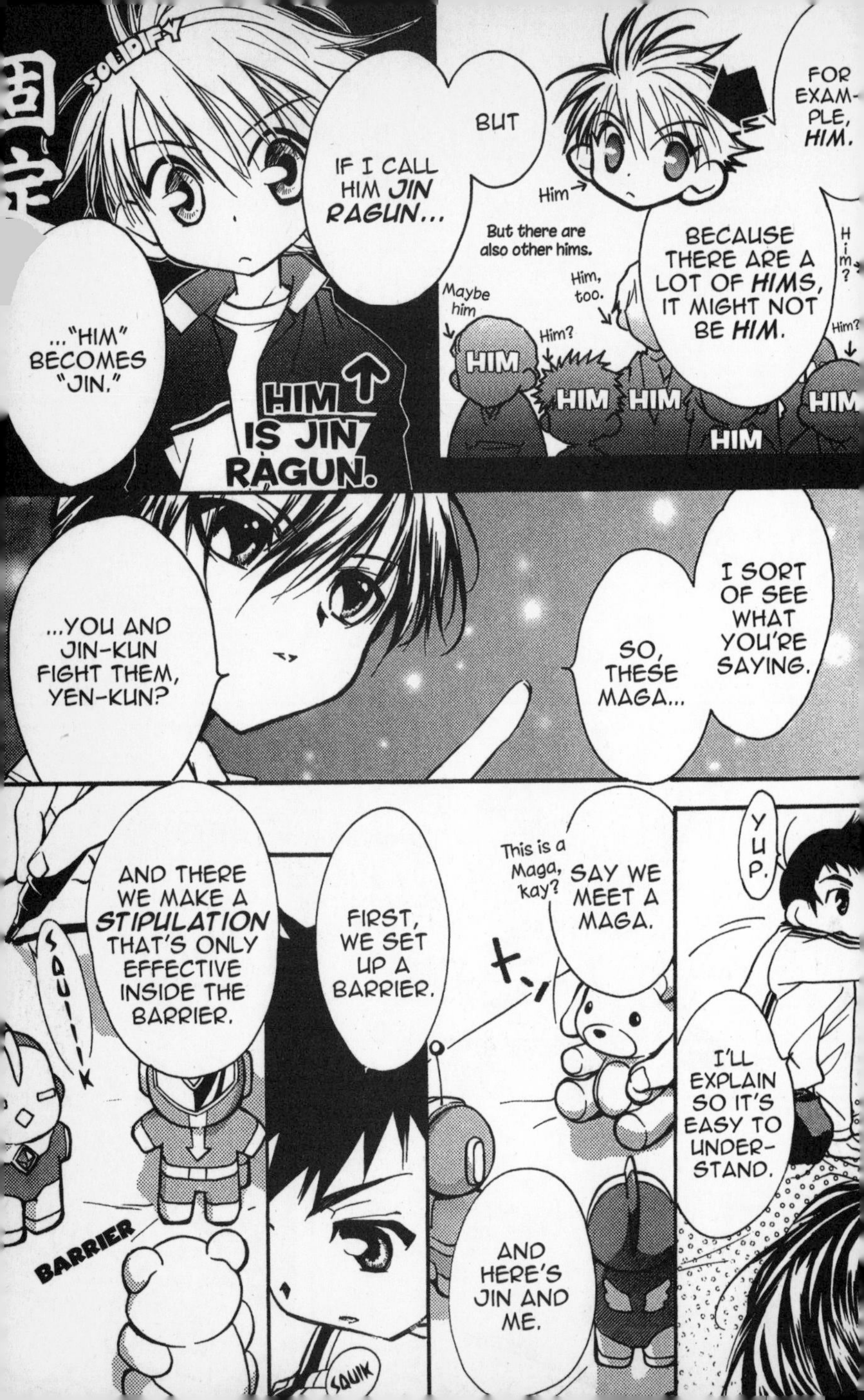
FOR EXAMPLE, HIM.
Him
BECAUSE THERE ARE A LOT OF HIMS, IT MIGHT NOT BE HIM.
Him?
But there are also other hims.
Him, too.
Maybe him
Him?
Him?
HIM
HIM
HIM
HIM
HIM
固定
SOLIDIFY
BUT
IF I CALL HIM JIN RAGUN...
..."HIM" BECOMES "JIN."
HIM IS JIN RAGUN.
I SORT OF SEE WHAT YOU'RE SAYING.
SO, THESE MAGA...
...YOU AND JIN-KUN FIGHT THEM, YEN-KUN?
YUP.
I'LL EXPLAIN SO IT'S EASY TO UNDER-STAND.
SAY WE MEET A MAGA.
This is a Maga, 'kay?
AND HERE'S JIN AND ME.
FIRST, WE SET UP A BARRIER.
AND THERE WE MAKE A STIPULATION THAT'S ONLY EFFECTIVE INSIDE THE BARRIER.
SQUIIIIK
BARRIER
SQUIK

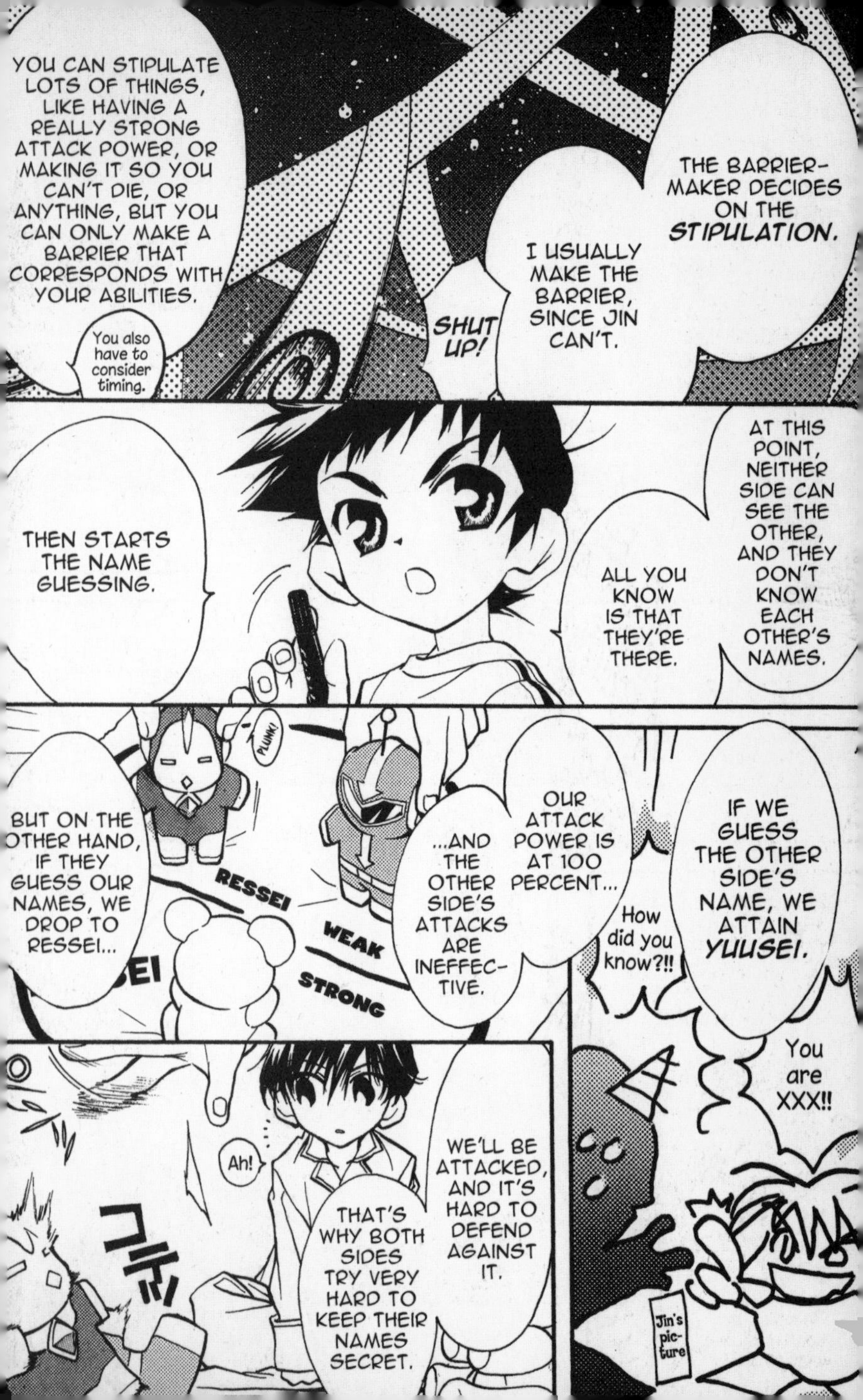
THE BARRIER-MAKER DECIDES ON THE STIPULATION.
I USUALLY MAKE THE BARRIER, SINCE JIN CAN'T.
SHUT UP!
YOU CAN STIPULATE LOTS OF THINGS, LIKE HAVING A REALLY STRONG ATTACK POWER, OR MAKING IT SO YOU CAN'T DIE, OR ANYTHING, BUT YOU CAN ONLY MAKE A BARRIER THAT CORRESPONDS WITH YOUR ABILITIES.
You also have to consider timing.
AT THIS POINT, NEITHER SIDE CAN SEE THE OTHER, AND THEY DON'T KNOW EACH OTHER'S NAMES.
ALL YOU KNOW IS THAT THEY'RE THERE.
THEN STARTS THE NAME GUESSING.
IF WE GUESS THE OTHER SIDE'S NAME, WE ATTAIN YUUSEI.
How did you know?!!
You are XXX!!
Jin's picture
OUR ATTACK POWER IS AT 100 PERCENT...
...AND THE OTHER SIDE'S ATTACKS ARE INEFFECTIVE.
PLUNK!
RESSEI
WEAK
STRONG
BUT ON THE OTHER HAND, IF THEY GUESS OUR NAMES, WE DROP TO RESSEI...
WE'LL BE ATTACKED, AND IT'S HARD TO DEFEND AGAINST IT.
THAT'S WHY BOTH SIDES TRY VERY HARD TO KEEP THEIR NAMES SECRET.
Ah!

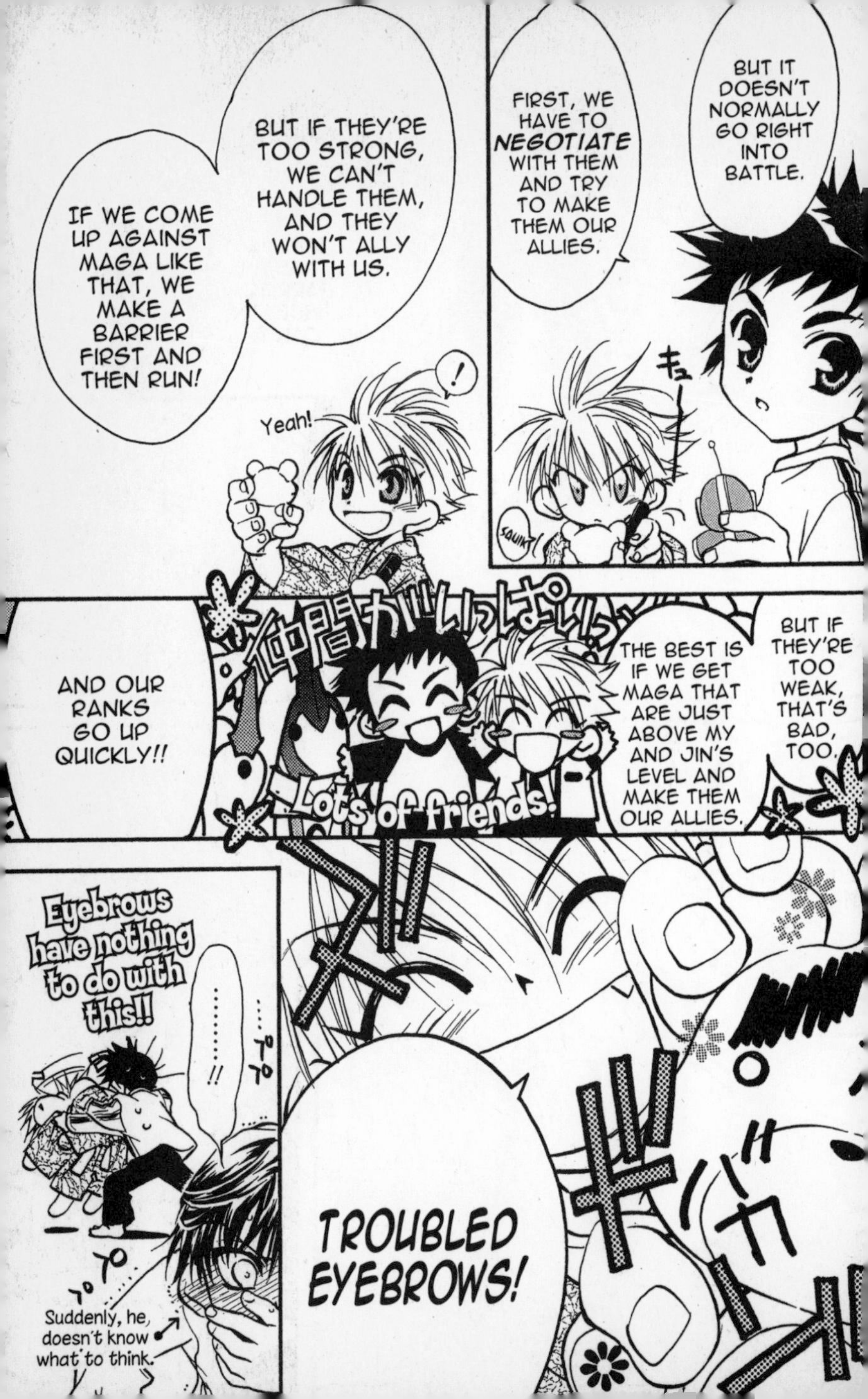

BUT IT DOESN'T NORMALLY GO RIGHT INTO BATTLE.
FIRST, WE HAVE TO ***NEGOTIATE*** WITH THEM AND TRY TO MAKE THEM OUR ALLIES.
キュ
SQUINT
BUT IF THEY'RE TOO STRONG, WE CAN'T HANDLE THEM, AND THEY WON'T ALLY WITH US.
IF WE COME UP AGAINST MAGA LIKE THAT, WE MAKE A BARRIER FIRST AND THEN RUN!
!
Yeah!
BUT IF THEY'RE TOO WEAK, THAT'S BAD, TOO.
THE BEST IS IF WE GET MAGA THAT ARE JUST ABOVE MY AND JIN'S LEVEL AND MAKE THEM OUR ALLIES.
仲間がいっぱいっ
Lots of friends!
AND OUR RANKS GO UP QUICKLY!!
TROUBLED EYEBROWS!
Eyebrows have nothing to do with this!!
.........!!
Suddenly, he doesn't know what to think.

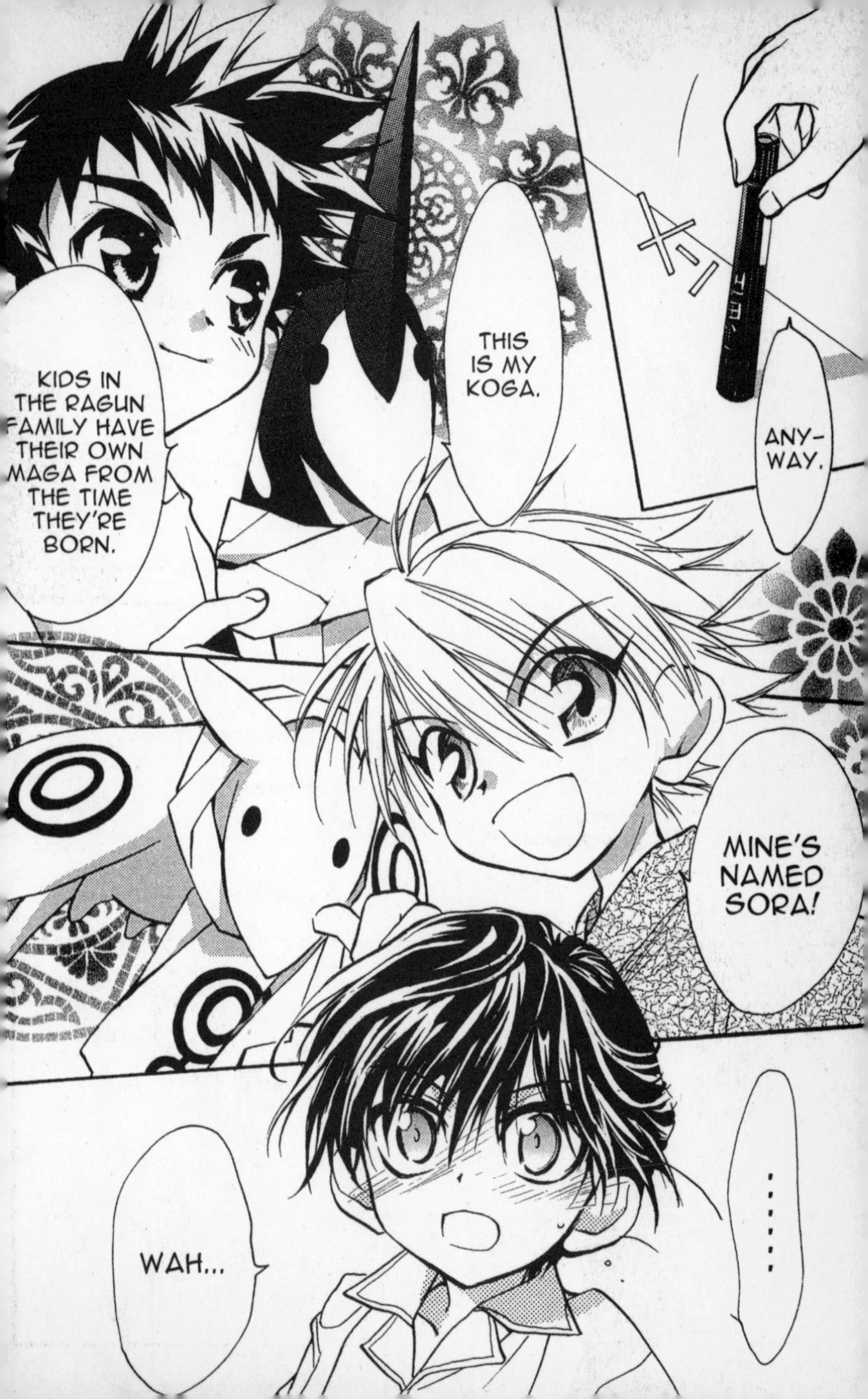
ANY-WAY.
THIS IS MY KOGA.
KIDS IN THE RAGUN FAMILY HAVE THEIR OWN MAGA FROM THE TIME THEY'RE BORN.
MINE'S NAMED SORA!
......
WAH...

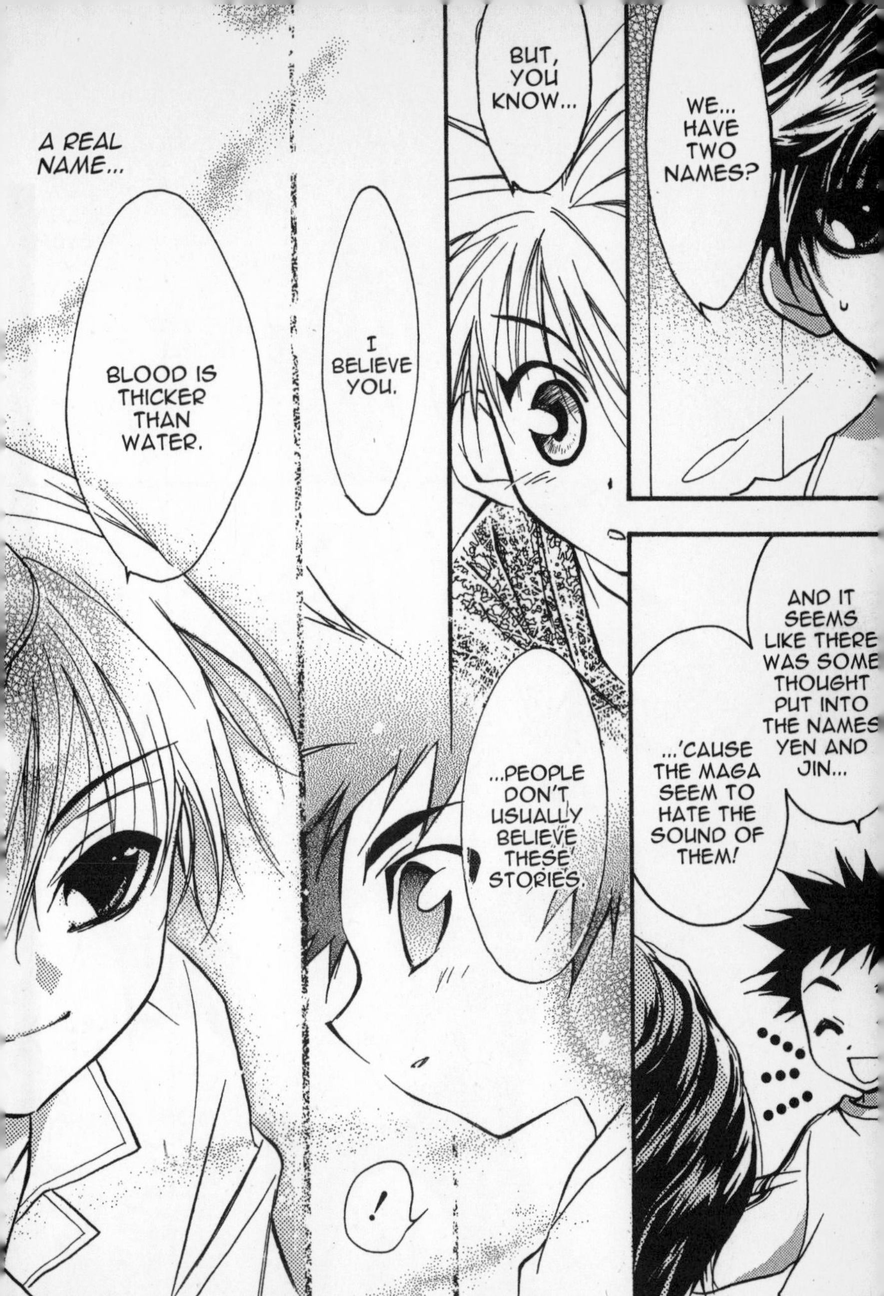

WE... HAVE TWO NAMES?
AND IT SEEMS LIKE THERE WAS SOME THOUGHT PUT INTO THE NAMES YEN AND JIN...
...'CAUSE THE MAGA SEEM TO HATE THE SOUND OF THEM!
BUT, YOU KNOW...
...PEOPLE DON'T USUALLY BELIEVE THESE STORIES.
I BELIEVE YOU.
!
A REAL NAME...
BLOOD IS THICKER THAN WATER.

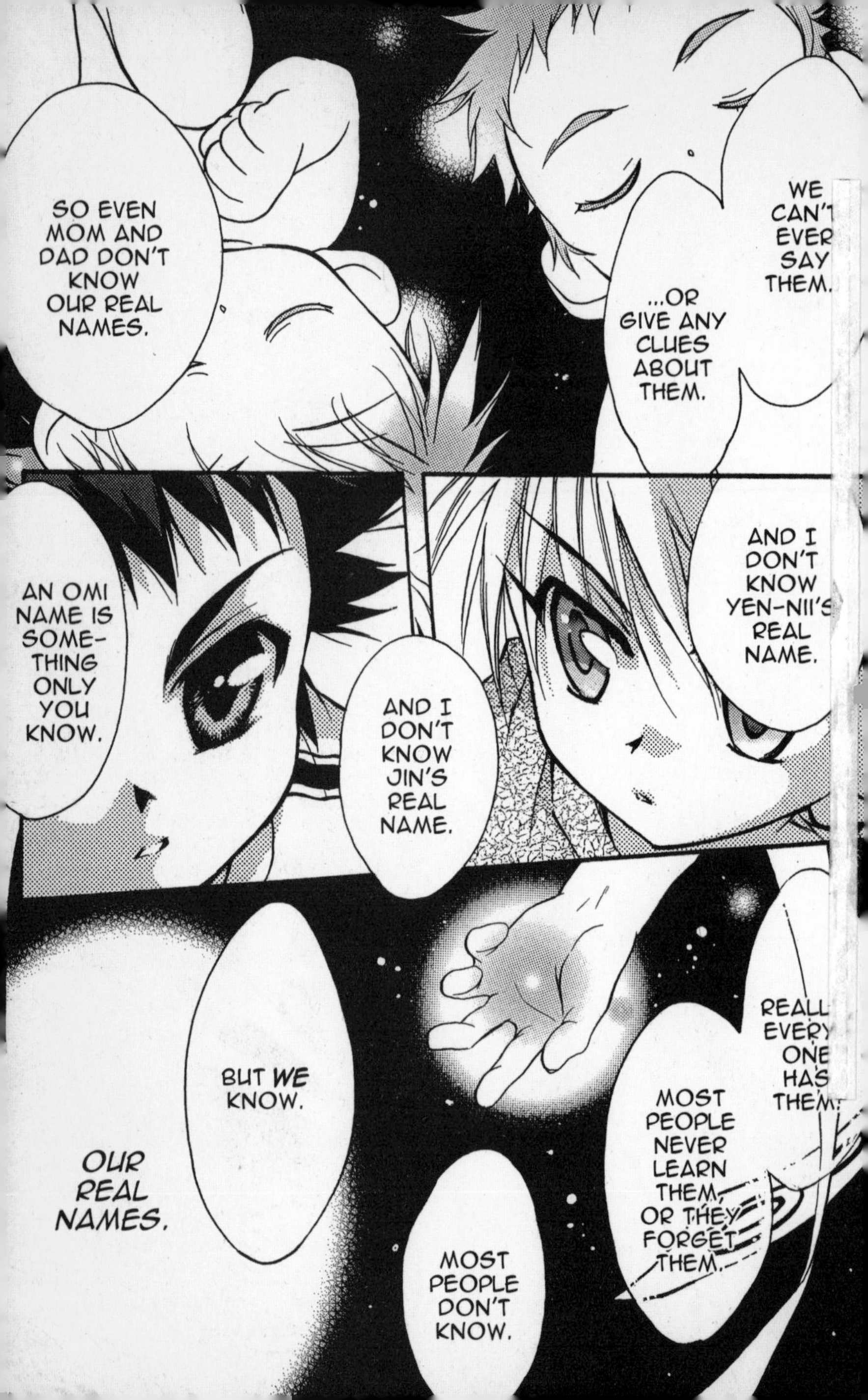
WE CAN'T EVER SAY THEM.
...OR GIVE ANY CLUES ABOUT THEM.
SO EVEN MOM AND DAD DON'T KNOW OUR REAL NAMES.
AND I DON'T KNOW YEN-NII'S REAL NAME.
AND I DON'T KNOW JIN'S REAL NAME.
AN OMI NAME IS SOME-THING ONLY YOU KNOW.
REALL EVERY ONE HAS THEM.
MOST PEOPLE NEVER LEARN THEM, OR THEY FORGET THEM.
MOST PEOPLE DON'T KNOW.
BUT WE KNOW.
OUR REAL NAMES.

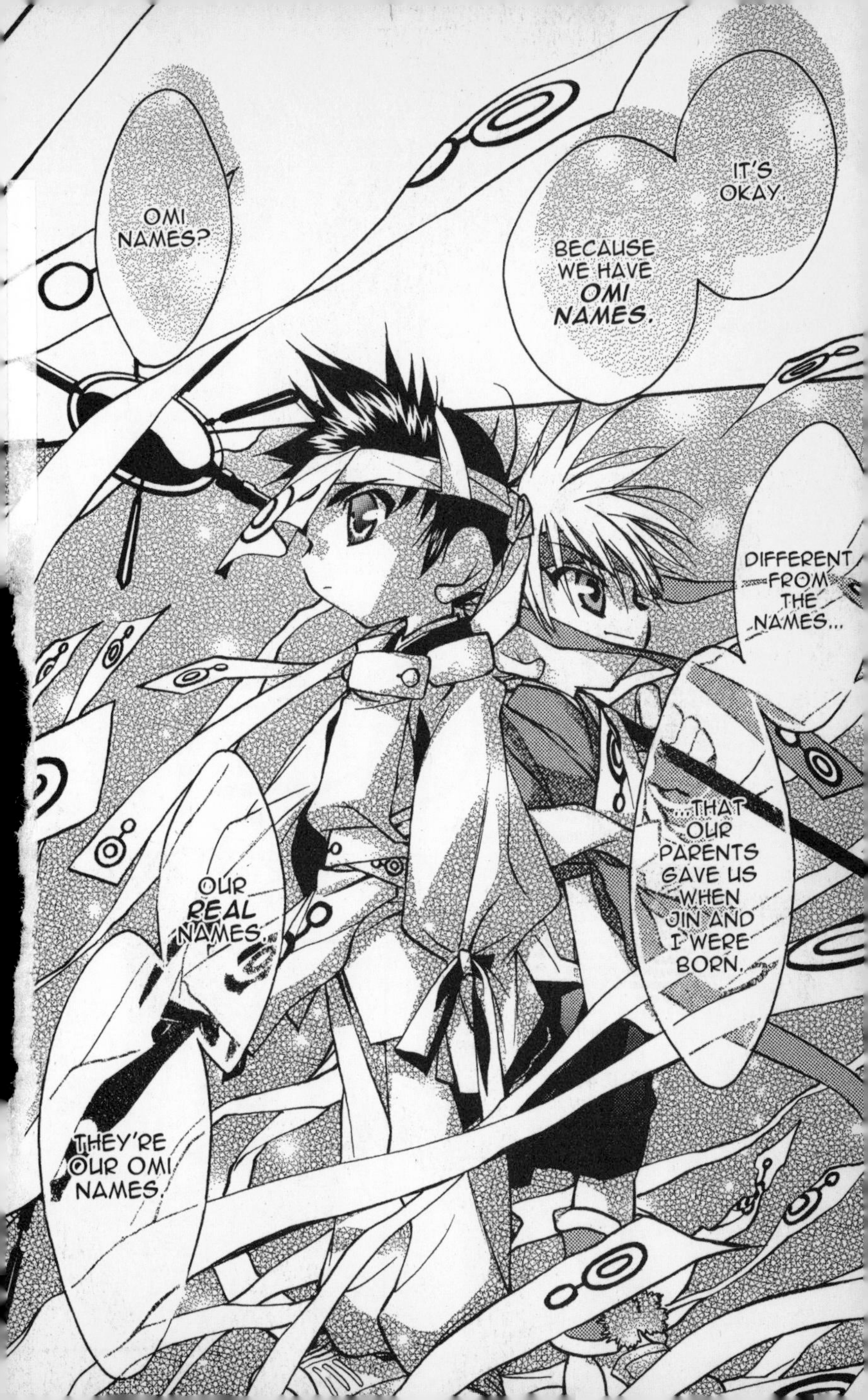
IT'S OKAY.
BECAUSE WE HAVE OMI NAMES.
OMI NAMES?
DIFFERENT FROM THE NAMES...
...THAT OUR PARENTS GAVE US WHEN JIN AND I WERE BORN.
OUR REAL NAMES.
THEY'RE OUR OMI NAMES.

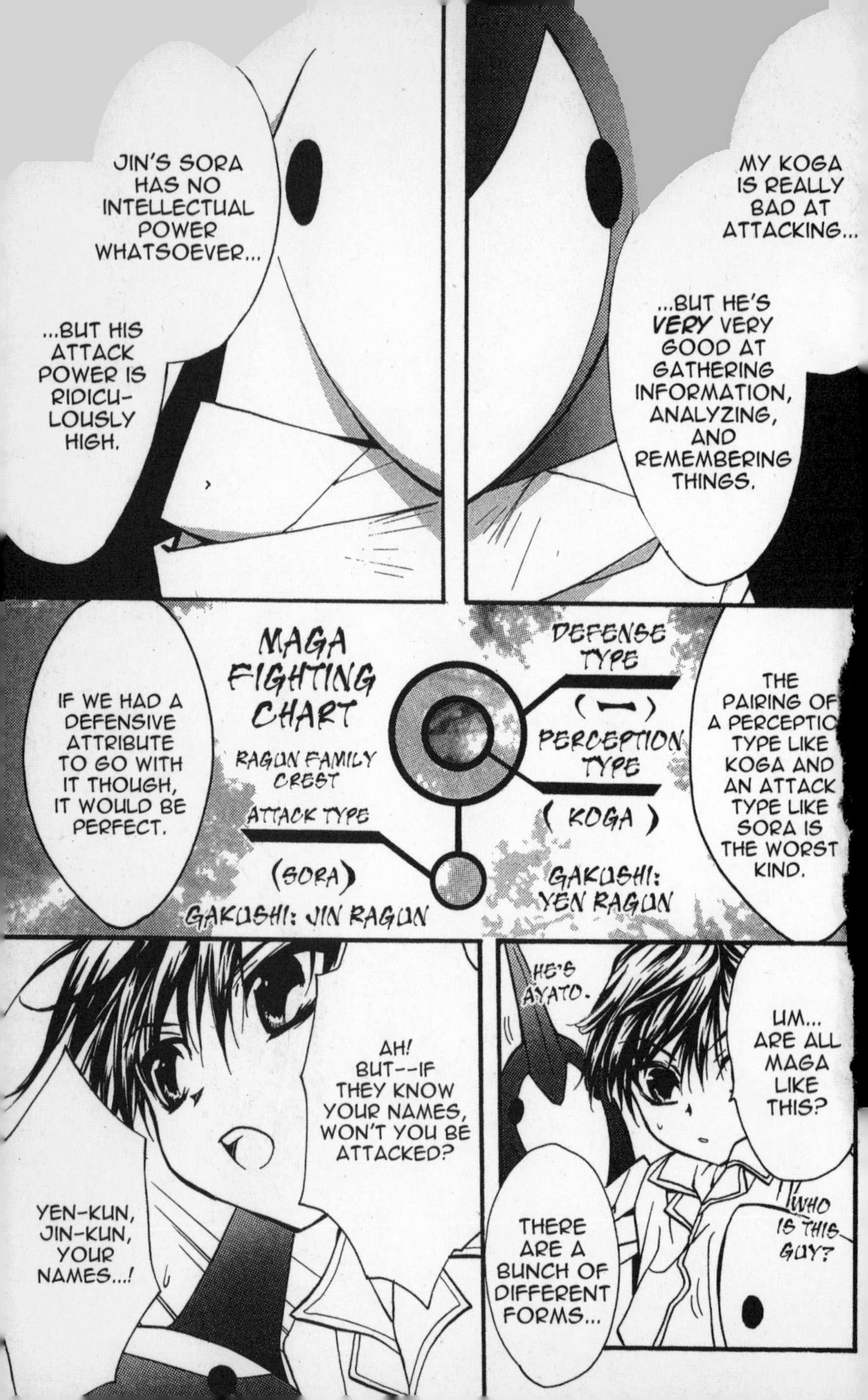
MY KOGA IS REALLY BAD AT ATTACKING...
...BUT HE'S VERY VERY GOOD AT GATHERING INFORMATION, ANALYZING, AND REMEMBERING THINGS.
JIN'S SORA HAS NO INTELLECTUAL POWER WHATSOEVER...
...BUT HIS ATTACK POWER IS RIDICULOUSLY HIGH.
THE PAIRING OF A PERCEPTIO TYPE LIKE KOGA AND AN ATTACK TYPE LIKE SORA IS THE WORST KIND.
MAGA FIGHTING CHART
DEFENSE TYPE
(—)
PERCEPTION TYPE
(KOGA)
GAKUSHI: YEN RAGUN
RAGUN FAMILY CREST
ATTACK TYPE
(SORA)
GAKUSHI: JIN RAGUN
IF WE HAD A DEFENSIVE ATTRIBUTE TO GO WITH IT THOUGH, IT WOULD BE PERFECT.
UM... ARE ALL MAGA LIKE THIS?
HE'S AYATO.
WHO IS THIS GUY?
THERE ARE A BUNCH OF DIFFERENT FORMS...
AH! BUT--IF THEY KNOW YOUR NAMES, WON'T YOU BE ATTACKED?
YEN-KUN, JIN-KUN, YOUR NAMES...!

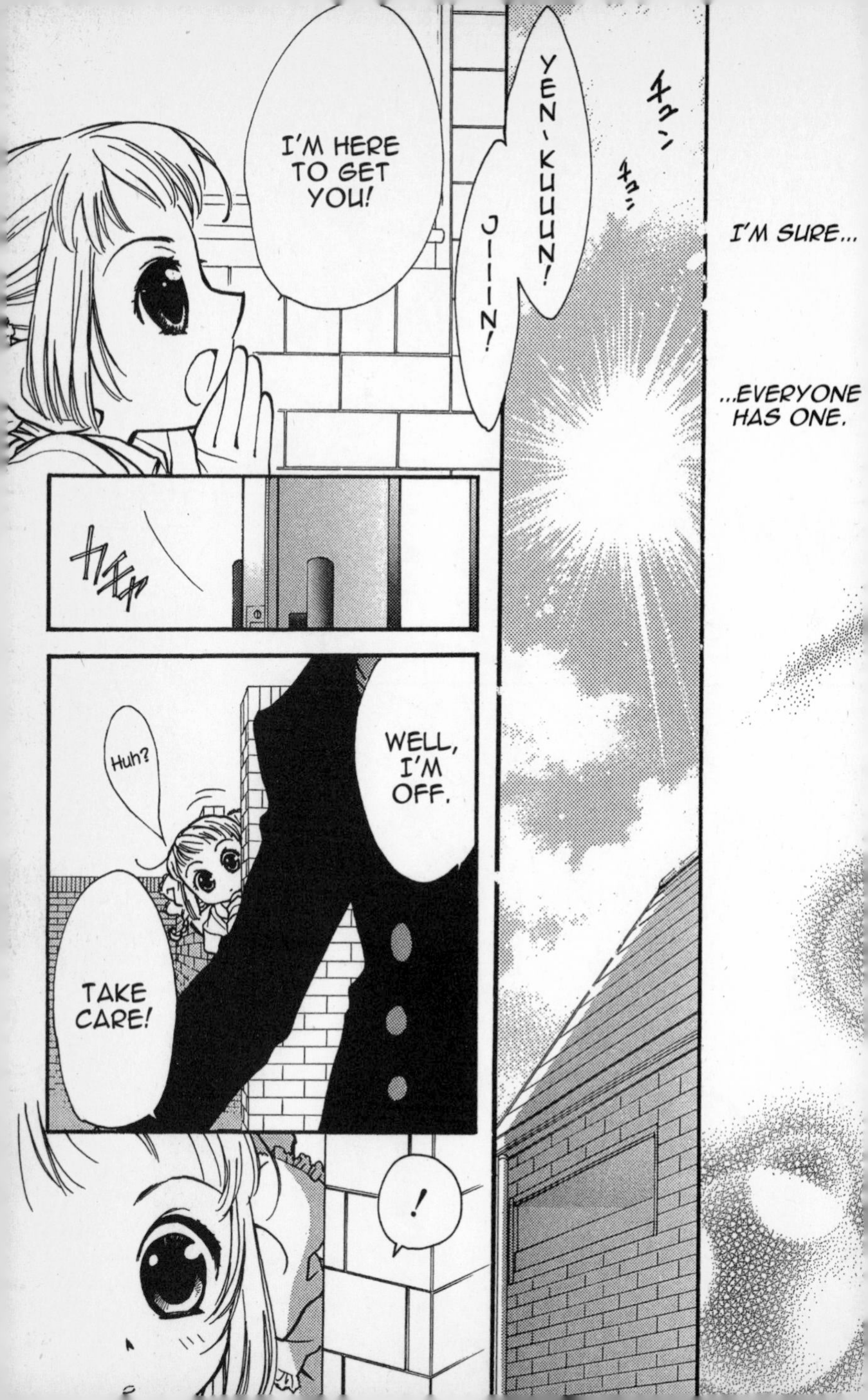
I'M SURE...
...EVERYONE HAS ONE.
チュン
チュン
YEN-KUUUN!
JIIIIN!
I'M HERE TO GET YOU!
カチャ
WELL, I'M OFF.
Huh?
TAKE CARE!
!

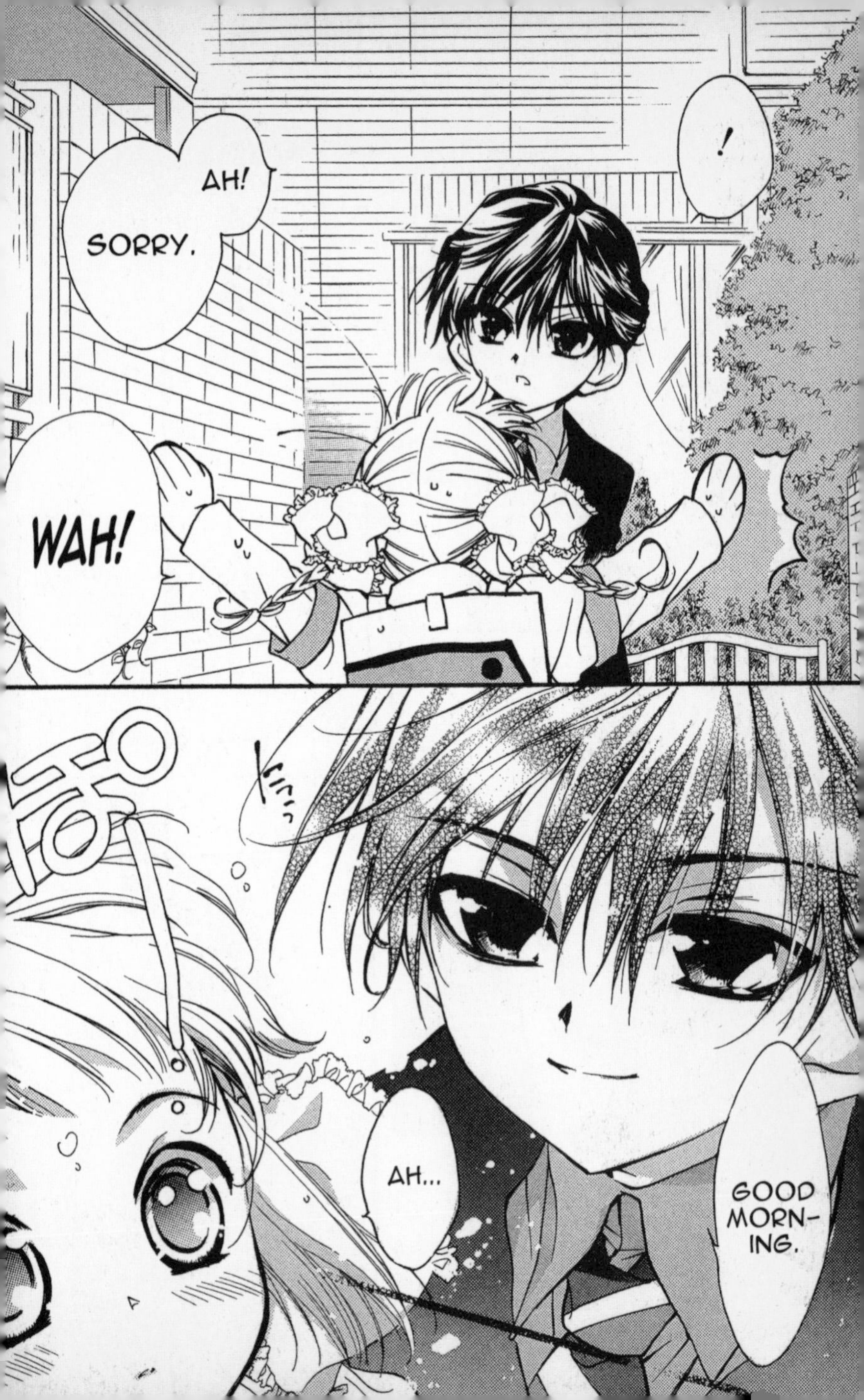
!
AH! SORRY.
WAH!
GOOD MORN-ING.
AH...

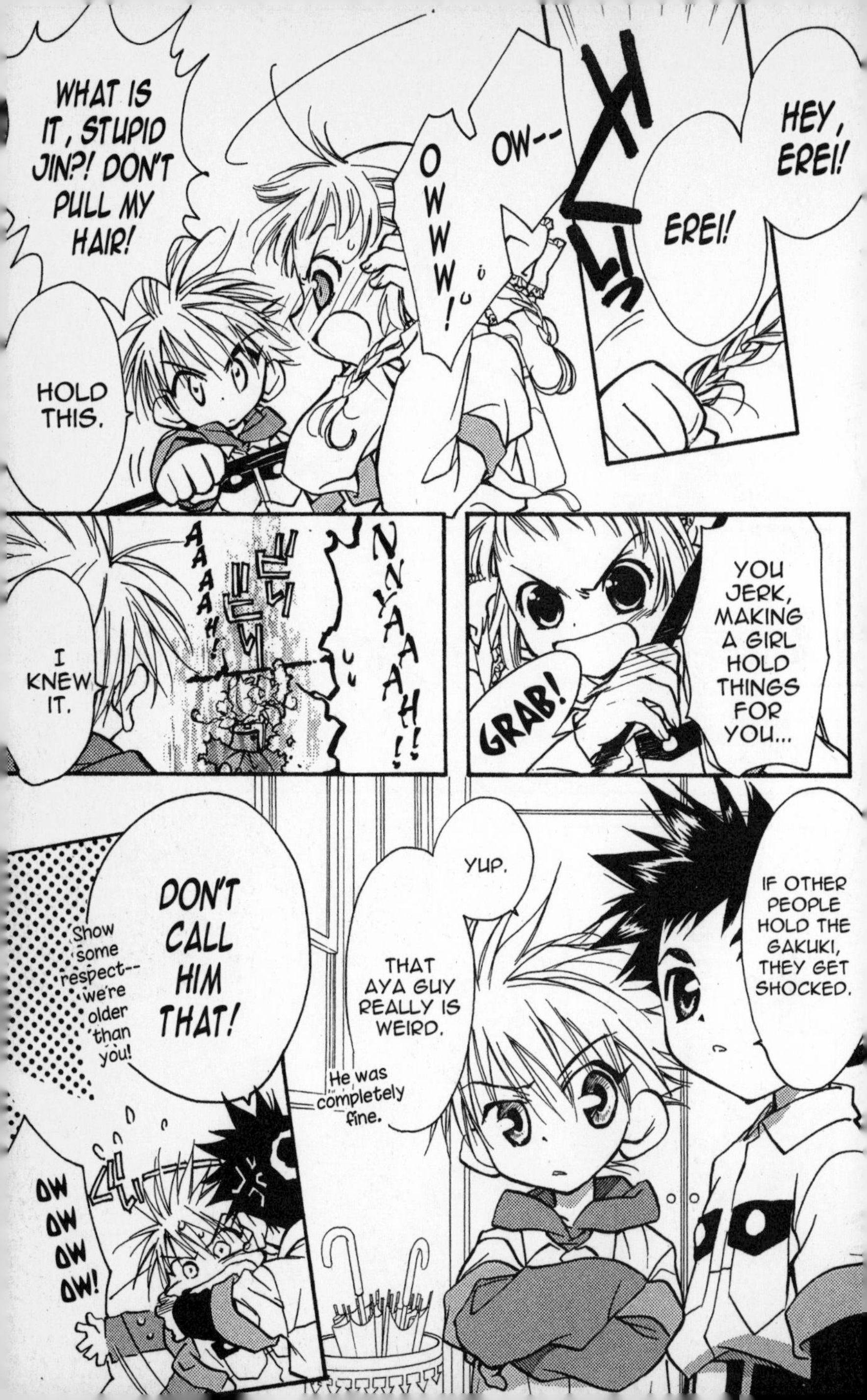
HEY, EREI!
EREI!
OW-- OWWWW!
WHAT IS IT, STUPID JIN?! DON'T PULL MY HAIR!
HOLD THIS.
YOU JERK, MAKING A GIRL HOLD THINGS FOR YOU...
GRAB!
NNYAAAAH!!
AAAAAH!
I KNEW IT.
IF OTHER PEOPLE HOLD THE GAKUKI, THEY GET SHOCKED.
YUP.
THAT AYA GUY REALLY IS WEIRD.
He was completely fine.
DON'T CALL HIM THAT!
Show some respect--we're older than you!
OW OW OW OW!

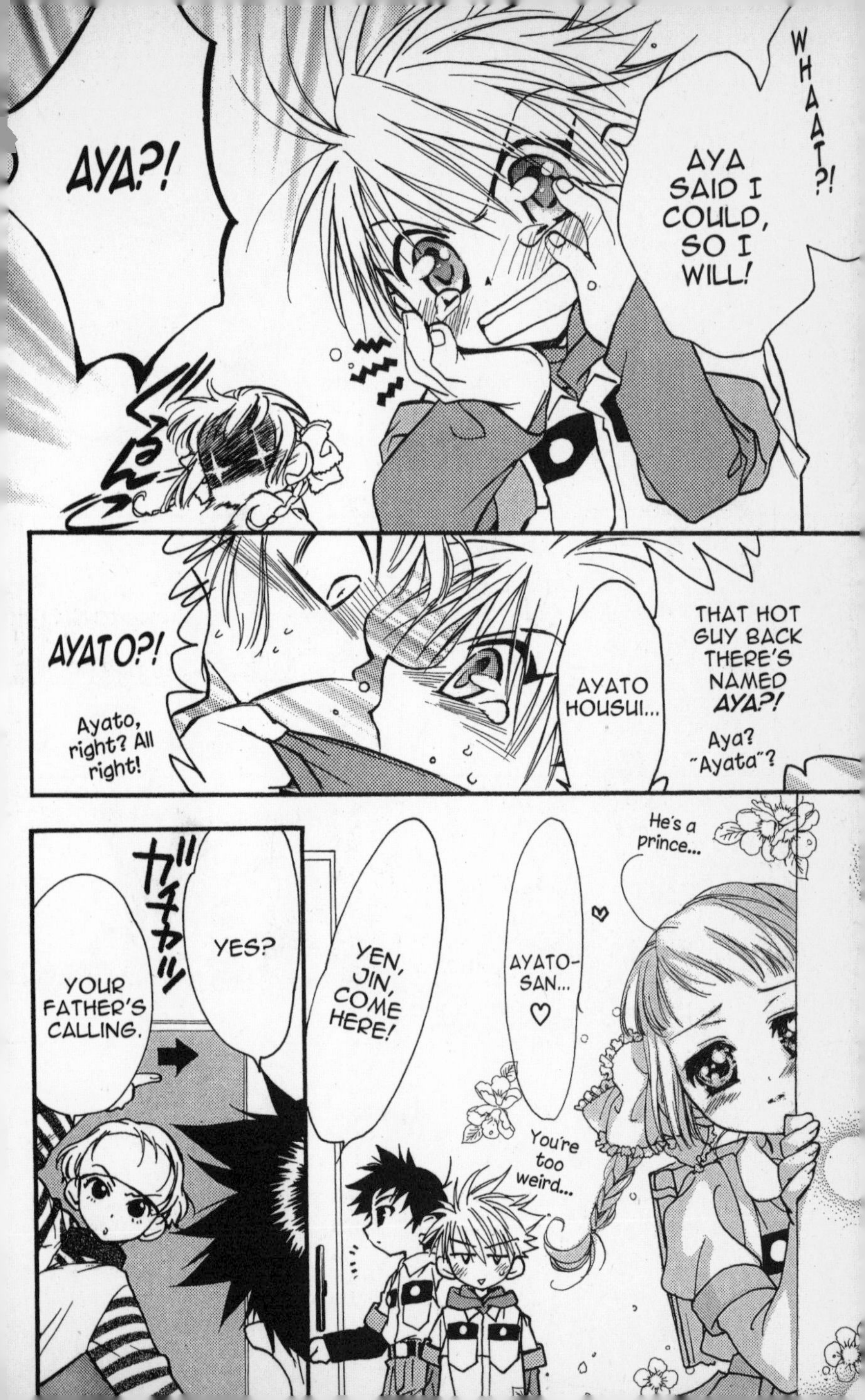
WHAAAT?!
AYA SAID I COULD, SO I WILL!
AYA?!
THAT HOT GUY BACK THERE'S NAMED AYA?!
Aya? "Ayata"?
AYATO HOUSUI...
AYATO?!
Ayato, right? All right!
He's a prince...
AYATO-SAN... ♡
You're too weird...
YEN, JIN, COME HERE!
YES?
ガチャッ
YOUR FATHER'S CALLING.

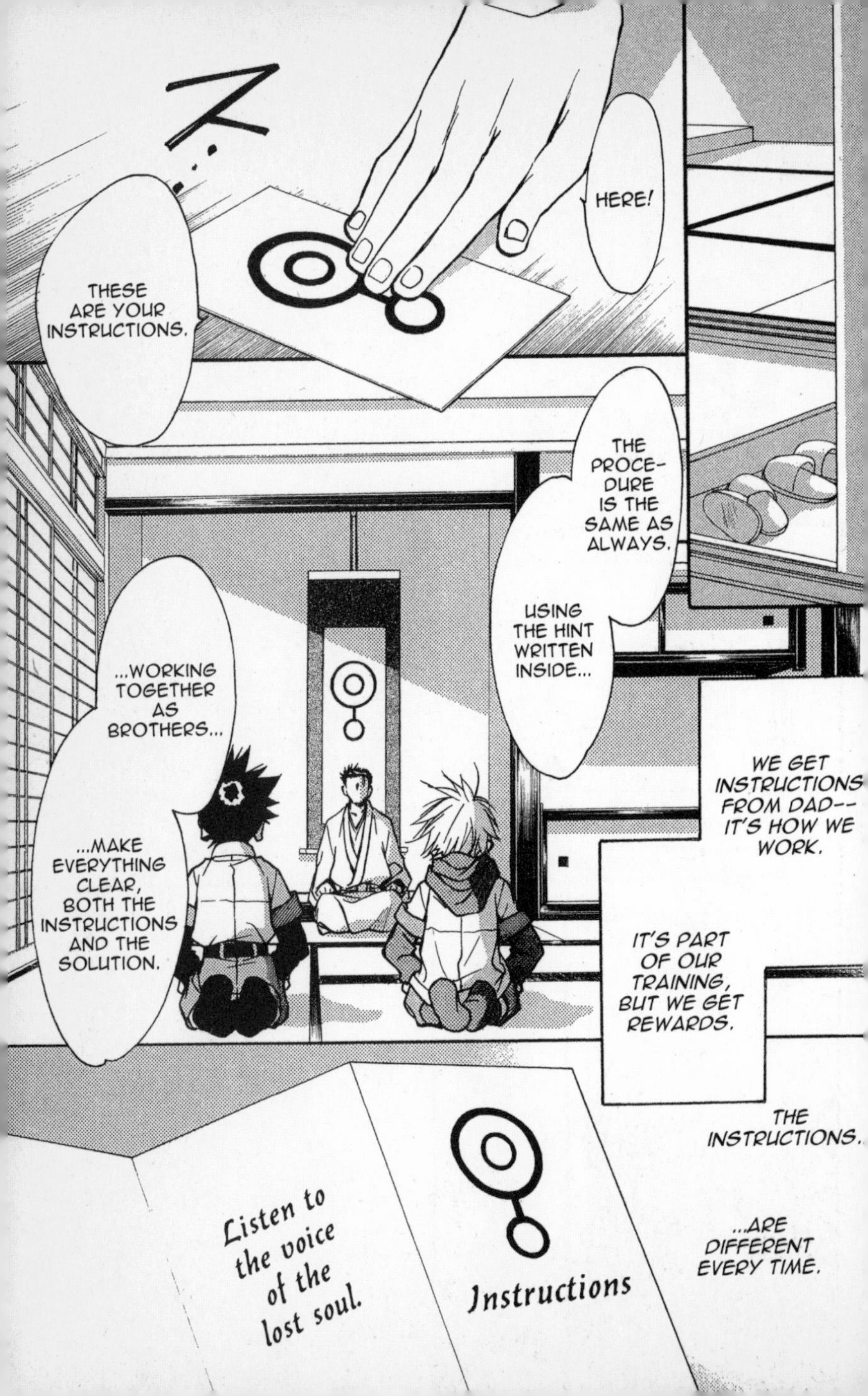
HERE!
THESE ARE YOUR INSTRUCTIONS.
THE PROCEDURE IS THE SAME AS ALWAYS.
USING THE HINT WRITTEN INSIDE...
...WORKING TOGETHER AS BROTHERS...
...MAKE EVERYTHING CLEAR, BOTH THE INSTRUCTIONS AND THE SOLUTION.
WE GET INSTRUCTIONS FROM DAD-- IT'S HOW WE WORK.
IT'S PART OF OUR TRAINING, BUT WE GET REWARDS.
THE INSTRUCTIONS.
...ARE DIFFERENT EVERY TIME.
Instructions
Listen to the voice of the lost soul.

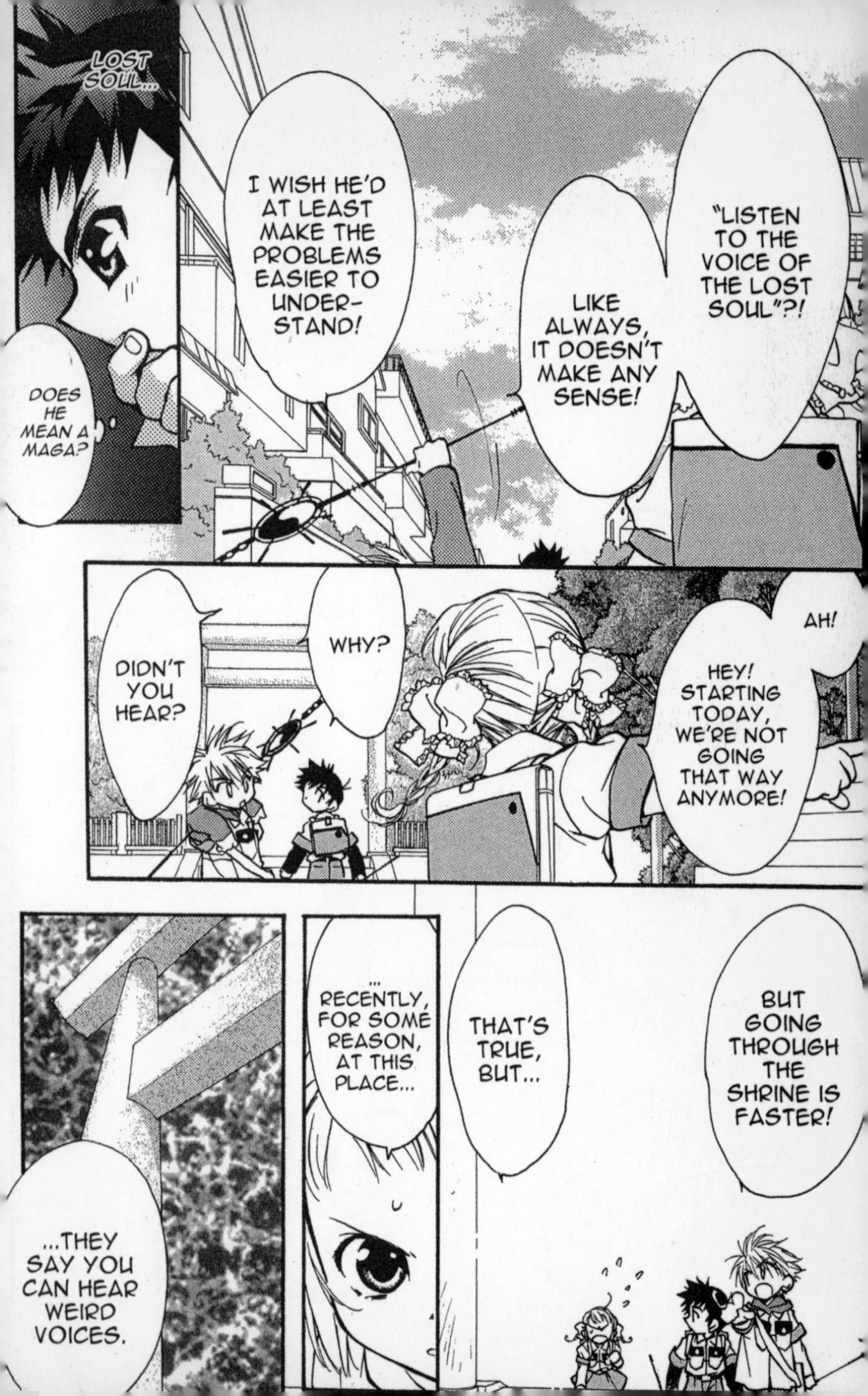
"LISTEN TO THE VOICE OF THE LOST SOUL"?!
LIKE ALWAYS, IT DOESN'T MAKE ANY SENSE!
I WISH HE'D AT LEAST MAKE THE PROBLEMS EASIER TO UNDER-STAND!
LOST SOUL...
DOES HE MEAN A MAGA?
AH!
HEY! STARTING TODAY, WE'RE NOT GOING THAT WAY ANYMORE!
WHY?
DIDN'T YOU HEAR?
BUT GOING THROUGH THE SHRINE IS FASTER!
THAT'S TRUE, BUT...
... RECENTLY, FOR SOME REASON, AT THIS PLACE...
...THEY SAY YOU CAN HEAR WEIRD VOICES.

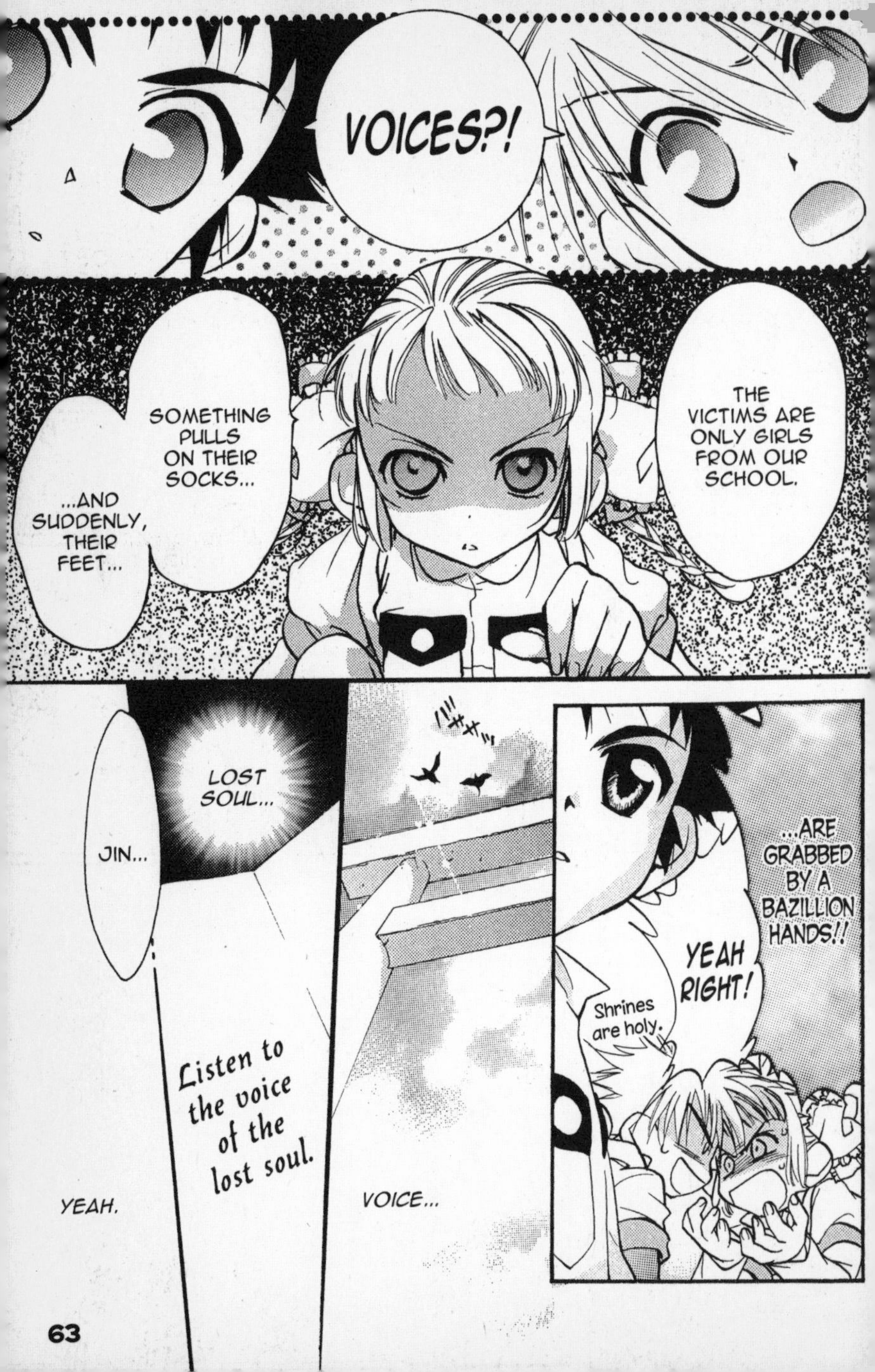
VOICES?!
THE VICTIMS ARE ONLY GIRLS FROM OUR SCHOOL.
SOMETHING PULLS ON THEIR SOCKS...
...AND SUDDENLY, THEIR FEET...
...ARE GRABBED BY A BAZILLION HANDS!!
YEAH RIGHT!
Shrines are holy.
VOICE...
LOST SOUL...
JIN...
Listen to the voice of the lost soul.
YEAH.

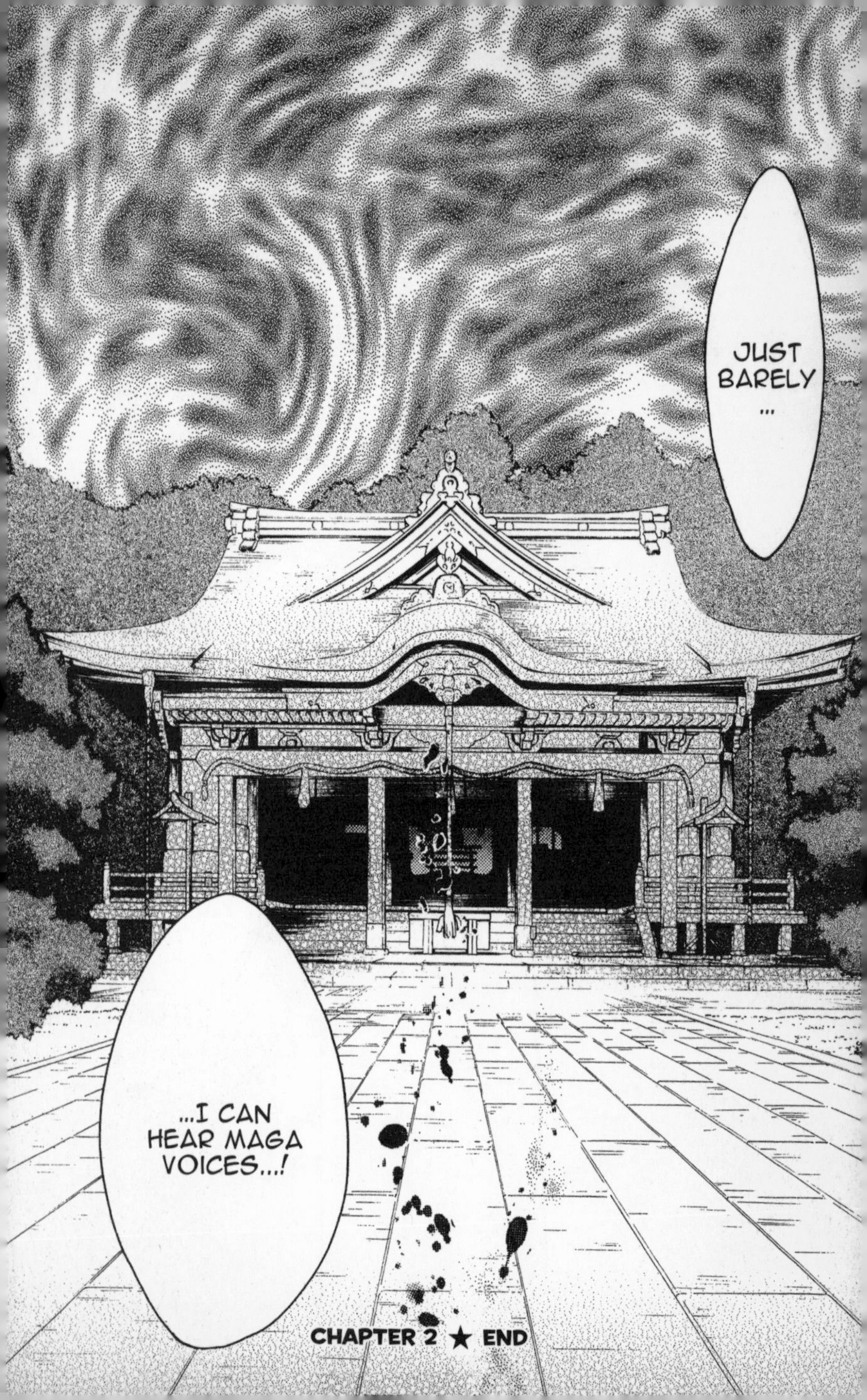
JUST BARELY ...
...I CAN HEAR MAGA VOICES...!
CHAPTER 2 ★ END

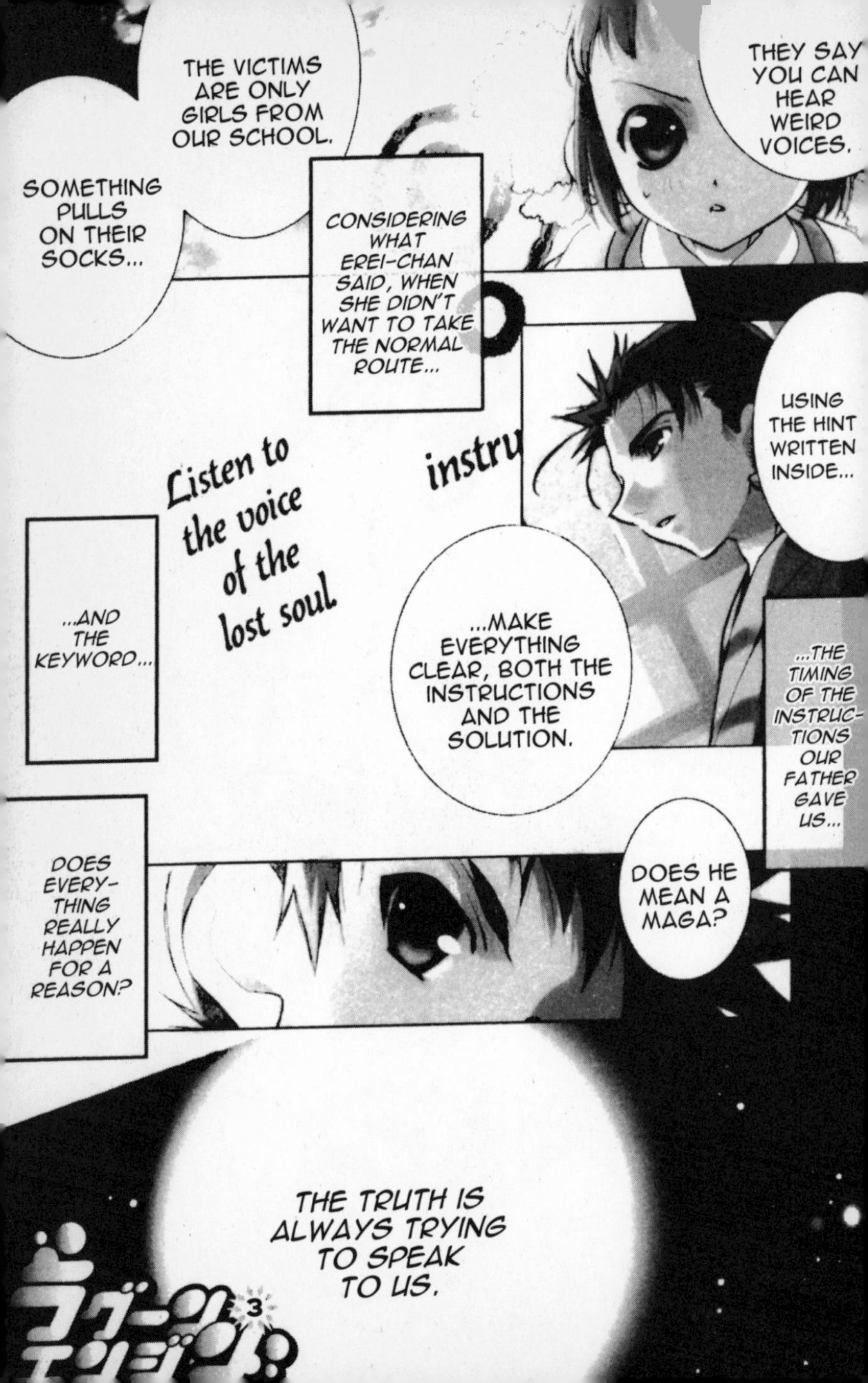
THEY SAY YOU CAN HEAR WEIRD VOICES.
THE VICTIMS ARE ONLY GIRLS FROM OUR SCHOOL.
SOMETHING PULLS ON THEIR SOCKS...
CONSIDERING WHAT EREI-CHAN SAID, WHEN SHE DIDN'T WANT TO TAKE THE NORMAL ROUTE...
USING THE HINT WRITTEN INSIDE...
...THE TIMING OF THE INSTRUC-TIONS OUR FATHER GAVE US...
instru
Listen to the voice of the lost soul
...AND THE KEYWORD...
...MAKE EVERYTHING CLEAR, BOTH THE INSTRUCTIONS AND THE SOLUTION.
DOES HE MEAN A MAGA?
DOES EVERY-THING REALLY HAPPEN FOR A REASON?
THE TRUTH IS ALWAYS TRYING TO SPEAK TO US.

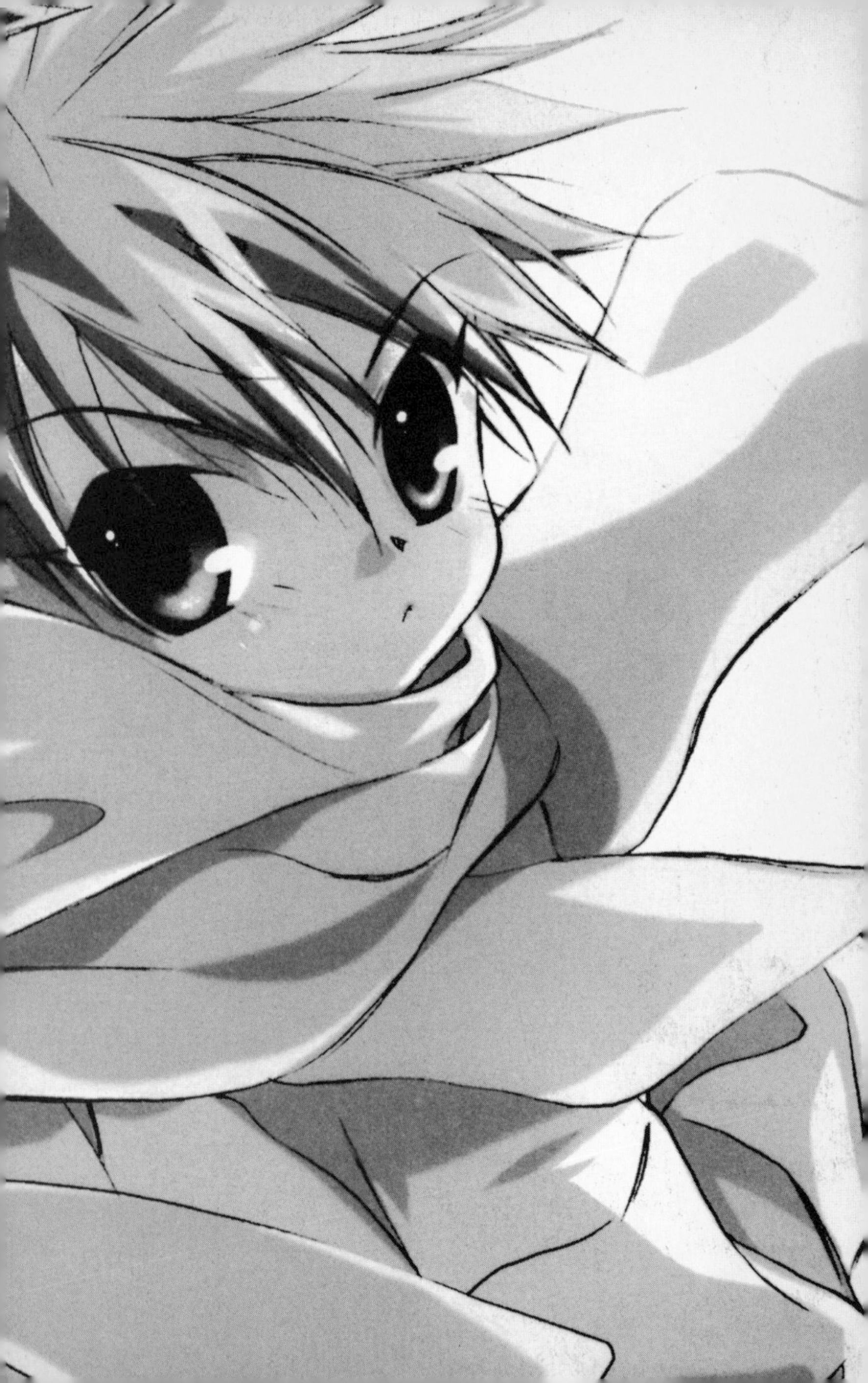

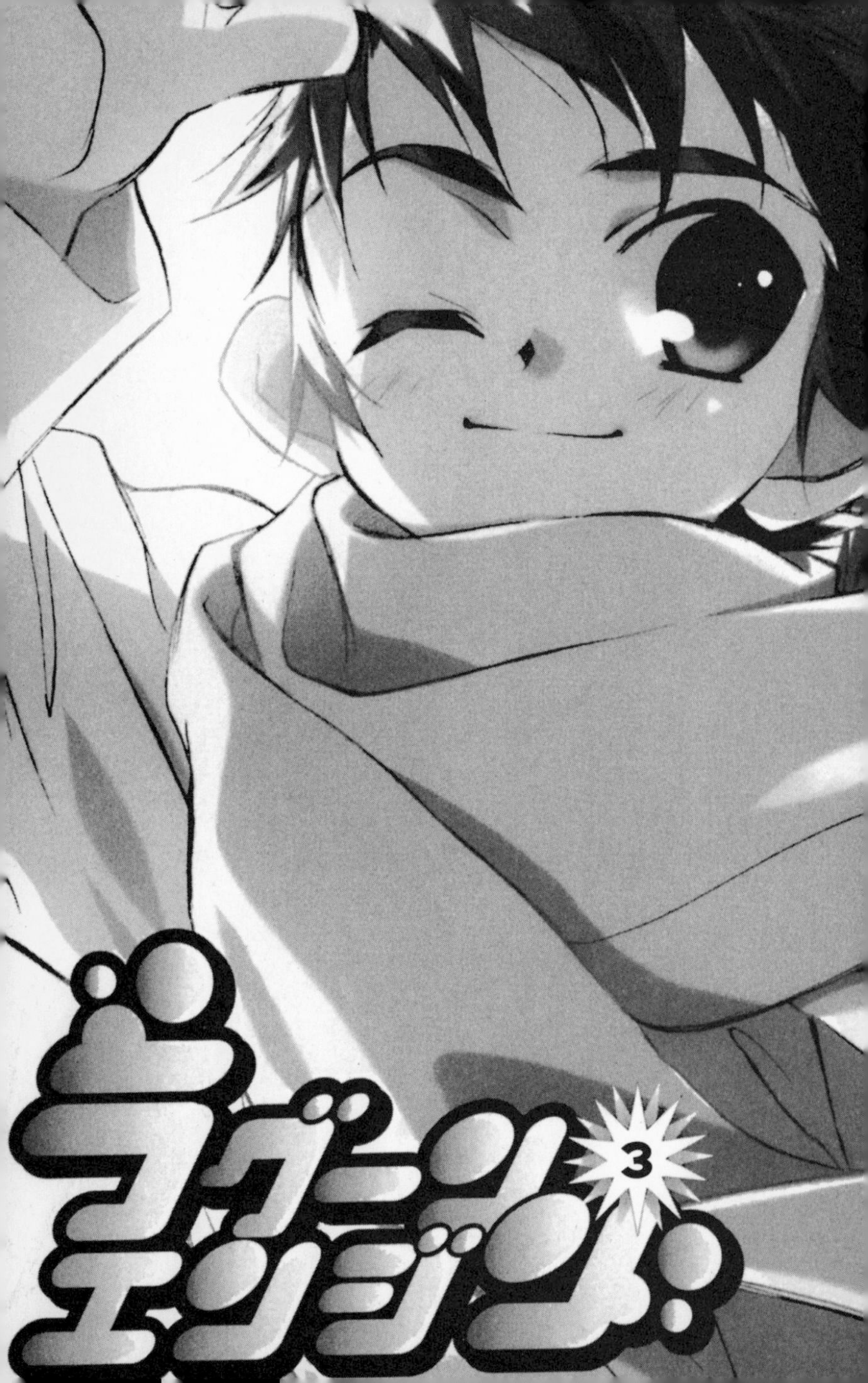
ラグーン
エンジン
3

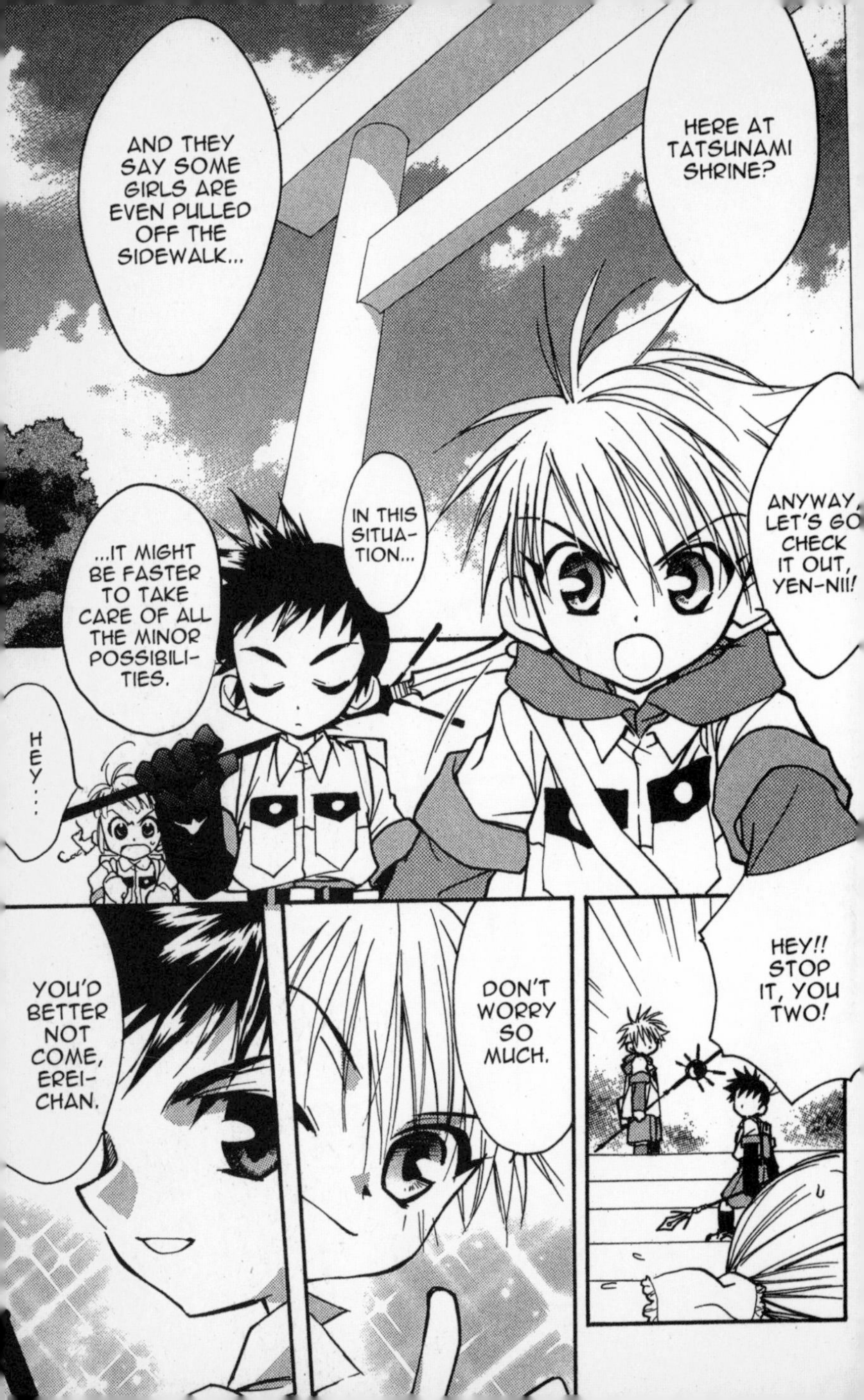
HERE AT TATSUNAMI SHRINE?
AND THEY SAY SOME GIRLS ARE EVEN PULLED OFF THE SIDEWALK...
ANYWAY, LET'S GO CHECK IT OUT, YEN-NII!
IN THIS SITUA-TION...
...IT MIGHT BE FASTER TO TAKE CARE OF ALL THE MINOR POSSIBILI-TIES.
HEY...
HEY!! STOP IT, YOU TWO!
DON'T WORRY SO MUCH.
YOU'D BETTER NOT COME, EREI-CHAN.

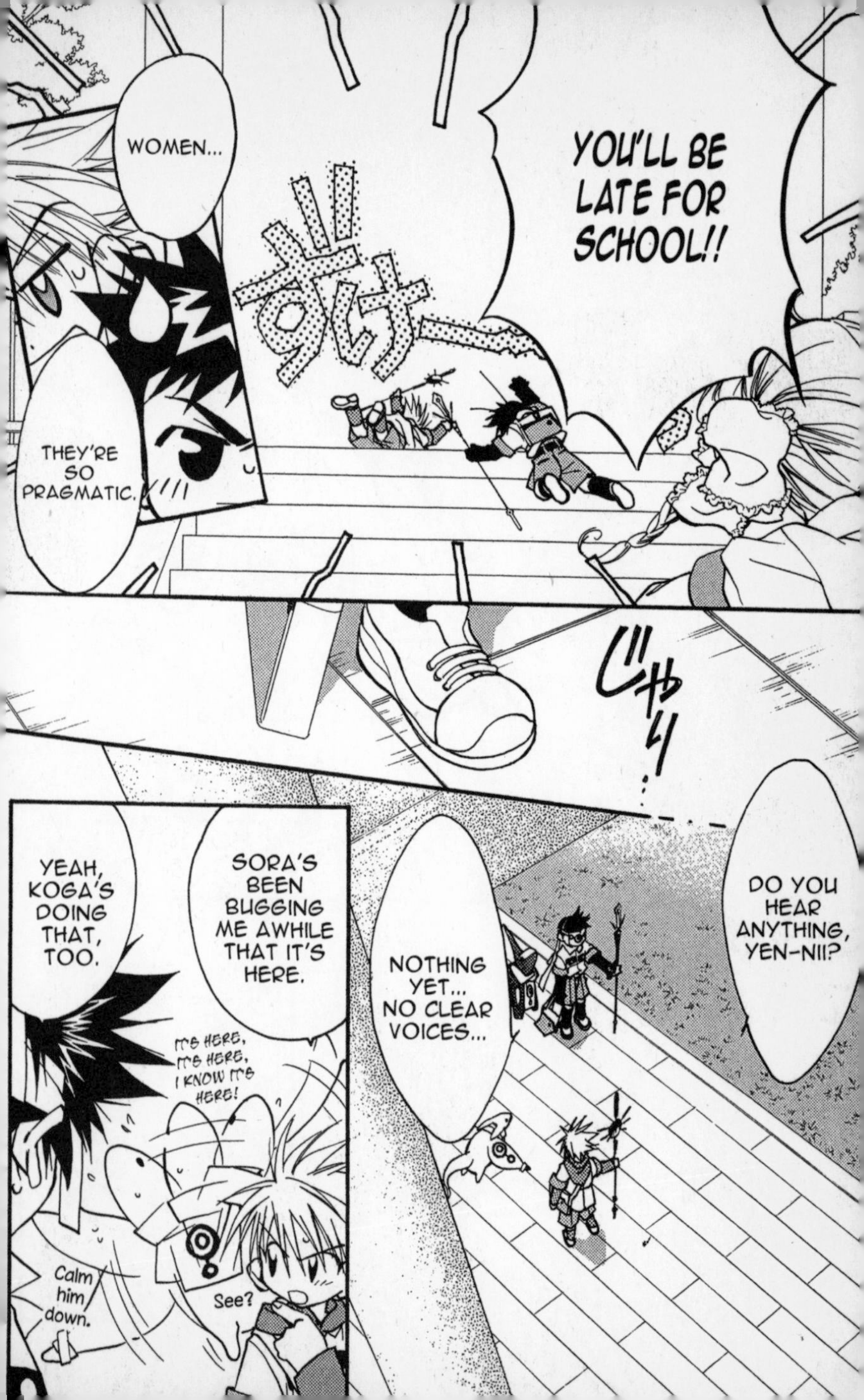
YOU'LL BE LATE FOR SCHOOL!!
WOMEN...
THEY'RE SO PRAGMATIC.
じゃり
DO YOU HEAR ANYTHING, YEN-NII?
NOTHING YET... NO CLEAR VOICES...
SORA'S BEEN BUGGING ME AWHILE THAT IT'S HERE.
YEAH, KOGA'S DOING THAT, TOO.
IT'S HERE, IT'S HERE, I KNOW IT'S HERE!
See?
Calm him down.

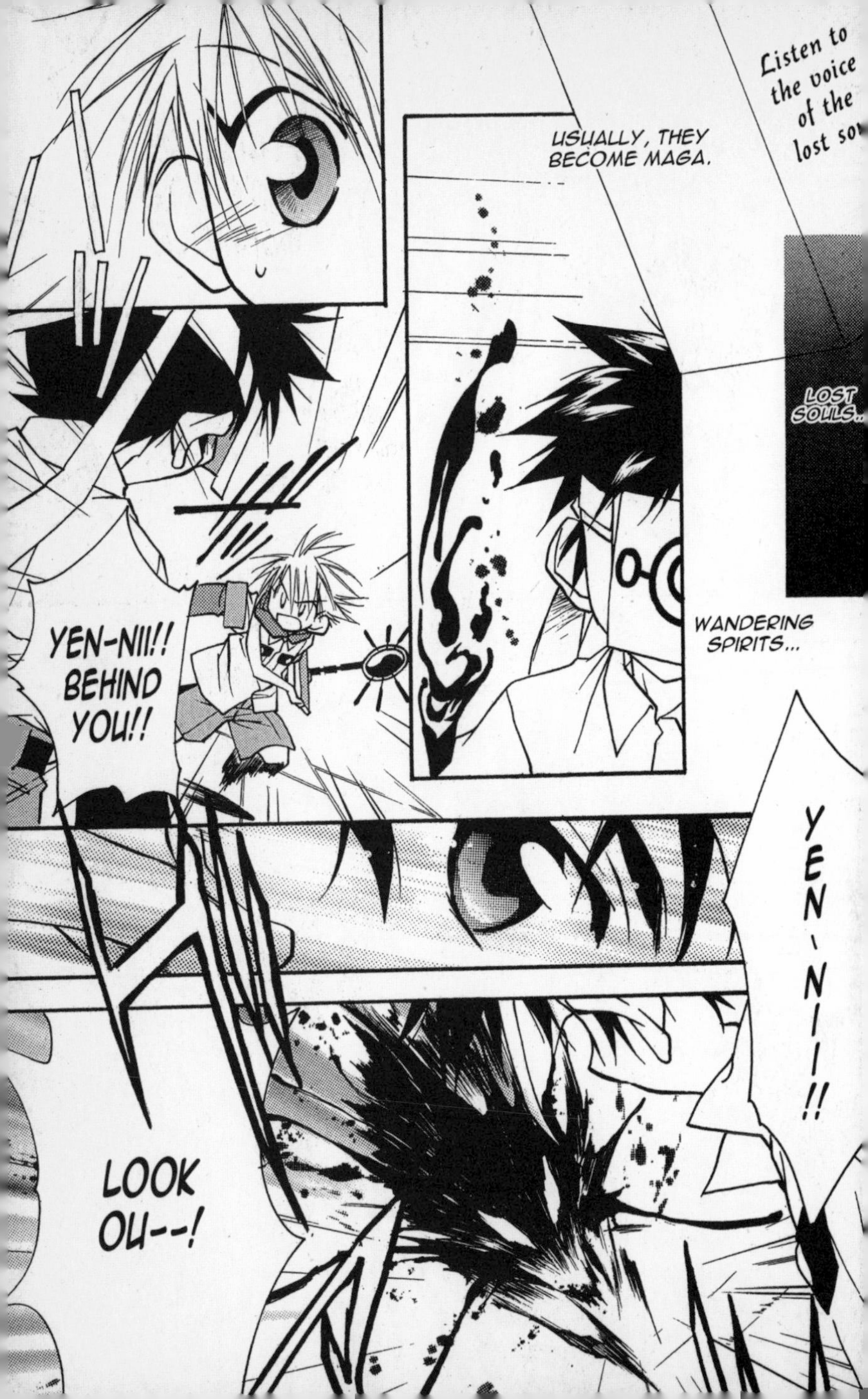

Listen to the voice of the lost
LOST SOULS...
USUALLY, THEY BECOME MAGA.
WANDERING SPIRITS...
YEN-NII!! BEHIND YOU!!
YEN-NIII!!
LOOK OU--!

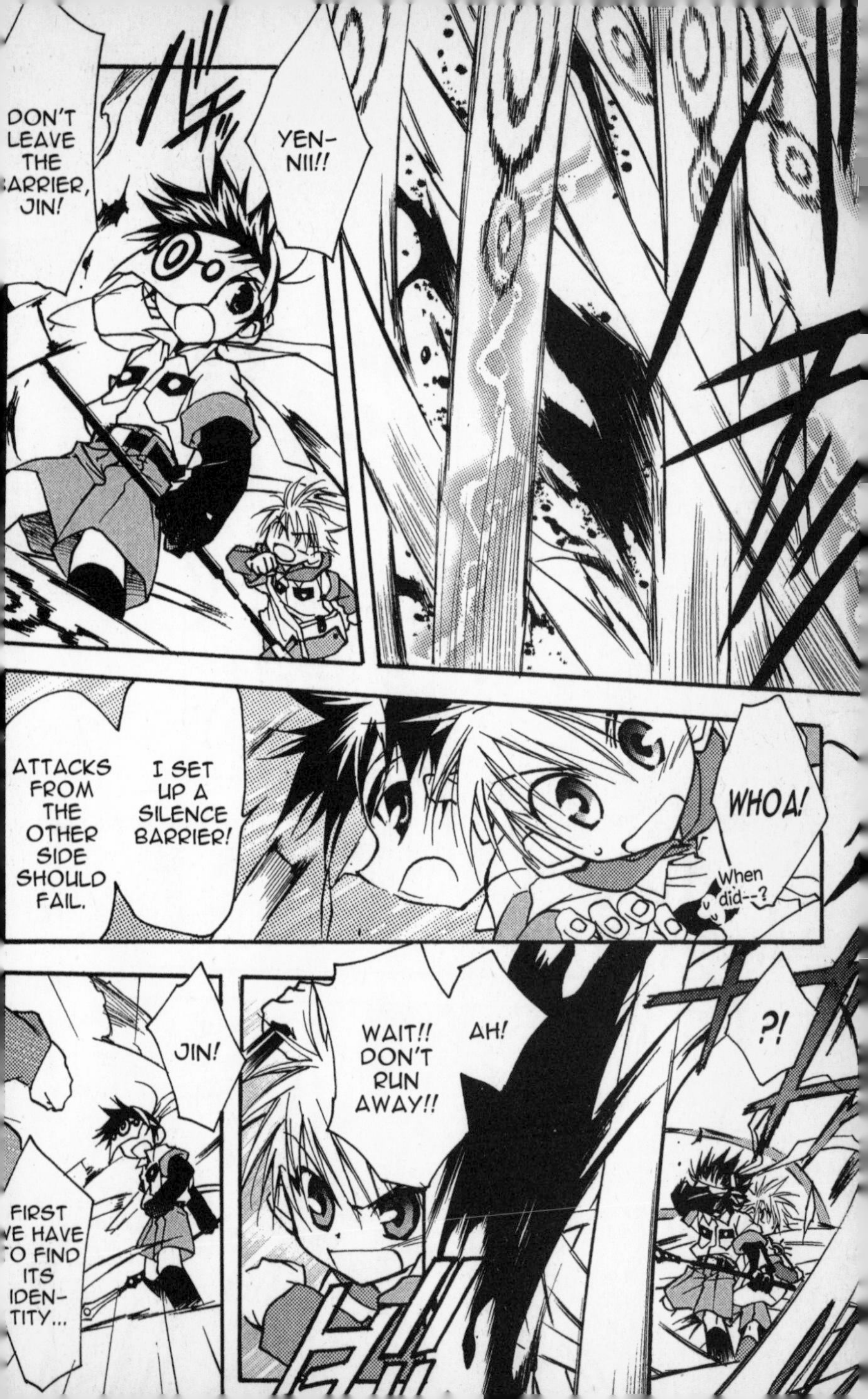
YEN-NII!!
DON'T LEAVE THE ARRIER, JIN!
WHOA!
When did--?
I SET UP A SILENCE BARRIER!
ATTACKS FROM THE OTHER SIDE SHOULD FAIL.
?!
AH!
WAIT!! DON'T RUN AWAY!!
JIN!
FIRST VE HAVE O FIND ITS IDENTITY...

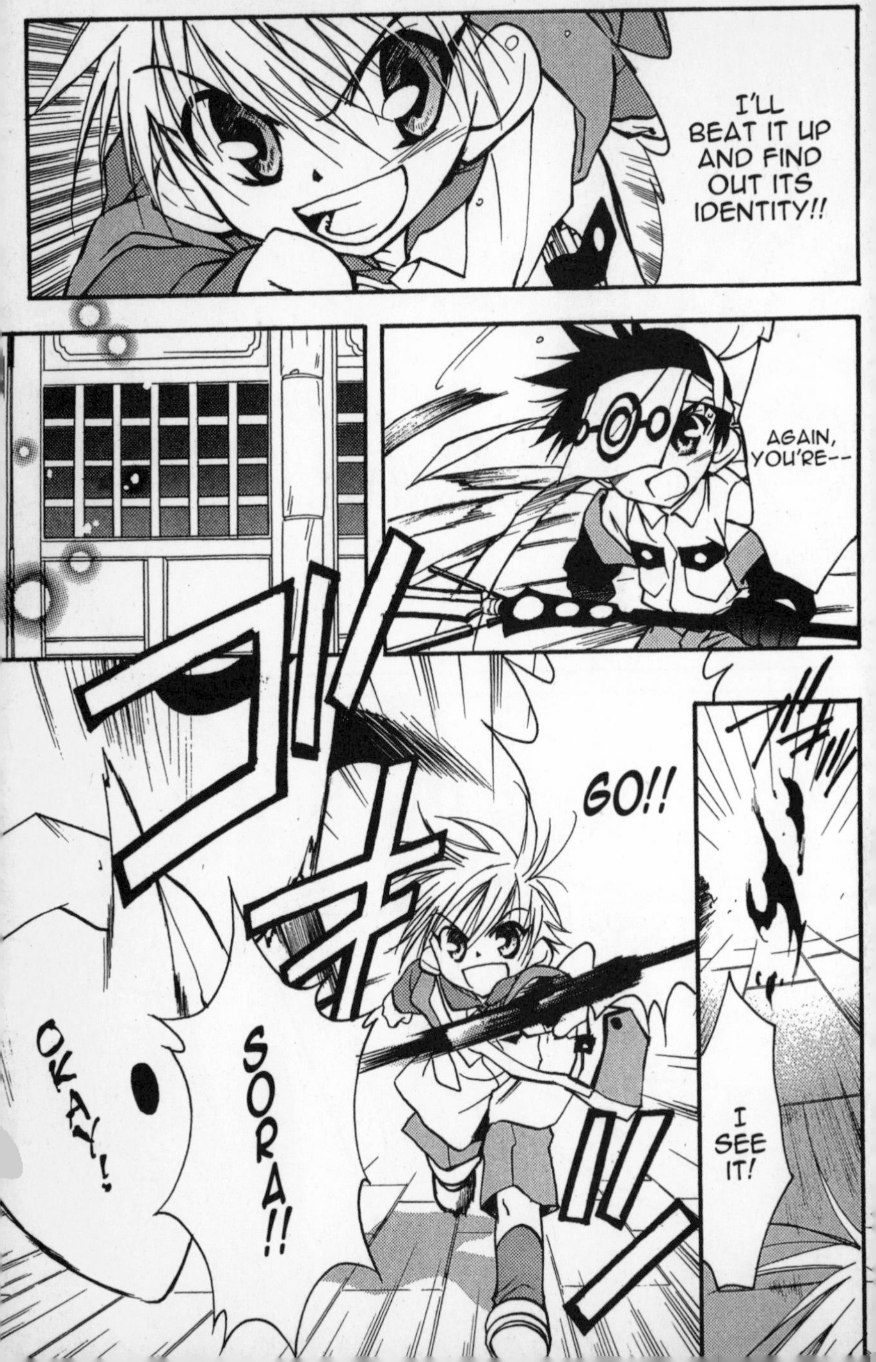
I'LL BEAT IT UP AND FIND OUT ITS IDENTITY!!
AGAIN, YOU'RE--
I SEE IT!
GO!!
SORA!!
OKAY!!

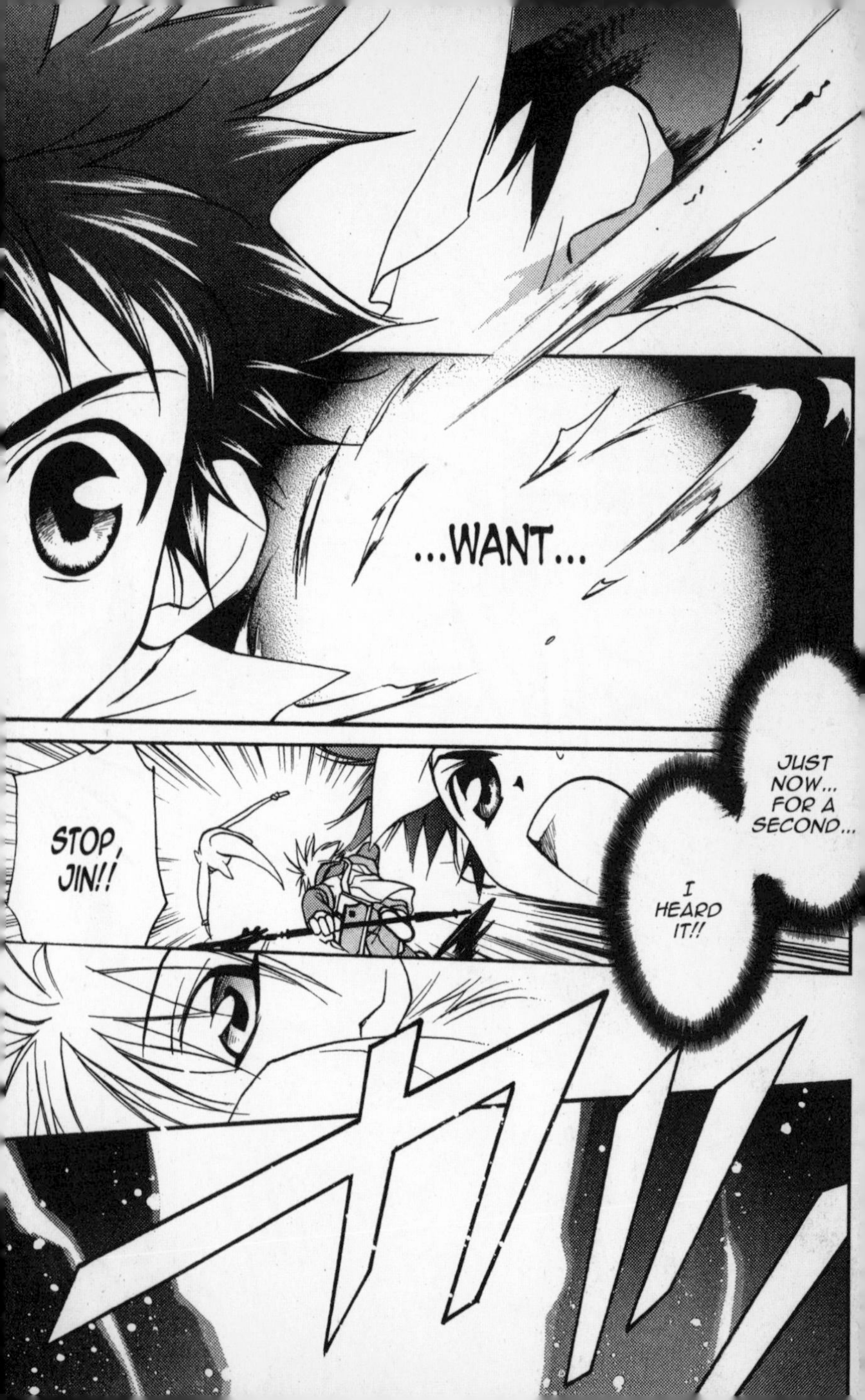
...WANT...
JUST NOW... FOR A SECOND...
I HEARD IT!!
STOP, JIN!!

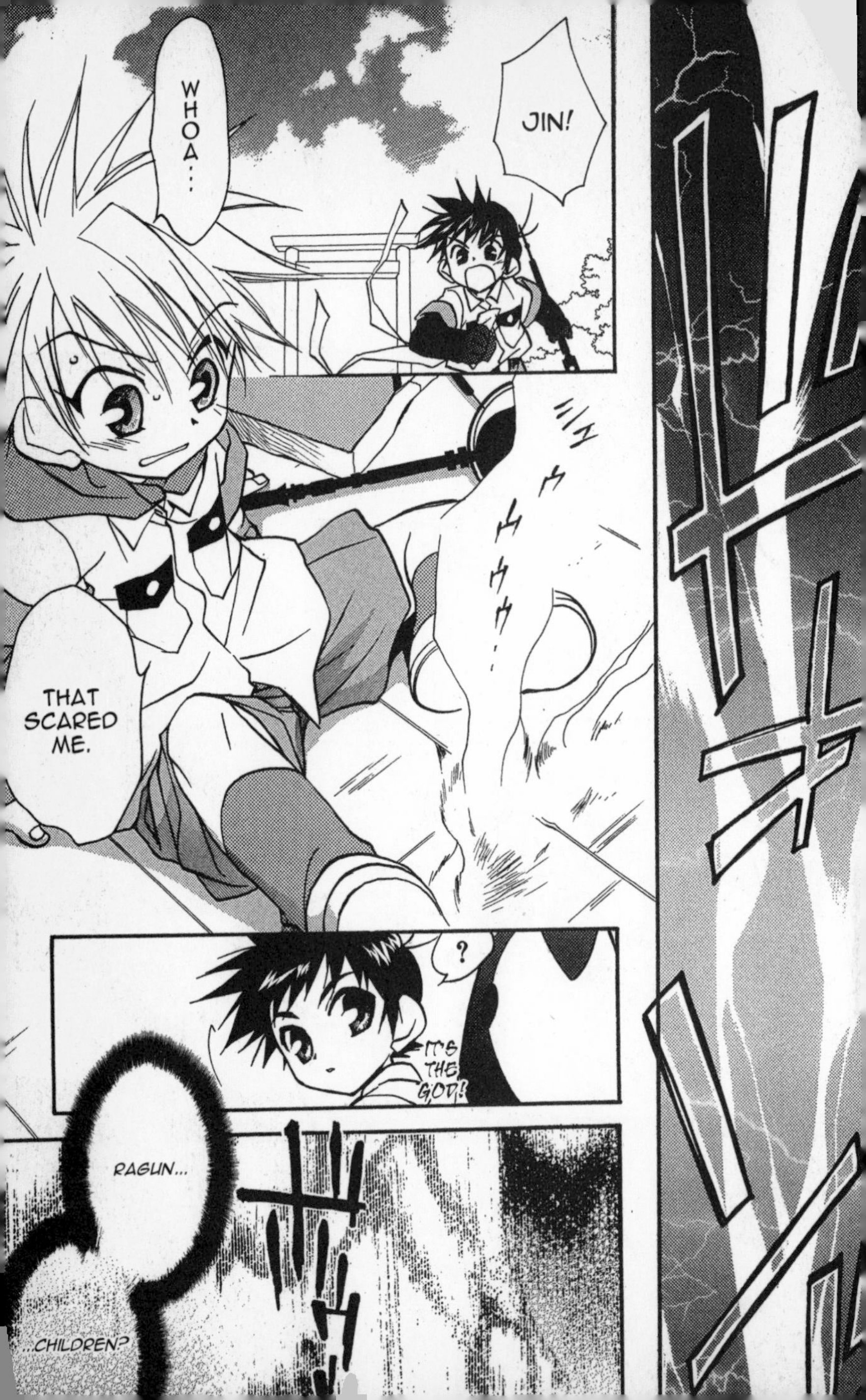
JIN!
WHOA...
THAT SCARED ME.
?
IT'S THE GOD!
RAGUN...
...CHILDREN?

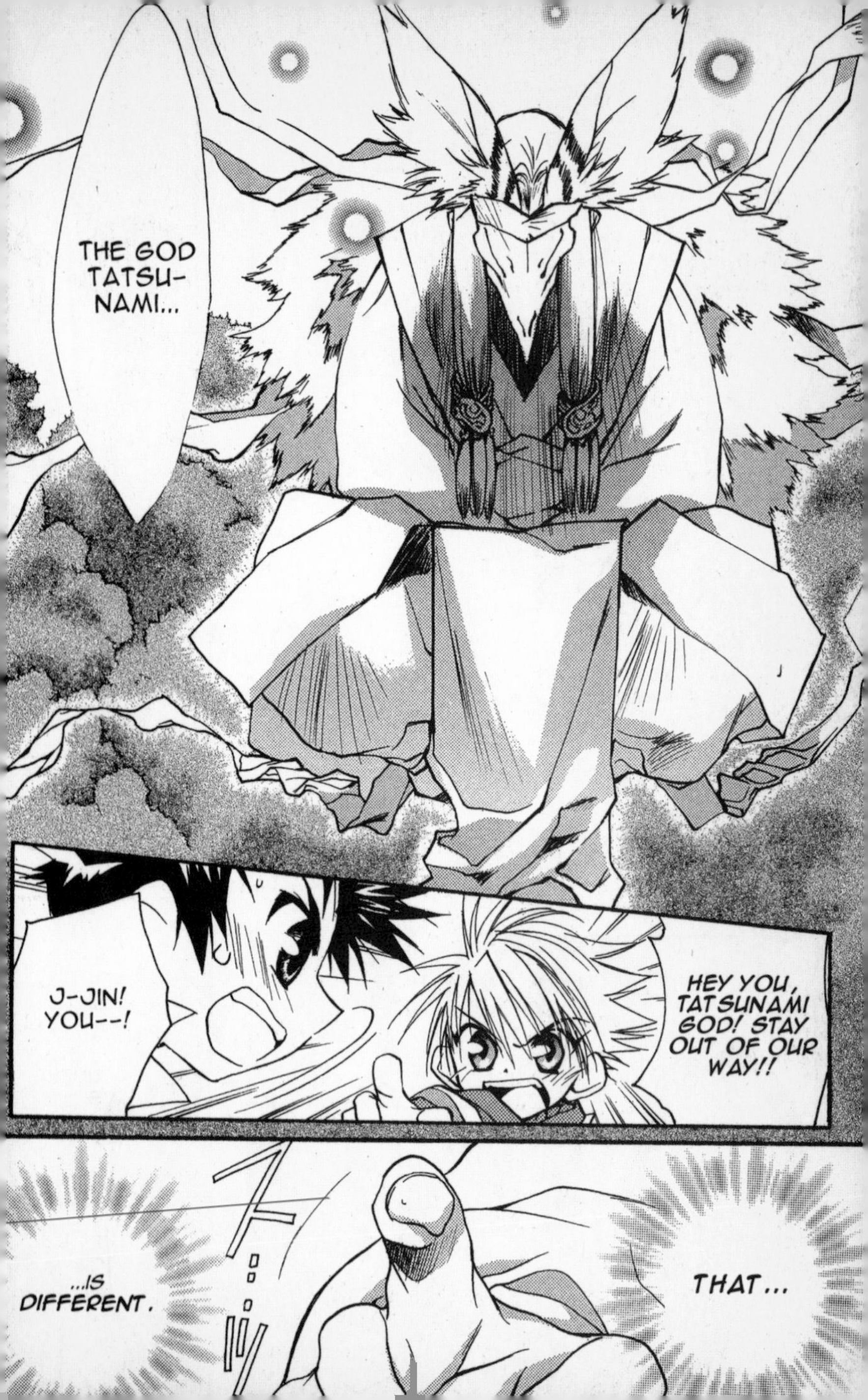
THE GOD TATSU-NAMI...
HEY YOU, TATSUNAMI GOD! STAY OUT OF OUR WAY!!
J-JIN! YOU--!
THAT...
...IS DIFFERENT.

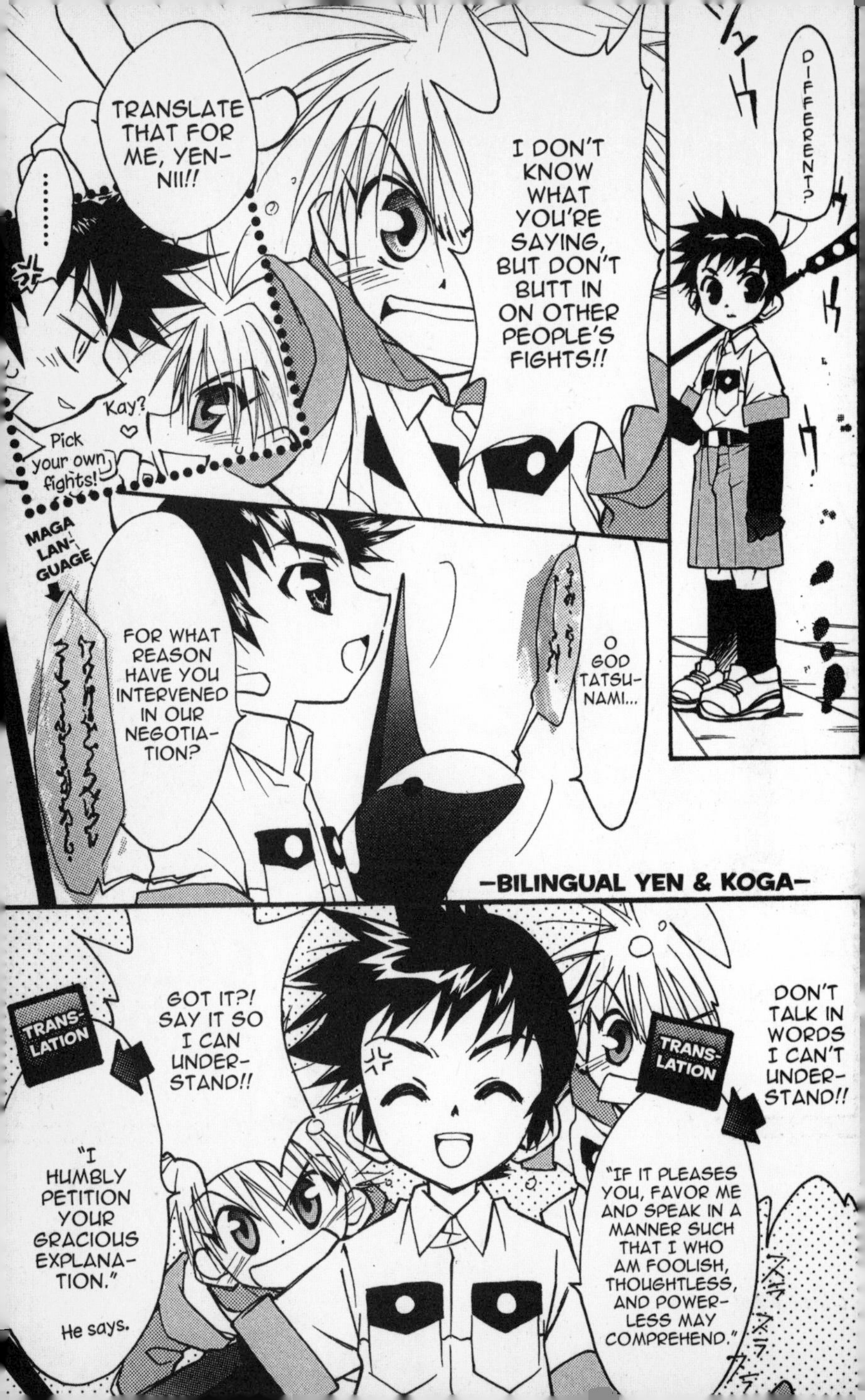
DIFFERENT?
I DON'T KNOW WHAT YOU'RE SAYING, BUT DON'T BUTT IN ON OTHER PEOPLE'S FIGHTS!!
TRANSLATE THAT FOR ME, YEN-NII!!
......
Kay? ♡
Pick your own fights!
O GOD TATSUNAMI...
FOR WHAT REASON HAVE YOU INTERVENED IN OUR NEGOTIATION?
MAGA LANGUAGE
—BILINGUAL YEN & KOGA—
DON'T TALK IN WORDS I CAN'T UNDERSTAND!!
TRANSLATION
"IF IT PLEASES YOU, FAVOR ME AND SPEAK IN A MANNER SUCH THAT I WHO AM FOOLISH, THOUGHTLESS, AND POWERLESS MAY COMPREHEND."
GOT IT?! SAY IT SO I CAN UNDERSTAND!!
TRANSLATION
"I HUMBLY PETITION YOUR GRACIOUS EXPLANATION."
He says.

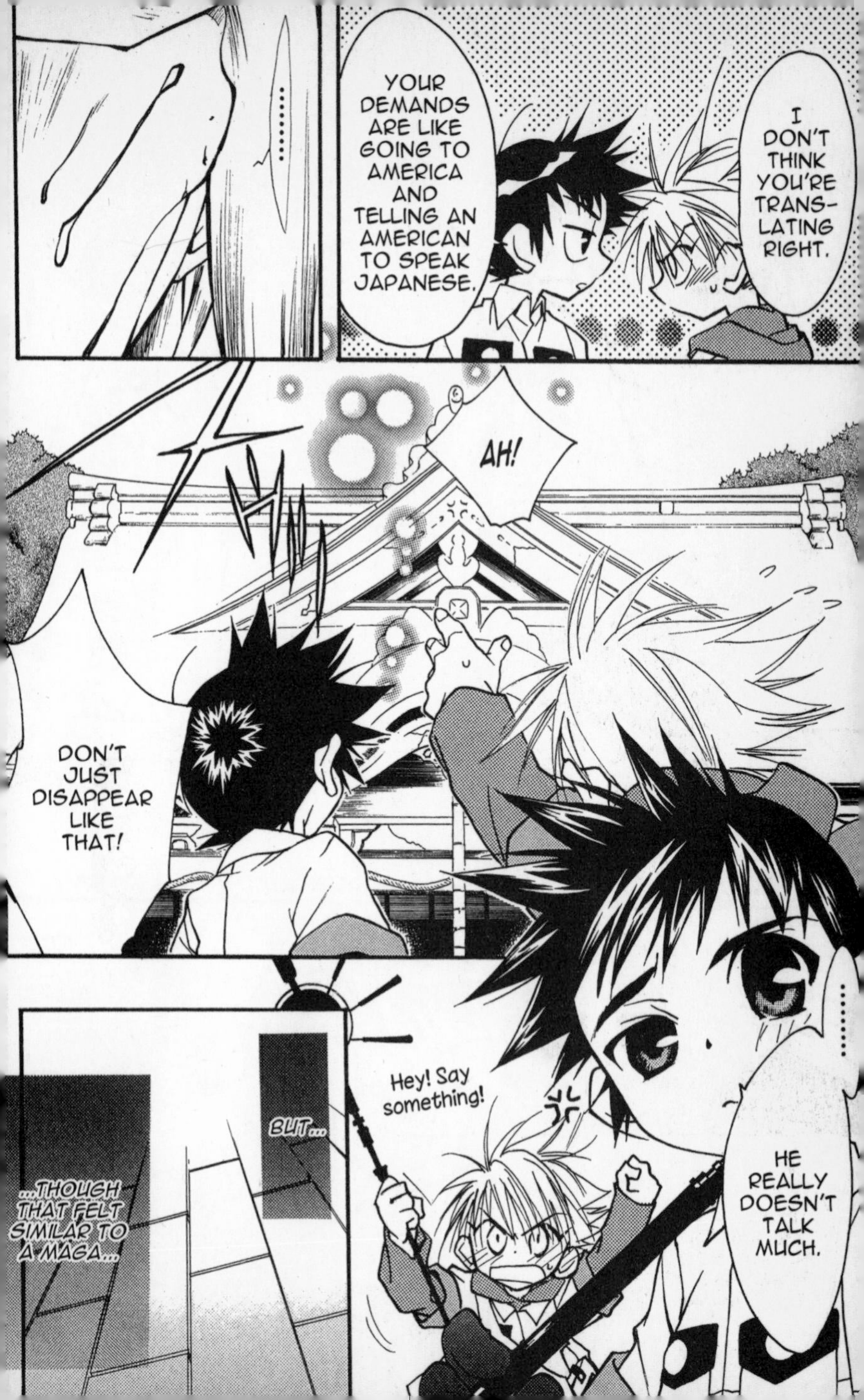
I DON'T THINK YOU'RE TRANS-LATING RIGHT.
YOUR DEMANDS ARE LIKE GOING TO AMERICA AND TELLING AN AMERICAN TO SPEAK JAPANESE.
......
AH!
DON'T JUST DISAPPEAR LIKE THAT!
......
HE REALLY DOESN'T TALK MUCH.
Hey! Say something!
BUT...
...THOUGH THAT FELT SIMILAR TO A MAGA...

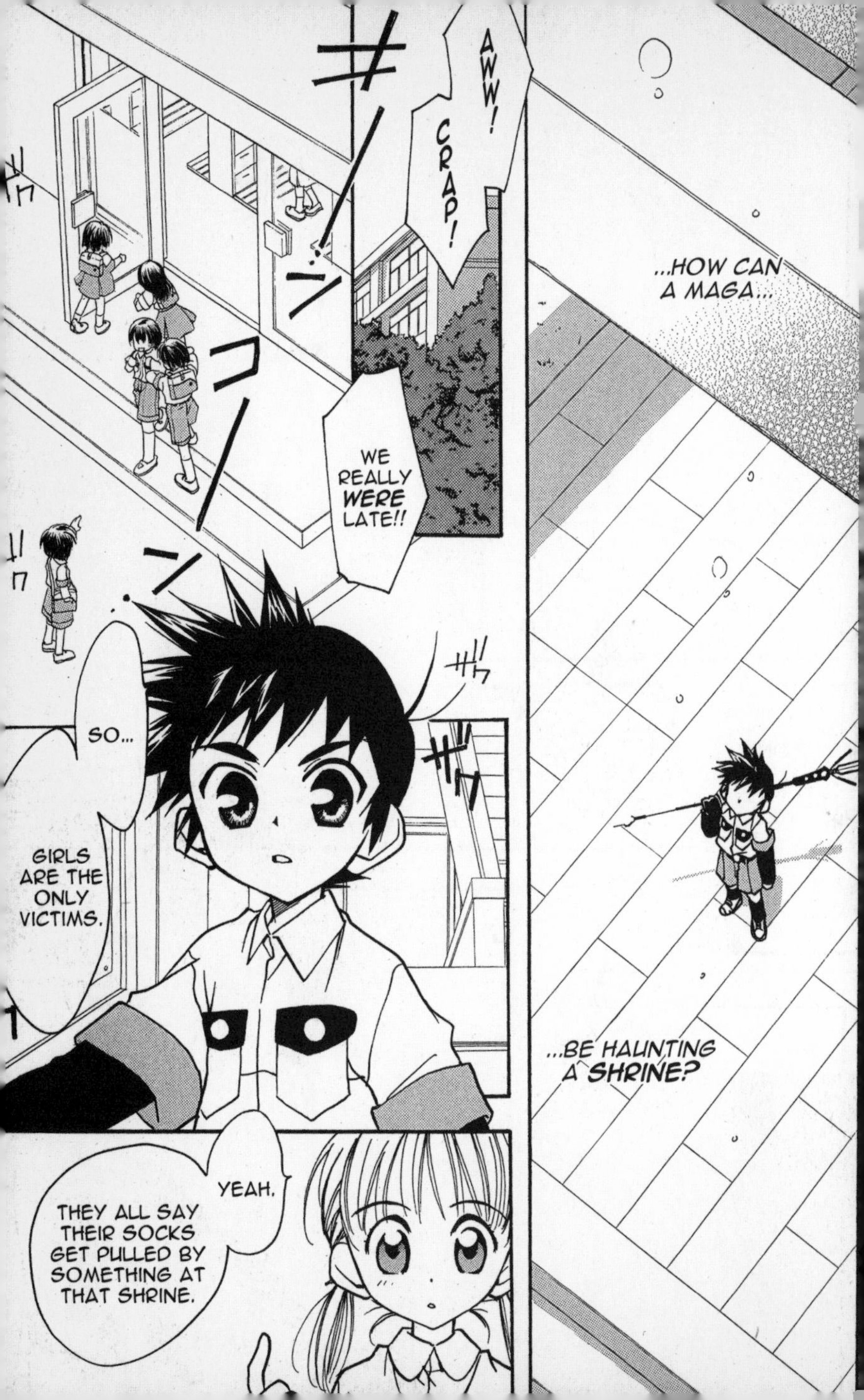
...HOW CAN A MAGA...
...BE HAUNTING A SHRINE?
AWW! CRAP!
WE REALLY WERE LATE!!
SO...
GIRLS ARE THE ONLY VICTIMS.
YEAH.
THEY ALL SAY THEIR SOCKS GET PULLED BY SOMETHING AT THAT SHRINE.

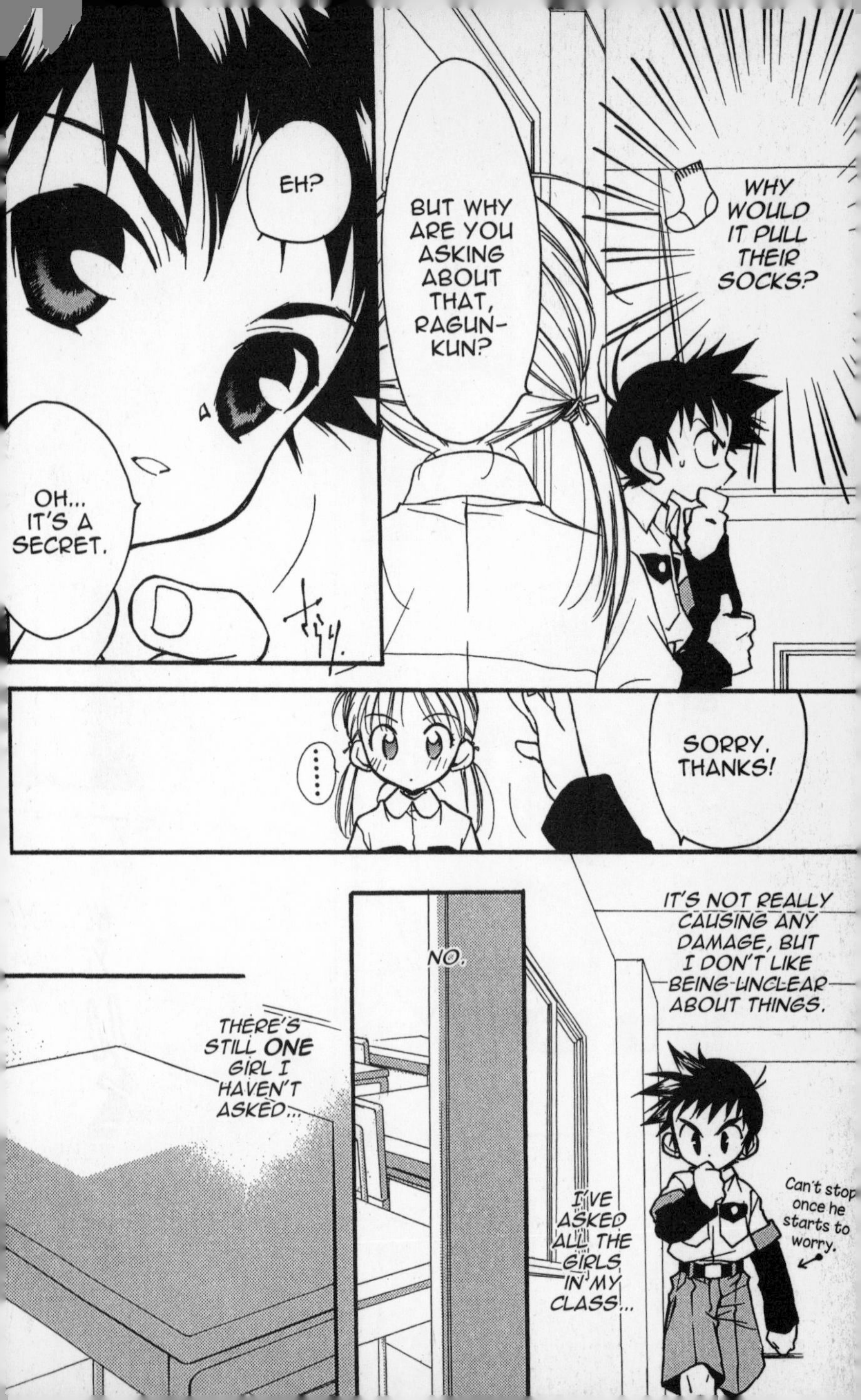

WHY WOULD IT PULL THEIR SOCKS?
BUT WHY ARE YOU ASKING ABOUT THAT, RAGUN-KUN?
EH?
OH... IT'S A SECRET.
SORRY. THANKS!
......
IT'S NOT REALLY CAUSING ANY DAMAGE, BUT I DON'T LIKE BEING UNCLEAR ABOUT THINGS.
Can't stop once he starts to worry.
I'VE ASKED ALL THE GIRLS IN MY CLASS...
NO.
THERE'S STILL ONE GIRL I HAVEN'T ASKED...

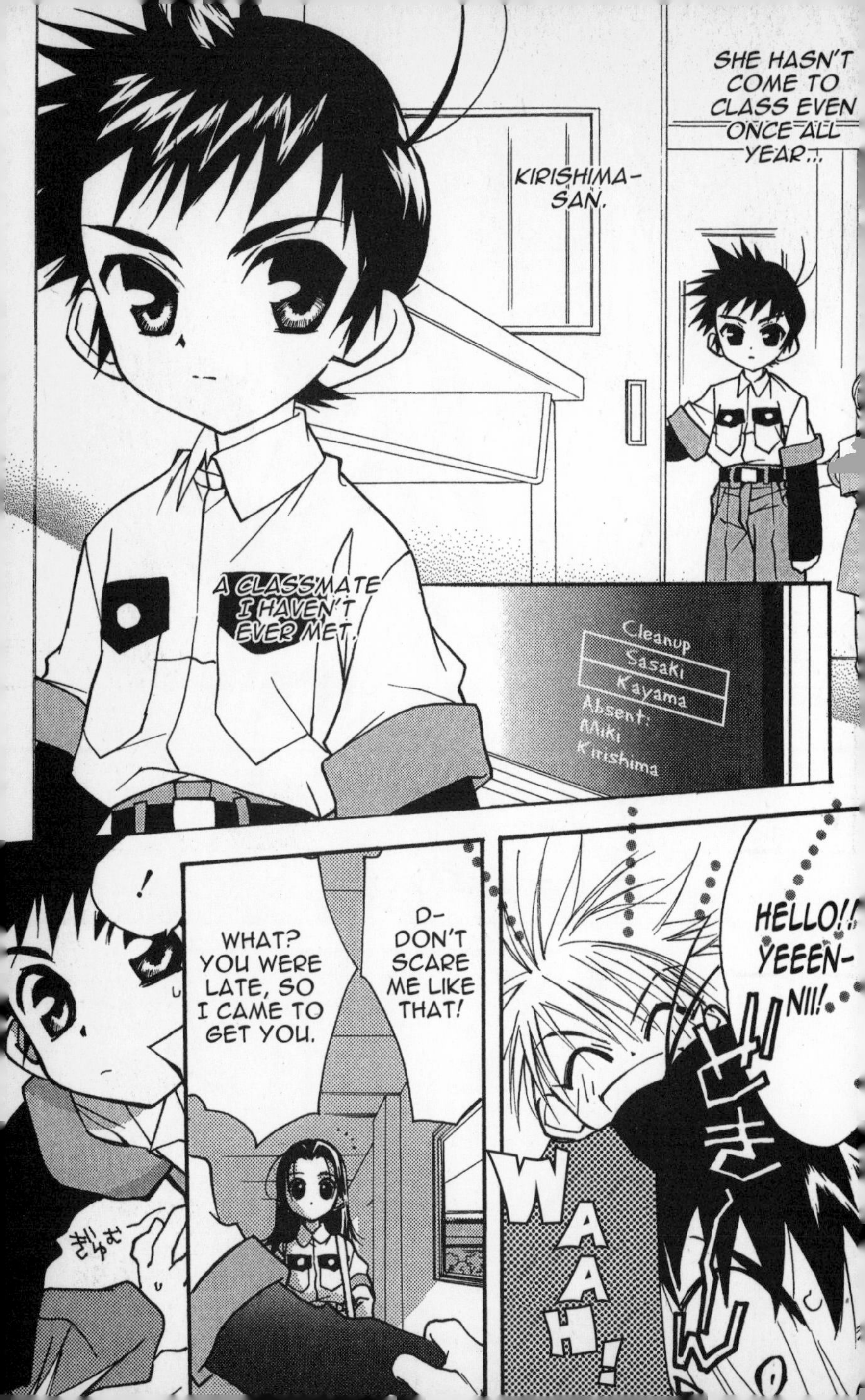
SHE HASN'T COME TO CLASS EVEN ONCE ALL YEAR...
KIRISHIMA-SAN.
A CLASSMATE I HAVEN'T EVER MET.
Cleanup
Sasaki
Kayama
Absent:
Miki
Kirishima
HELLO!! YEEEN-NII!
WAAAH!
D-DON'T SCARE ME LIKE THAT!
WHAT? YOU WERE LATE, SO I CAME TO GET YOU.
!

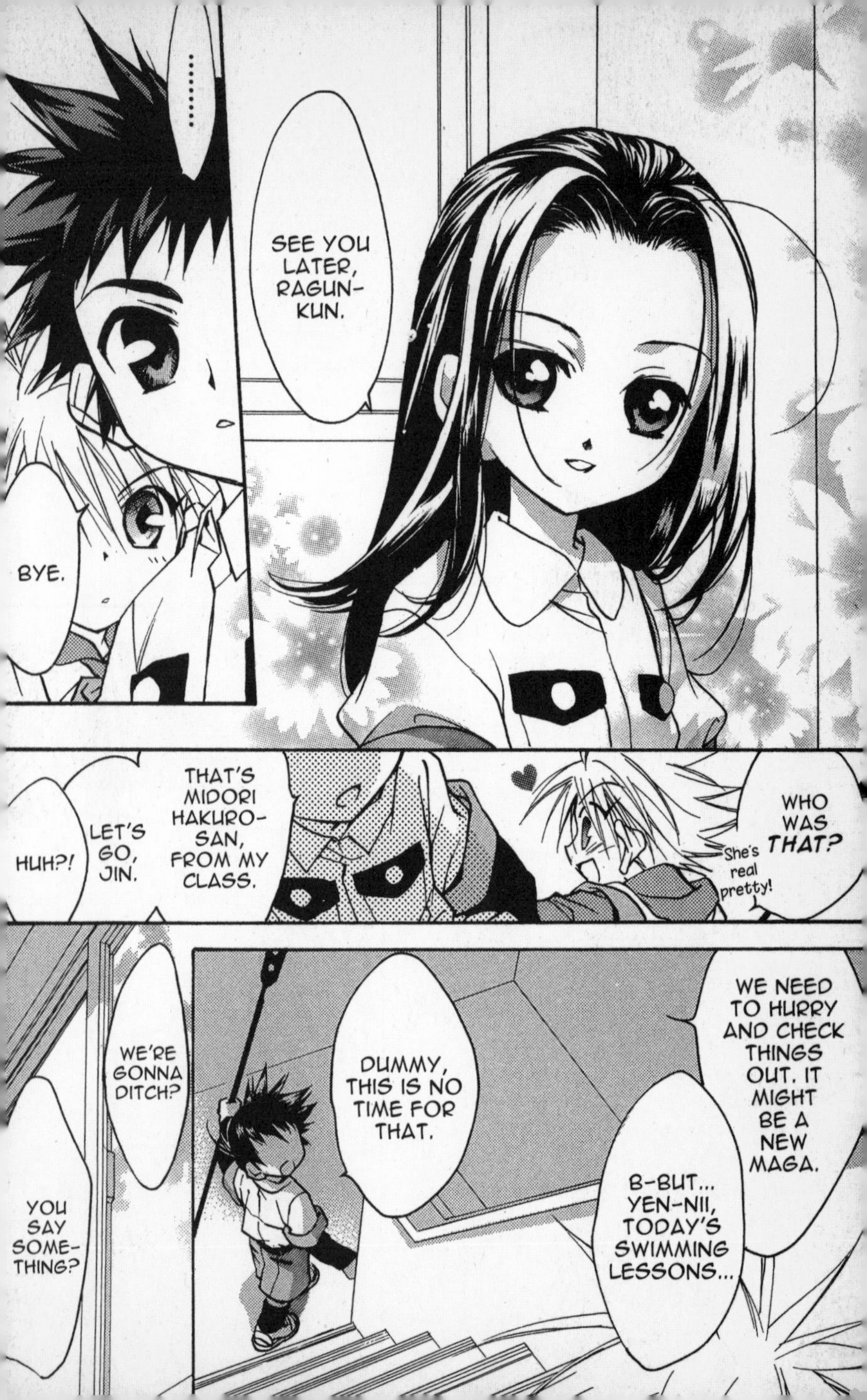
SEE YOU LATER, RAGUN-KUN.
......
BYE.
WHO WAS *THAT?*
She's real pretty!
THAT'S MIDORI HAKURO-SAN, FROM MY CLASS.
LET'S GO, JIN.
HUH?!
WE NEED TO HURRY AND CHECK THINGS OUT. IT MIGHT BE A NEW MAGA.
B-BUT... YEN-NII, TODAY'S SWIMMING LESSONS...
DUMMY, THIS IS NO TIME FOR THAT.
WE'RE GONNA DITCH?
YOU SAY SOMETHING?

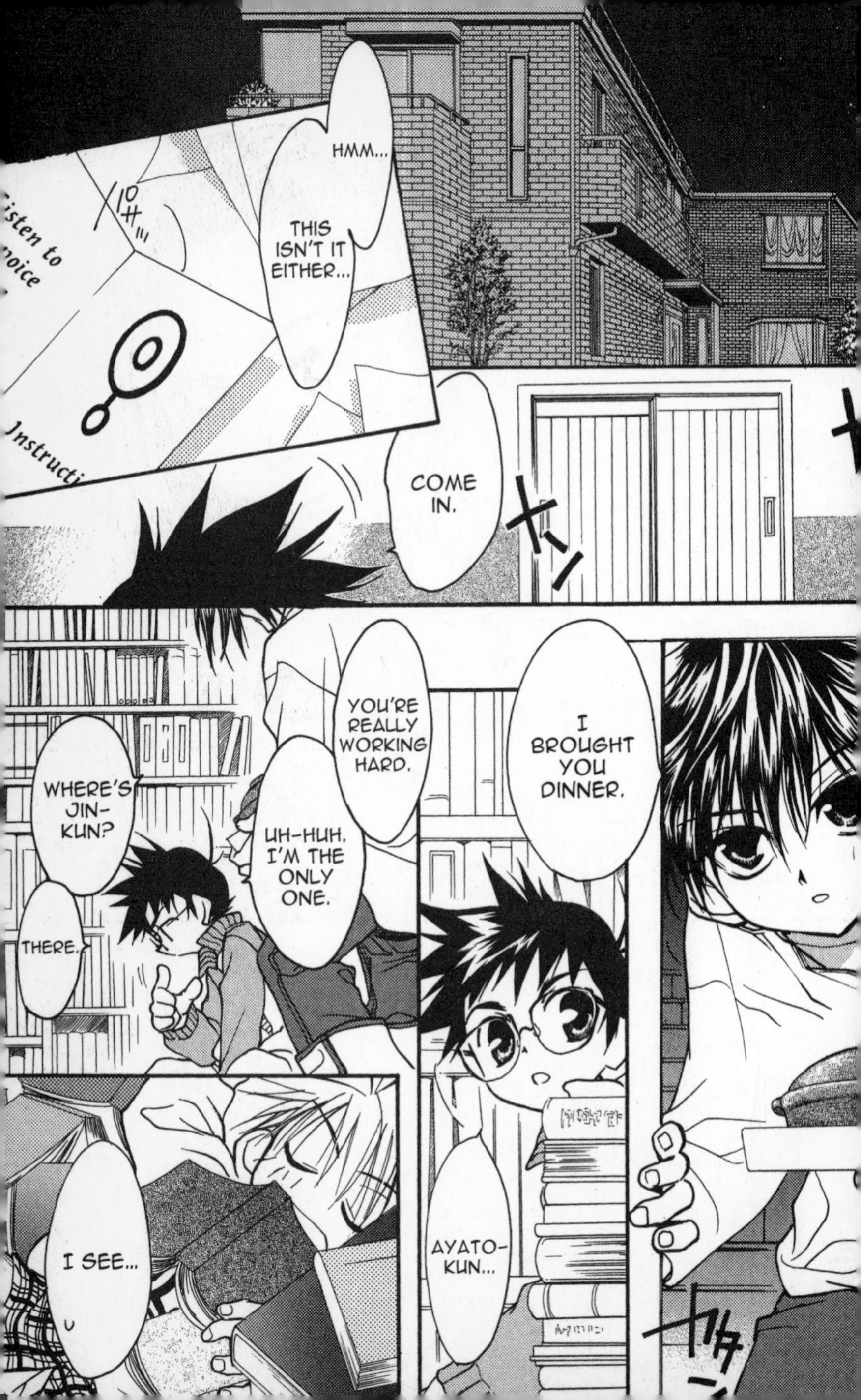

HMM...
THIS ISN'T IT EITHER...
isten to
oice
Instructi
COME IN.
I BROUGHT YOU DINNER.
AYATO-KUN...
YOU'RE REALLY WORKING HARD.
UH-HUH. I'M THE ONLY ONE.
WHERE'S JIN-KUN?
THERE.
I SEE...

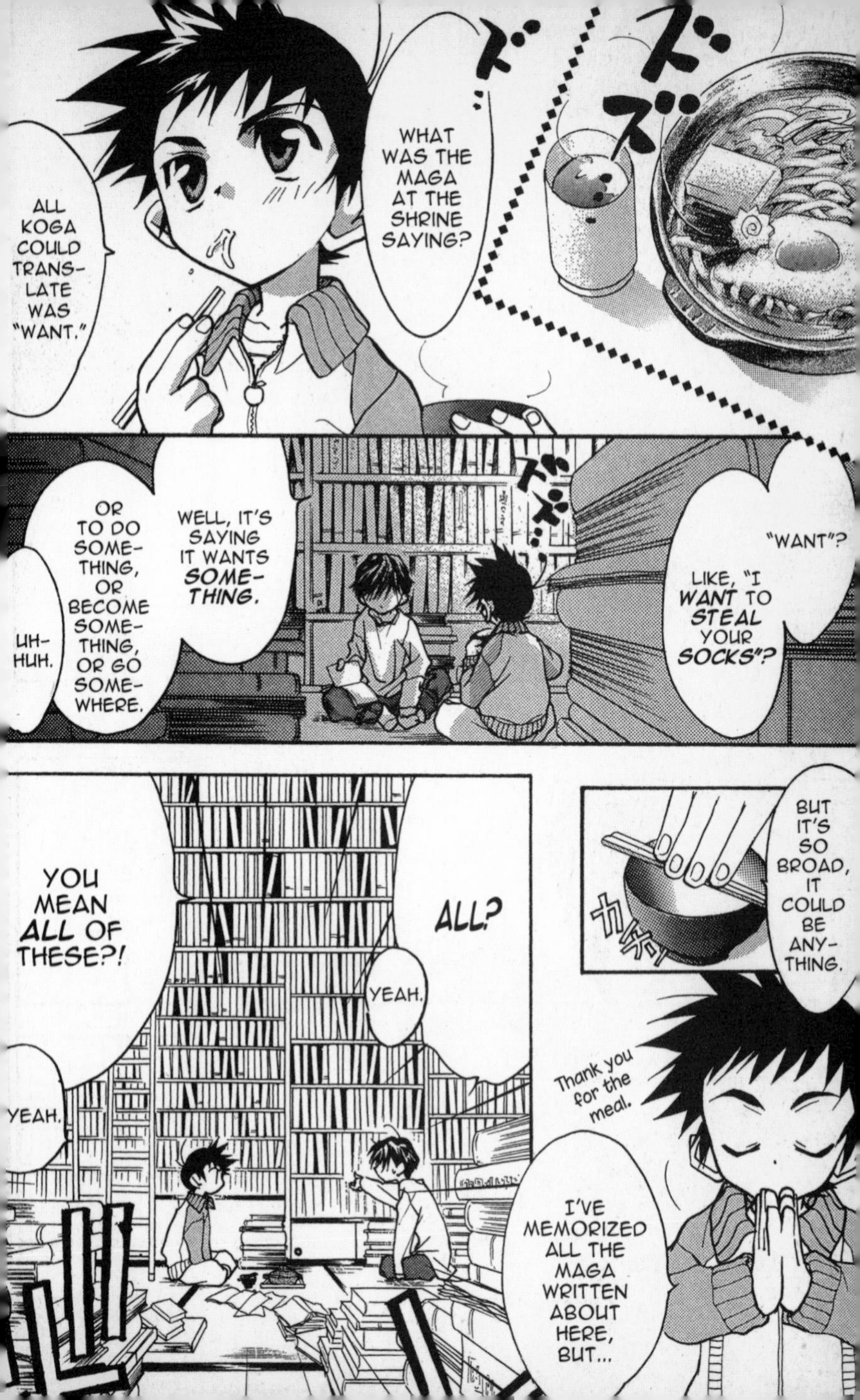
WHAT WAS THE MAGA AT THE SHRINE SAYING?
ALL KOGA COULD TRANSLATE WAS "WANT."
"WANT"? LIKE, "I WANT TO STEAL YOUR SOCKS"?
WELL, IT'S SAYING IT WANTS SOMETHING.
OR TO DO SOMETHING, OR BECOME SOMETHING, OR GO SOMEWHERE.
UH-HUH.
BUT IT'S SO BROAD, IT COULD BE ANYTHING.
Thank you for the meal.
I'VE MEMORIZED ALL THE MAGA WRITTEN ABOUT HERE, BUT...
ALL?
YEAH.
YOU MEAN ALL OF THESE?!
YEAH.

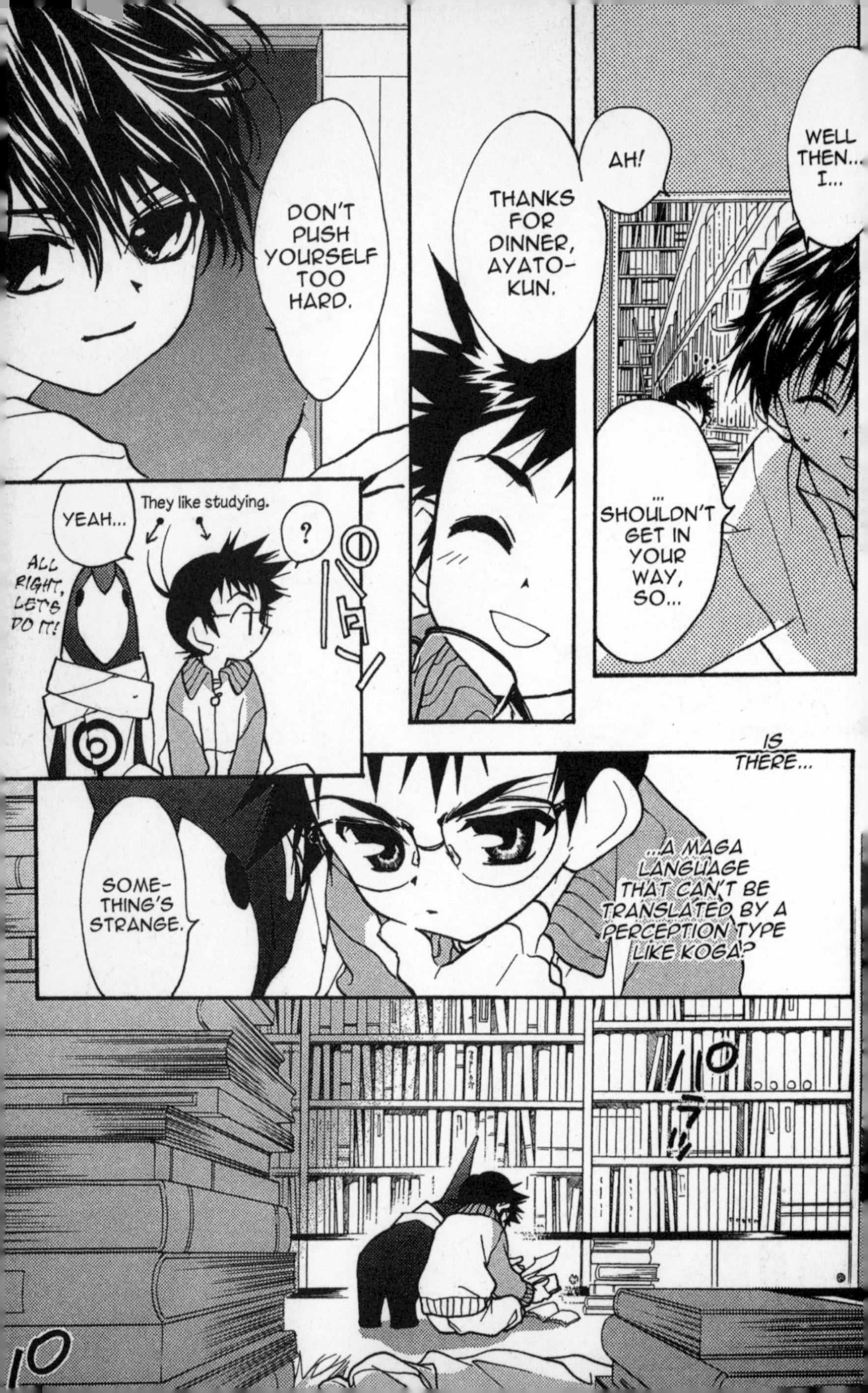
WELL THEN... I...
... SHOULDN'T GET IN YOUR WAY, SO...
AH!
THANKS FOR DINNER, AYATO-KUN.
DON'T PUSH YOURSELF TOO HARD.
?
YEAH...
They like studying.
ALL RIGHT, LET'S DO IT!
IS THERE...
...A MAGA LANGUAGE THAT CAN'T BE TRANSLATED BY A PERCEPTION TYPE LIKE KOGA?
SOME-THING'S STRANGE.

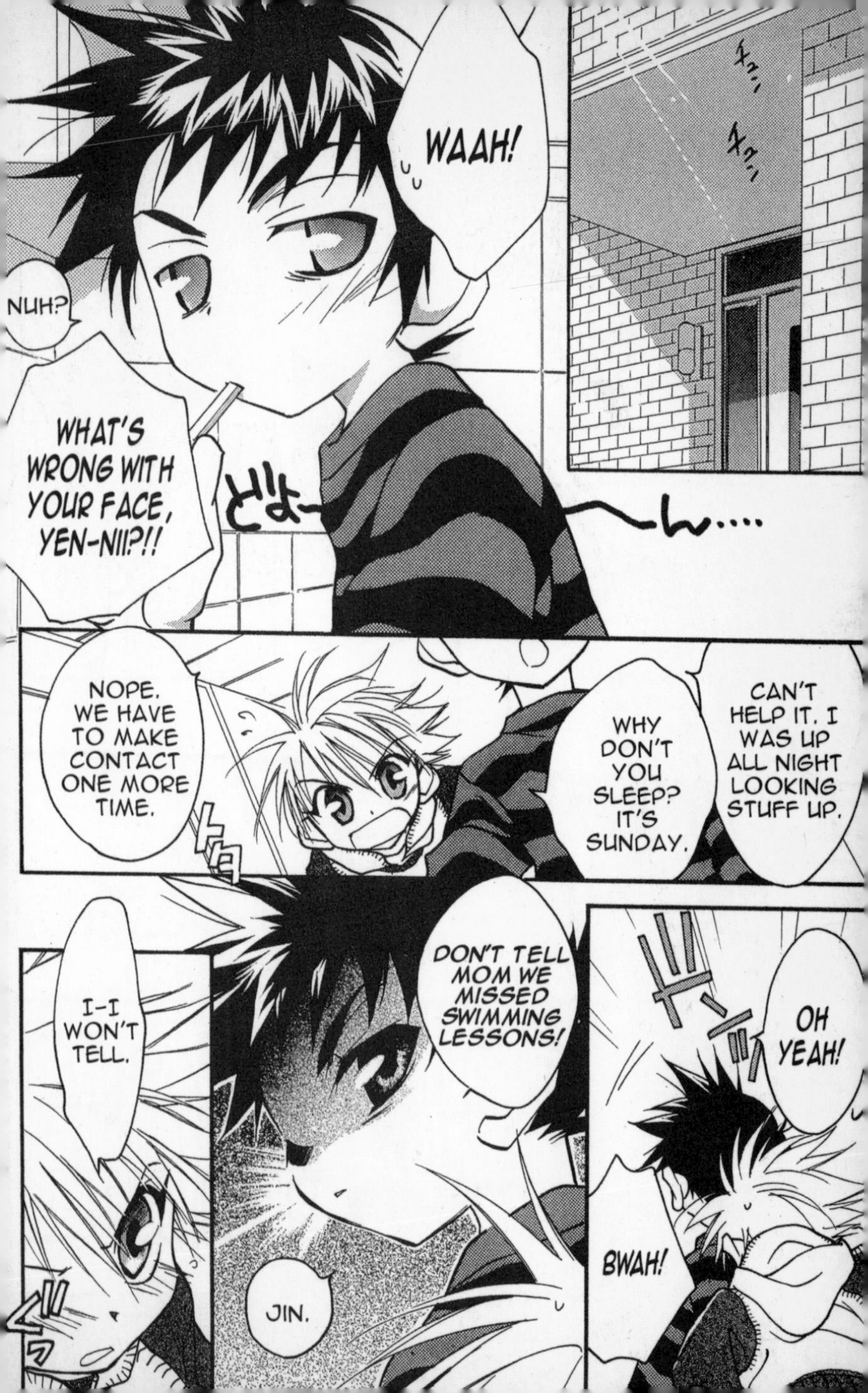
WAAH!
どよ〜〜ん....
NUH?
WHAT'S WRONG WITH YOUR FACE, YEN-NII?!!
CAN'T HELP IT. I WAS UP ALL NIGHT LOOKING STUFF UP.
WHY DON'T YOU SLEEP? IT'S SUNDAY.
NOPE. WE HAVE TO MAKE CONTACT ONE MORE TIME.
OH YEAH!
BWAH!
DON'T TELL MOM WE MISSED SWIMMING LESSONS!
JIN.
I-I WON'T TELL.

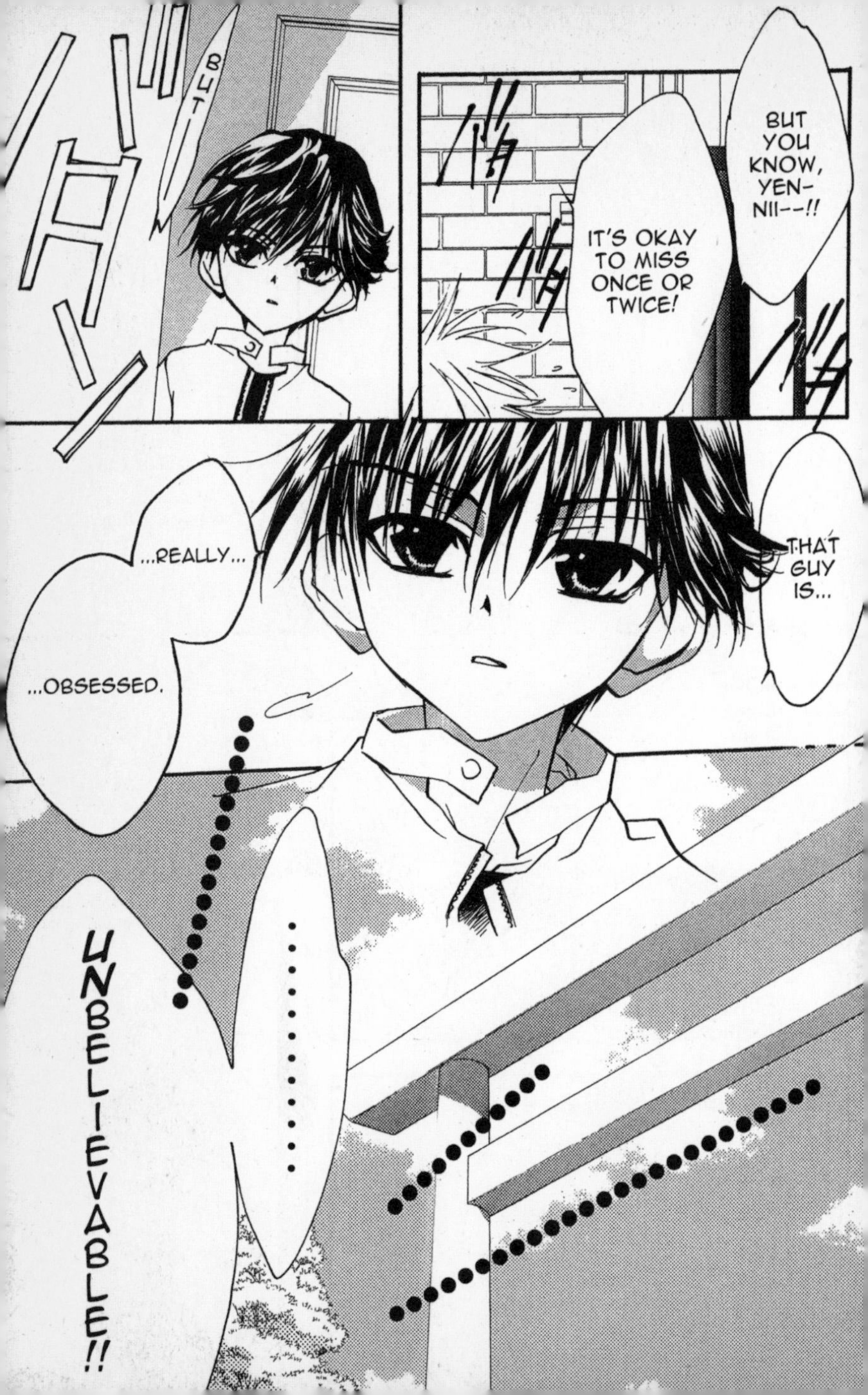
BUT YOU KNOW, YEN-NII--!!
IT'S OKAY TO MISS ONCE OR TWICE!
BUT
THAT GUY IS...
...REALLY...
...OBSESSED.
......
UNBELIEVABLE!!

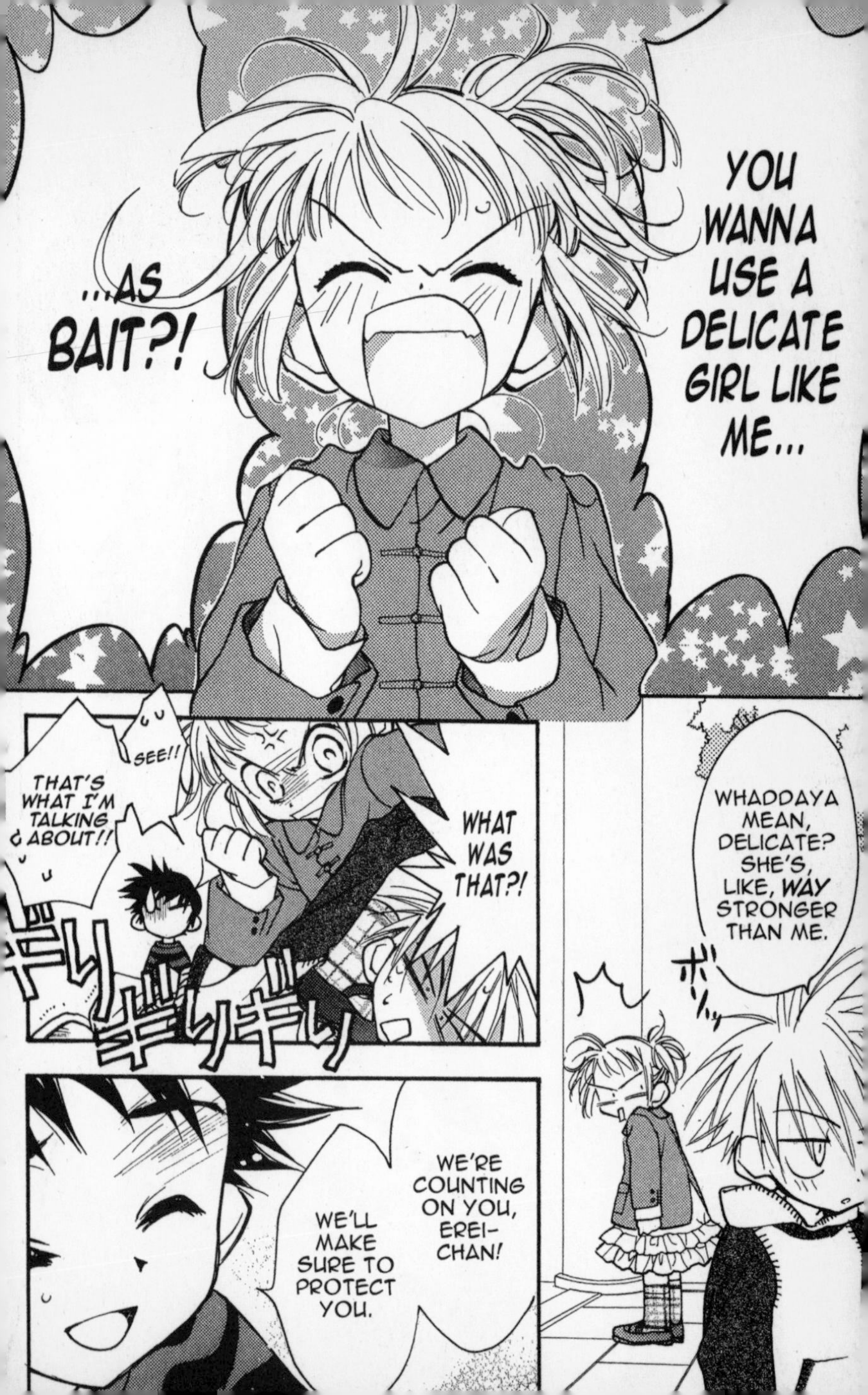
YOU WANNA USE A DELICATE GIRL LIKE ME...
...AS BAIT?!
WHADDAYA MEAN, DELICATE? SHE'S, LIKE, WAY STRONGER THAN ME.
ボソッ
WHAT WAS THAT?!
SEE!!
THAT'S WHAT I'M TALKING ABOUT!!
ギリギリ
WE'RE COUNTING ON YOU, EREI-CHAN!
WE'LL MAKE SURE TO PROTECT YOU.

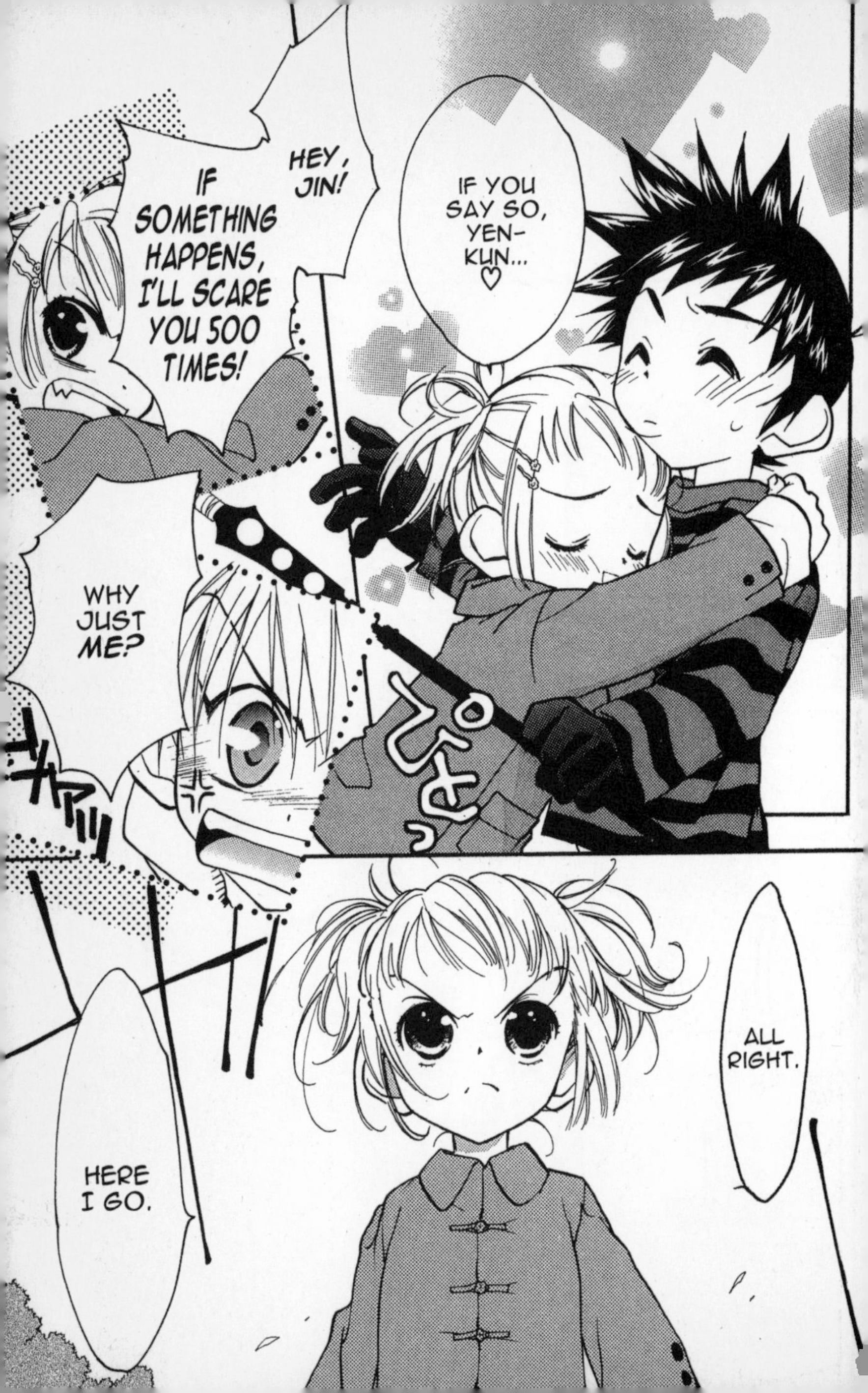

IF YOU SAY SO, YEN-KUN...♡
HEY, JIN!
IF SOMETHING HAPPENS, I'LL SCARE YOU 500 TIMES!
ぴとっ
WHY JUST ME?
ALL RIGHT.
HERE I GO.

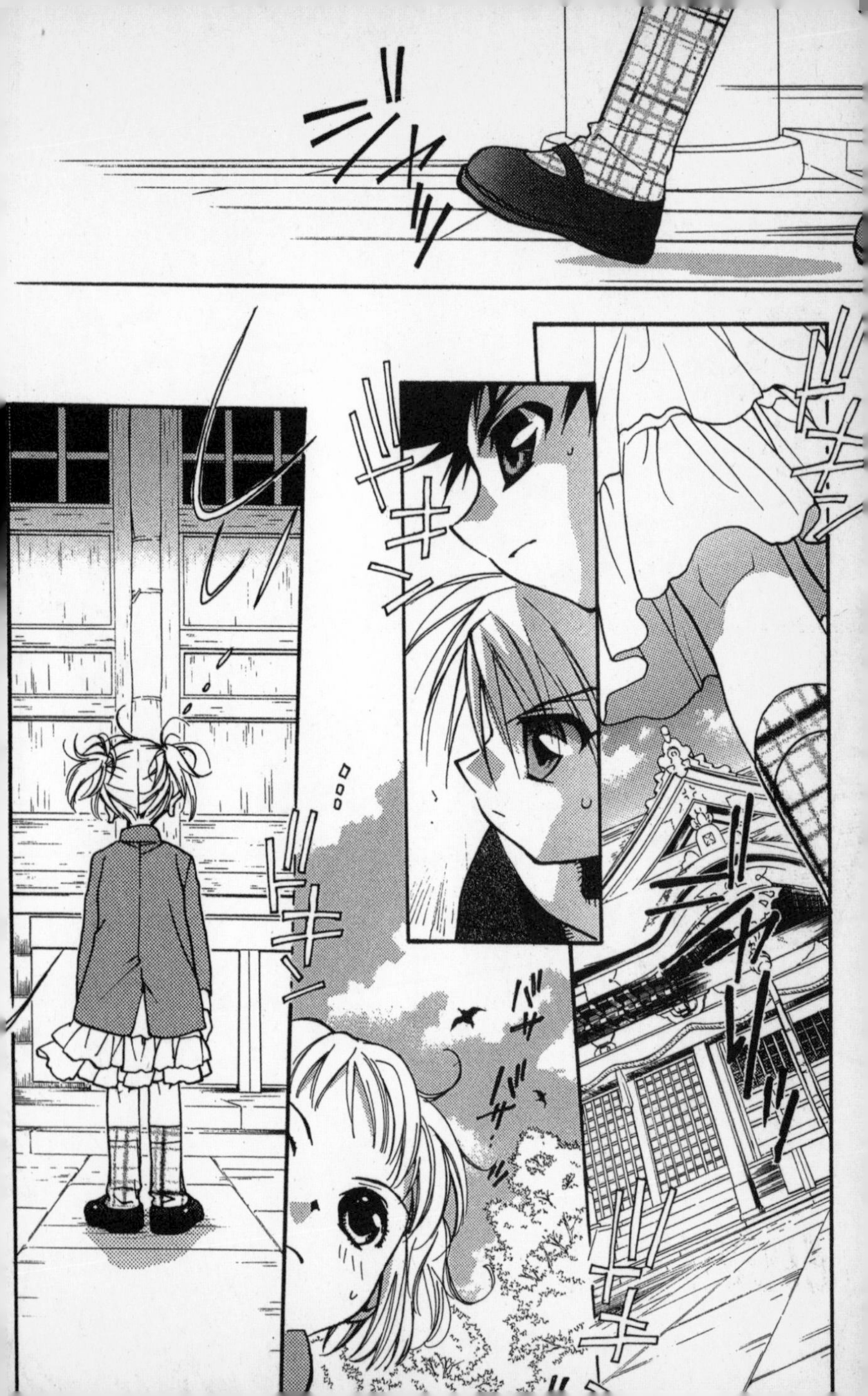
ジャッ
ドキ…
ジャリッ
ドキ
ドキーン
バサ
バサッ
…
ドキーン

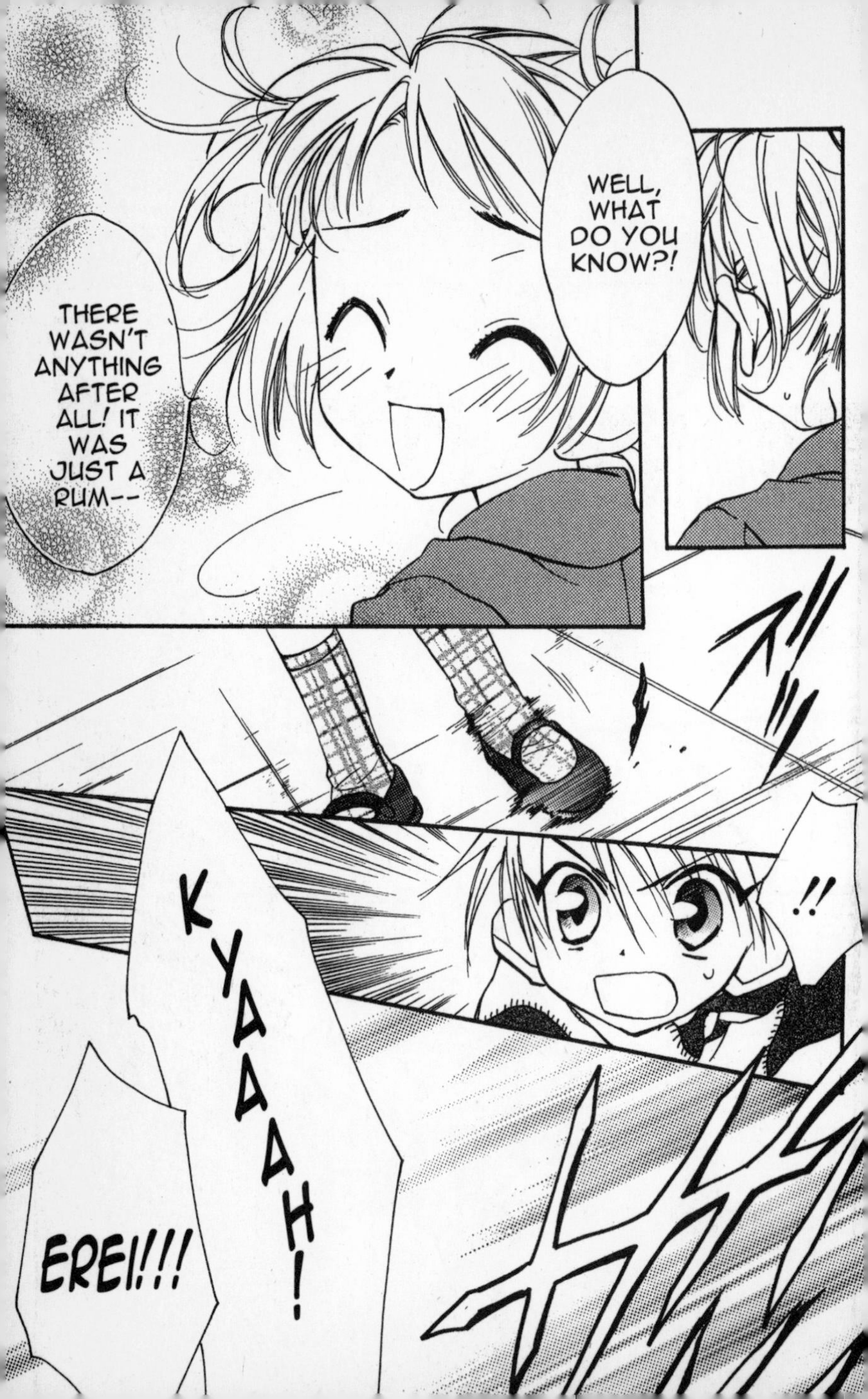
WELL, WHAT DO YOU KNOW?!
THERE WASN'T ANYTHING AFTER ALL! IT WAS JUST A RUM--
!!
KYAAAH!
EREI!!!

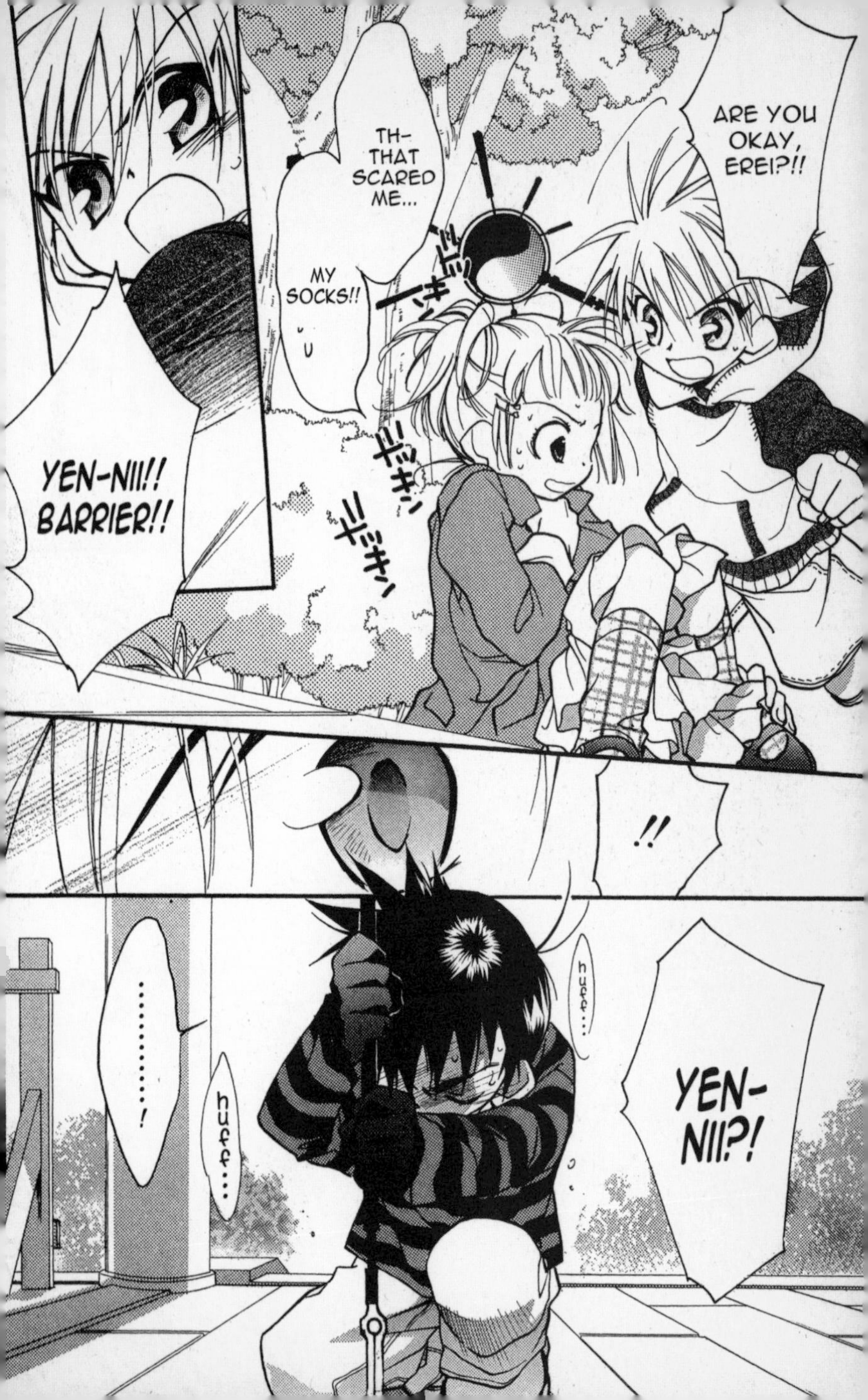
ARE YOU OKAY, EREI?!!
TH-THAT SCARED ME...
MY SOCKS!!
YEN-NII!! BARRIER!!
!!
YEN-NII?!
huff...
......!
huff...

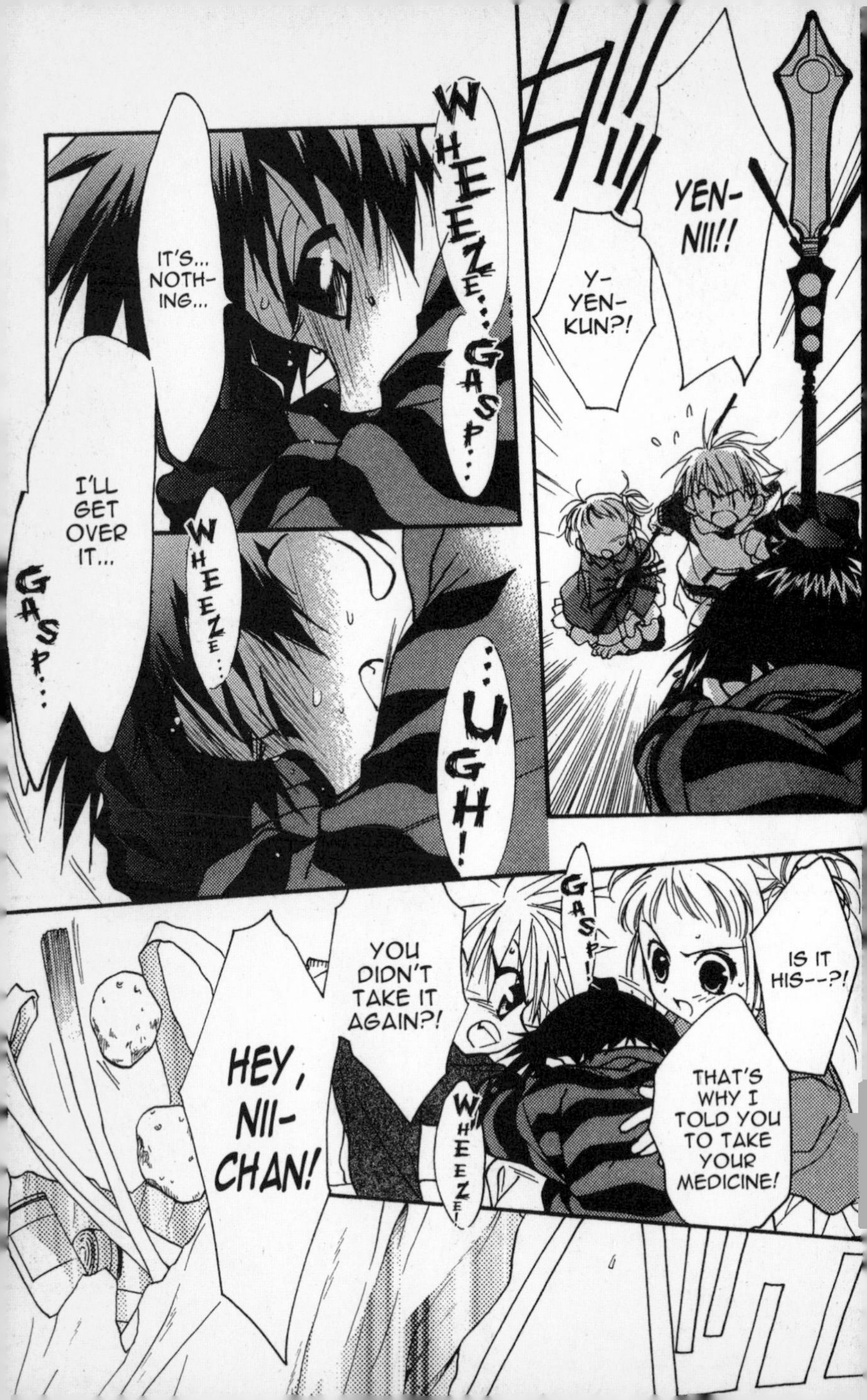
YEN-NII!!
Y-YEN-KUN?!
WHEEZE... GASP...
IT'S... NOTHING...
...UGH!
WHEEZE...
I'LL GET OVER IT...
GASP...
IS IT HIS--?!
THAT'S WHY I TOLD YOU TO TAKE YOUR MEDICINE!
GASP!
WHEEZE!
YOU DIDN'T TAKE IT AGAIN?!
HEY, NII-CHAN!

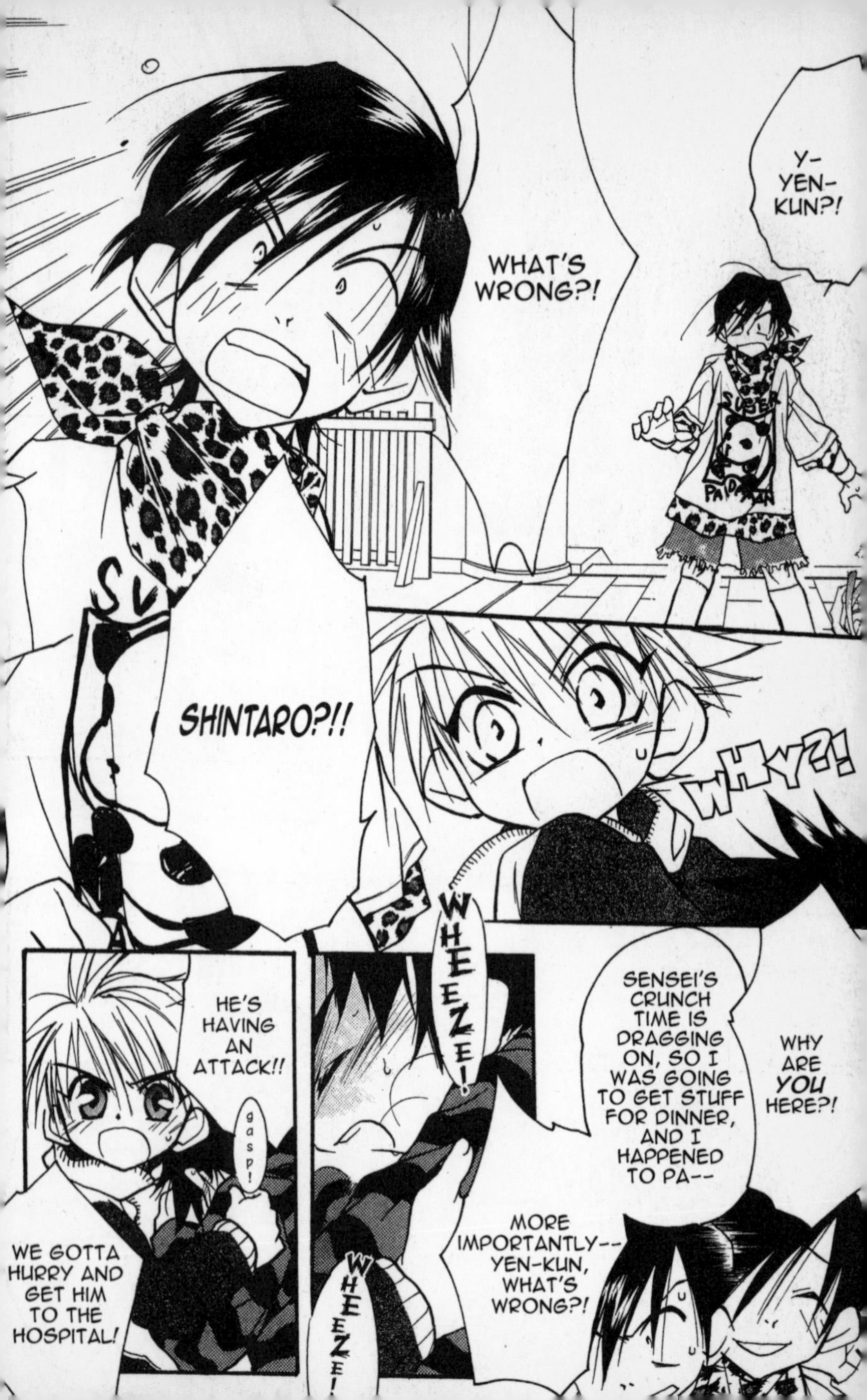
Y-
YEN-
KUN?!
WHAT'S WRONG?!
SHINTARO?!!
WHY?!
WHY ARE YOU HERE?!
SENSEI'S CRUNCH TIME IS DRAGGING ON, SO I WAS GOING TO GET STUFF FOR DINNER, AND I HAPPENED TO PA--
MORE IMPORTANTLY-- YEN-KUN, WHAT'S WRONG?!
WHEEZE!
WHEEZE!
HE'S HAVING AN ATTACK!!
gasp!
WE GOTTA HURRY AND GET HIM TO THE HOSPITAL!

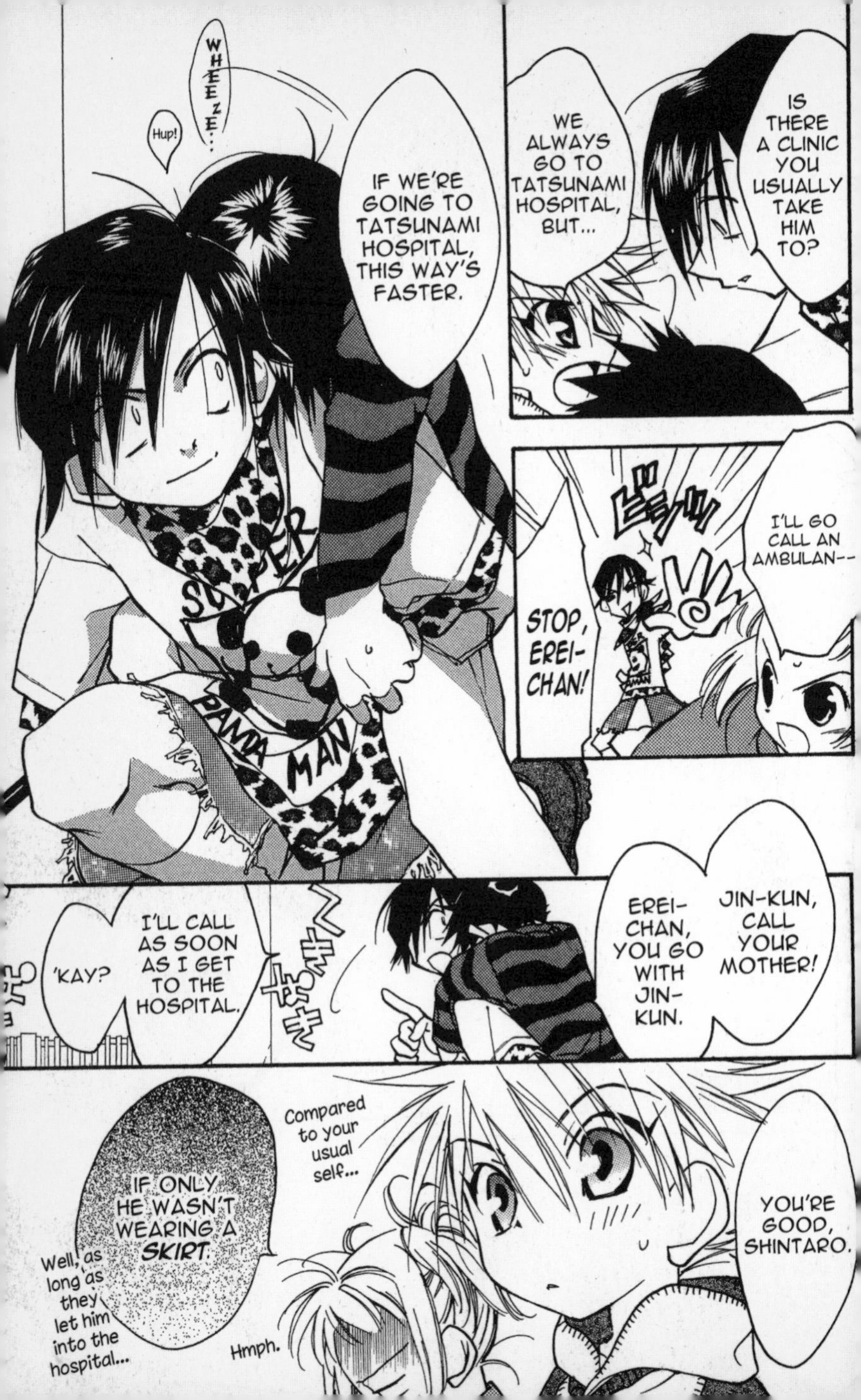
IS THERE A CLINIC YOU USUALLY TAKE HIM TO?
WE ALWAYS GO TO TATSUNAMI HOSPITAL, BUT...
I'LL GO CALL AN AMBULAN--
STOP, EREI-CHAN!
IF WE'RE GOING TO TATSUNAMI HOSPITAL, THIS WAY'S FASTER.
WHEEZE...
Hup!
SUPER PANDA MAN
JIN-KUN, CALL YOUR MOTHER!
EREI-CHAN, YOU GO WITH JIN-KUN.
I'LL CALL AS SOON AS I GET TO THE HOSPITAL.
'KAY?
YOU'RE GOOD, SHINTARO.
Compared to your usual self...
IF ONLY HE WASN'T WEARING A SKIRT.
Well, as long as they let him into the hospital...
Hmph.

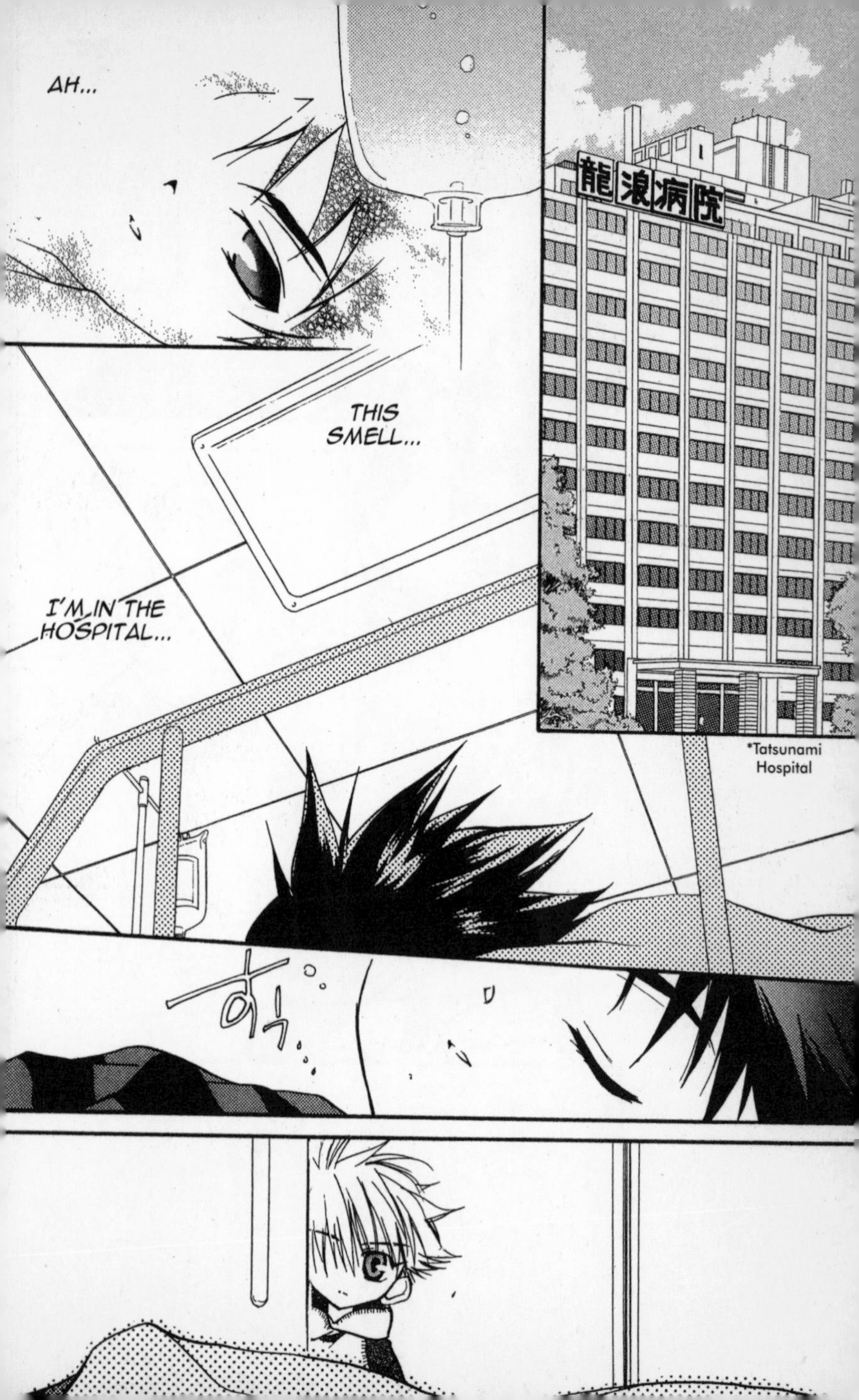
龍浪病院
*Tatsunami Hospital
AH...
THIS SMELL...
I'M IN THE HOSPITAL...
すぅ

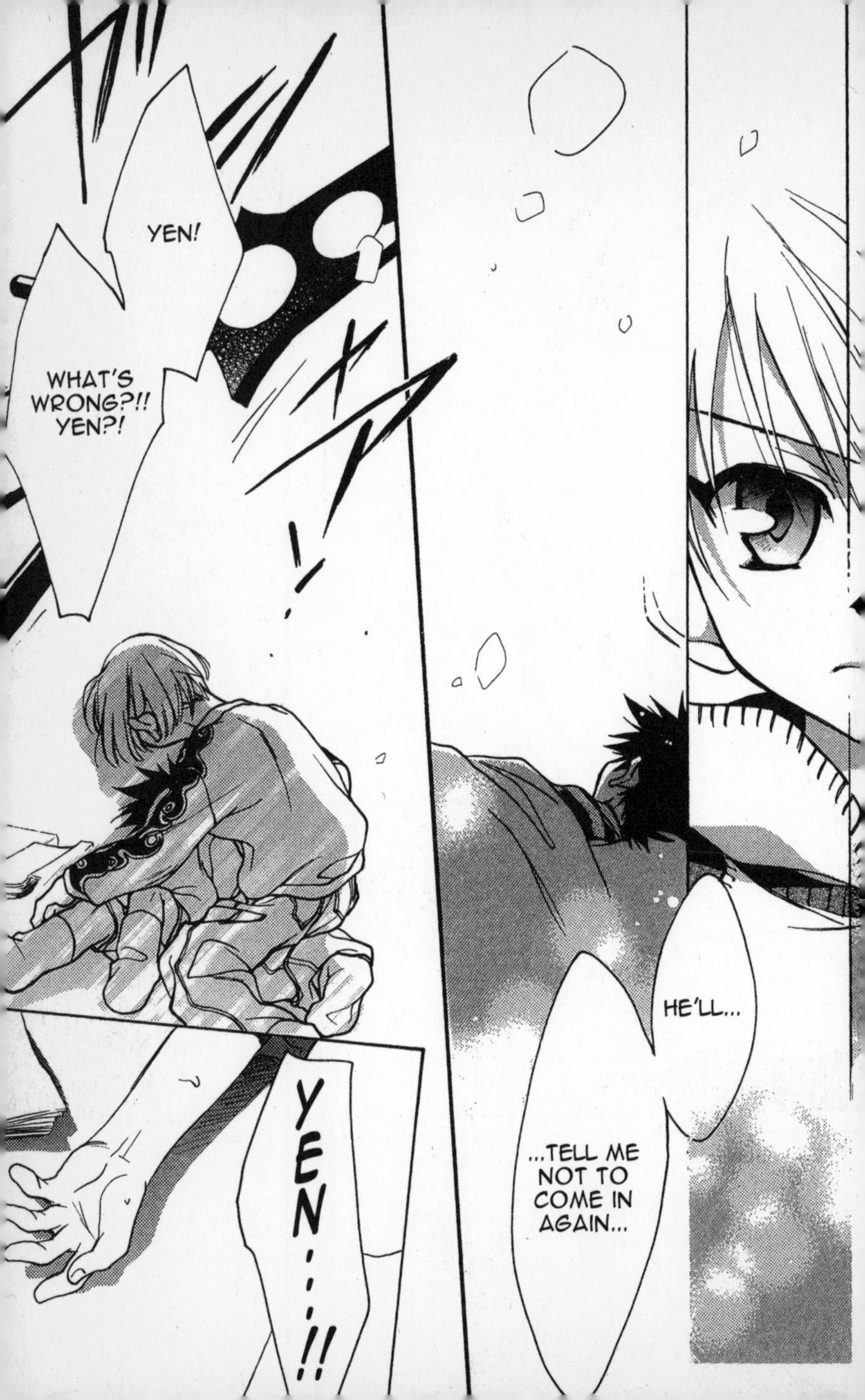
HE'LL...
...TELL ME NOT TO COME IN AGAIN...
YEN!
WHAT'S WRONG?!! YEN?!
YEN...!!

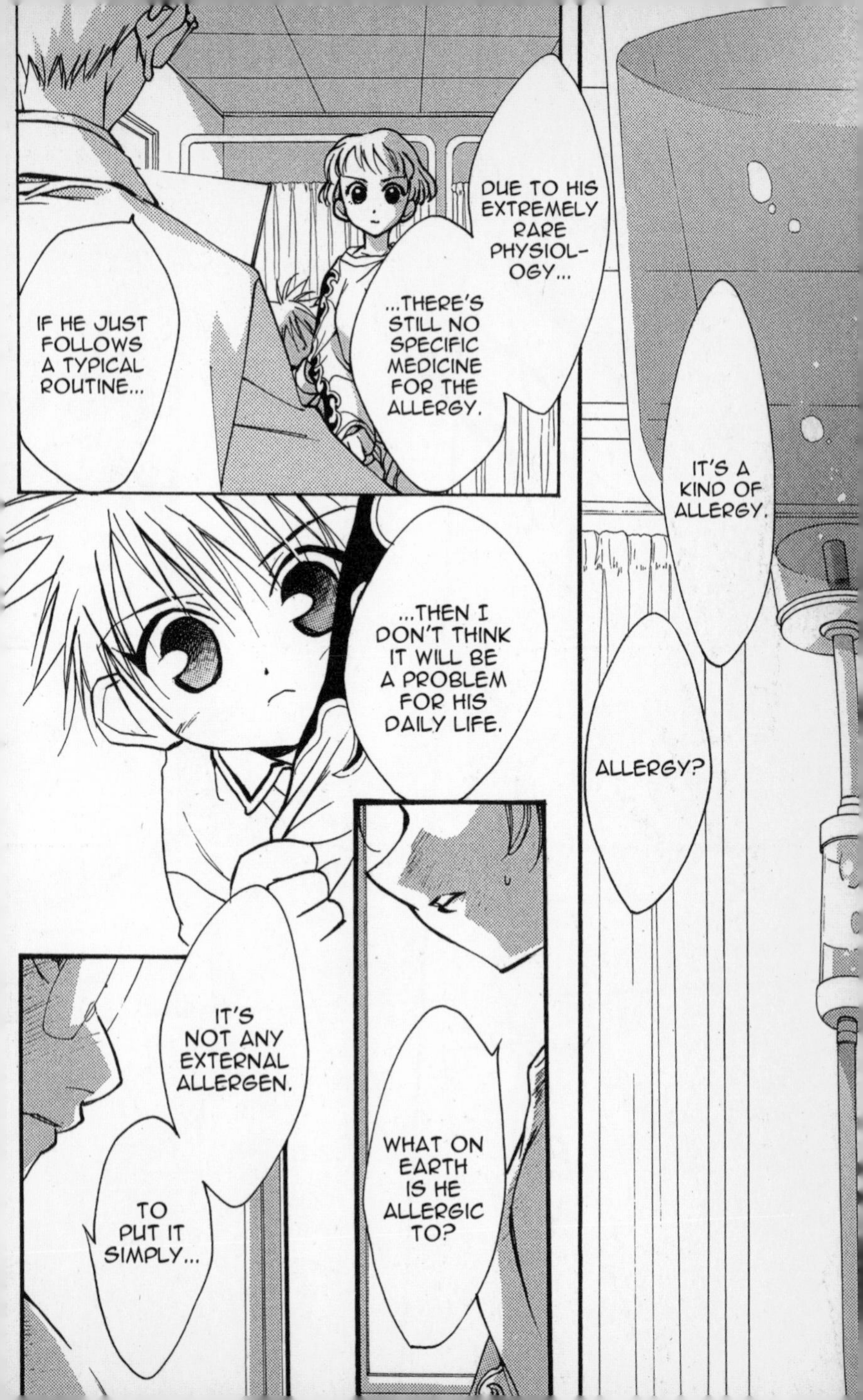
IT'S A KIND OF ALLERGY.
ALLERGY?
DUE TO HIS EXTREMELY RARE PHYSIOLOGY...
...THERE'S STILL NO SPECIFIC MEDICINE FOR THE ALLERGY.
IF HE JUST FOLLOWS A TYPICAL ROUTINE...
...THEN I DON'T THINK IT WILL BE A PROBLEM FOR HIS DAILY LIFE.
WHAT ON EARTH IS HE ALLERGIC TO?
IT'S NOT ANY EXTERNAL ALLERGEN.
TO PUT IT SIMPLY...

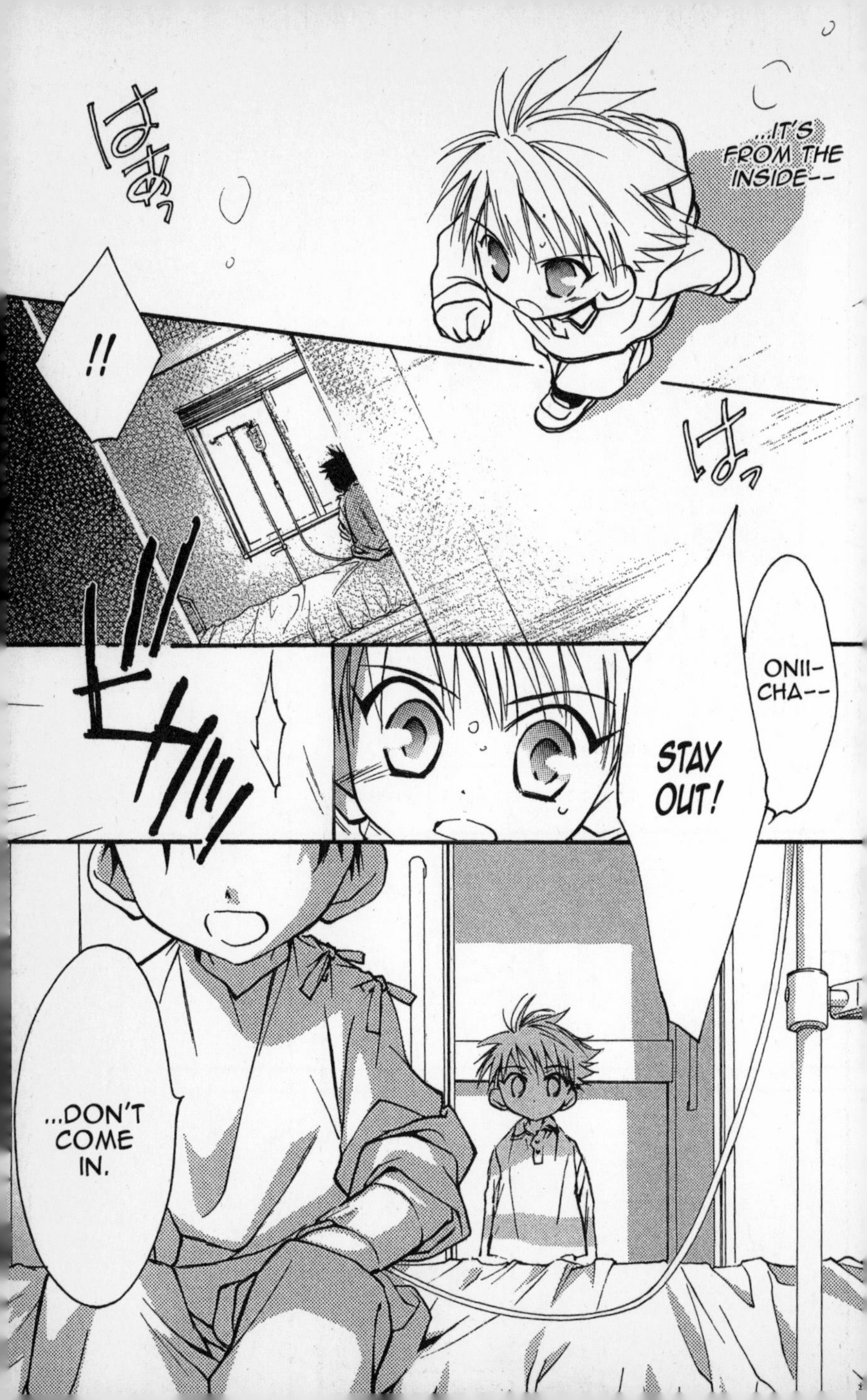

...IT'S FROM THE INSIDE--
はぁっ
はっ
!!
ONII-CHA--
STAY OUT!
...DON'T COME IN.

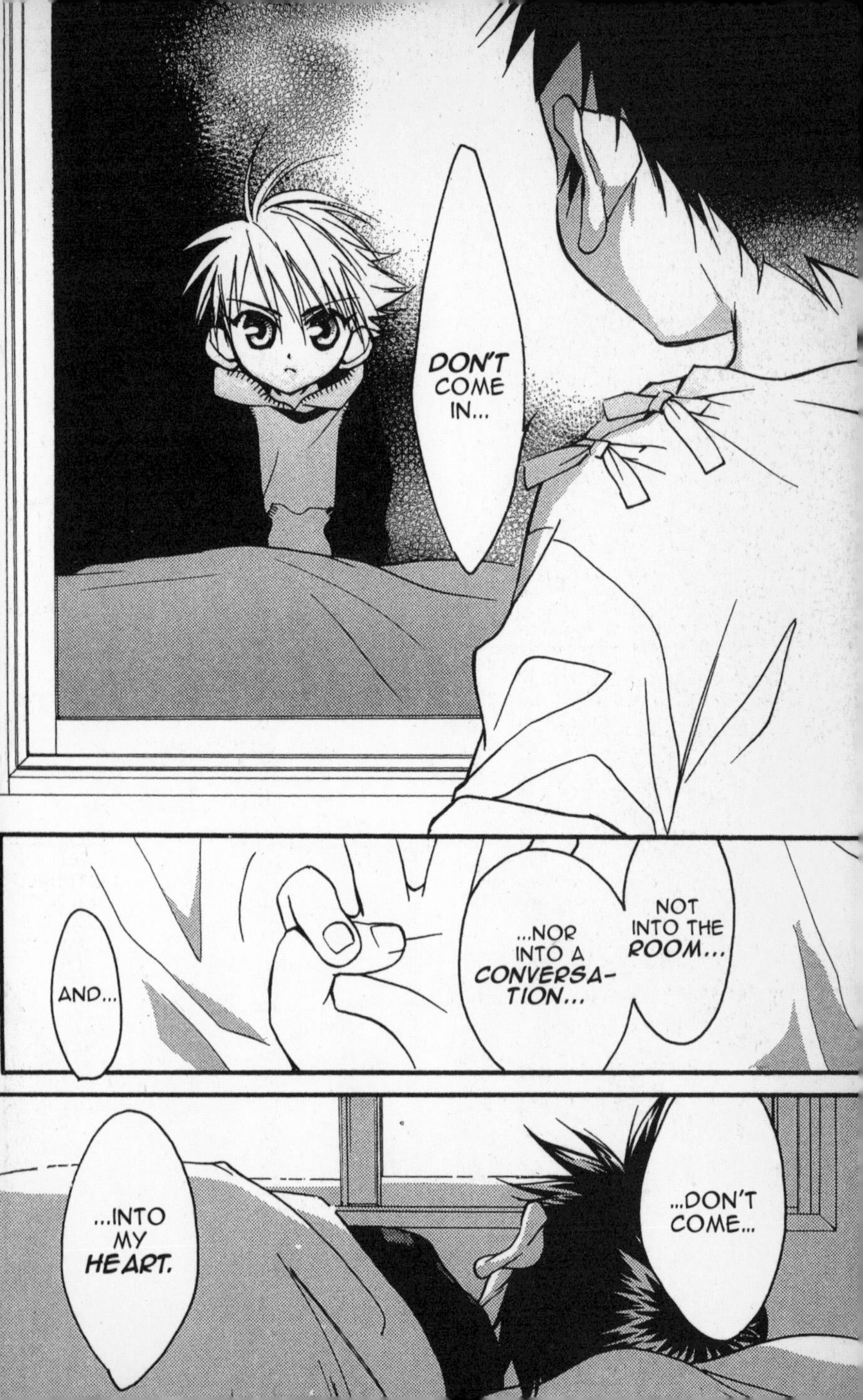
DON'T COME IN...
NOT INTO THE ROOM...
...NOR INTO A CONVERSATION...
AND...
...DON'T COME...
...INTO MY HEART.

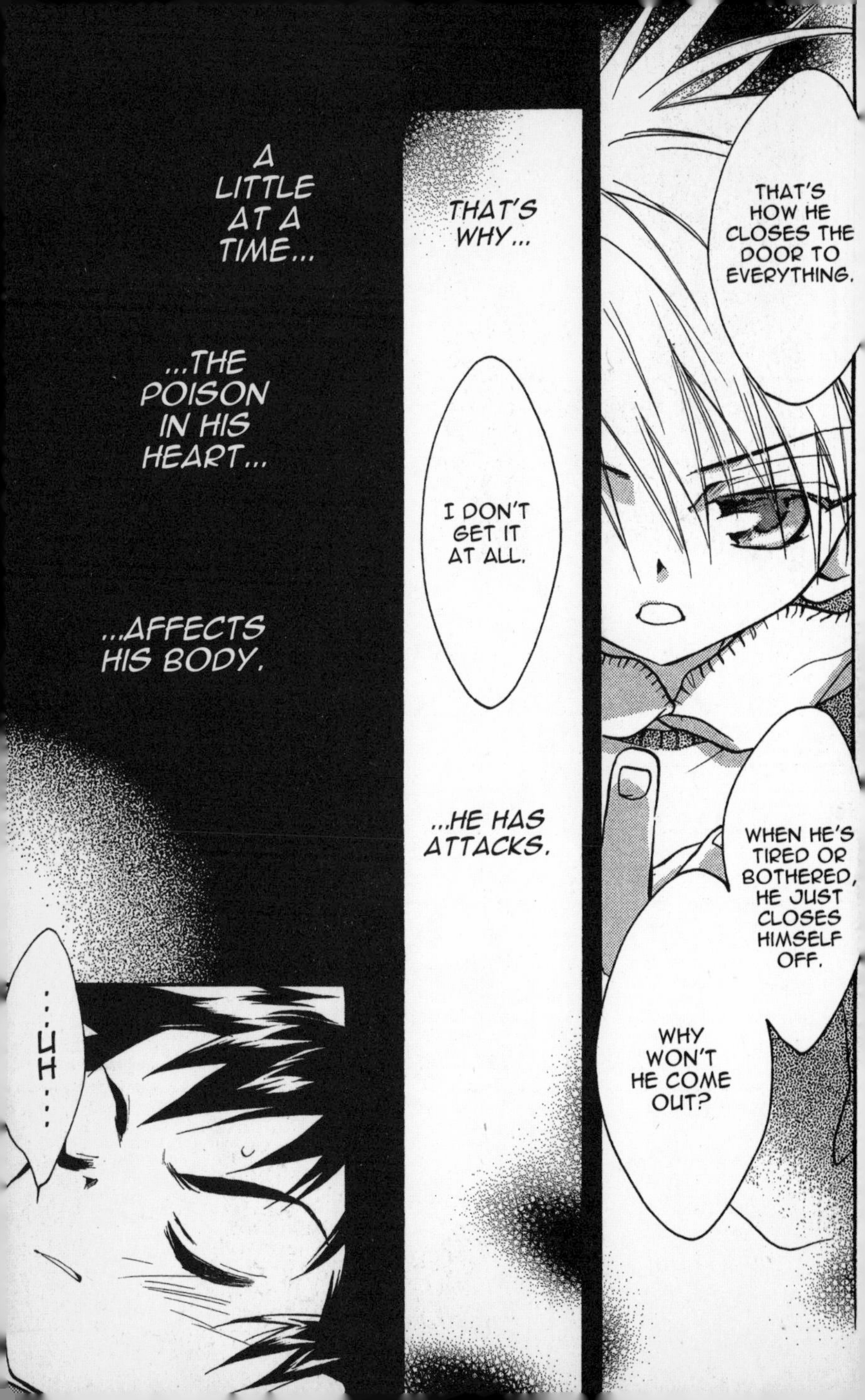
THAT'S HOW HE CLOSES THE DOOR TO EVERYTHING.
WHEN HE'S TIRED OR BOTHERED, HE JUST CLOSES HIMSELF OFF.
WHY WON'T HE COME OUT?
THAT'S WHY...
I DON'T GET IT AT ALL.
...HE HAS ATTACKS.
A LITTLE AT A TIME...
...THE POISON IN HIS HEART...
...AFFECTS HIS BODY.
...UH...

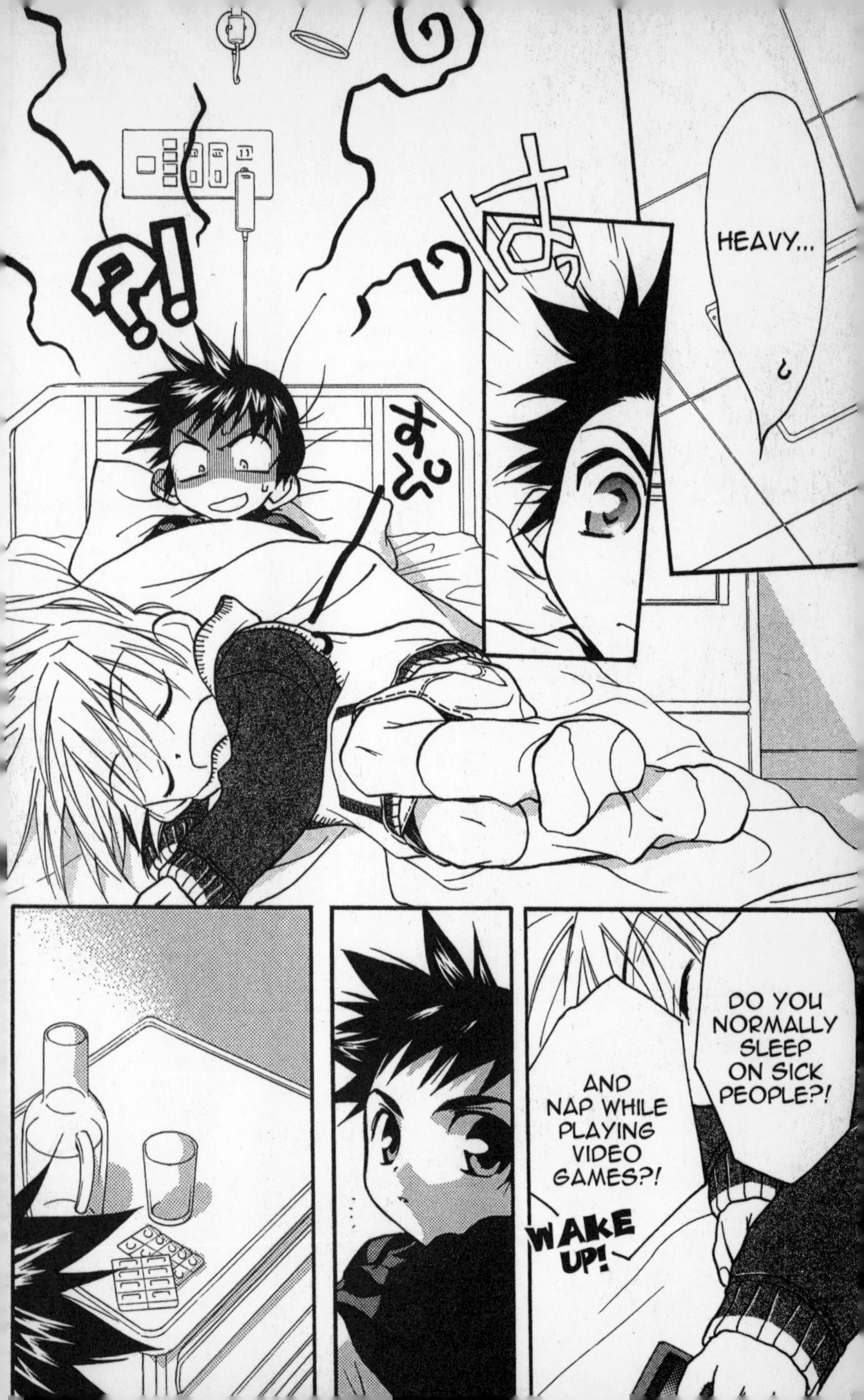
HEAVY...
?!
DO YOU NORMALLY SLEEP ON SICK PEOPLE?!
AND NAP WHILE PLAYING VIDEO GAMES?!
WAKE UP!

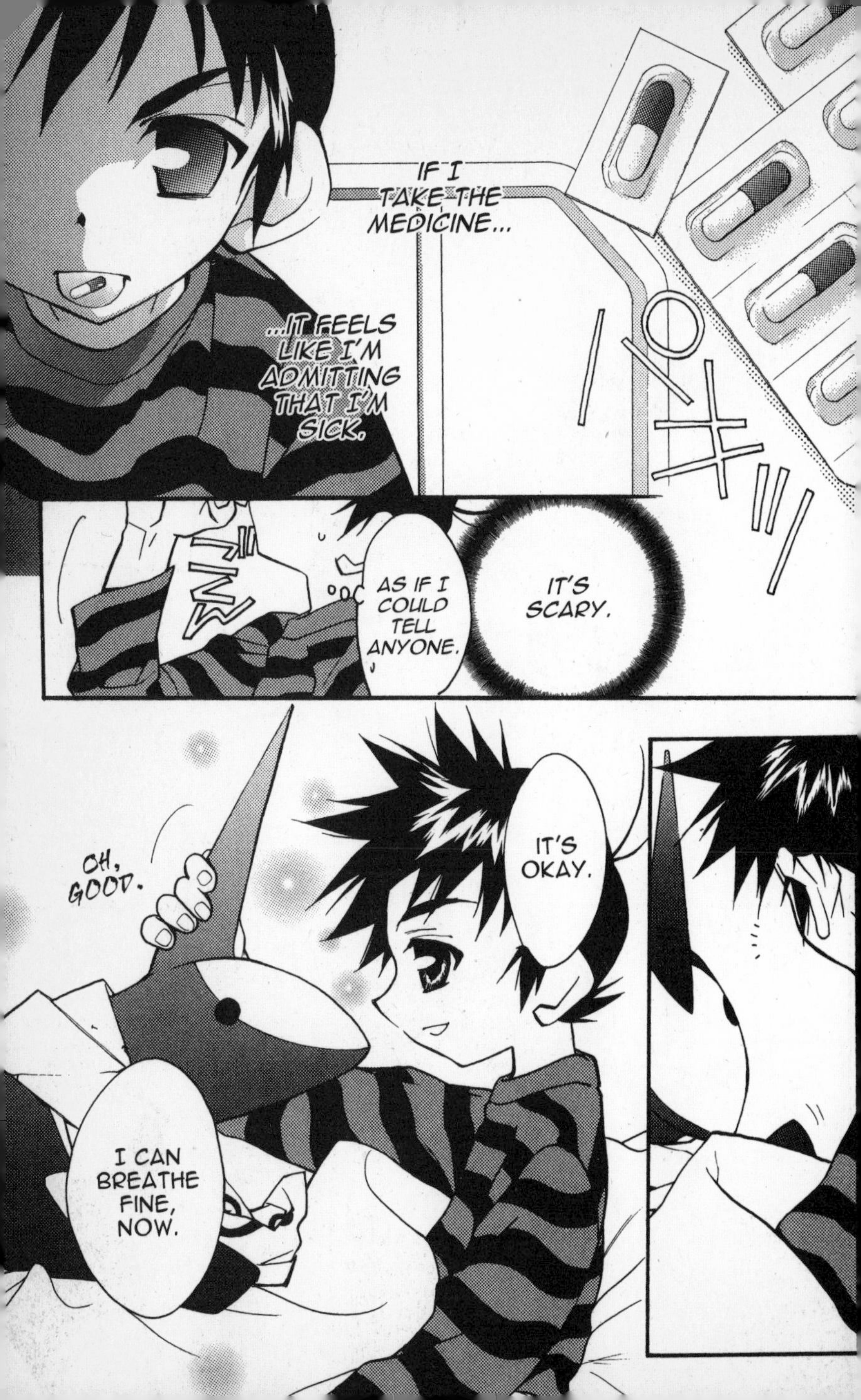
IF I TAKE THE MEDICINE...
...IT FEELS LIKE I'M ADMITTING THAT I'M SICK.
IT'S SCARY.
AS IF I COULD TELL ANYONE.
IT'S OKAY.
OH, GOOD.
I CAN BREATHE FINE, NOW.

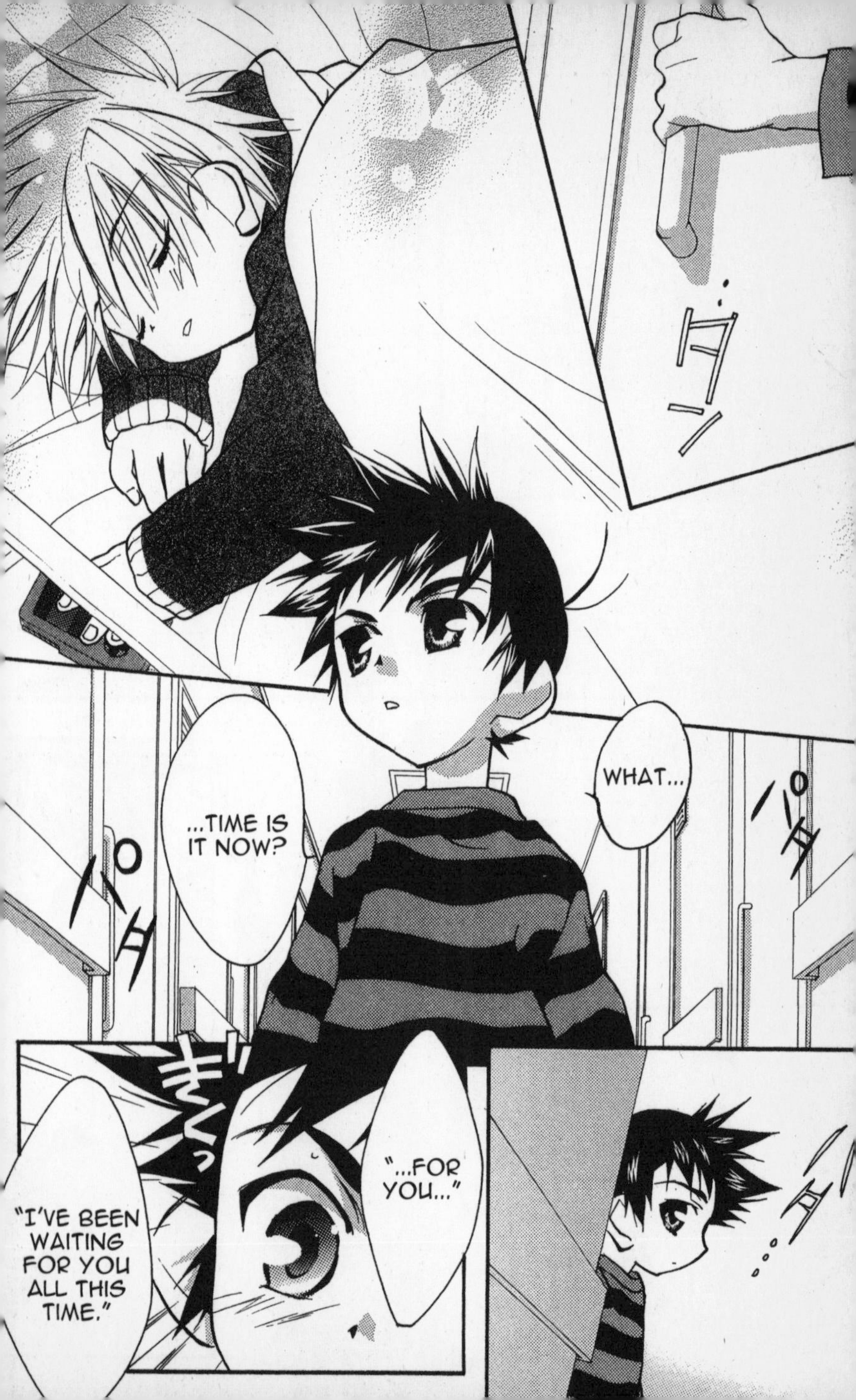

WHAT...
...TIME IS IT NOW?
"...FOR YOU..."
"I'VE BEEN WAITING FOR YOU ALL THIS TIME."

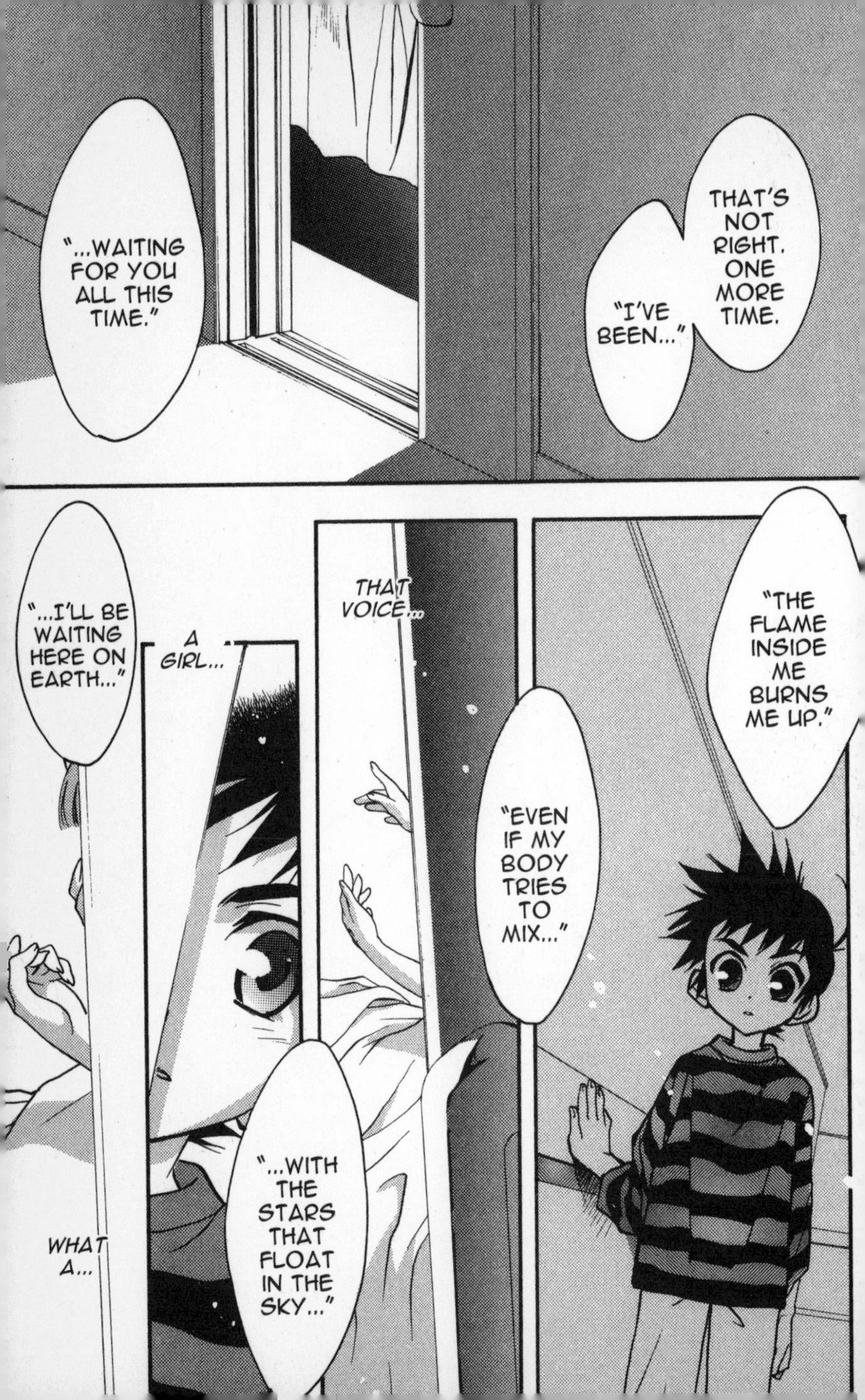
THAT'S NOT RIGHT. ONE MORE TIME.
"I'VE BEEN..."
"...WAITING FOR YOU ALL THIS TIME."
"THE FLAME INSIDE ME BURNS ME UP."
"EVEN IF MY BODY TRIES TO MIX..."
THAT VOICE...
"...WITH THE STARS THAT FLOAT IN THE SKY..."
A GIRL...
"...I'LL BE WAITING HERE ON EARTH..."
WHAT A...

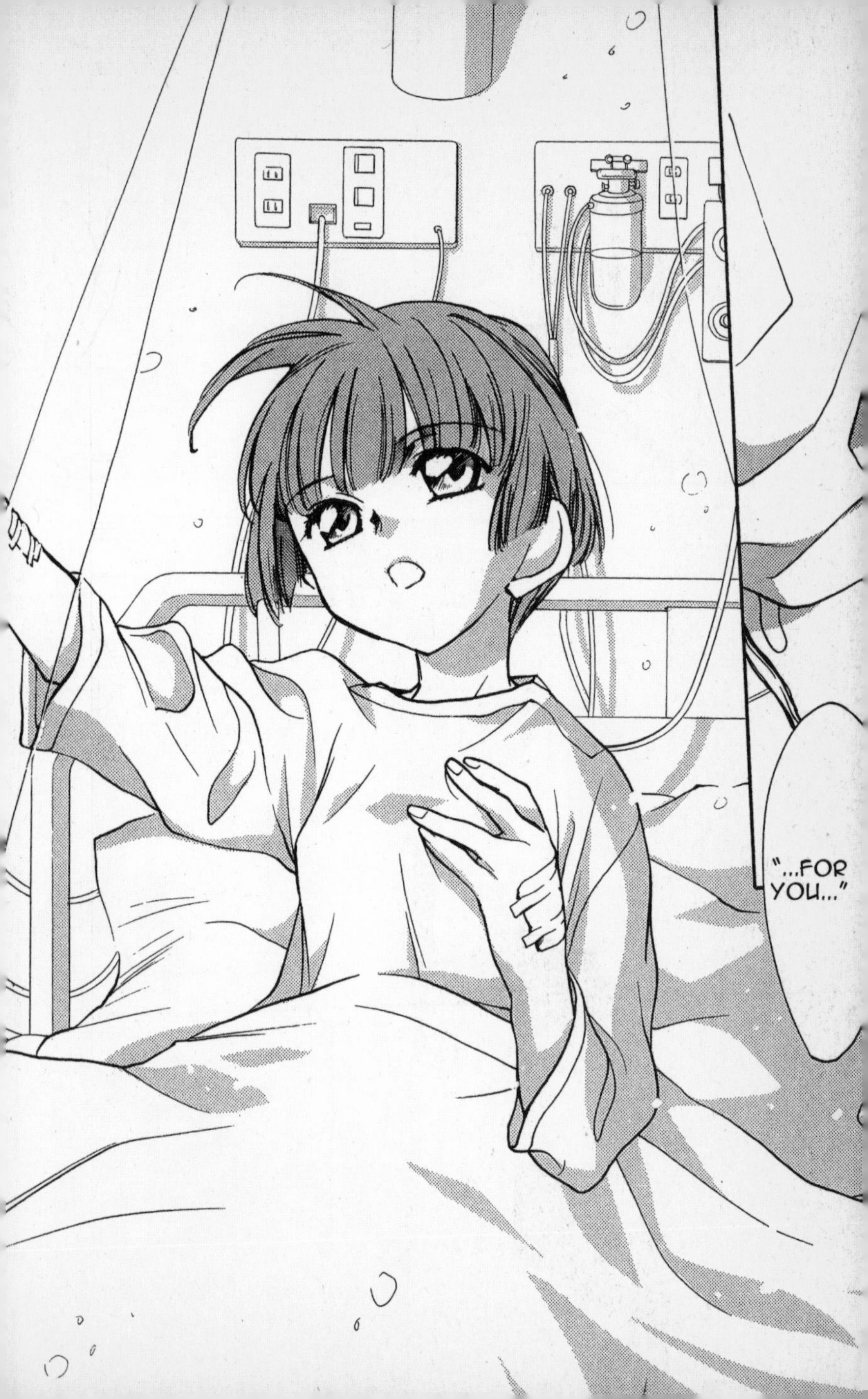
"...FOR YOU..."

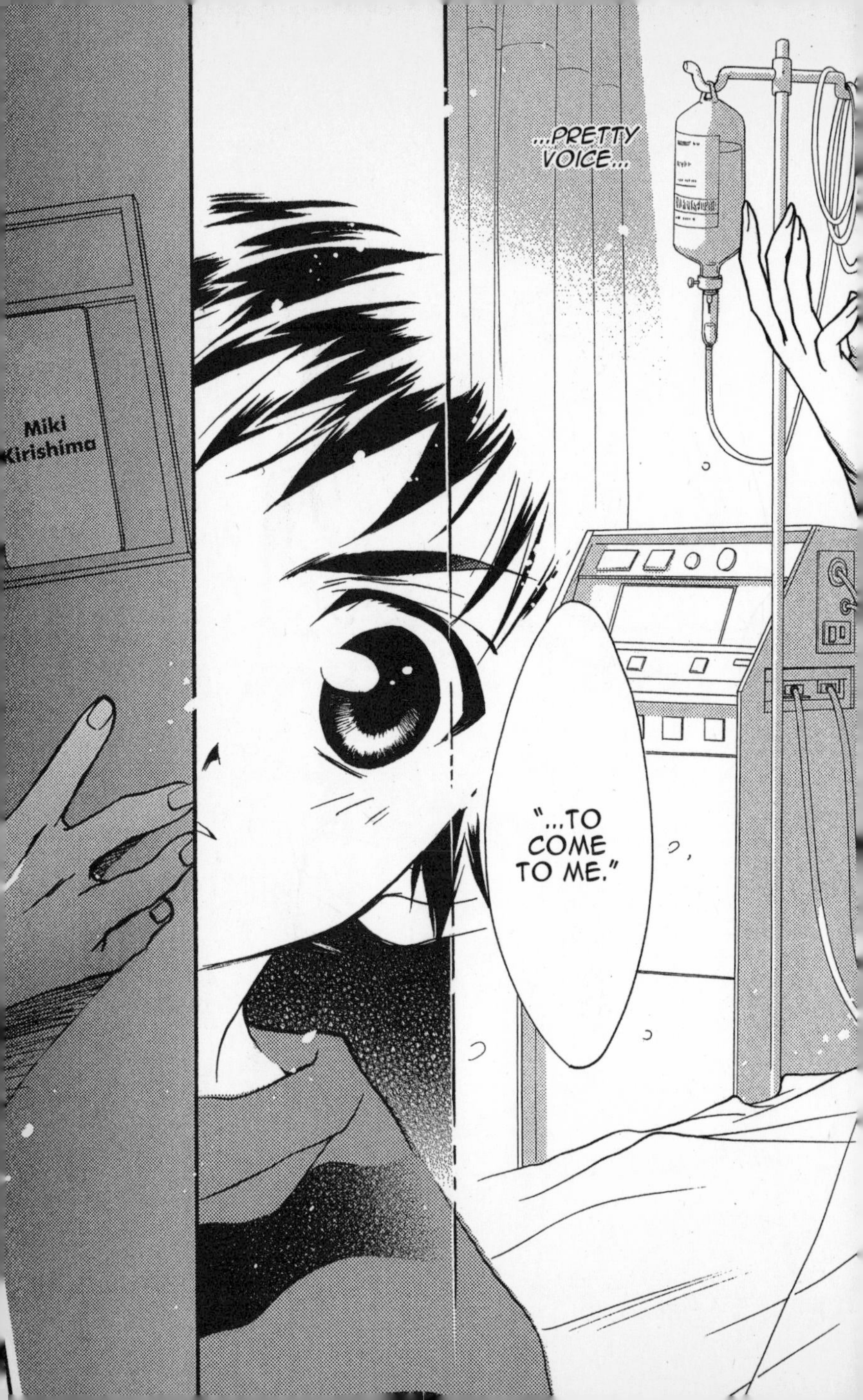
...PRETTY VOICE...
"...TO COME TO ME."
Miki Kirishima

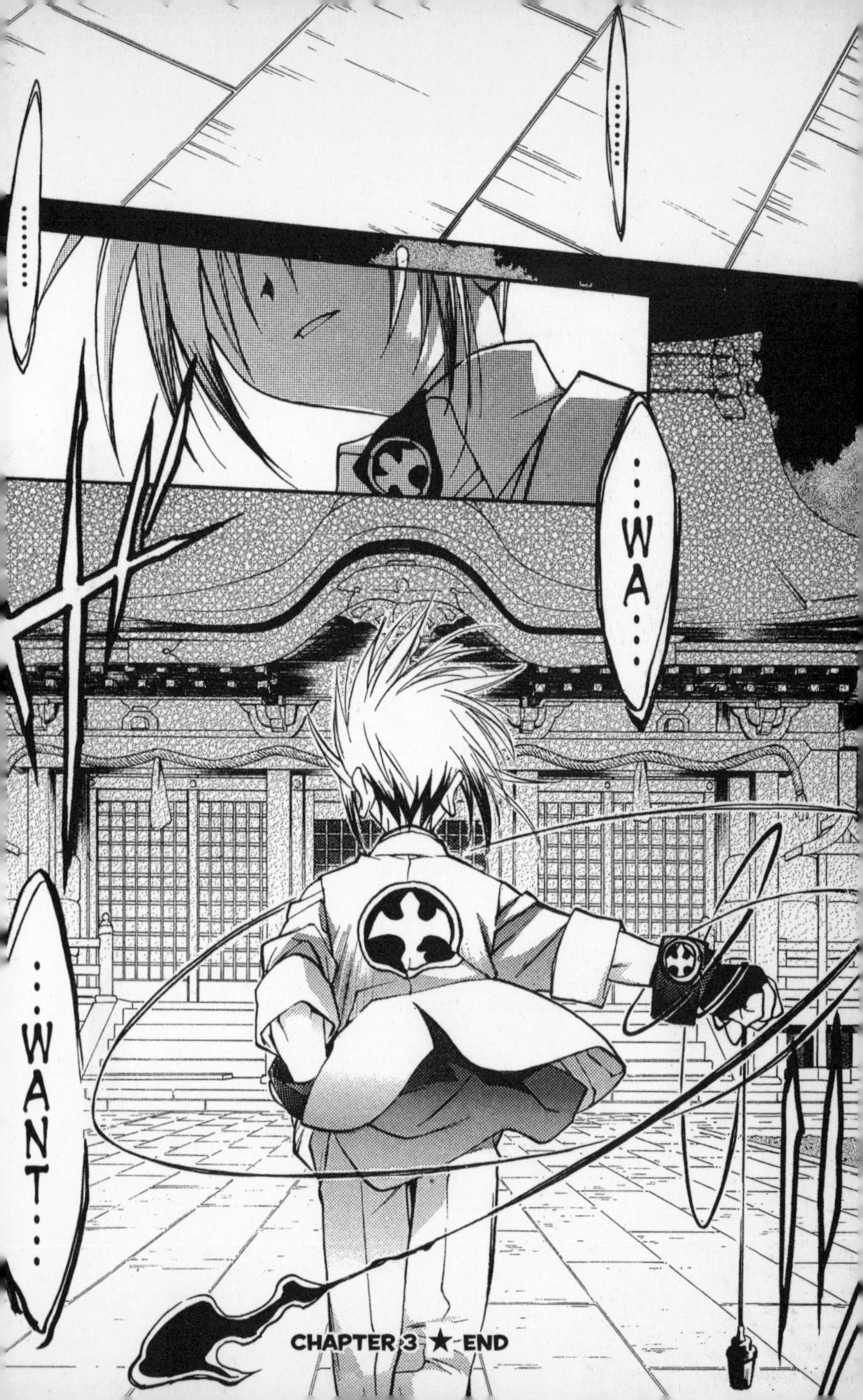
......
......
...WA...
...WANT...
CHAPTER 3 ★ END

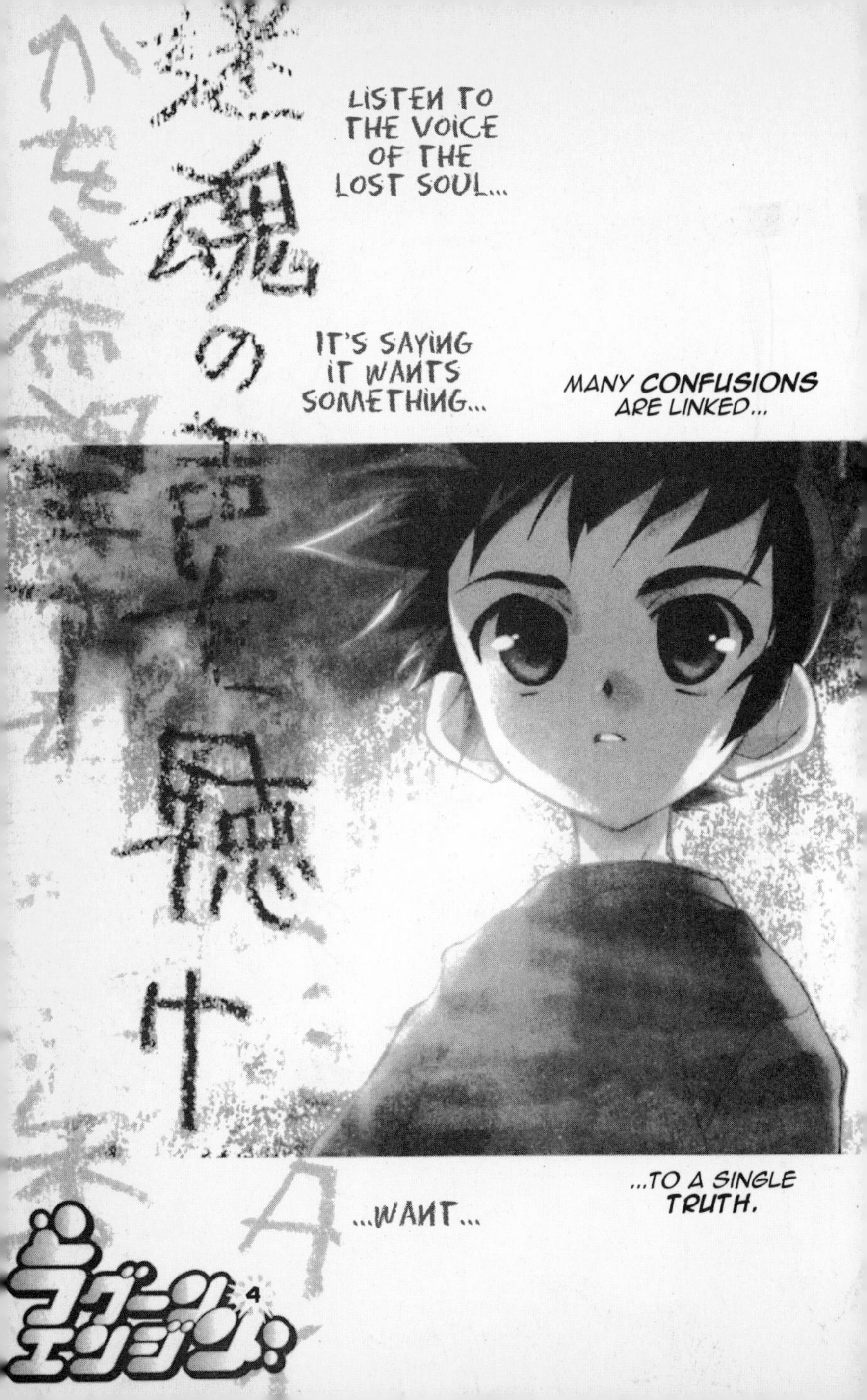

LISTEN TO THE VOICE OF THE LOST SOUL...
MANY **CONFUSIONS** ARE LINKED...
IT'S SAYING IT WANTS SOMETHING...
...TO A SINGLE **TRUTH.**
...WANT...

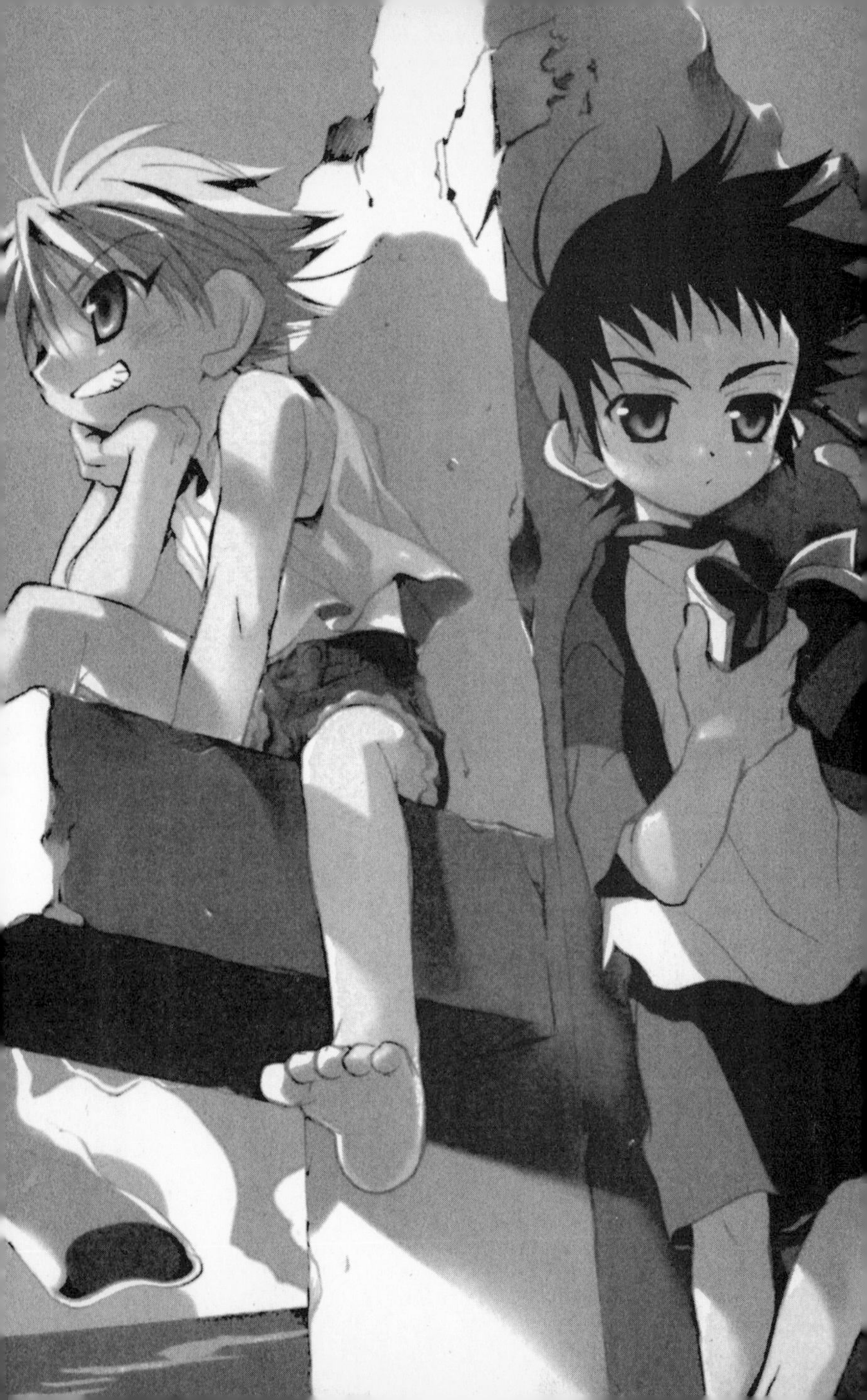

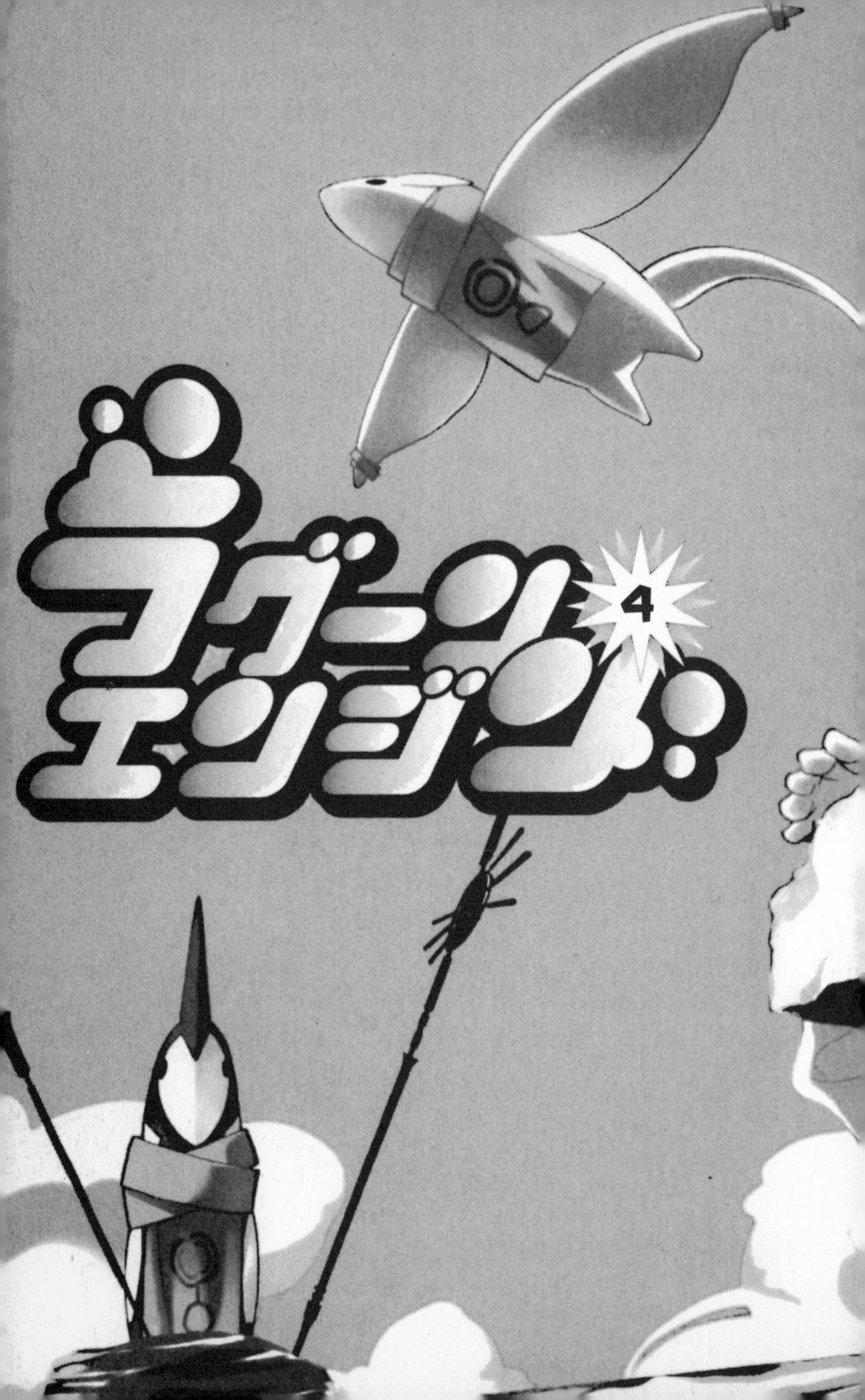
ラグーン
エンジン
4

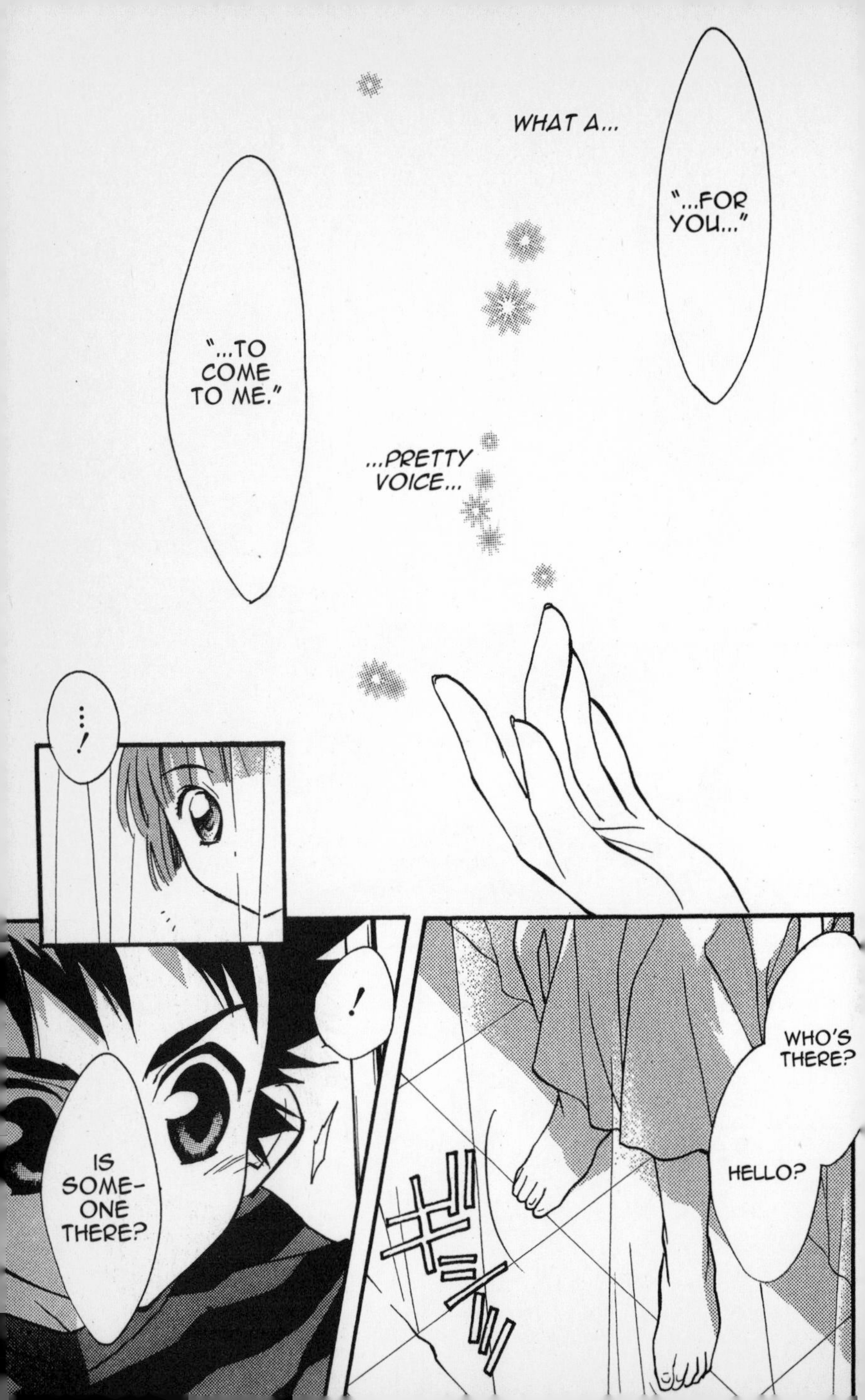
"...FOR YOU..."
WHAT A...
"...TO COME TO ME."
...PRETTY VOICE...
...!
WHO'S THERE?
HELLO?
!
IS SOME-ONE THERE?

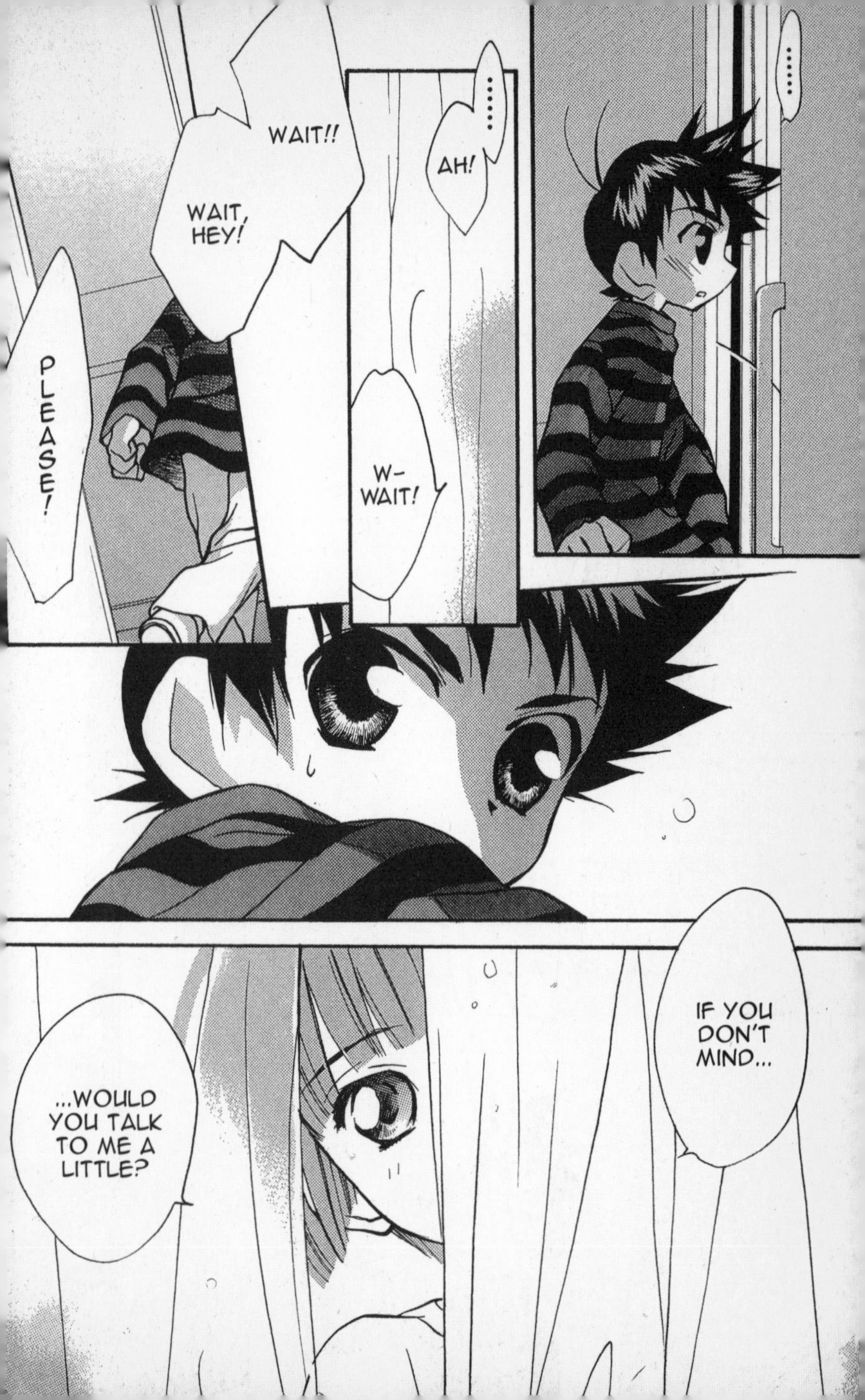
......
......
AH!
W-WAIT!
WAIT!!
WAIT, HEY!
PLEASE!
IF YOU DON'T MIND...
...WOULD YOU TALK TO ME A LITTLE?

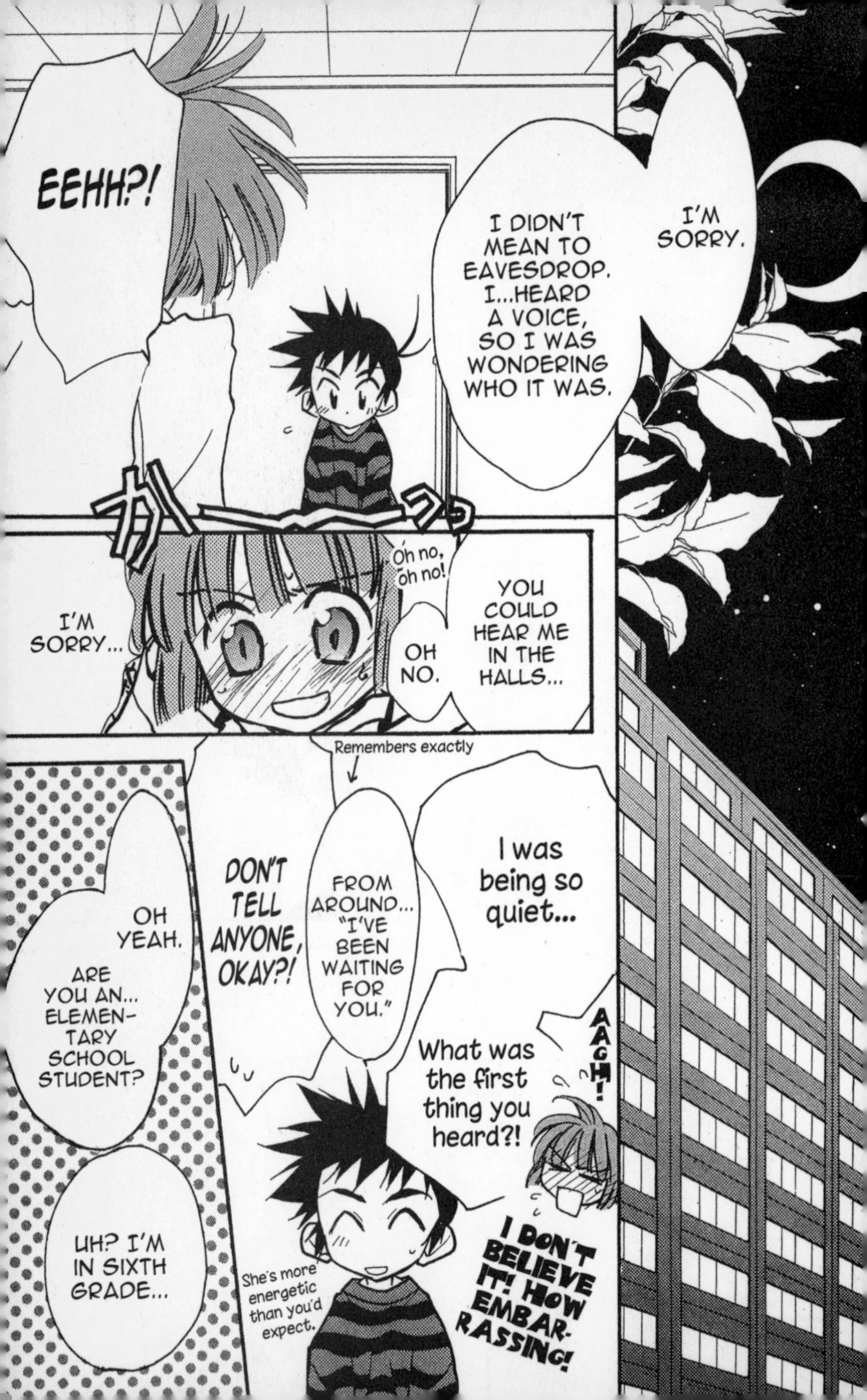
I'M SORRY.
I DIDN'T MEAN TO EAVESDROP. I...HEARD A VOICE, SO I WAS WONDERING WHO IT WAS.
EEHH?!
Oh no, oh no!
YOU COULD HEAR ME IN THE HALLS...
OH NO.
I'M SORRY...
I was being so quiet...
Remembers exactly
FROM AROUND... "I'VE BEEN WAITING FOR YOU."
DON'T TELL ANYONE, OKAY?!
AAGH!
What was the first thing you heard?!
I DON'T BELIEVE IT! HOW EMBARRASSING!
She's more energetic than you'd expect.
OH YEAH.
ARE YOU AN... ELEMENTARY SCHOOL STUDENT?
UH? I'M IN SIXTH GRADE...

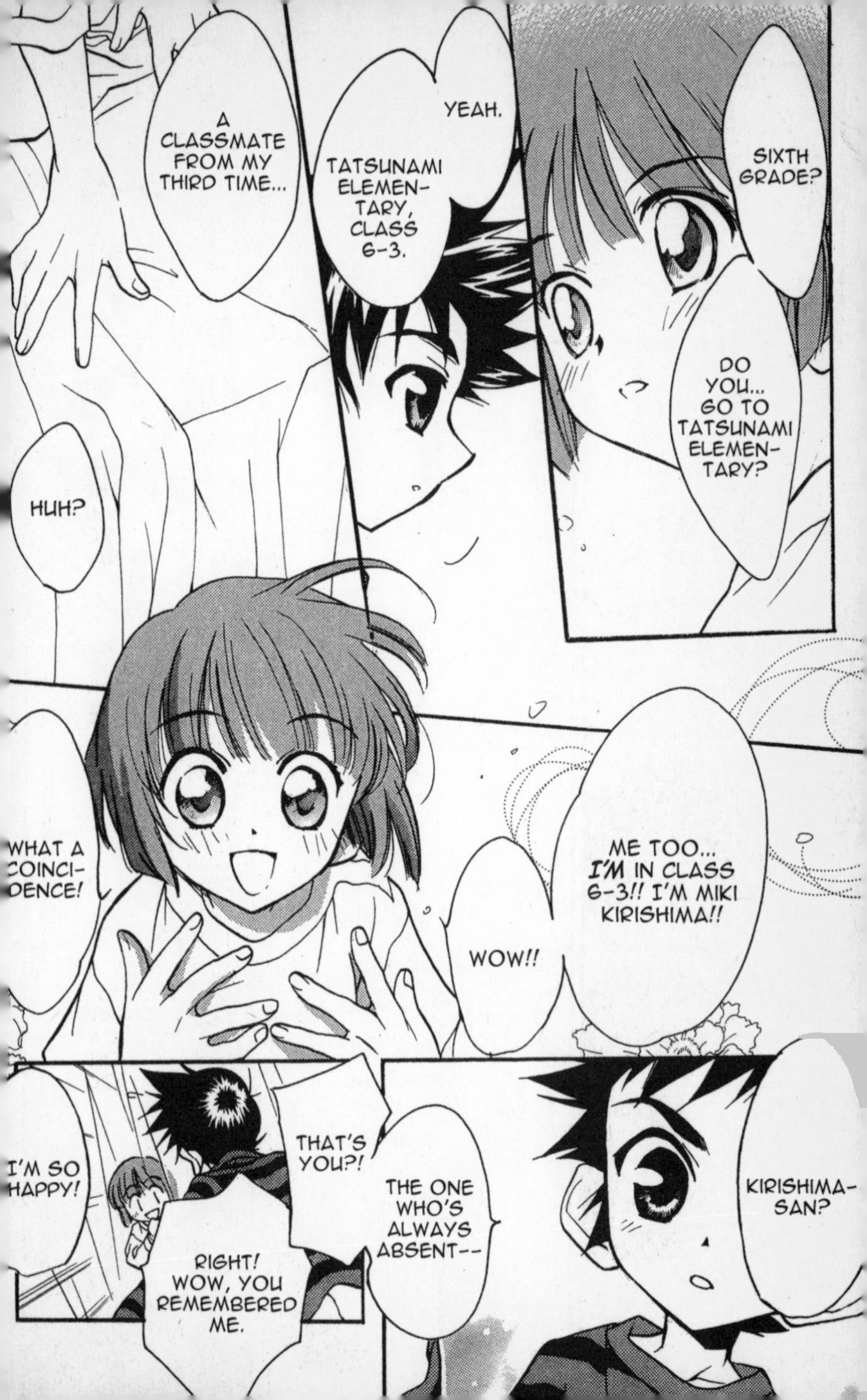
SIXTH GRADE?
DO YOU... GO TO TATSUNAMI ELEMENTARY?
YEAH.
TATSUNAMI ELEMENTARY, CLASS 6-3.
A CLASSMATE FROM MY THIRD TIME...
HUH?
ME TOO... *I'M* IN CLASS 6-3!! I'M MIKI KIRISHIMA!!
WOW!!
WHAT A COINCIDENCE!
KIRISHIMA-SAN?
THE ONE WHO'S ALWAYS ABSENT--
THAT'S YOU?!
RIGHT! WOW, YOU REMEMBERED ME.
I'M SO HAPPY!

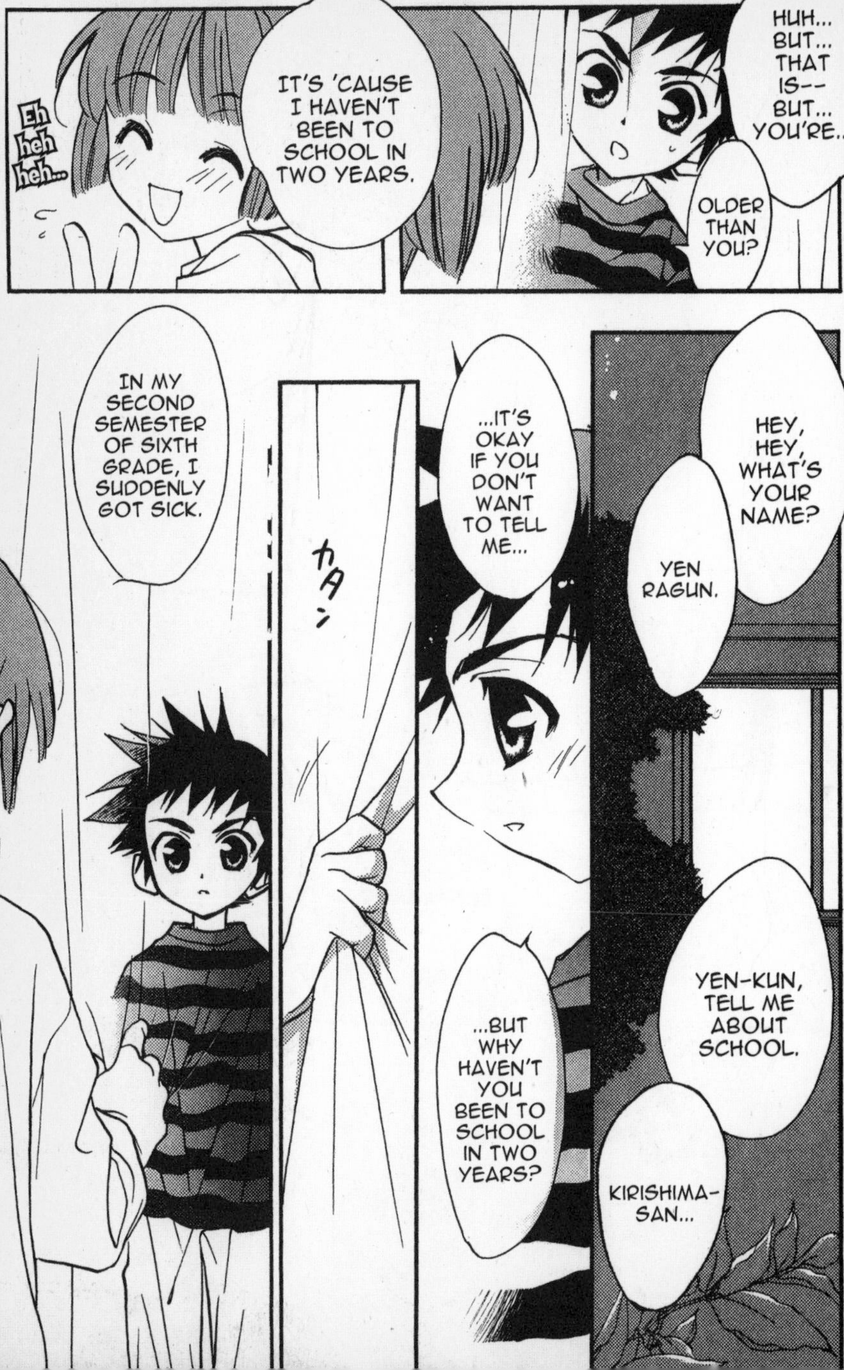
HUH... BUT... THAT IS-- BUT... YOU'RE...
OLDER THAN YOU?
IT'S 'CAUSE I HAVEN'T BEEN TO SCHOOL IN TWO YEARS.
Eh heh heh...
HEY, HEY, WHAT'S YOUR NAME?
YEN RAGUN.
YEN-KUN, TELL ME ABOUT SCHOOL.
KIRISHIMA-SAN...
...BUT WHY HAVEN'T YOU BEEN TO SCHOOL IN TWO YEARS?
...IT'S OKAY IF YOU DON'T WANT TO TELL ME...
IN MY SECOND SEMESTER OF SIXTH GRADE, I SUDDENLY GOT SICK.

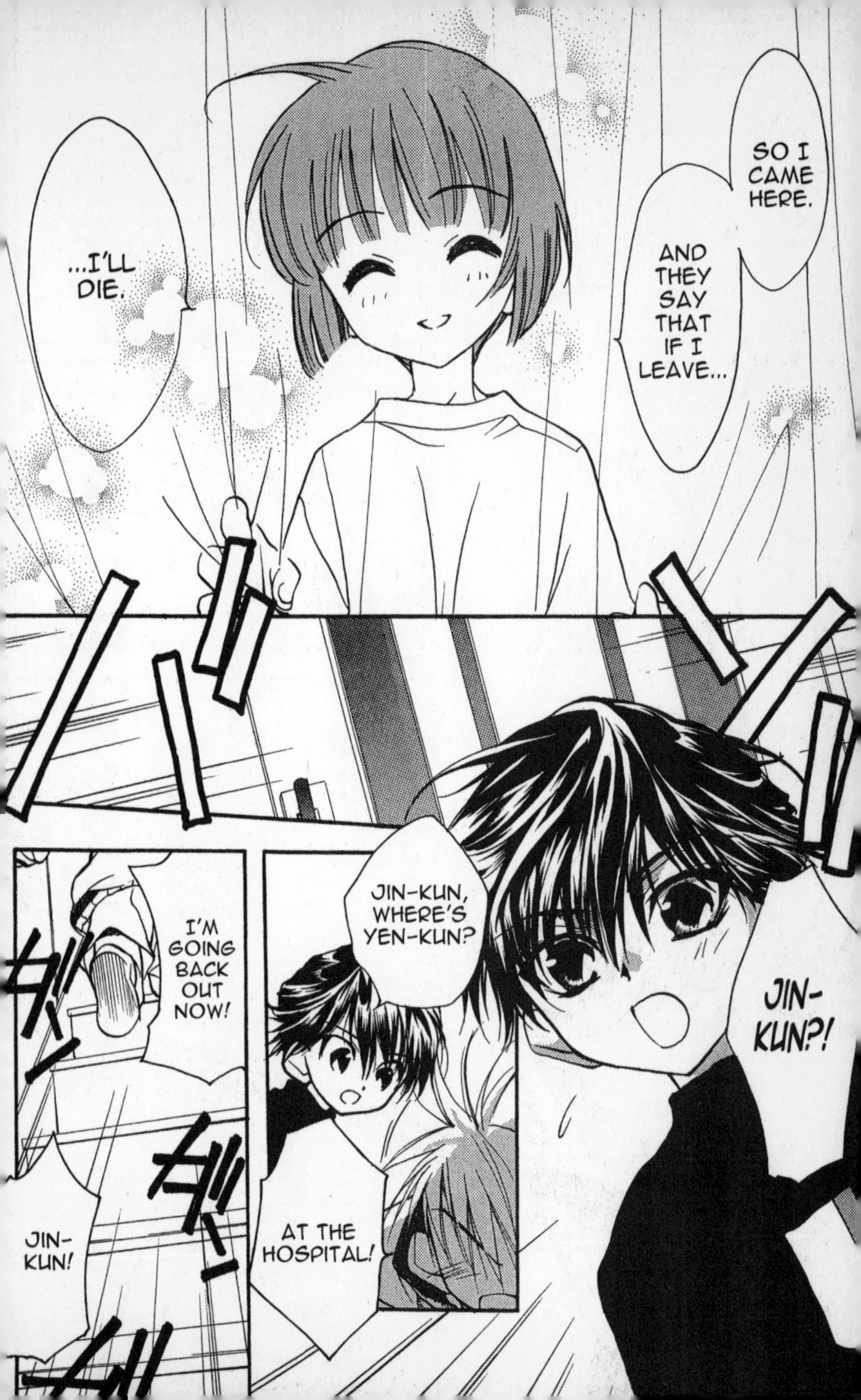
SO I CAME HERE.
AND THEY SAY THAT IF I LEAVE...
...I'LL DIE.
JIN-KUN?!
JIN-KUN, WHERE'S YEN-KUN?
AT THE HOSPITAL!
I'M GOING BACK OUT NOW!
JIN-KUN!

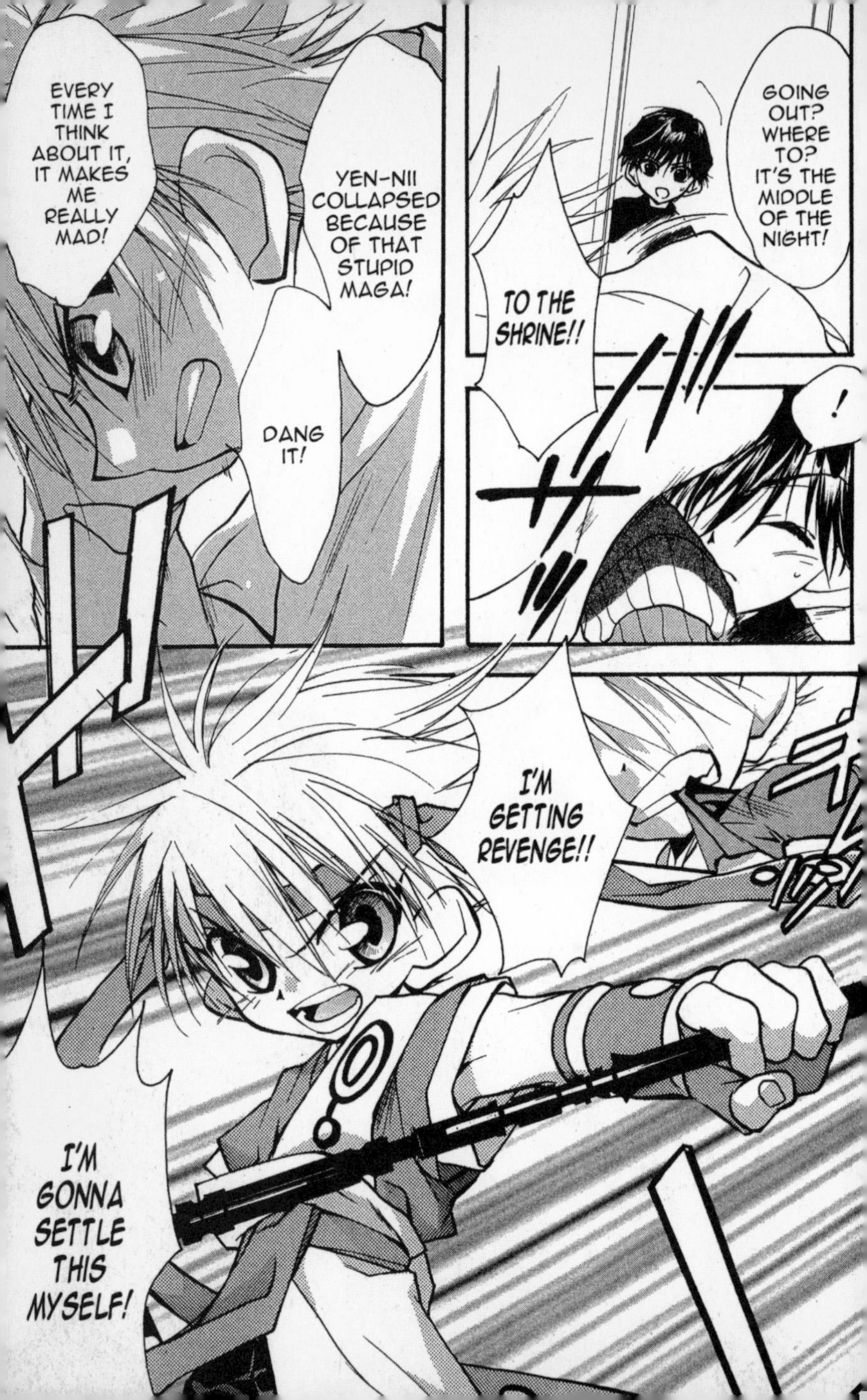
GOING OUT? WHERE TO? IT'S THE MIDDLE OF THE NIGHT!
TO THE SHRINE!!
!
YEN-NII COLLAPSED BECAUSE OF THAT STUPID MAGA!
EVERY TIME I THINK ABOUT IT, IT MAKES ME REALLY MAD!
DANG IT!
I'M GETTING REVENGE!!
I'M GONNA SETTLE THIS MYSELF!

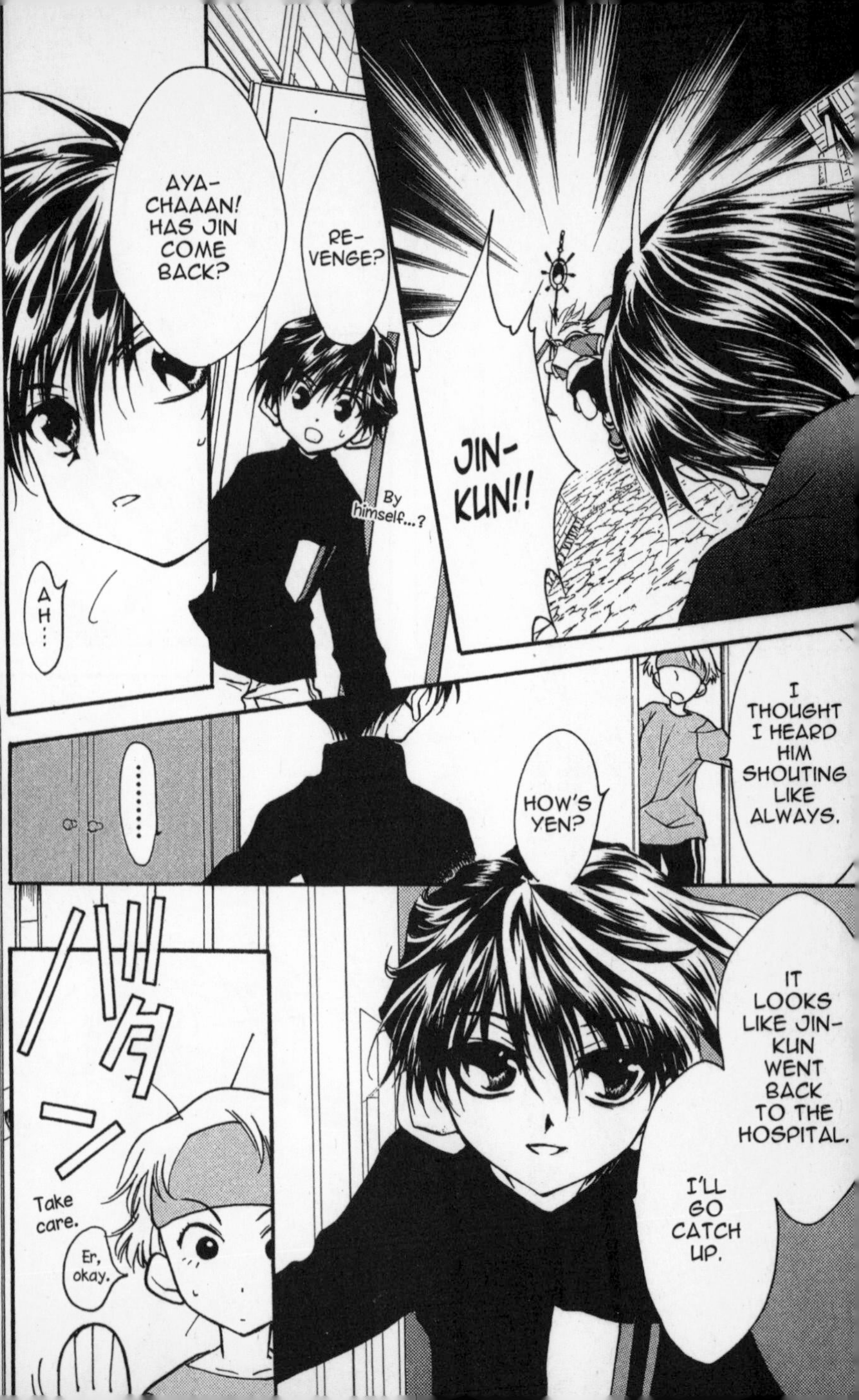
JIN-KUN!!
RE-VENGE?
AYA-CHAAAN! HAS JIN COME BACK?
By himself...?
AH...
I THOUGHT I HEARD HIM SHOUTING LIKE ALWAYS.
HOW'S YEN?
....
IT LOOKS LIKE JIN-KUN WENT BACK TO THE HOSPITAL.
I'LL GO CATCH UP.
Take care.
Er, okay.

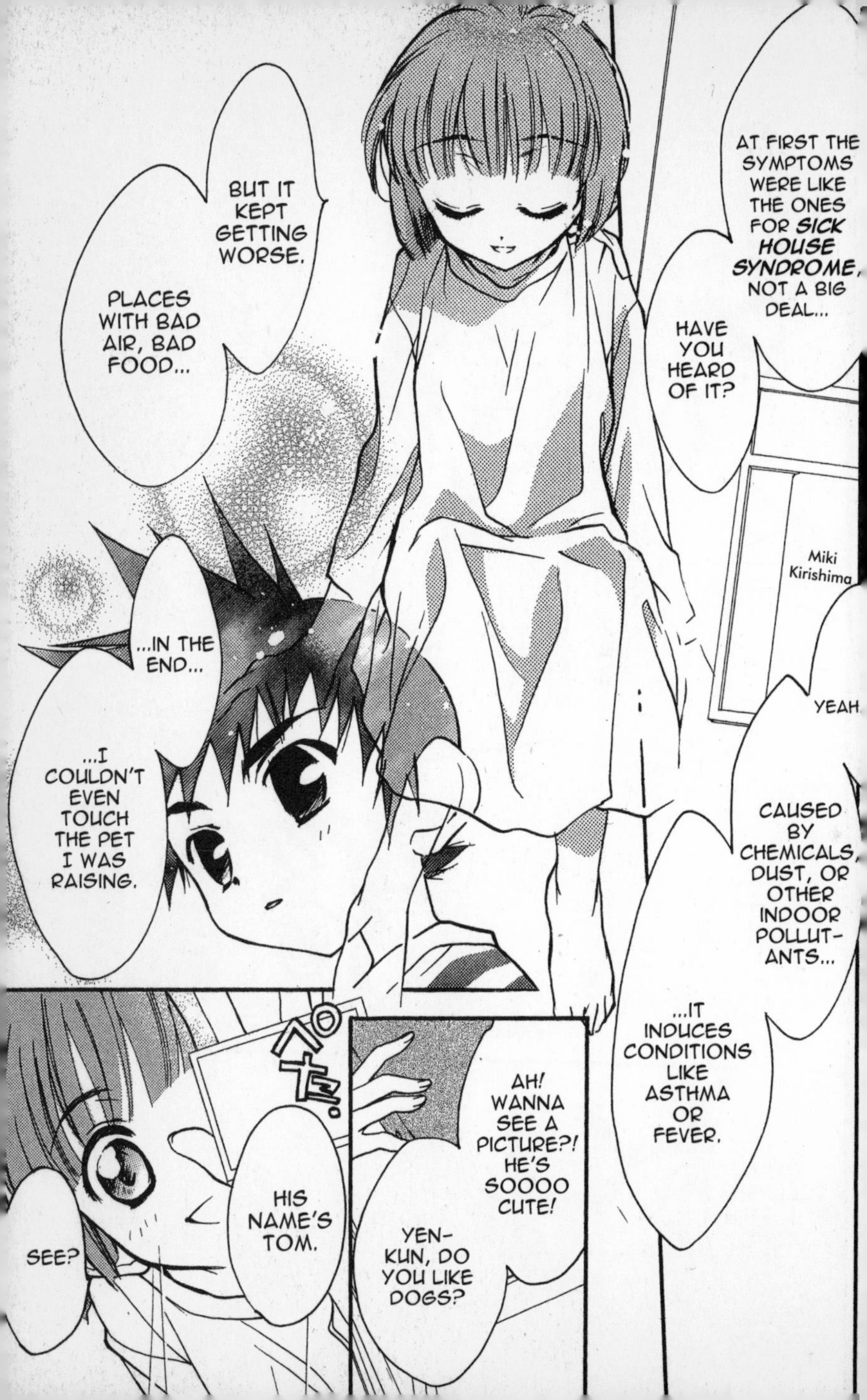
AT FIRST THE SYMPTOMS WERE LIKE THE ONES FOR **SICK HOUSE SYNDROME**, NOT A BIG DEAL...
HAVE YOU HEARD OF IT?
YEAH.
CAUSED BY CHEMICALS, DUST, OR OTHER INDOOR POLLUT-ANTS...
...IT INDUCES CONDITIONS LIKE ASTHMA OR FEVER.
Miki Kirishima
BUT IT KEPT GETTING WORSE.
PLACES WITH BAD AIR, BAD FOOD...
...IN THE END...
...I COULDN'T EVEN TOUCH THE PET I WAS RAISING.
AH! WANNA SEE A PICTURE?! HE'S SOOOO CUTE!
YEN-KUN, DO YOU LIKE DOGS?
HIS NAME'S TOM.
SEE?

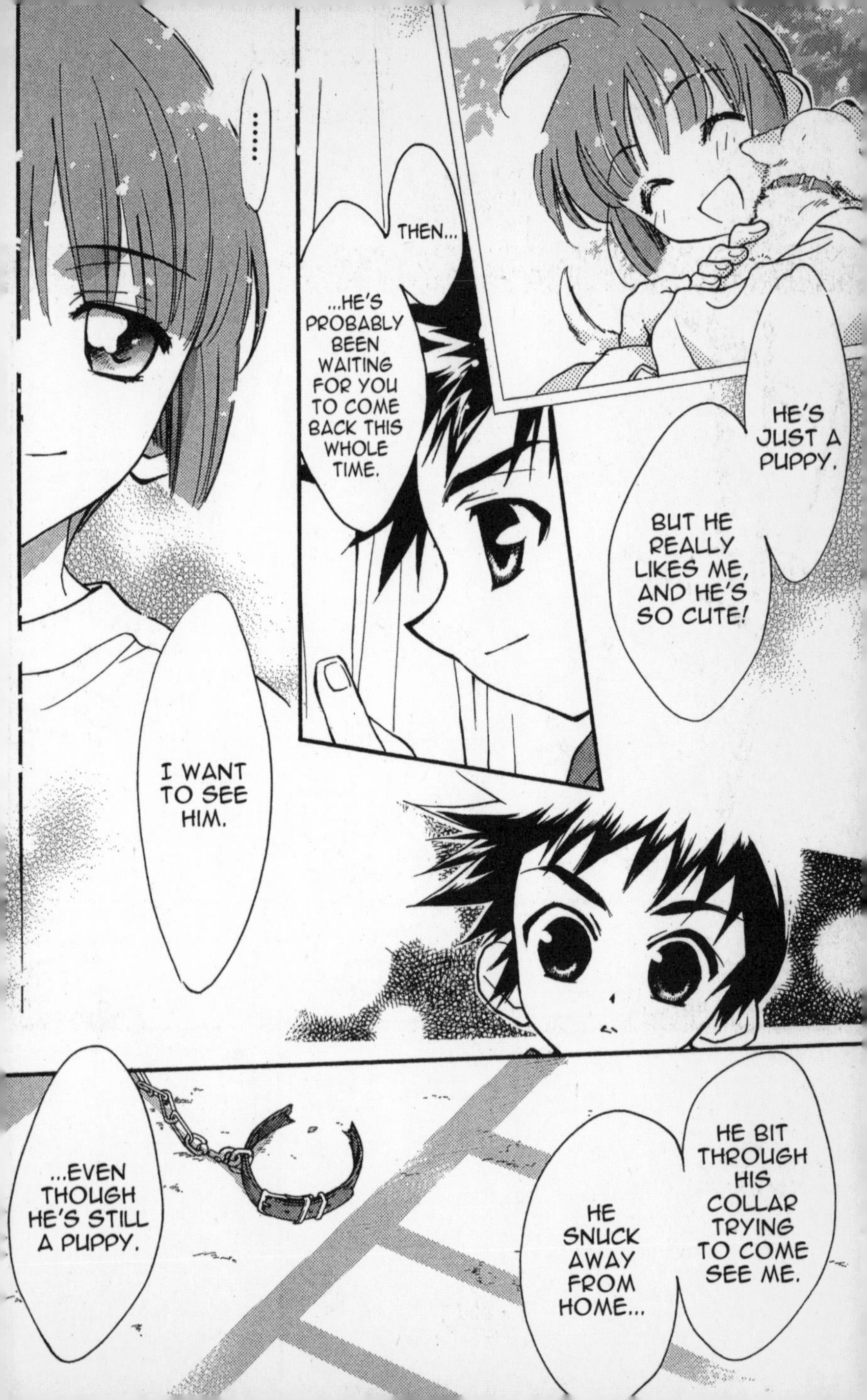
HE'S JUST A PUPPY.
BUT HE REALLY LIKES ME, AND HE'S SO CUTE!
THEN...
...HE'S PROBABLY BEEN WAITING FOR YOU TO COME BACK THIS WHOLE TIME.
......
I WANT TO SEE HIM.
HE BIT THROUGH HIS COLLAR TRYING TO COME SEE ME.
HE SNUCK AWAY FROM HOME...
...EVEN THOUGH HE'S STILL A PUPPY.

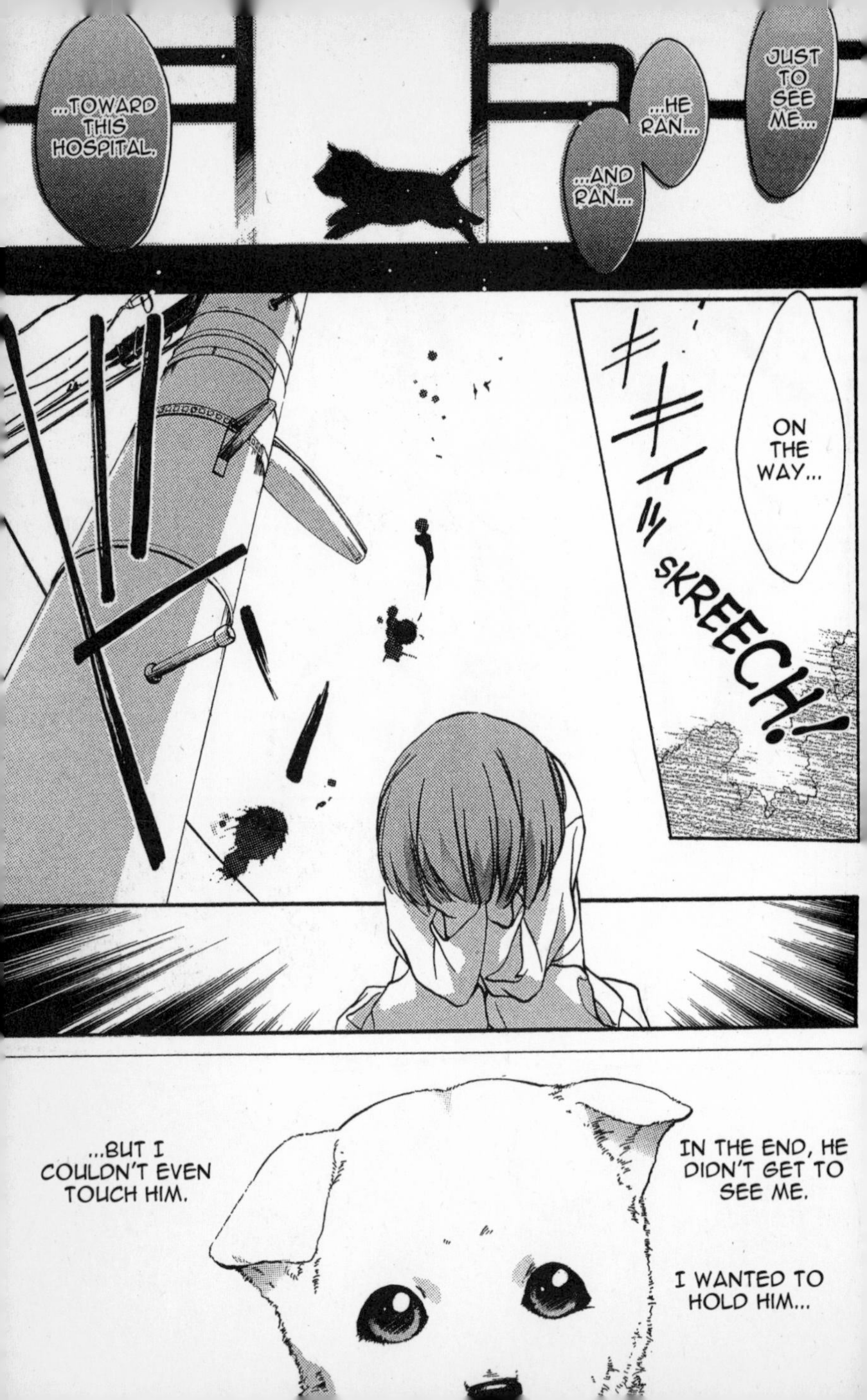
JUST TO SEE ME...
...HE RAN...
...AND RAN...
...TOWARD THIS HOSPITAL.
ON THE WAY...
SKREECH!!
IN THE END, HE DIDN'T GET TO SEE ME.
I WANTED TO HOLD HIM...
...BUT I COULDN'T EVEN TOUCH HIM.

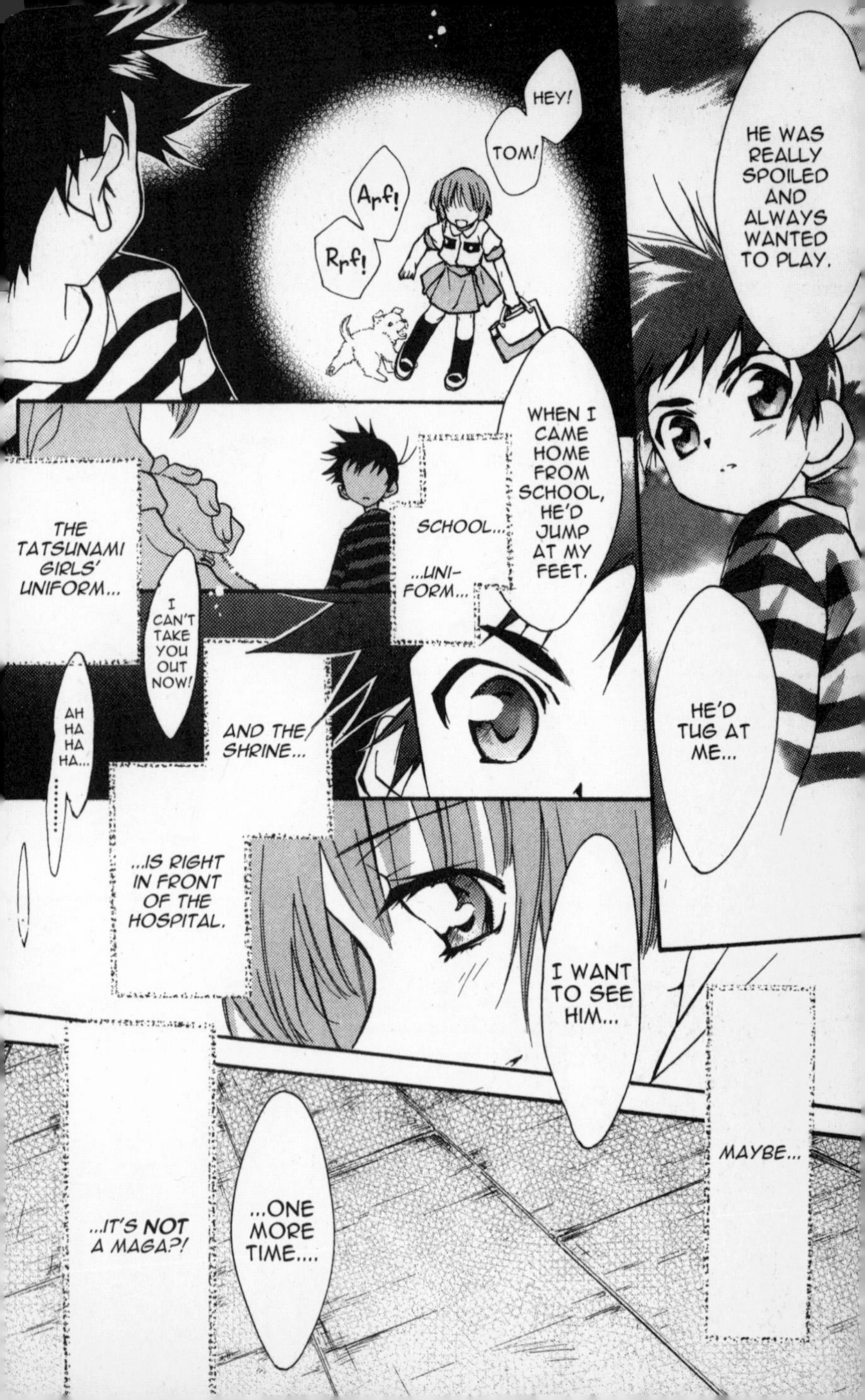
HE WAS REALLY SPOILED AND ALWAYS WANTED TO PLAY.
HEY!
TOM!
Arf!
Rpf!
WHEN I CAME HOME FROM SCHOOL, HE'D JUMP AT MY FEET.
HE'D TUG AT ME...
SCHOOL...
...UNI-FORM...
THE TATSUNAMI GIRLS' UNIFORM...
I CAN'T TAKE YOU OUT NOW!
AH HA HA HA...
......
AND THE SHRINE...
...IS RIGHT IN FRONT OF THE HOSPITAL.
I WANT TO SEE HIM...
MAYBE...
...ONE MORE TIME....
...IT'S **NOT** A MAGA?!

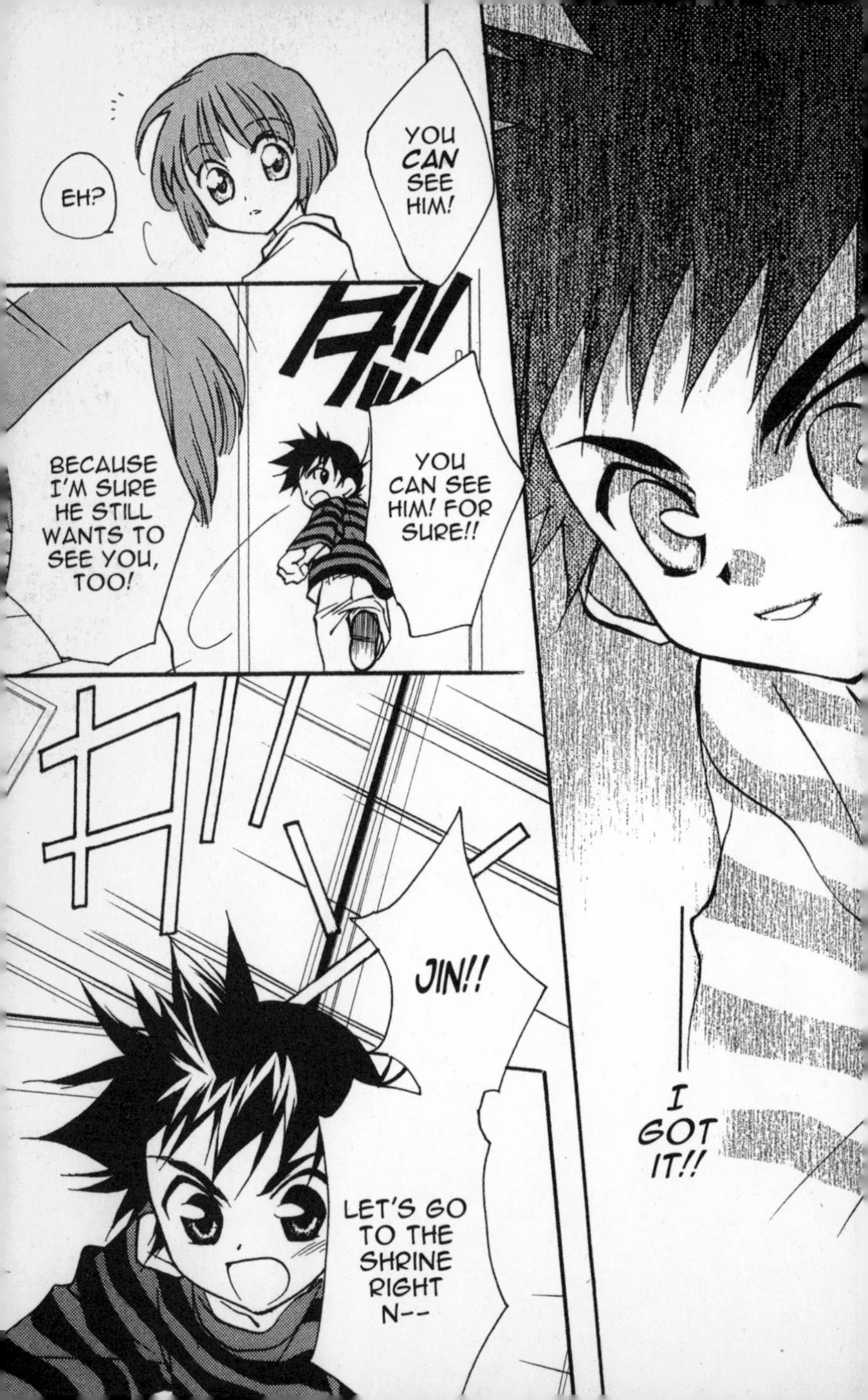

I GOT IT!!
YOU CAN SEE HIM!
EH?
YOU CAN SEE HIM! FOR SURE!!
BECAUSE I'M SURE HE STILL WANTS TO SEE YOU, TOO!
JIN!!
LET'S GO TO THE SHRINE RIGHT N--

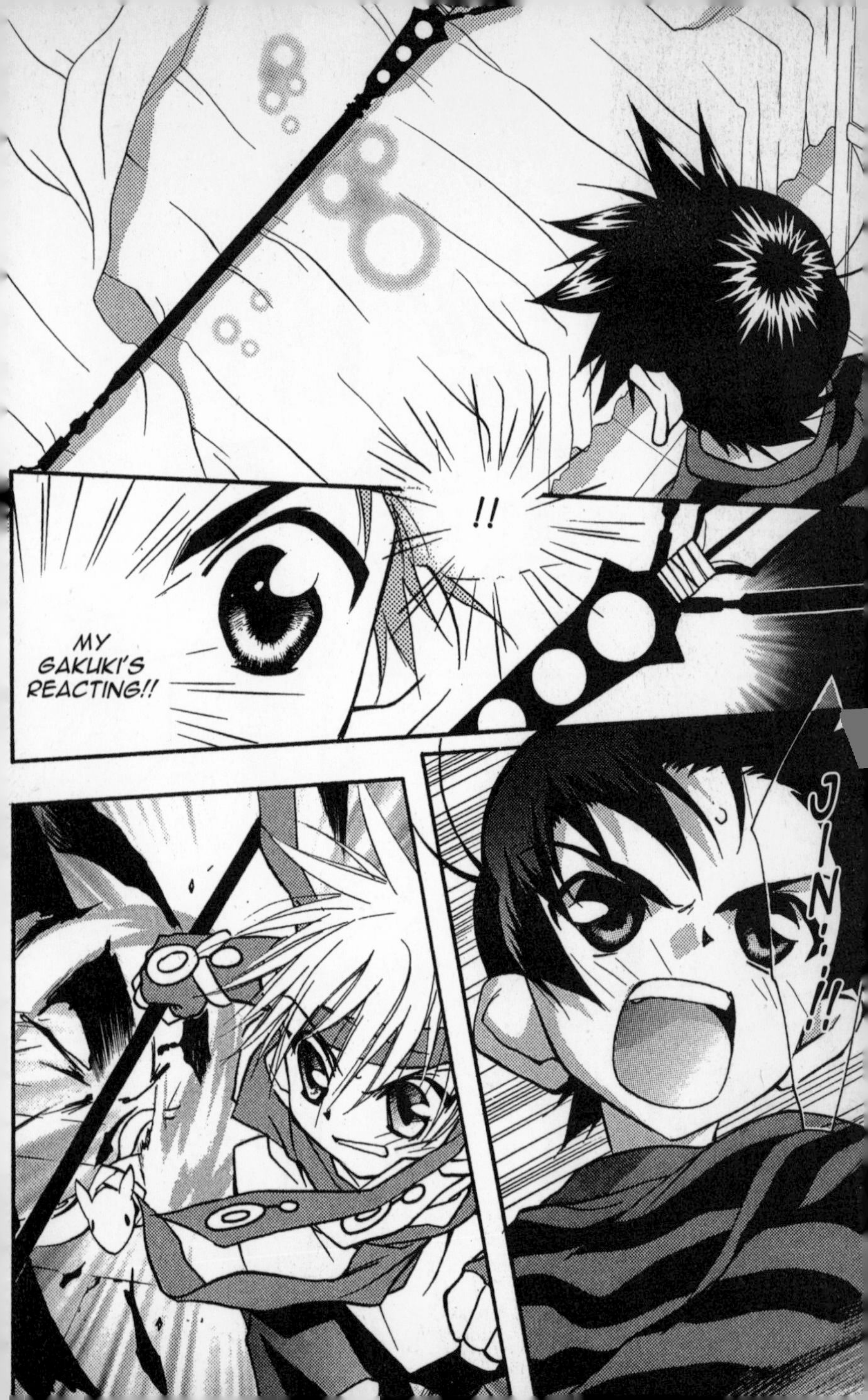
!!
MY GAKUKI'S REACTING!!
JIN...!!

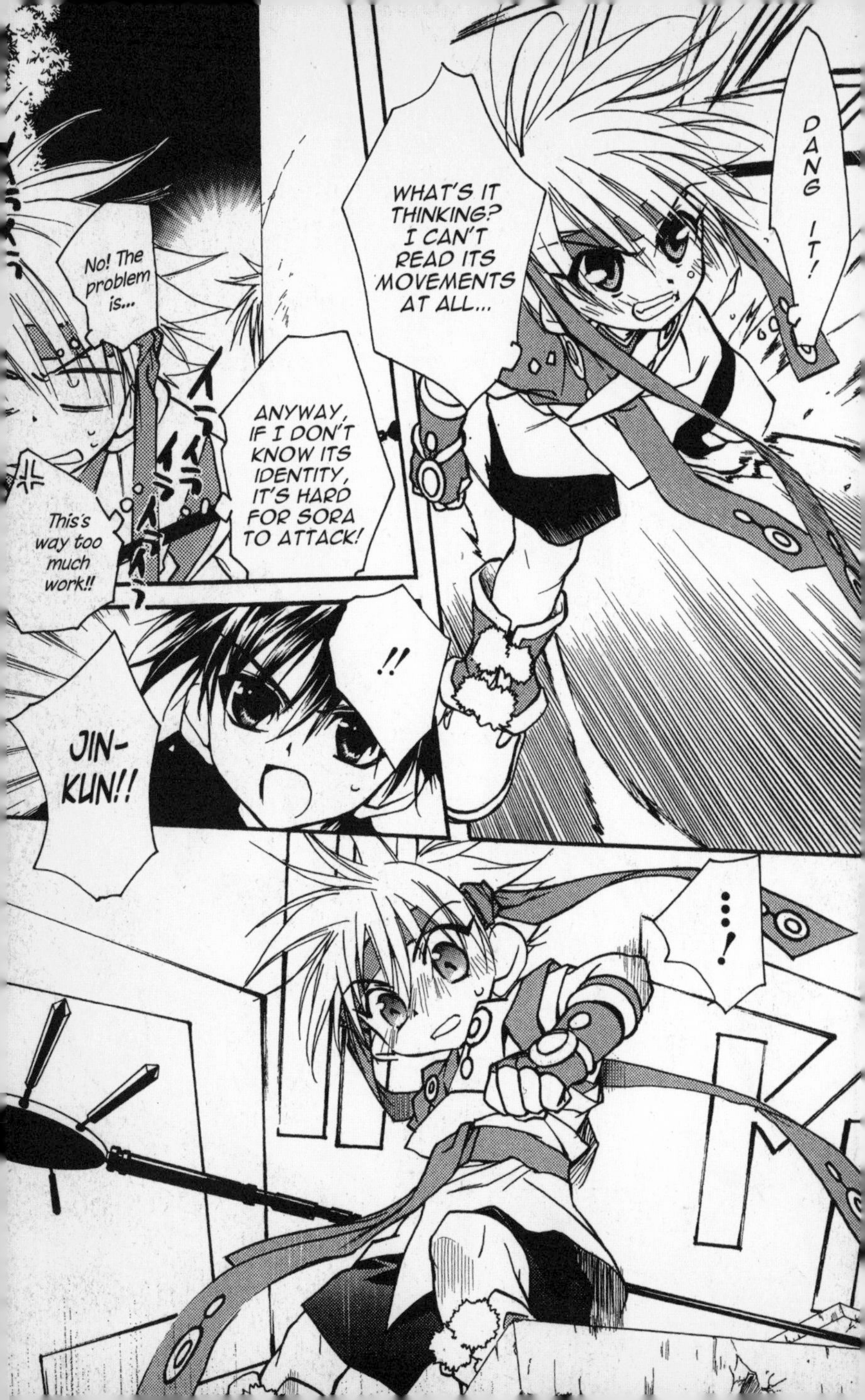
DANG IT!
WHAT'S IT THINKING? I CAN'T READ ITS MOVEMENTS AT ALL...
ANYWAY, IF I DON'T KNOW ITS IDENTITY, IT'S HARD FOR SORA TO ATTACK!
No! The problem is...
This's way too much work!!
!!
JIN-KUN!!
...!

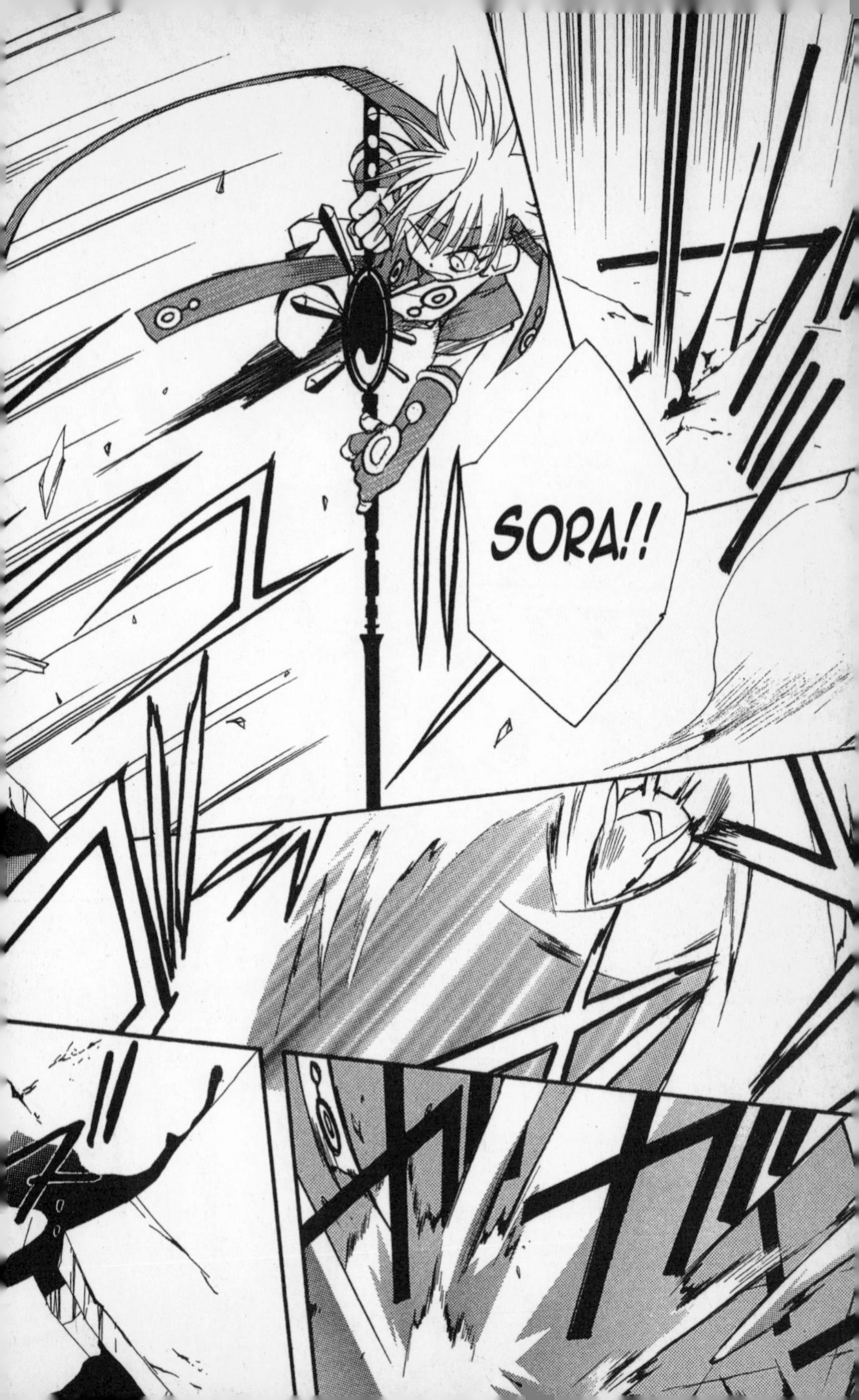
SORA!!

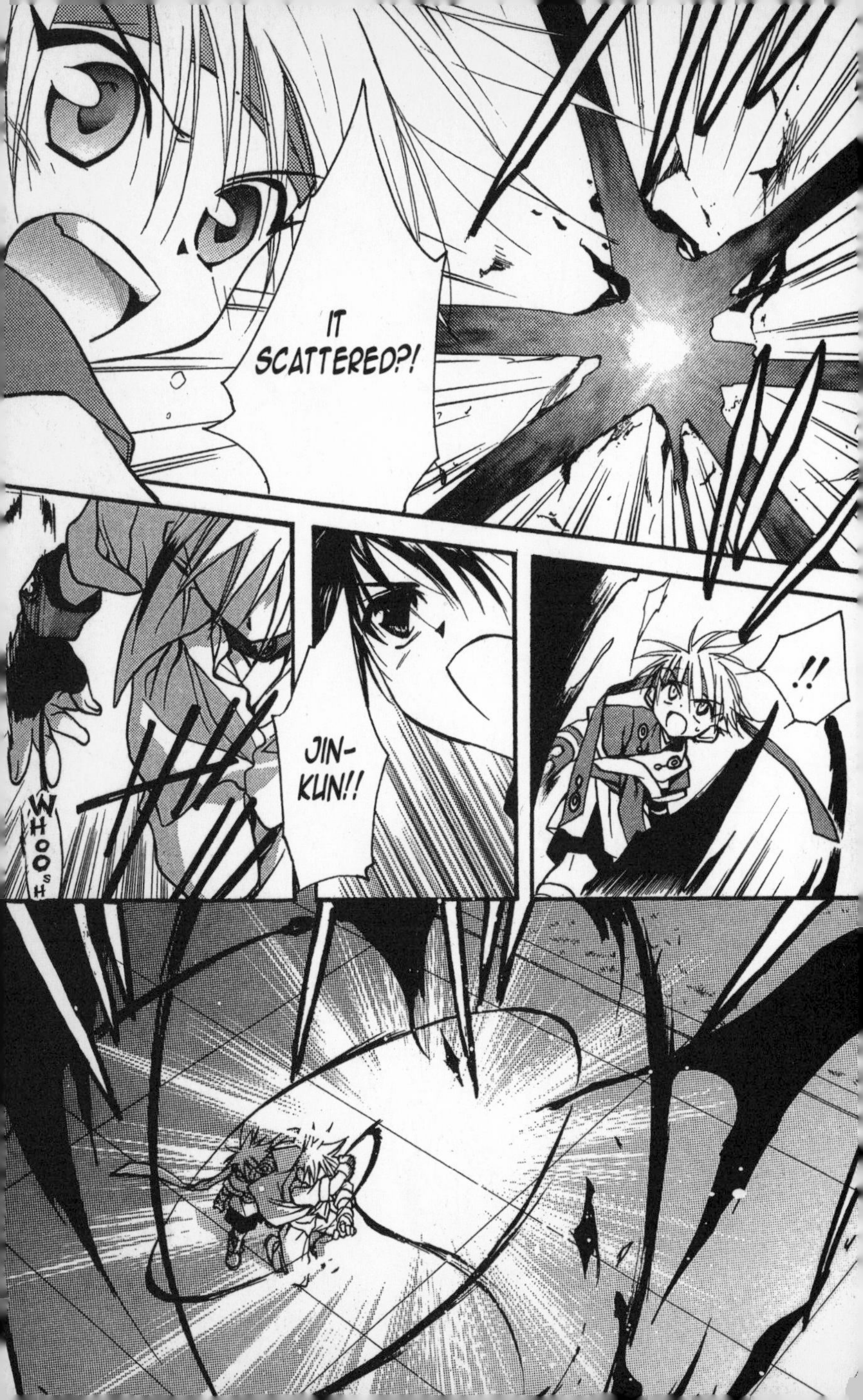
IT SCATTERED?!
!!
JIN-KUN!!
WHOOSH

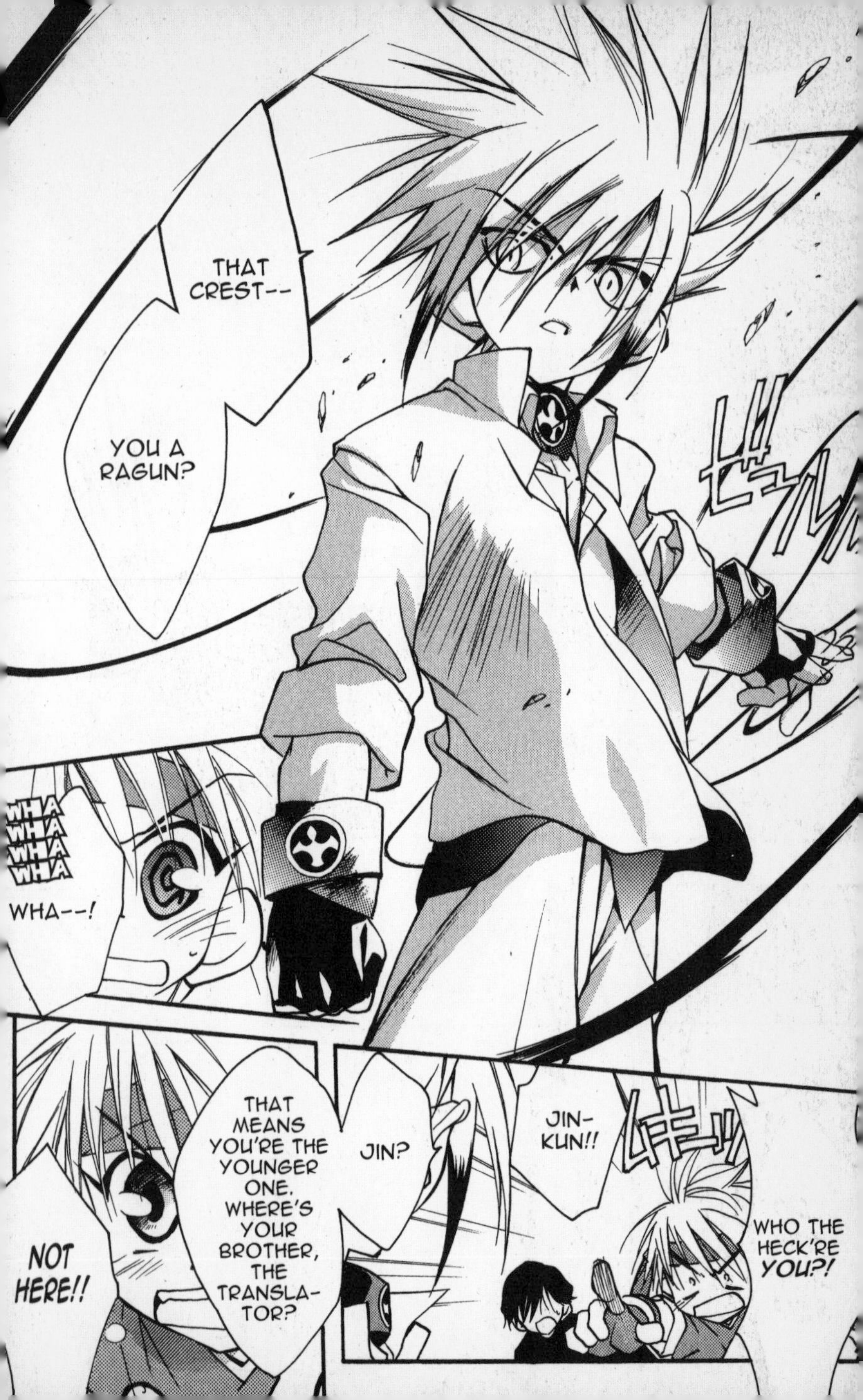
THAT CREST--
YOU A RAGUN?
WHA WHA WHA WHA
WHA--!
JIN-KUN!!
JIN?
WHO THE HECK'RE YOU?!
THAT MEANS YOU'RE THE YOUNGER ONE. WHERE'S YOUR BROTHER, THE TRANSLATOR?
NOT HERE!!

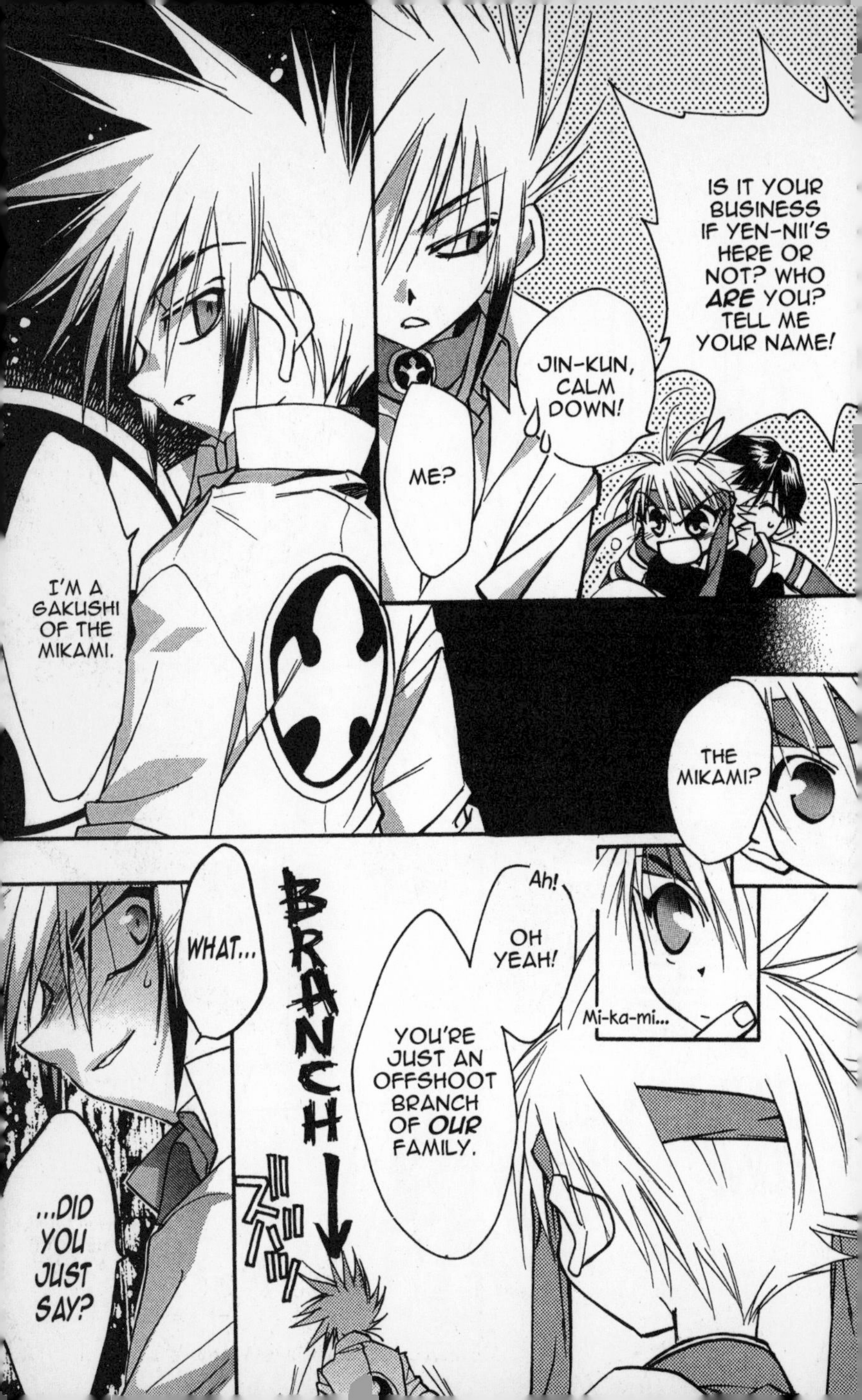
IS IT YOUR BUSINESS IF YEN-NII'S HERE OR NOT? WHO ARE YOU? TELL ME YOUR NAME!
JIN-KUN, CALM DOWN!
ME?
I'M A GAKUSHI OF THE MIKAMI.
THE MIKAMI?
Mi-ka-mi...
Ah!
OH YEAH!
YOU'RE JUST AN OFFSHOOT BRANCH OF OUR FAMILY.
BRANCH
WHAT...
...DID YOU JUST SAY?

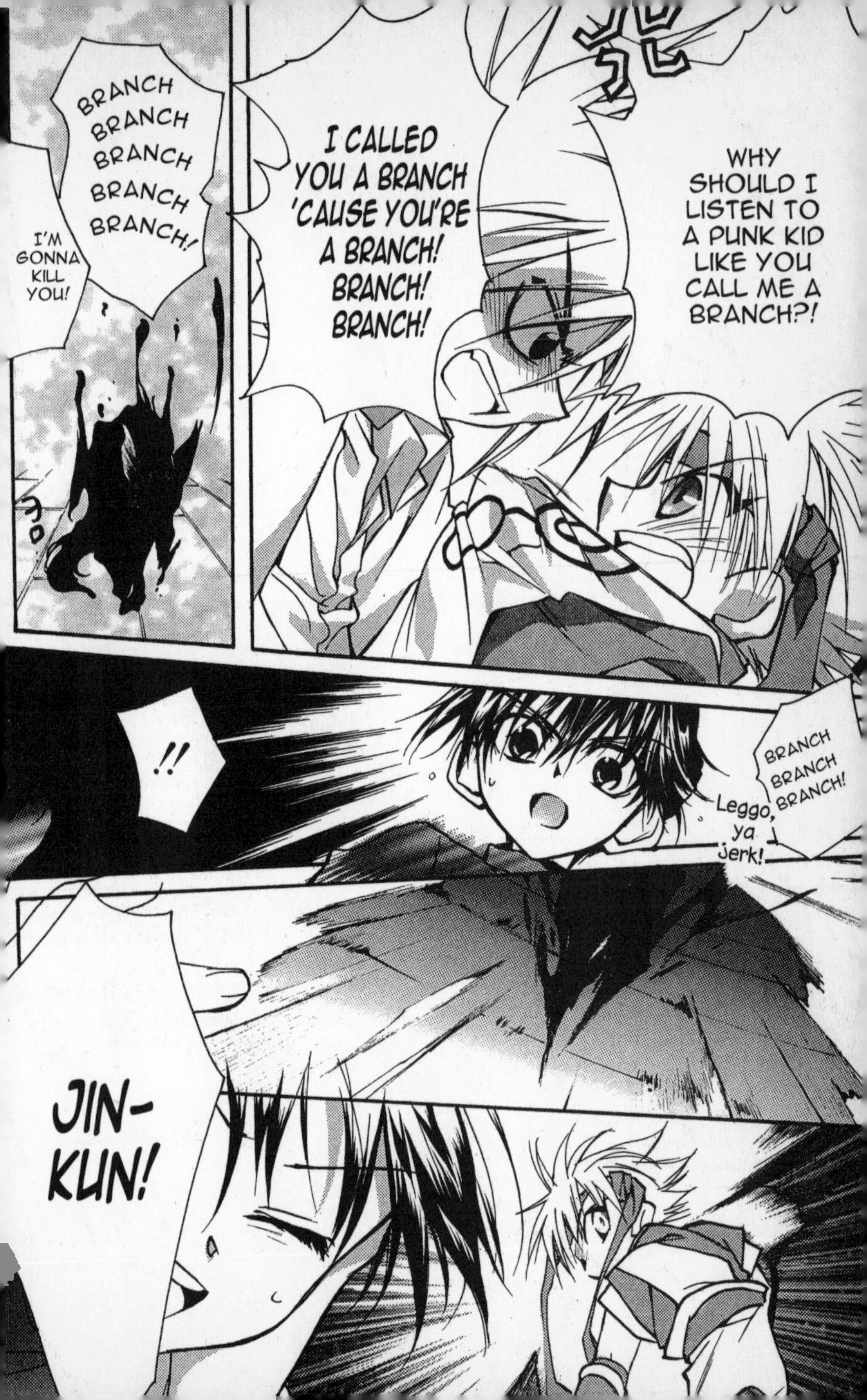
WHY SHOULD I LISTEN TO A PUNK KID LIKE YOU CALL ME A BRANCH?!
I CALLED YOU A BRANCH 'CAUSE YOU'RE A BRANCH! BRANCH! BRANCH!
BRANCH BRANCH BRANCH BRANCH BRANCH!
I'M GONNA KILL YOU!
BRANCH BRANCH BRANCH!
Leggo, ya jerk!
!!
JIN-KUN!

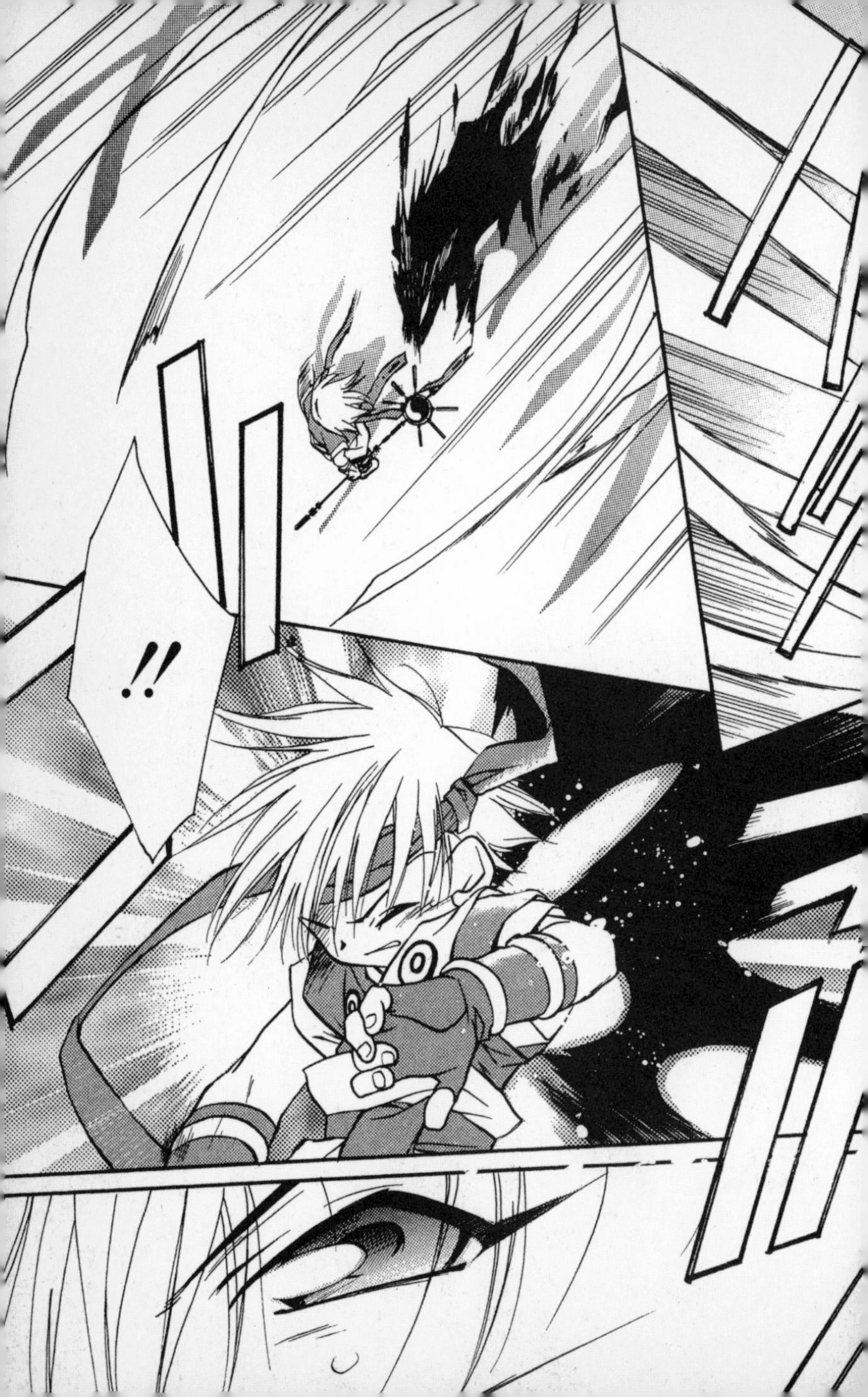
!!

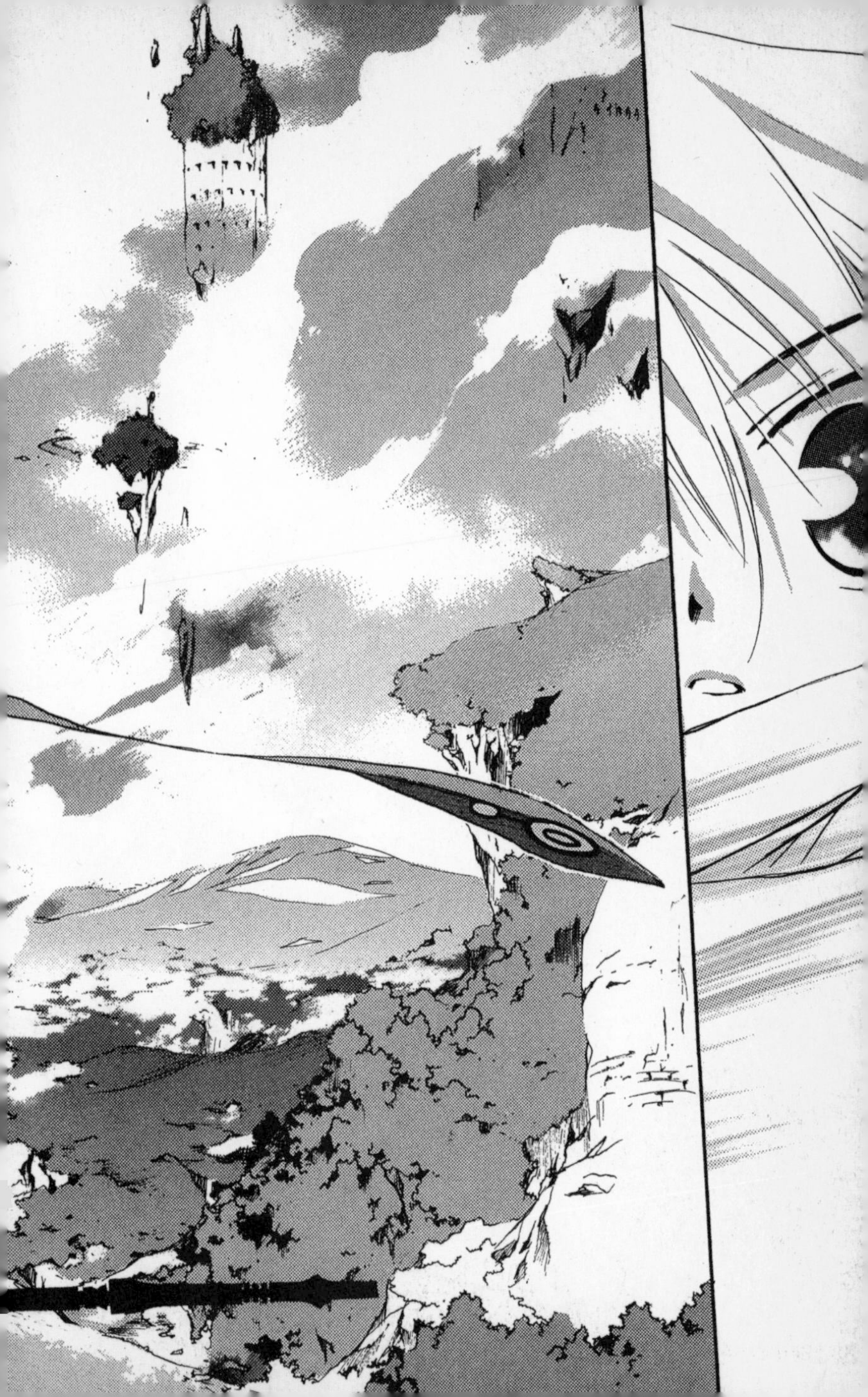

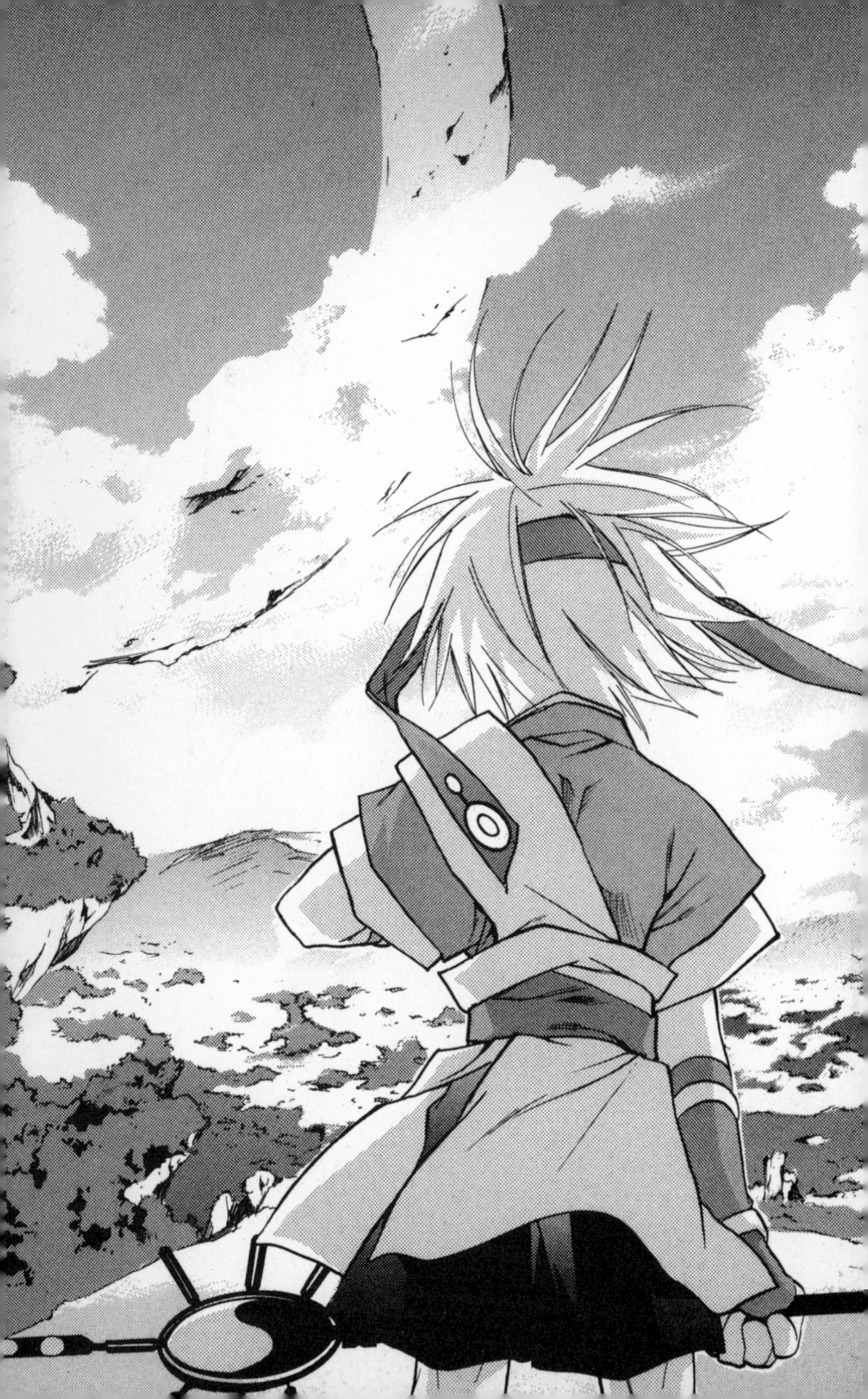

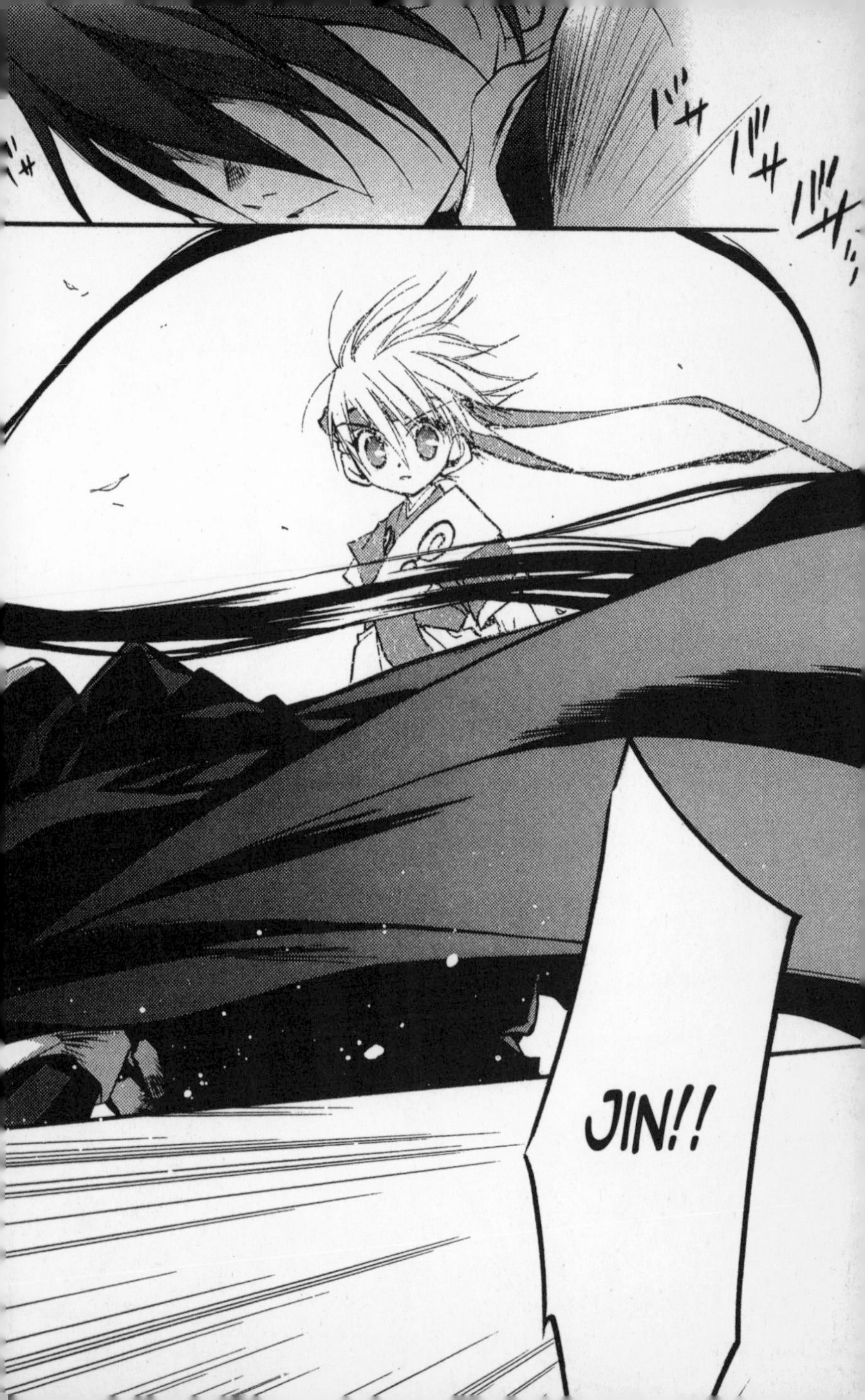
JIN!!

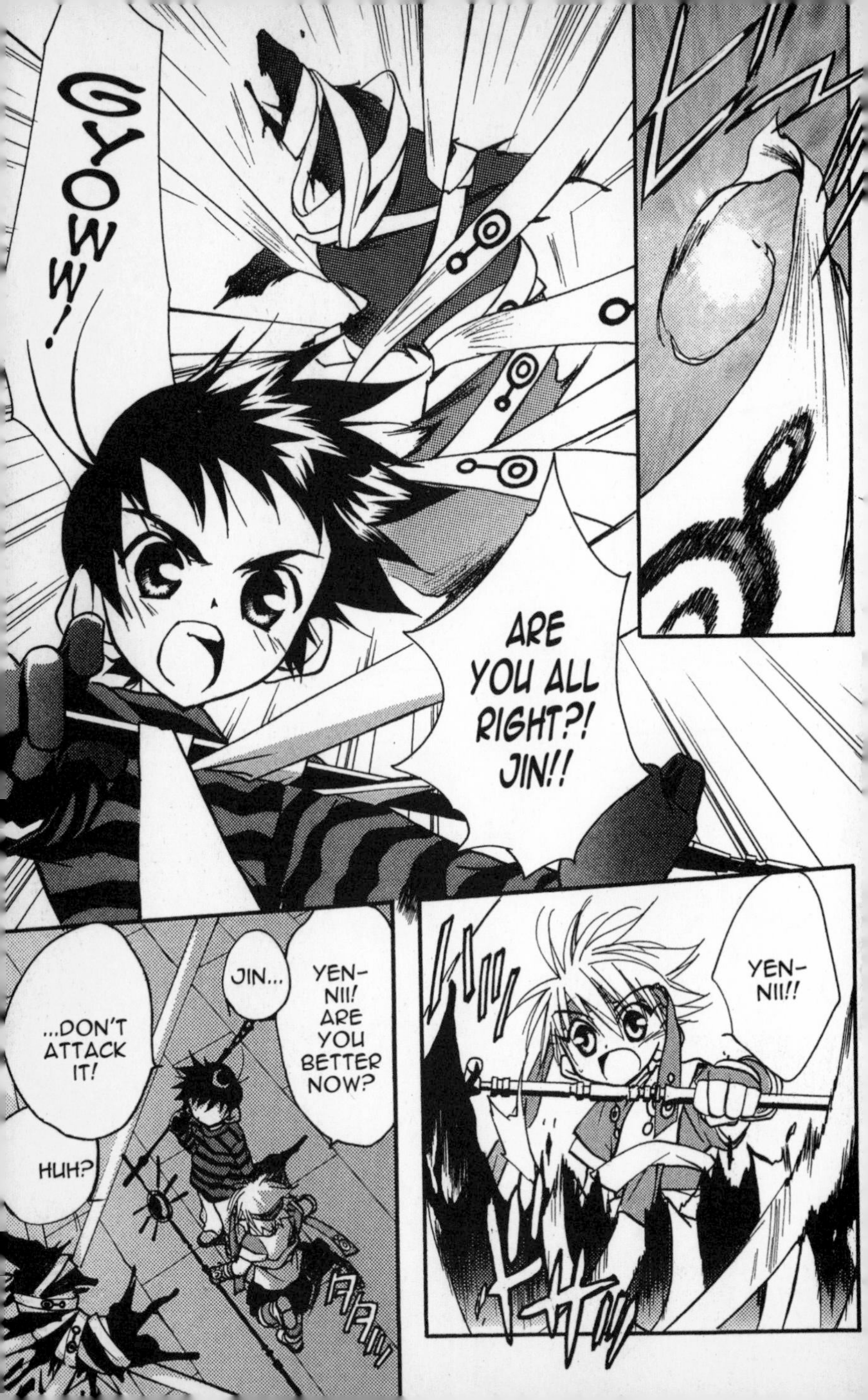
GYOWW!
ARE YOU ALL RIGHT?! JIN!!
YEN-NII!!
YEN-NII! ARE YOU BETTER NOW?
JIN...
...DON'T ATTACK IT!
HUH?

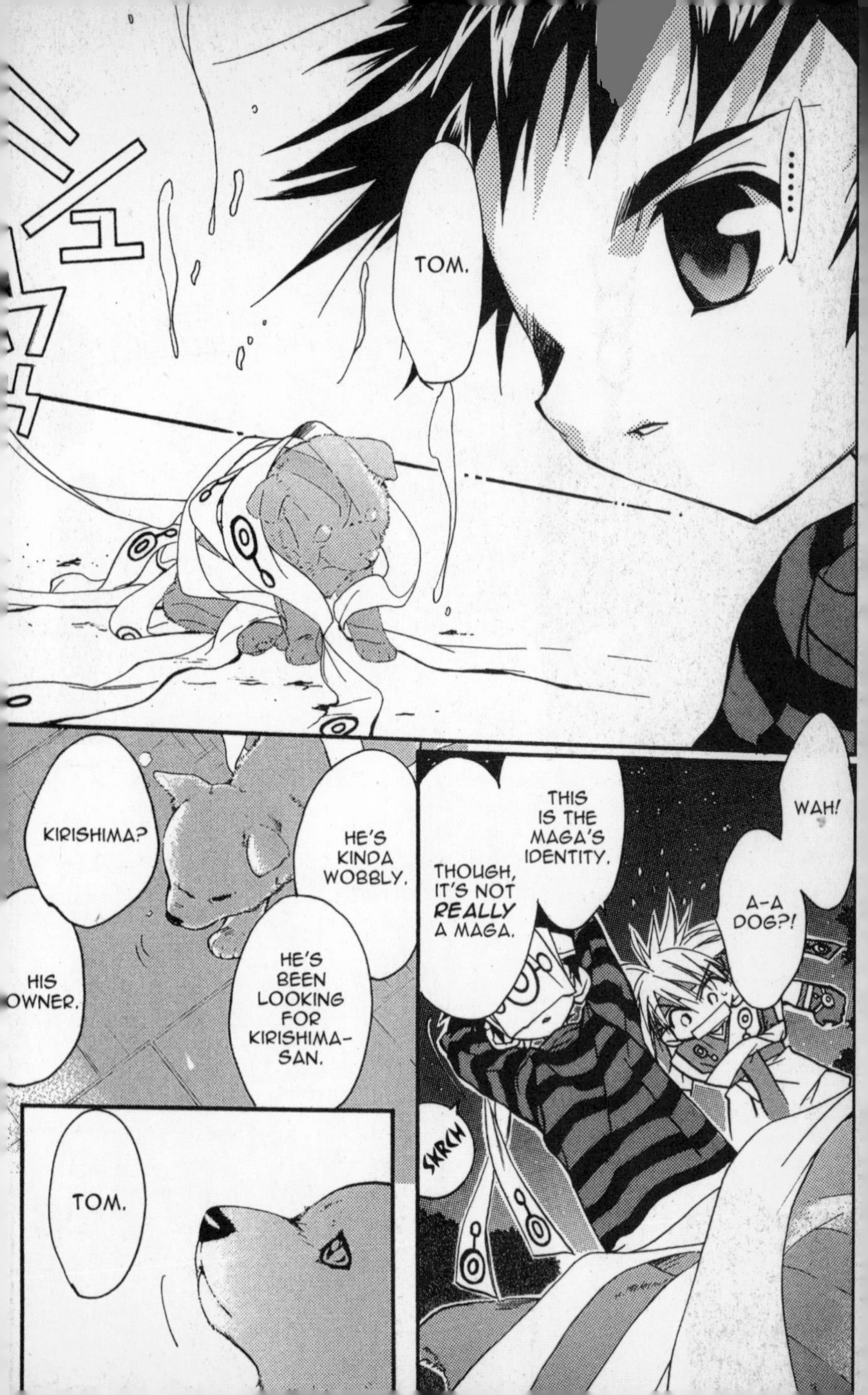
TOM.
WAH!
A-A DOG?!
THIS IS THE MAGA'S IDENTITY.
THOUGH, IT'S NOT REALLY A MAGA.
SKRCH
HE'S KINDA WOBBLY.
KIRISHIMA?
HE'S BEEN LOOKING FOR KIRISHIMA-SAN.
HIS OWNER.
TOM.

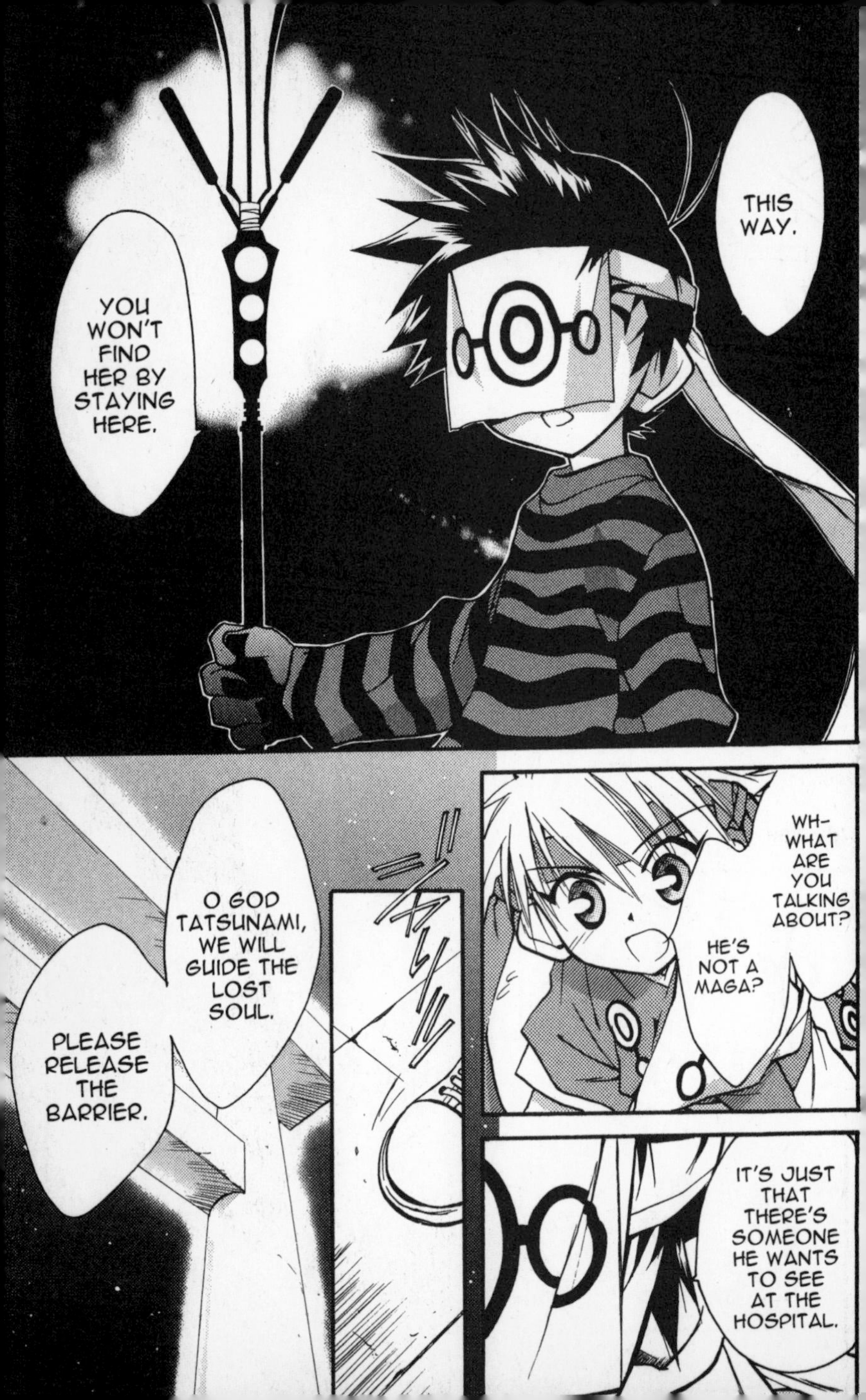
THIS WAY.
YOU WON'T FIND HER BY STAYING HERE.
WH-WHAT ARE YOU TALKING ABOUT?
HE'S NOT A MAGA?
IT'S JUST THAT THERE'S SOMEONE HE WANTS TO SEE AT THE HOSPITAL.
O GOD TATSUNAMI, WE WILL GUIDE THE LOST SOUL.
PLEASE RELEASE THE BARRIER.

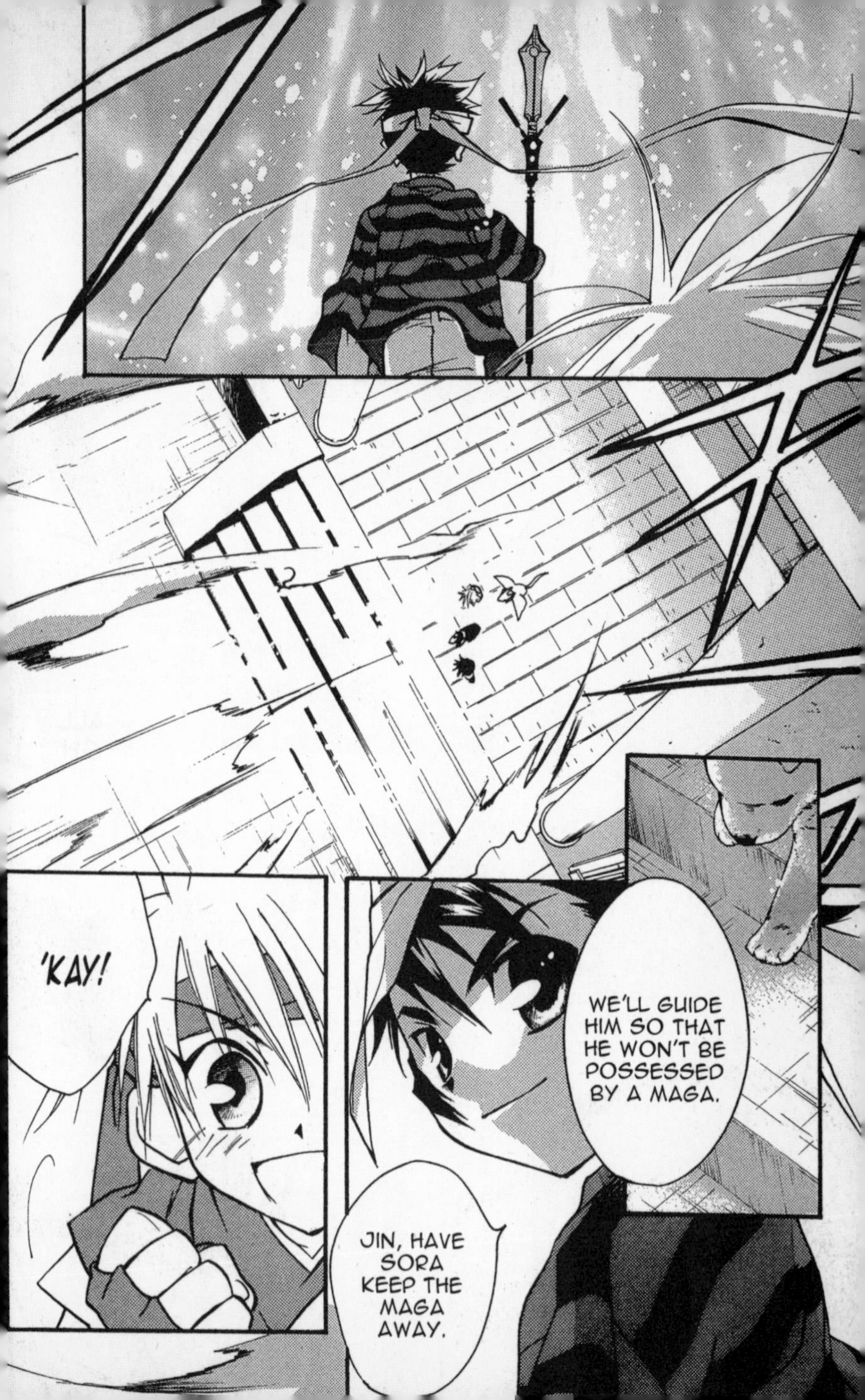
WE'LL GUIDE HIM SO THAT HE WON'T BE POSSESSED BY A MAGA.
JIN, HAVE SORA KEEP THE MAGA AWAY.
'KAY!

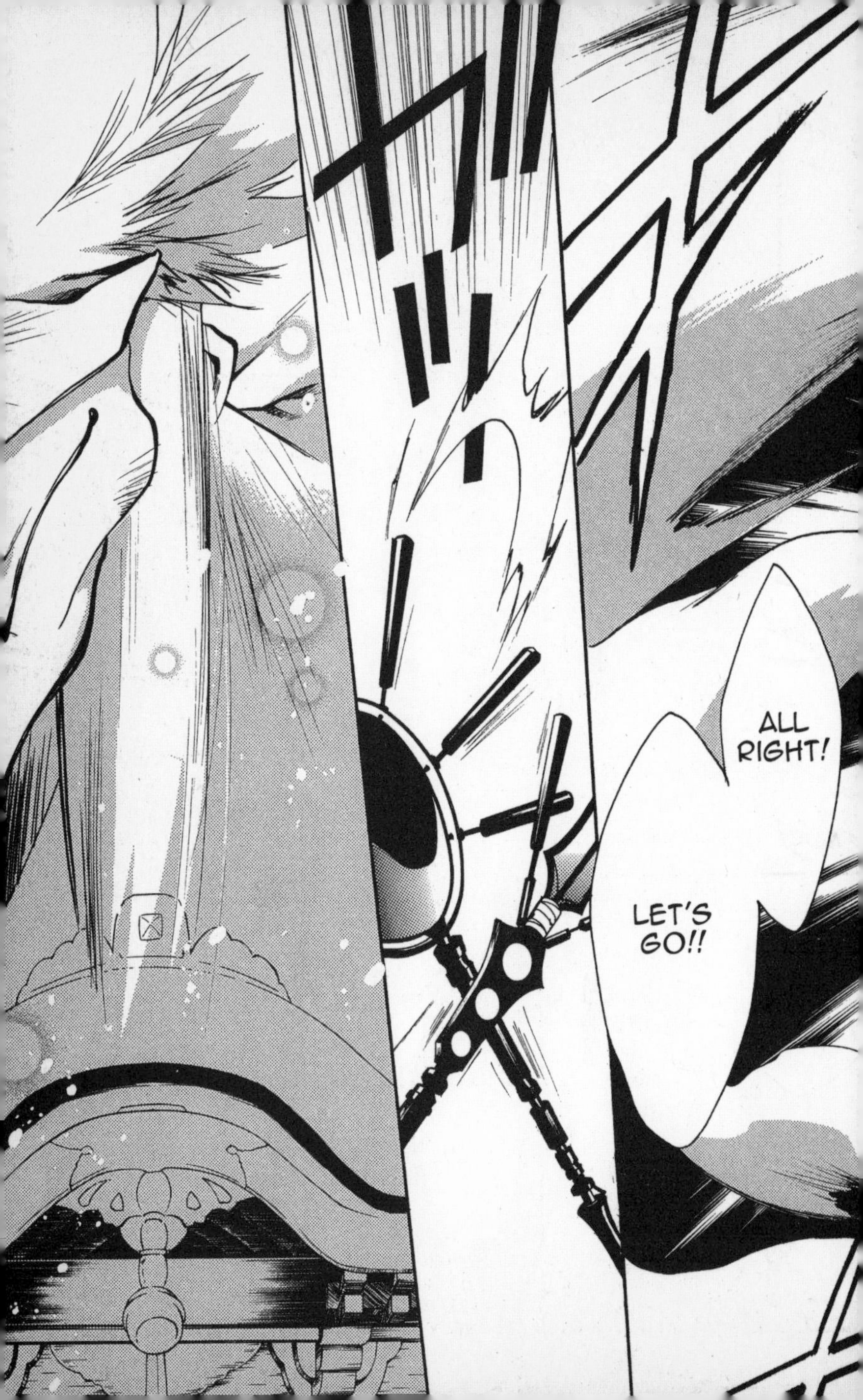
ALL RIGHT!
LET'S GO!!

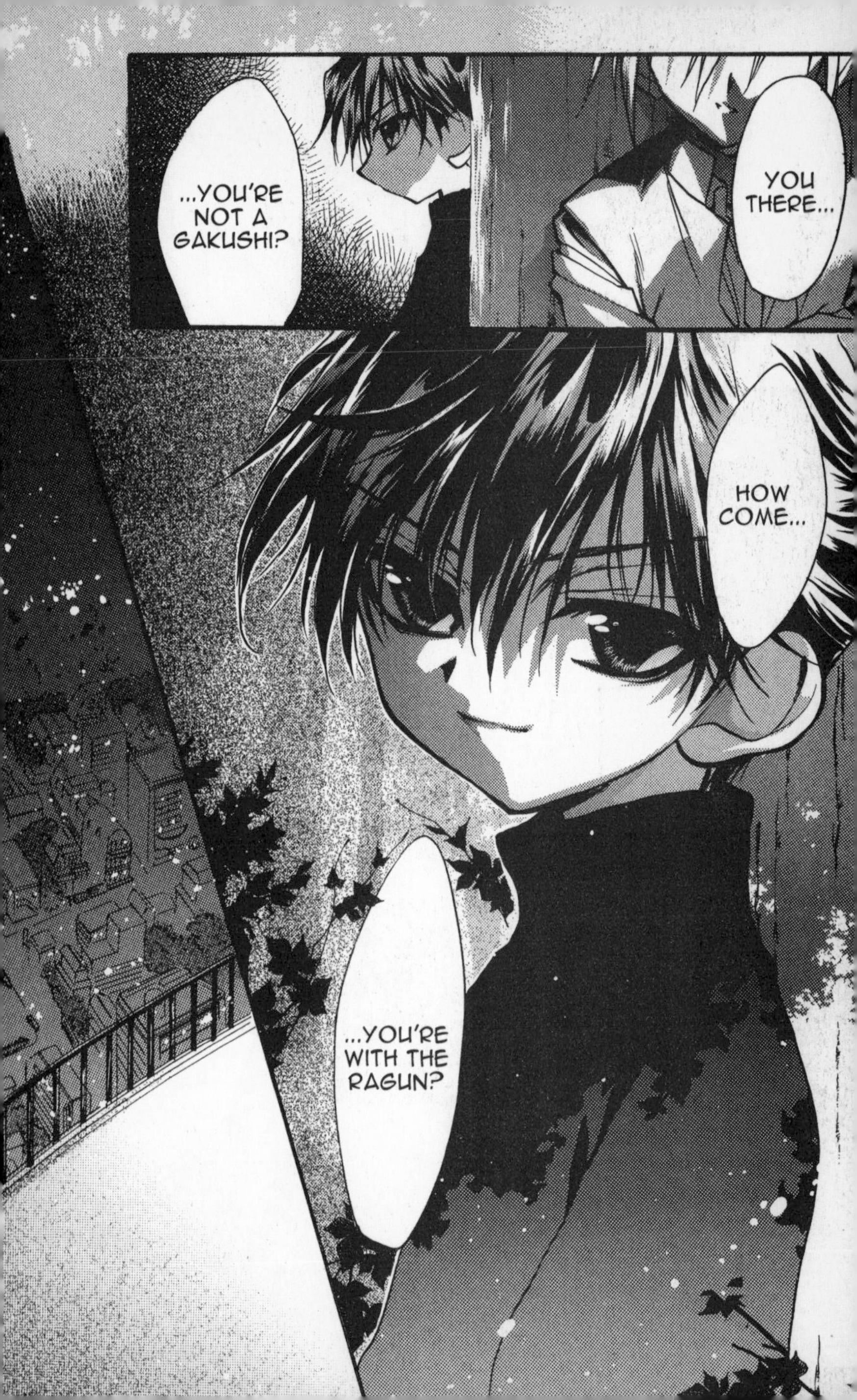
YOU THERE...
...YOU'RE NOT A GAKUSHI?
HOW COME...
...YOU'RE WITH THE RAGUN?

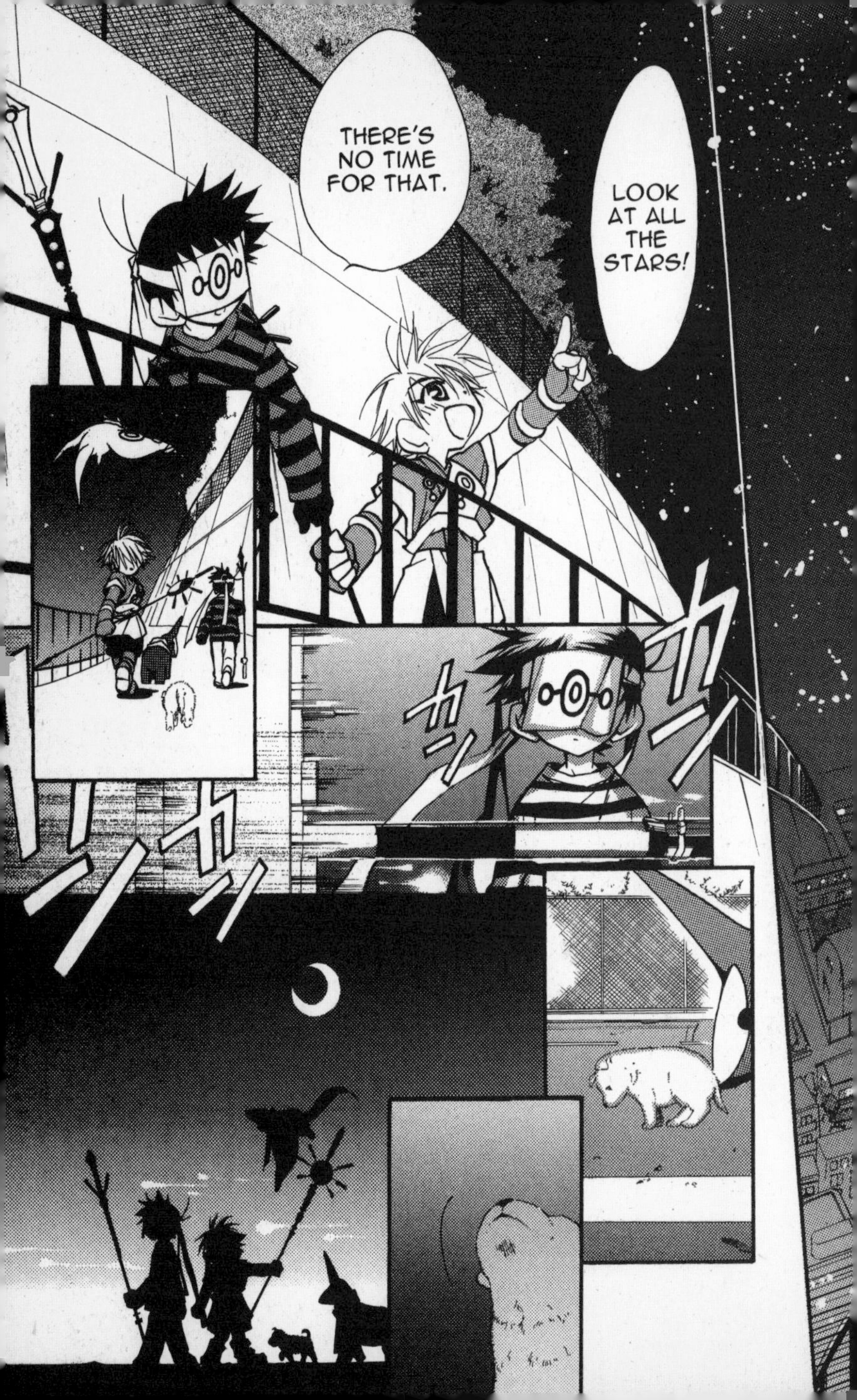
LOOK AT ALL THE STARS!
THERE'S NO TIME FOR THAT.

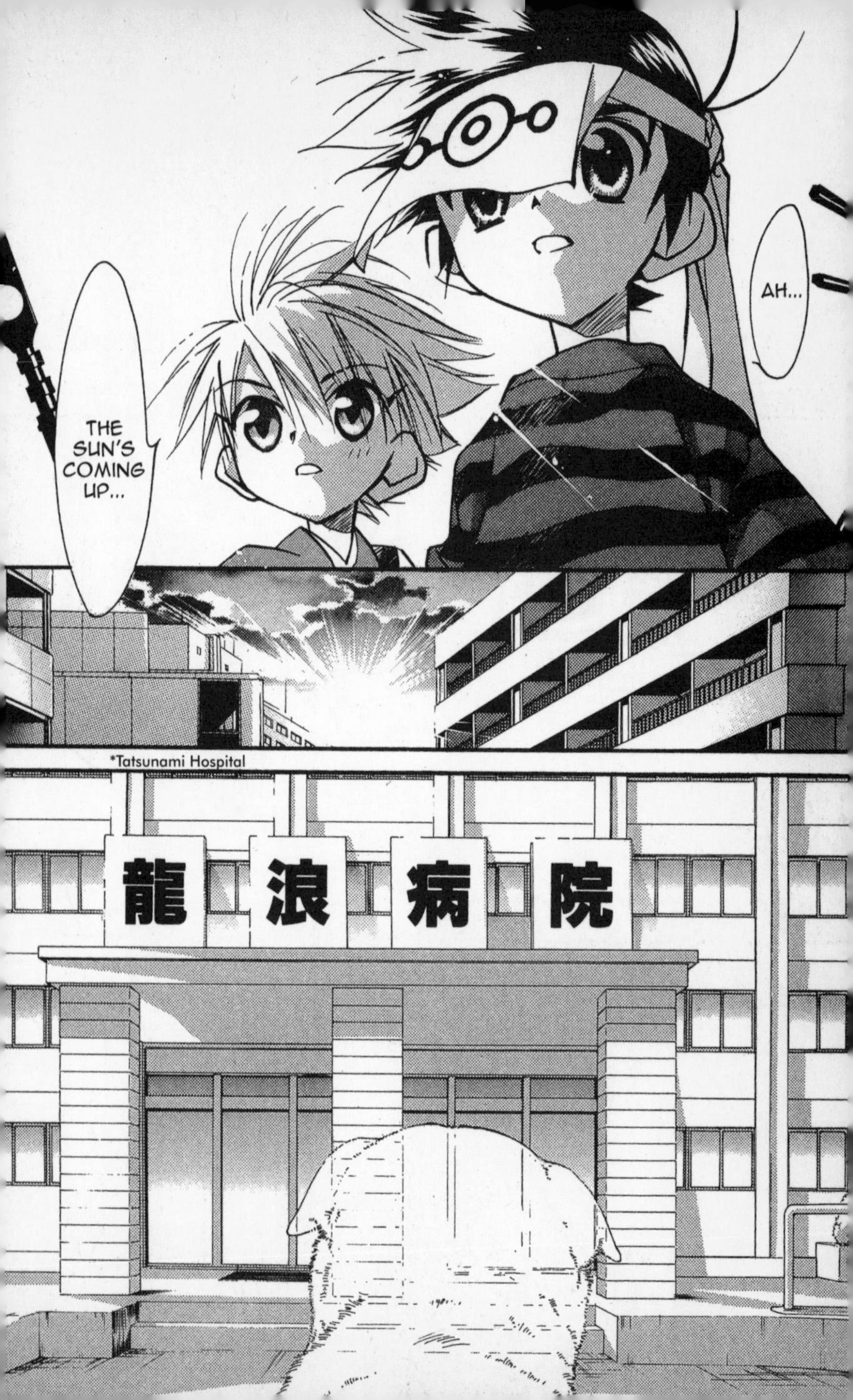
AH...
THE SUN'S COMING UP...
*Tatsunami Hospital
龍浪病院

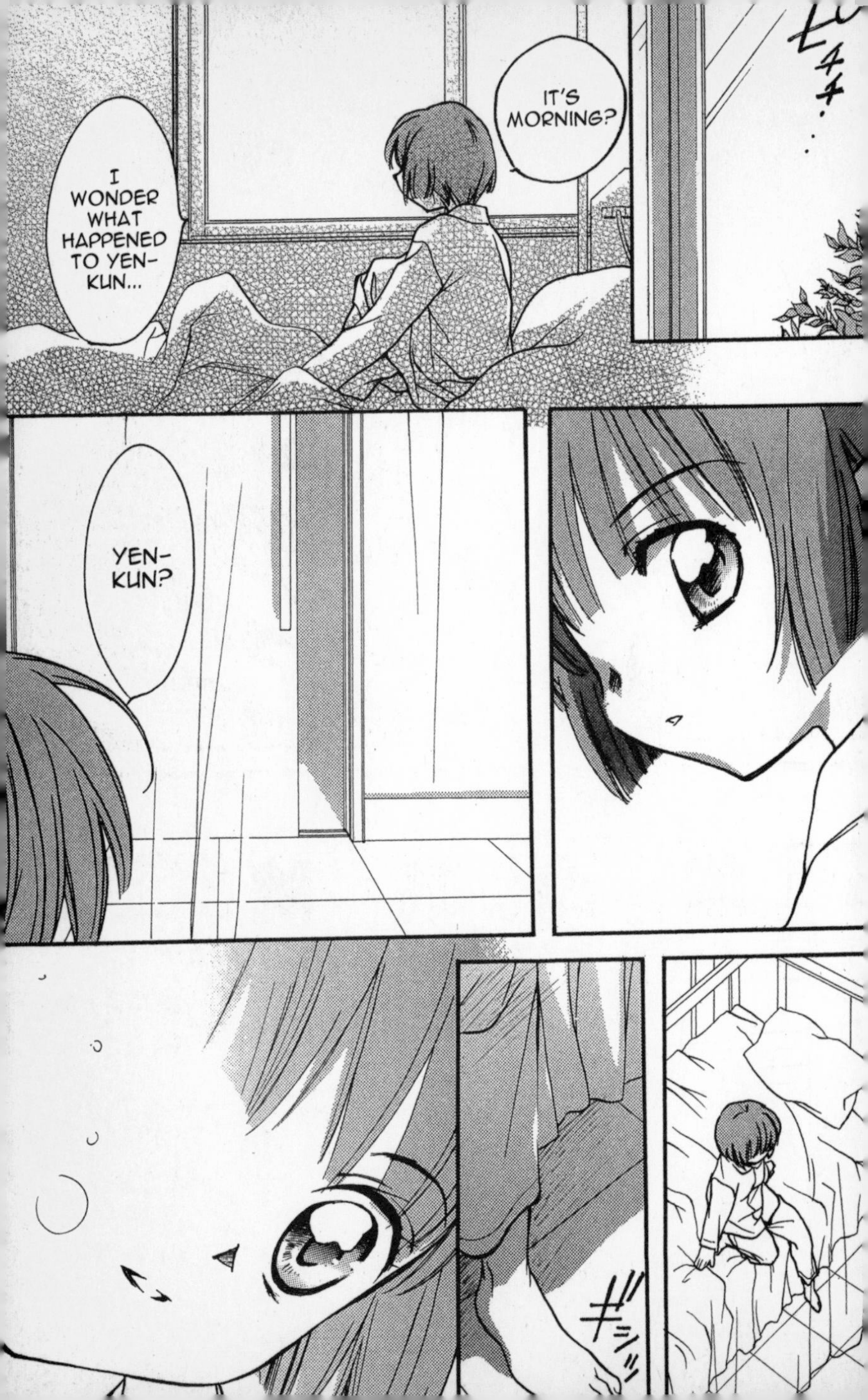
IT'S MORNING?
I WONDER WHAT HAPPENED TO YEN-KUN...
YEN-KUN?

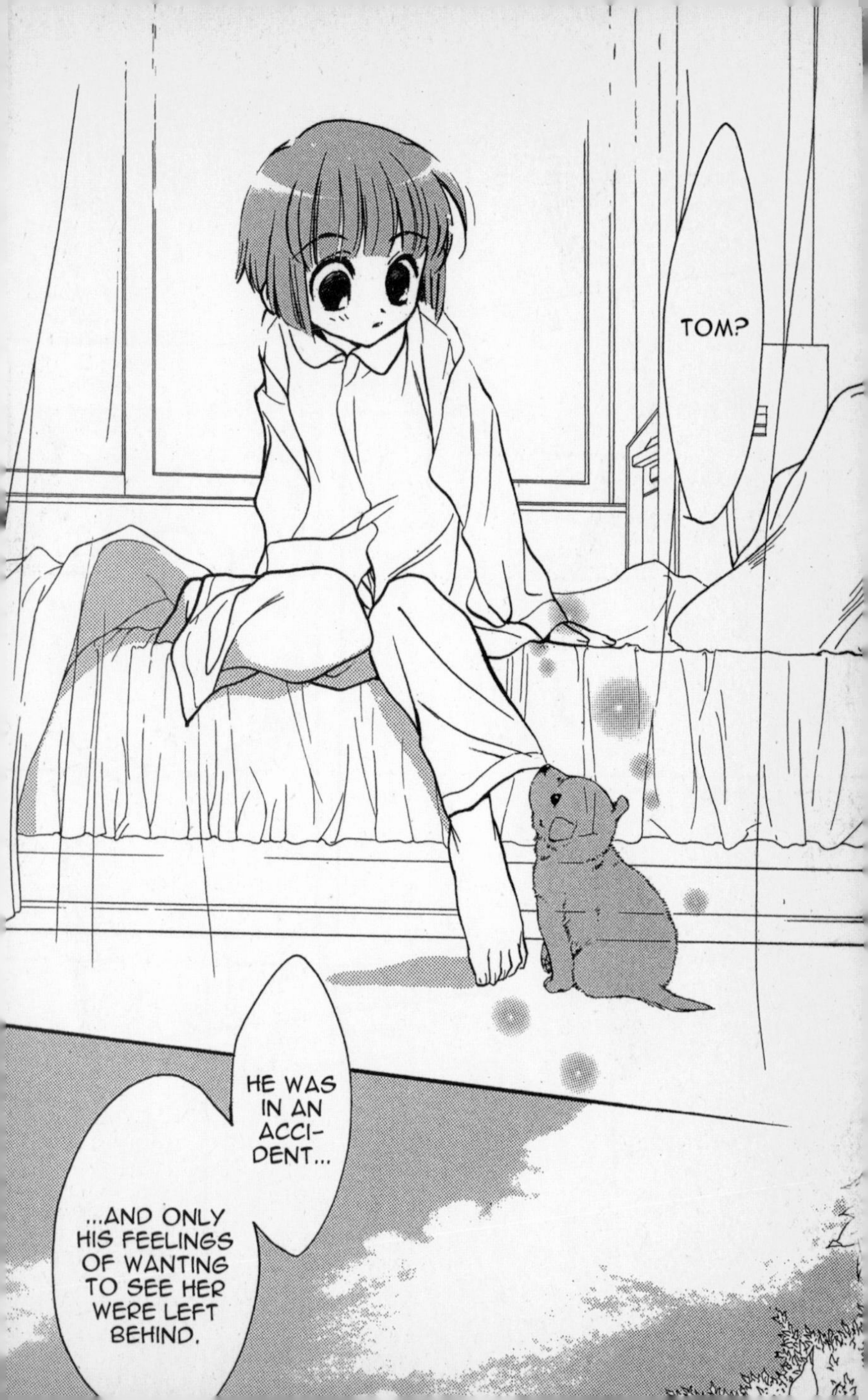
TOM?
HE WAS IN AN ACCI-DENT...
...AND ONLY HIS FEELINGS OF WANTING TO SEE HER WERE LEFT BEHIND.

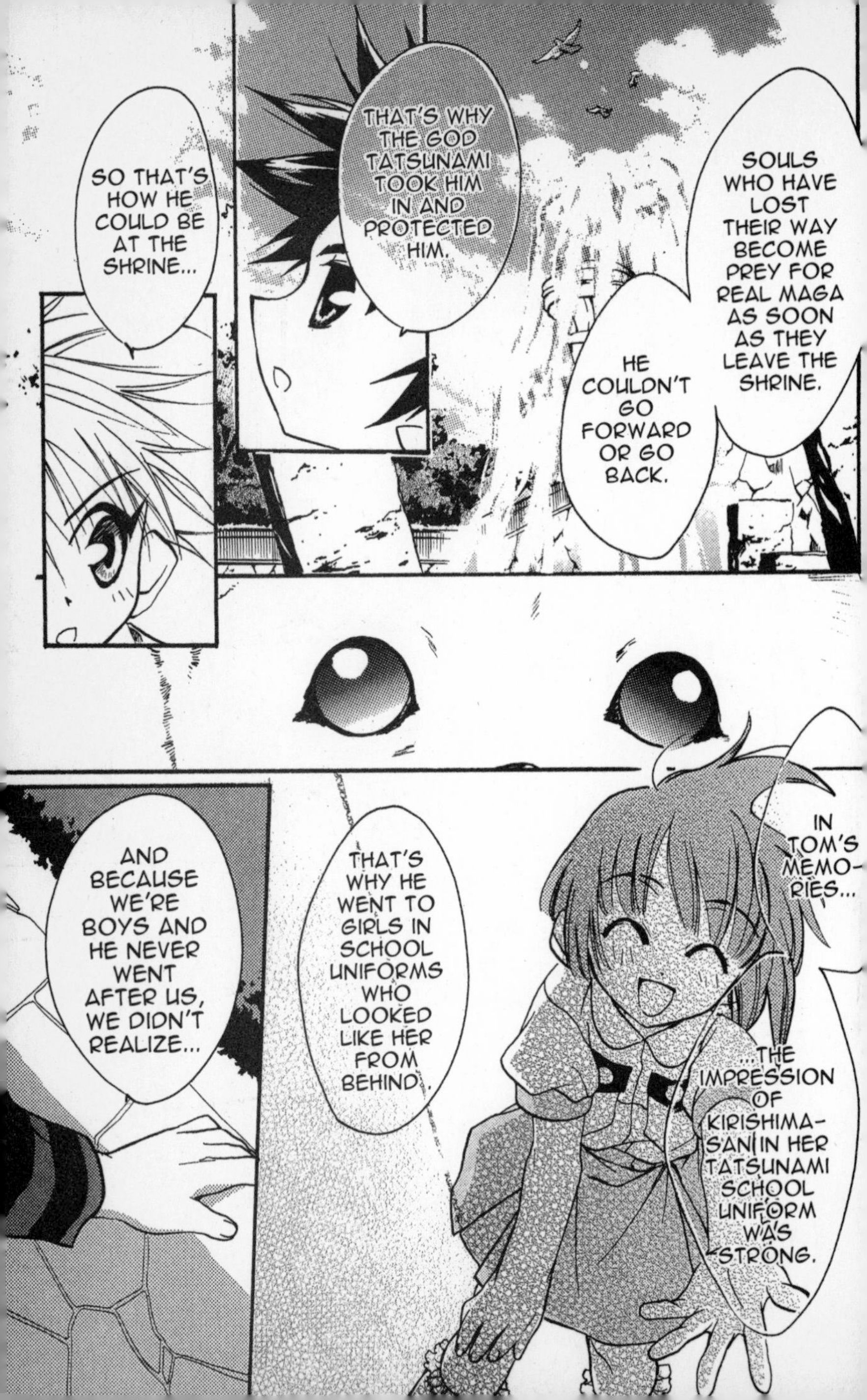
SOULS WHO HAVE LOST THEIR WAY BECOME PREY FOR REAL MAGA AS SOON AS THEY LEAVE THE SHRINE.
HE COULDN'T GO FORWARD OR GO BACK.
THAT'S WHY THE GOD TATSUNAMI TOOK HIM IN AND PROTECTED HIM.
SO THAT'S HOW HE COULD BE AT THE SHRINE...
IN TOM'S MEMO-RIES...
...THE IMPRESSION OF KIRISHIMA-SAN IN HER TATSUNAMI SCHOOL UNIFORM WAS STRONG.
THAT'S WHY HE WENT TO GIRLS IN SCHOOL UNIFORMS WHO LOOKED LIKE HER FROM BEHIND.
AND BECAUSE WE'RE BOYS AND HE NEVER WENT AFTER US, WE DIDN'T REALIZE...

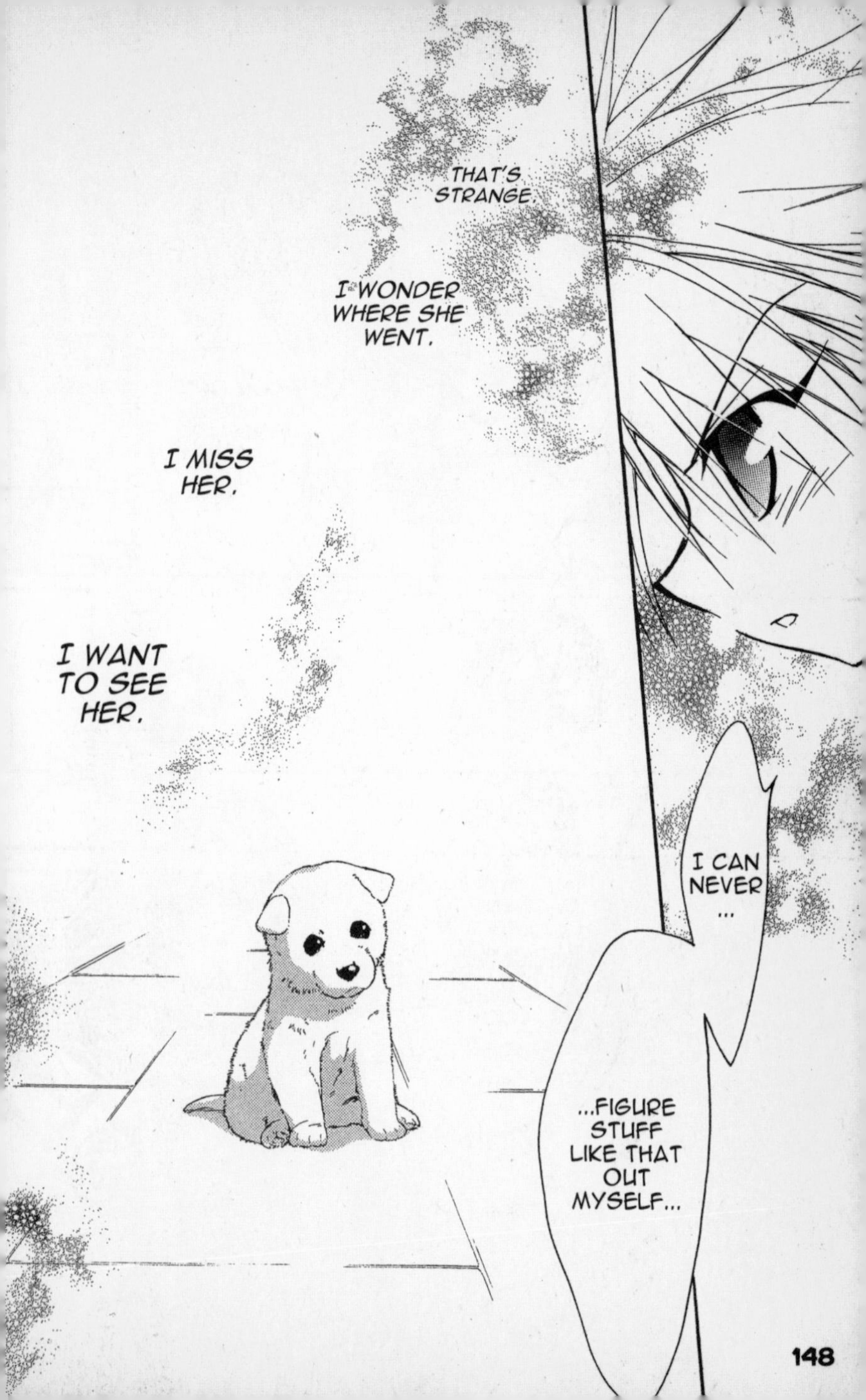
I CAN NEVER ...
...FIGURE STUFF LIKE THAT OUT MYSELF...
THAT'S STRANGE.
I WONDER WHERE SHE WENT.
I MISS HER.
I WANT TO SEE HER.

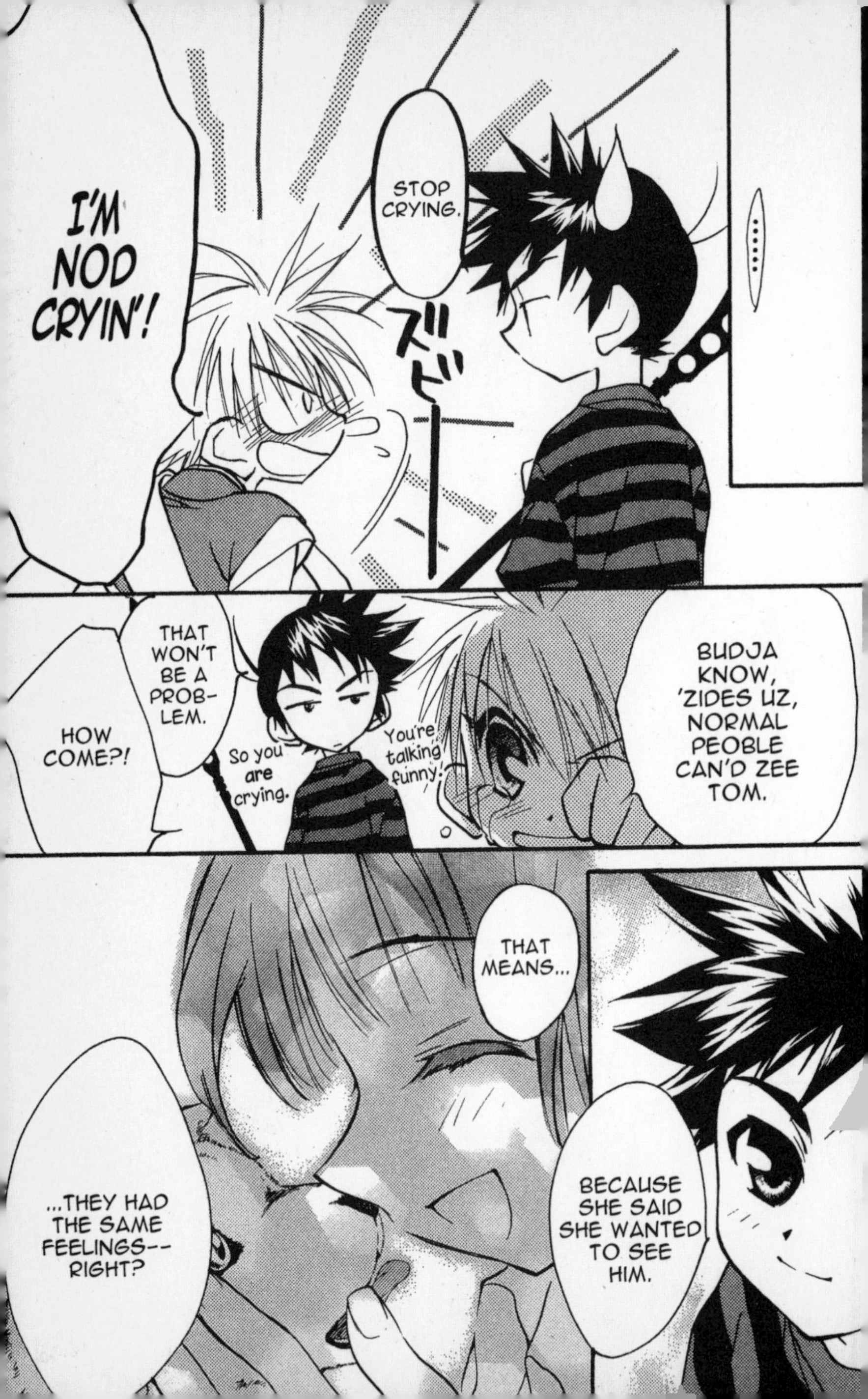
......
STOP CRYING.
ズビー
I'M NOD CRYIN'!
BUDJA KNOW, 'ZIDES UZ, NORMAL PEOBLE CAN'D ZEE TOM.
You're talking funny!
So you are crying.
THAT WON'T BE A PROB-LEM.
HOW COME?!
THAT MEANS...
BECAUSE SHE SAID SHE WANTED TO SEE HIM.
...THEY HAD THE SAME FEELINGS--RIGHT?

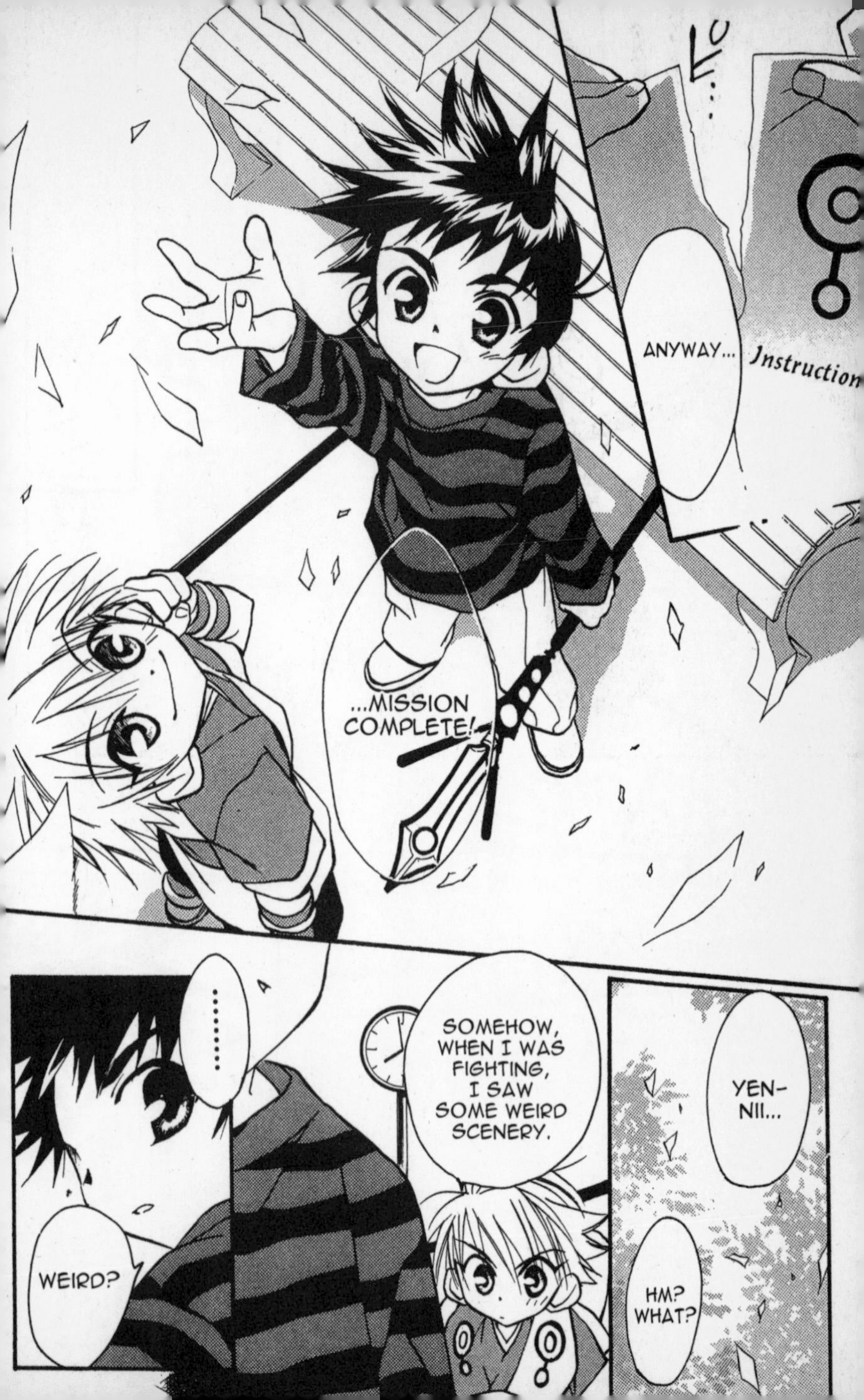

Instruction
ANYWAY...
...MISSION COMPLETE!
YEN-NII...
HM? WHAT?
SOMEHOW, WHEN I WAS FIGHTING, I SAW SOME WEIRD SCENERY.
......
WEIRD?

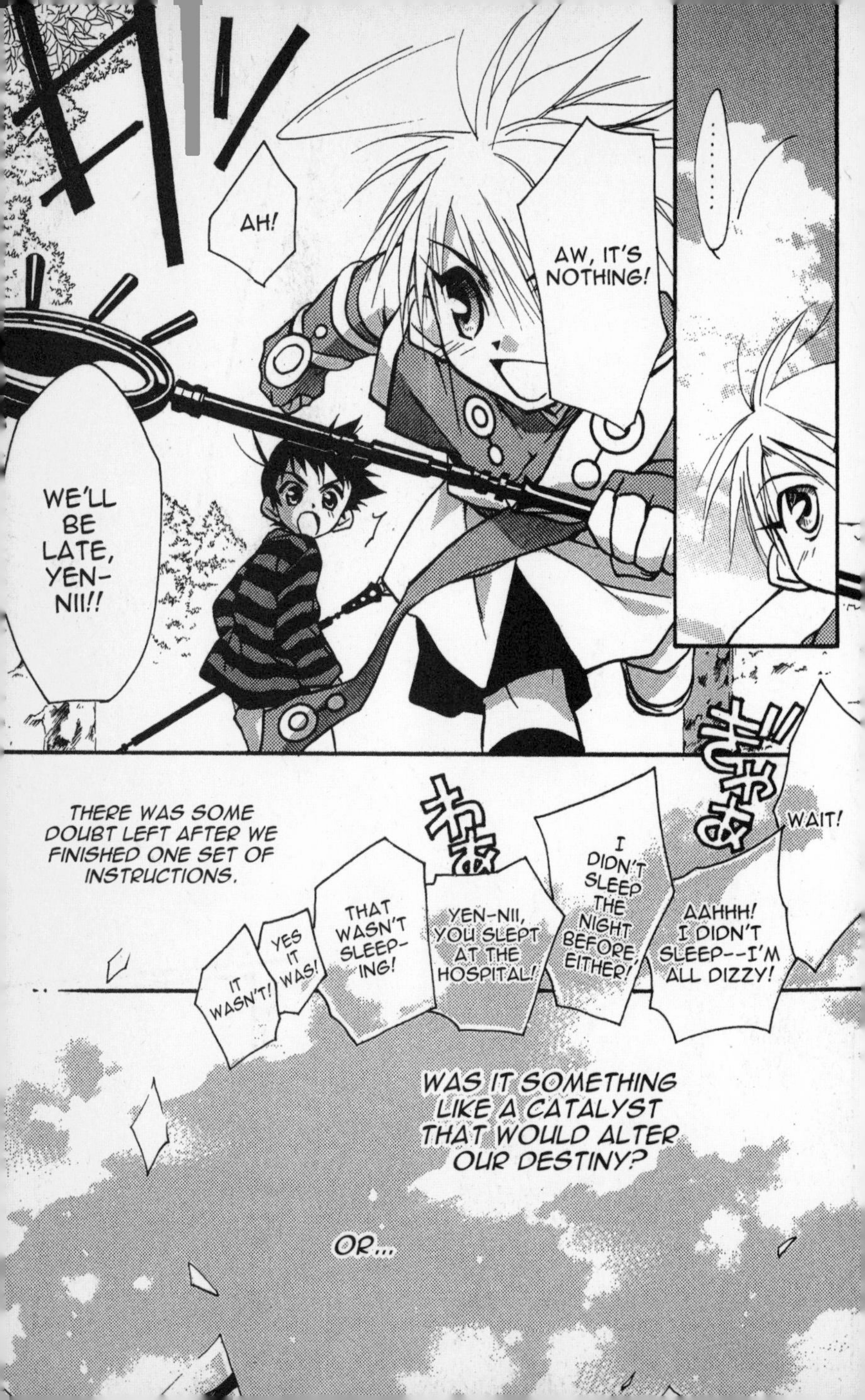
......
AW, IT'S NOTHING!
AH!
WE'LL BE LATE, YEN-NII!!
WAIT!
AAHHH! I DIDN'T SLEEP--I'M ALL DIZZY!
I DIDN'T SLEEP THE NIGHT BEFORE, EITHER!
YEN-NII, YOU SLEPT AT THE HOSPITAL!
THAT WASN'T SLEEPING!
YES IT WAS!
IT WASN'T!
THERE WAS SOME DOUBT LEFT AFTER WE FINISHED ONE SET OF INSTRUCTIONS.
WAS IT SOMETHING LIKE A CATALYST THAT WOULD ALTER OUR DESTINY?
OR...

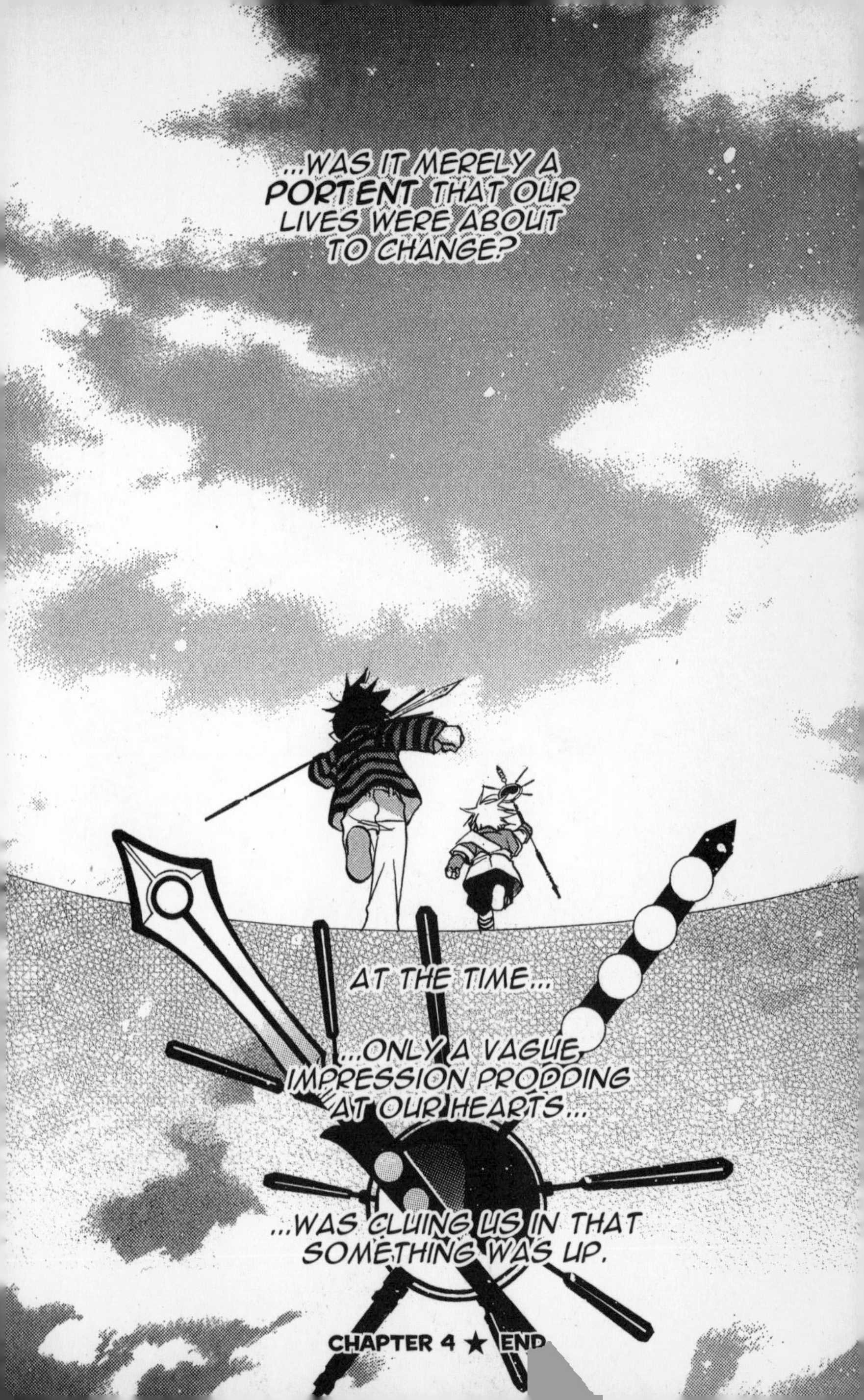
...WAS IT MERELY A PORTENT THAT OUR LIVES WERE ABOUT TO CHANGE?
AT THE TIME...
...ONLY A VAGUE IMPRESSION PRODDING AT OUR HEARTS...
...WAS CLUING US IN THAT SOMETHING WAS UP.
CHAPTER 4 ★ END

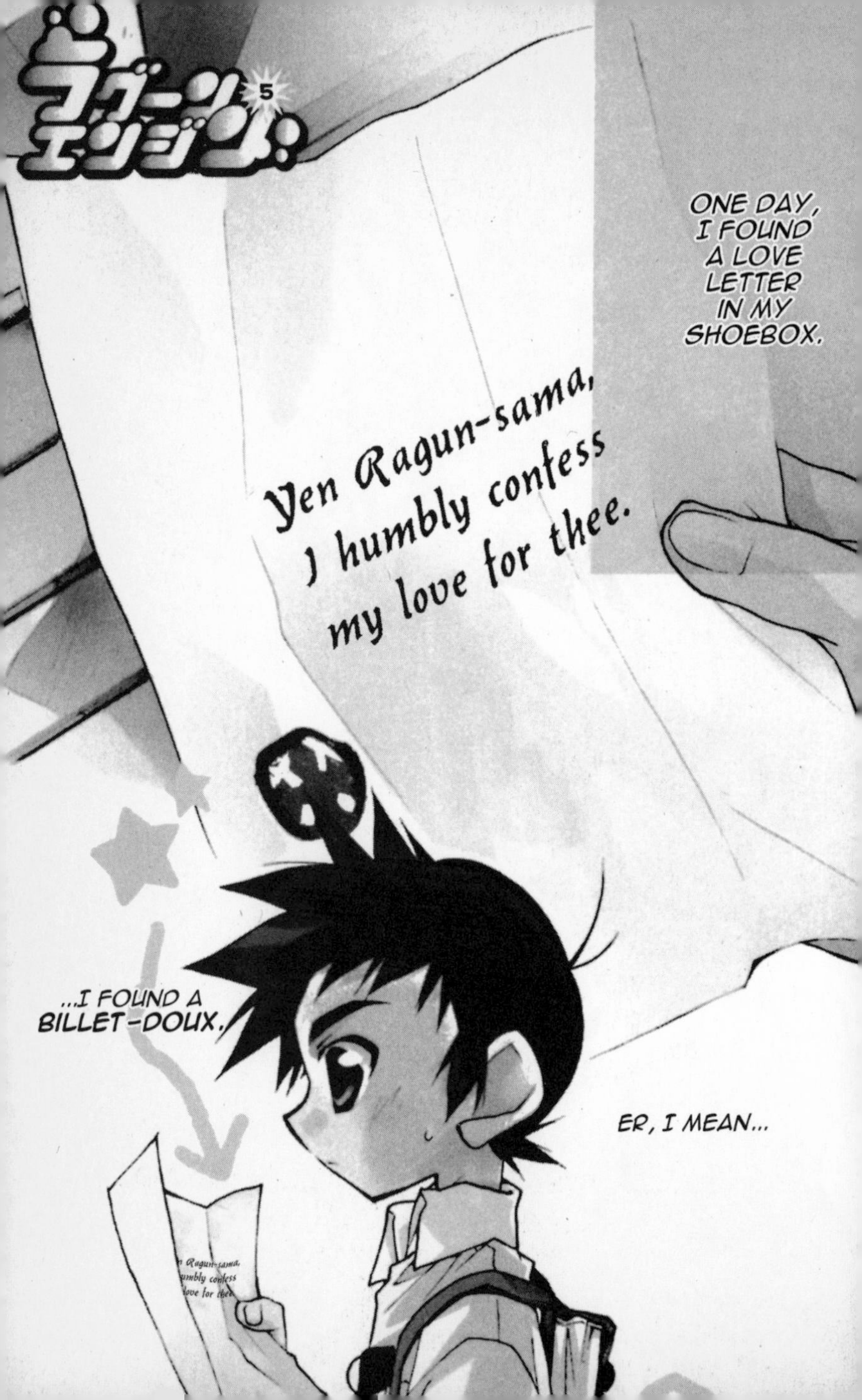
ラグーンエンジン 5
ONE DAY, I FOUND A LOVE LETTER IN MY SHOEBOX.
Yen Ragun-sama, I humbly confess my love for thee.
ER, I MEAN...
...I FOUND A BILLET-DOUX.

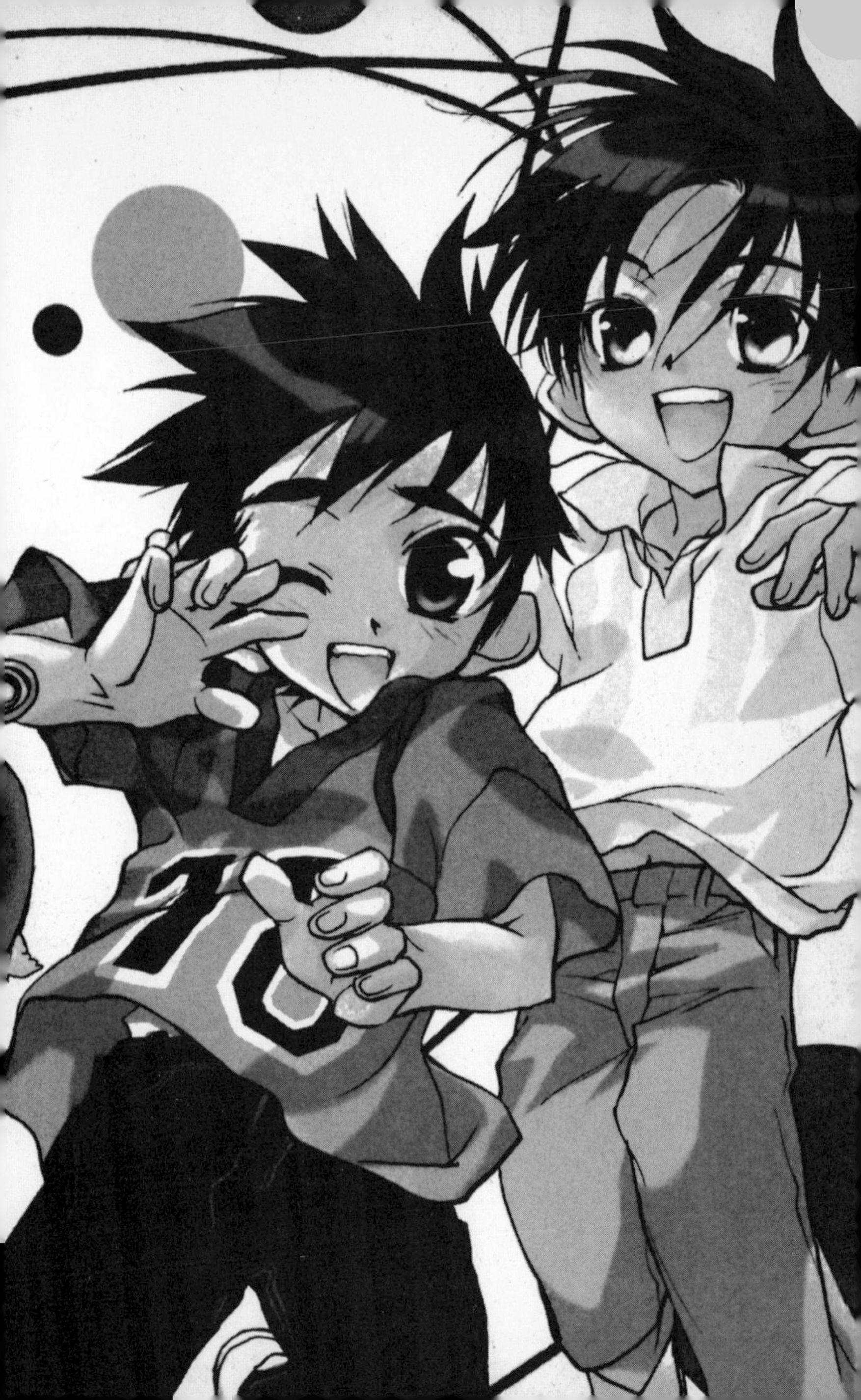

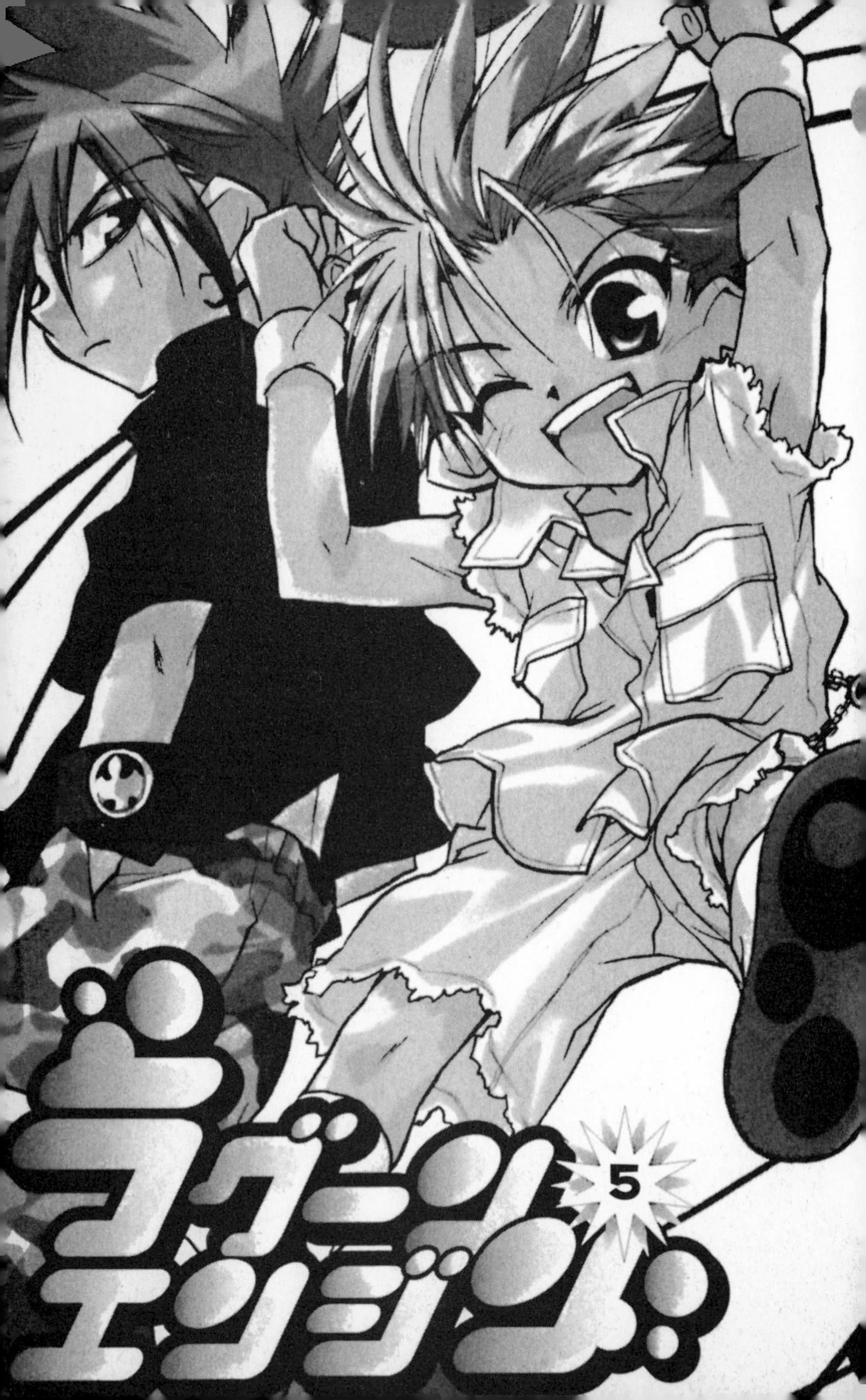
ラグーン
エンジン
5

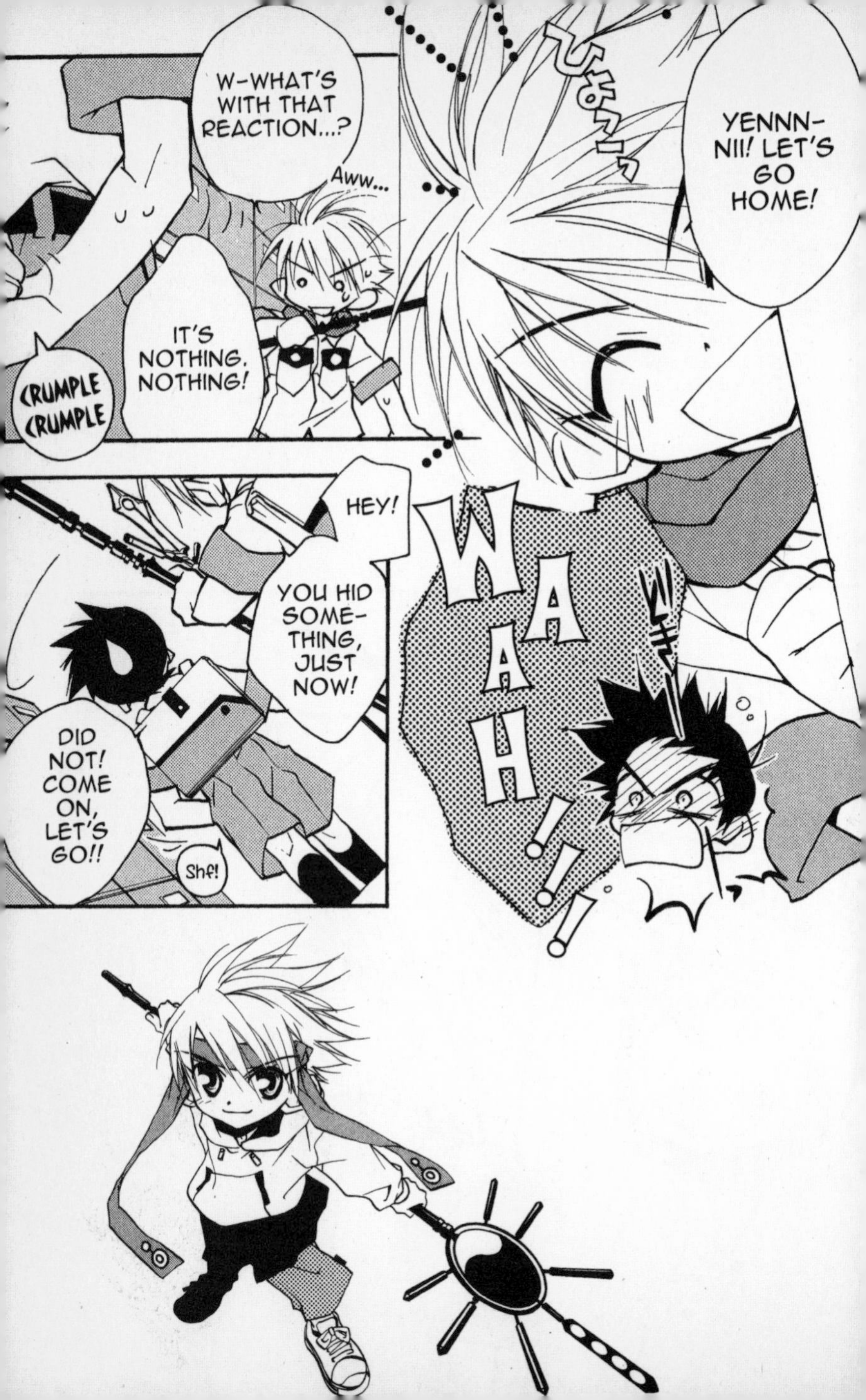
YENNN-NII! LET'S GO HOME!
WAAH!!!
W-WHAT'S WITH THAT REACTION...?
Aww...
IT'S NOTHING. NOTHING!
CRUMPLE CRUMPLE
HEY!
YOU HID SOME-THING, JUST NOW!
DID NOT! COME ON, LET'S GO!!
Shf!

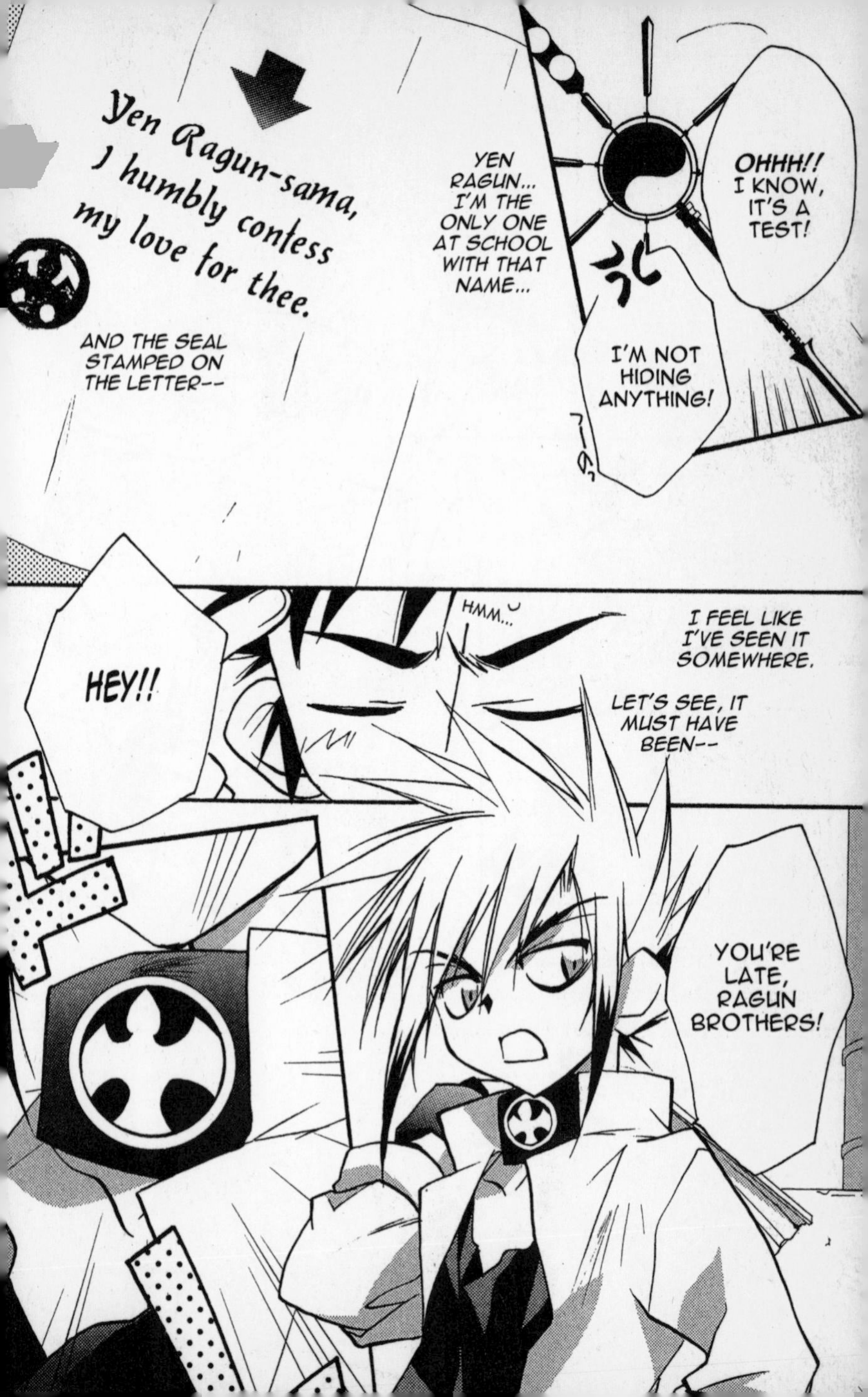
OHHH!! I KNOW, IT'S A TEST!
I'M NOT HIDING ANYTHING!
YEN RAGUN... I'M THE ONLY ONE AT SCHOOL WITH THAT NAME...
Yen Ragun-sama, I humbly confess my love for thee.
AND THE SEAL STAMPED ON THE LETTER--
I FEEL LIKE I'VE SEEN IT SOMEWHERE.
HMM...
LET'S SEE, IT MUST HAVE BEEN--
HEY!!
YOU'RE LATE, RAGUN BROTHERS!

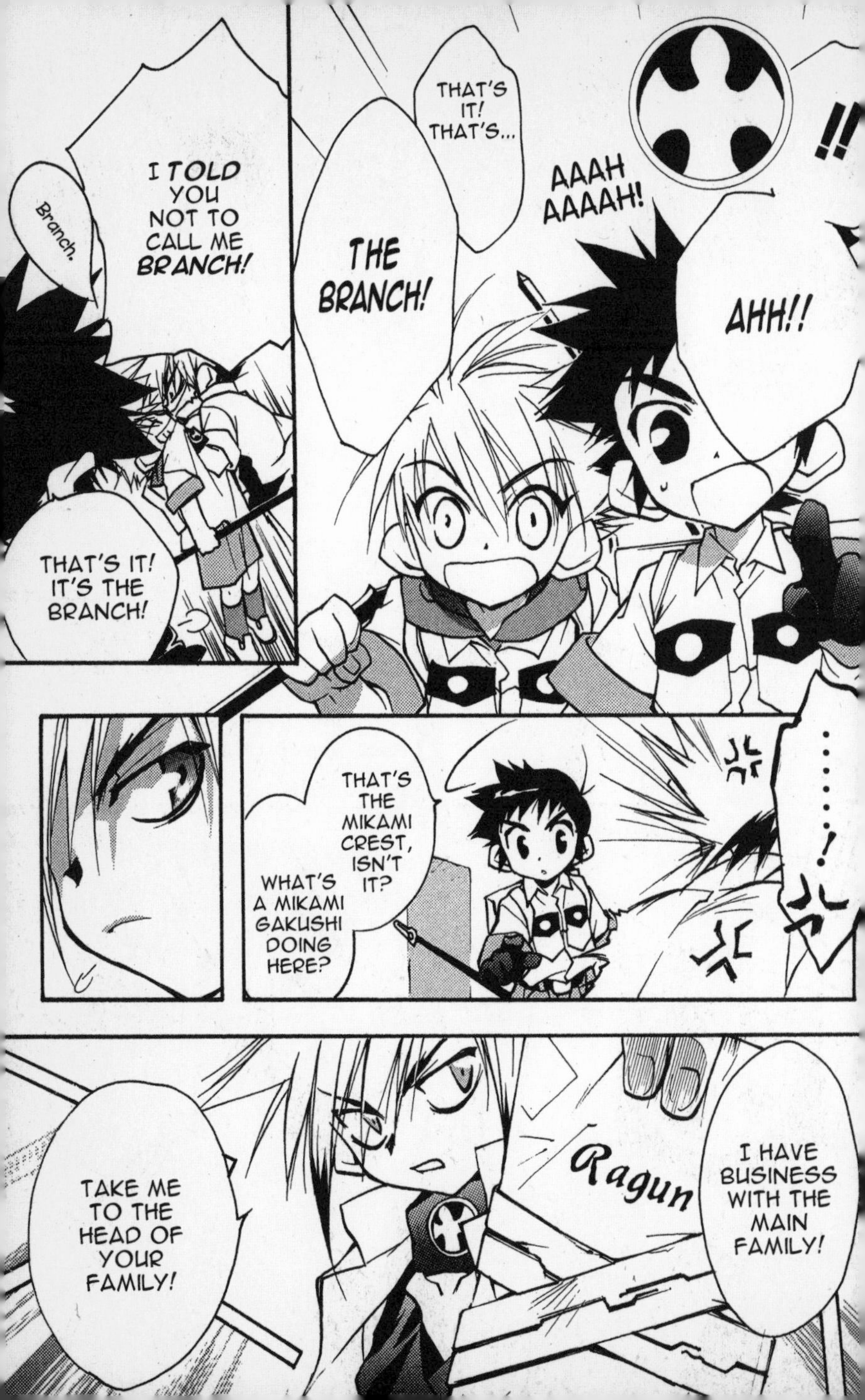
!!
AAAH AAAAH!
AHH!!
THAT'S IT! THAT'S...
THE BRANCH!
I TOLD YOU NOT TO CALL ME BRANCH!
Branch.
THAT'S IT! IT'S THE BRANCH!
......!
THAT'S THE MIKAMI CREST, ISN'T IT?
WHAT'S A MIKAMI GAKUSHI DOING HERE?
I HAVE BUSINESS WITH THE MAIN FAMILY!
Ragun
TAKE ME TO THE HEAD OF YOUR FAMILY!

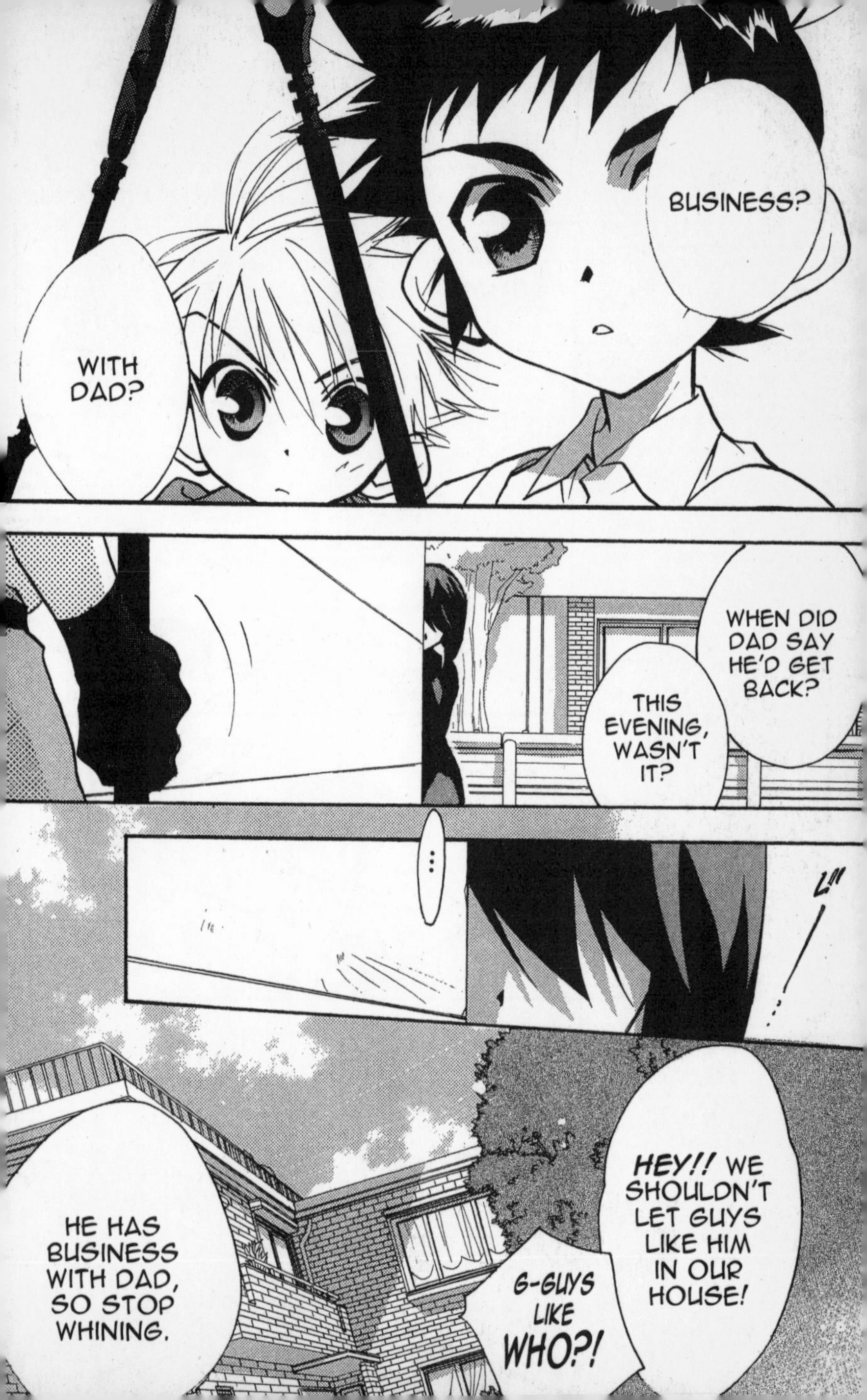
BUSINESS?
WITH DAD?
WHEN DID DAD SAY HE'D GET BACK?
THIS EVENING, WASN'T IT?
...
HEY!! WE SHOULDN'T LET GUYS LIKE HIM IN OUR HOUSE!
G-GUYS LIKE WHO?!
HE HAS BUSINESS WITH DAD, SO STOP WHINING.

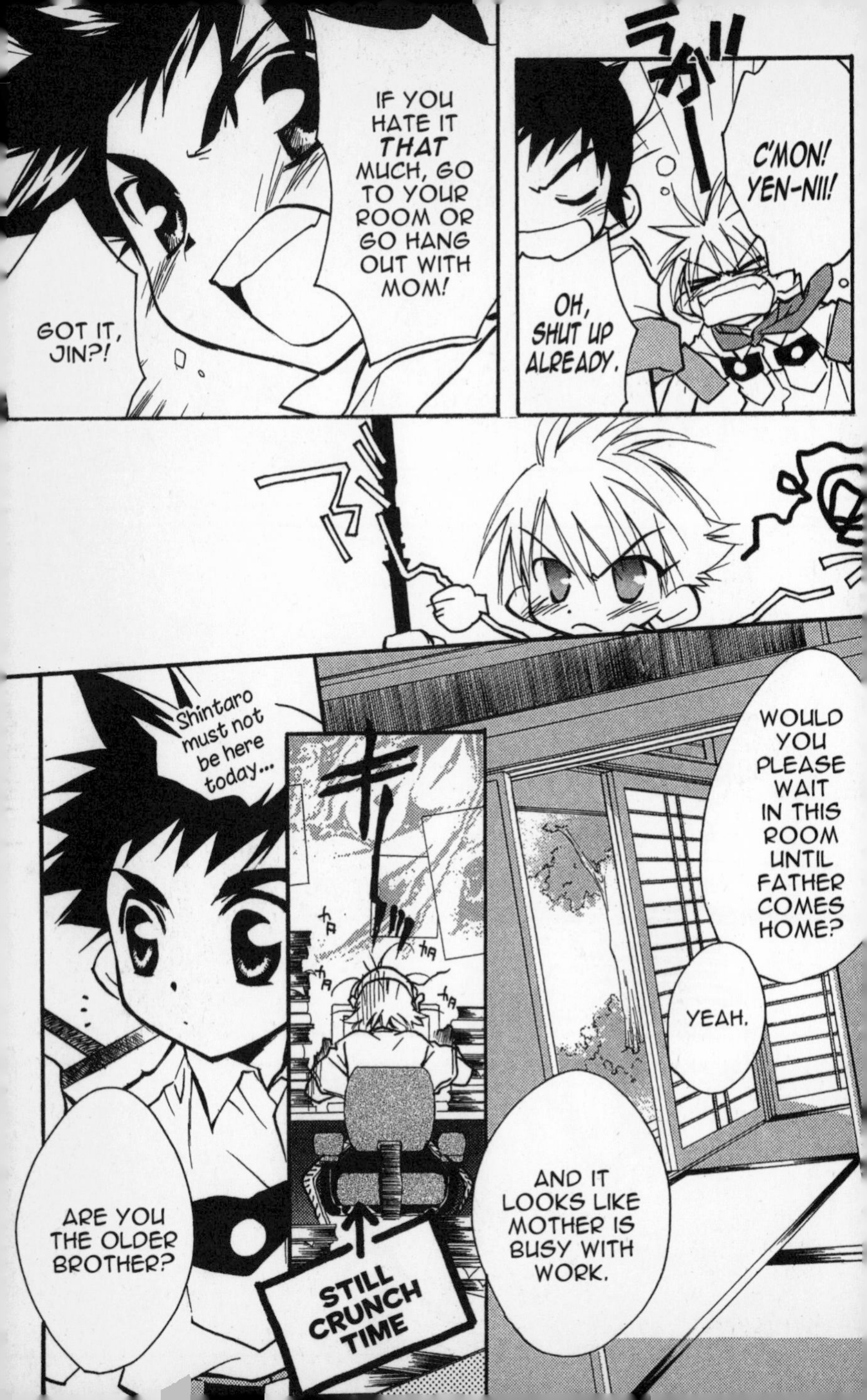
C'MON! YEN-NII!
OH, SHUT UP ALREADY.
IF YOU HATE IT THAT MUCH, GO TO YOUR ROOM OR GO HANG OUT WITH MOM!
GOT IT, JIN?!
WOULD YOU PLEASE WAIT IN THIS ROOM UNTIL FATHER COMES HOME?
YEAH.
AND IT LOOKS LIKE MOTHER IS BUSY WITH WORK.
STILL CRUNCH TIME
Shintaro must not be here today...
ARE YOU THE OLDER BROTHER?

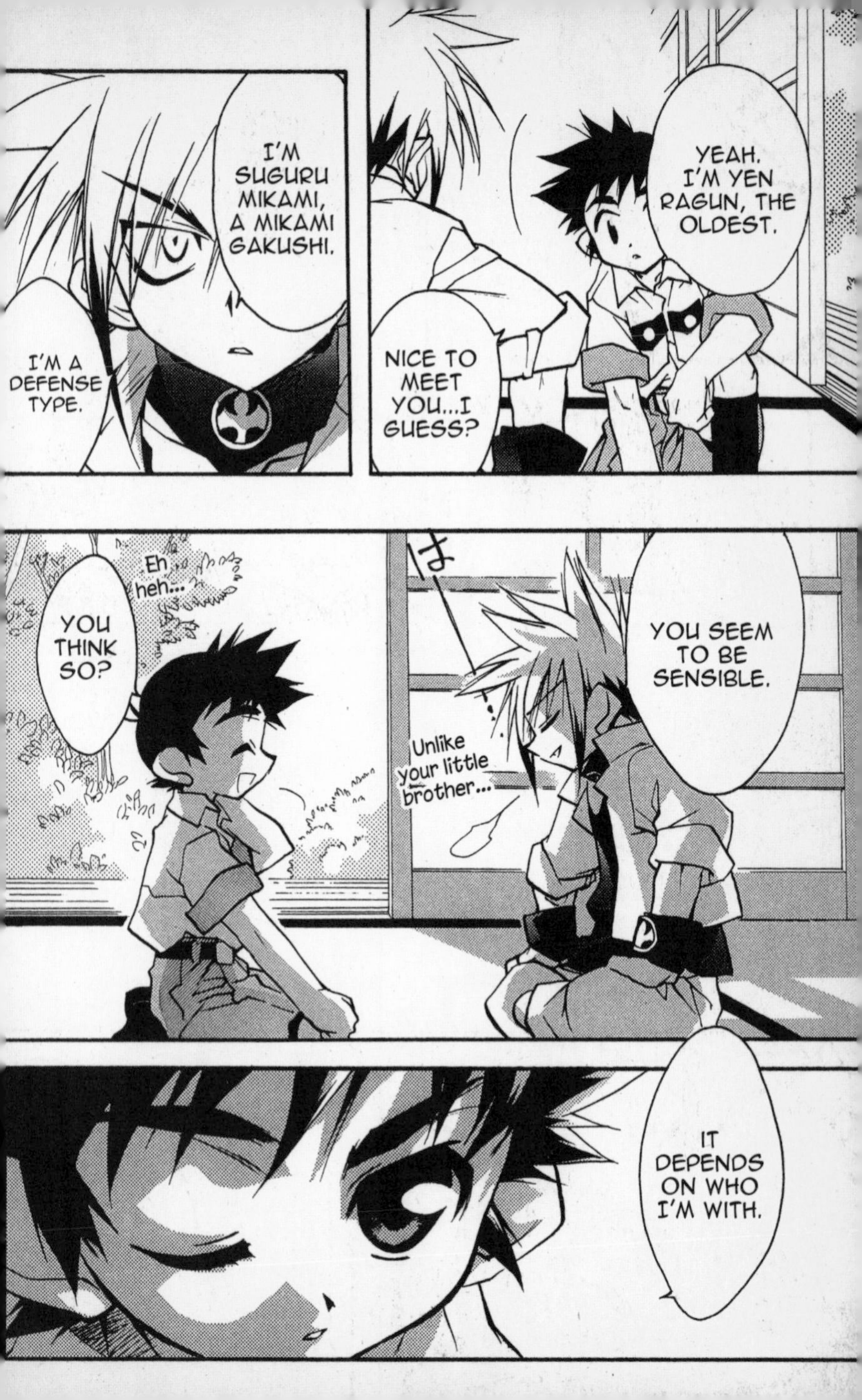
YEAH. I'M YEN RAGUN, THE OLDEST.
NICE TO MEET YOU...I GUESS?
I'M SUGURU MIKAMI, A MIKAMI GAKUSHI.
I'M A DEFENSE TYPE.
は
YOU SEEM TO BE SENSIBLE.
Unlike your little brother...
YOU THINK SO?
Eh heh...
IT DEPENDS ON WHO I'M WITH.

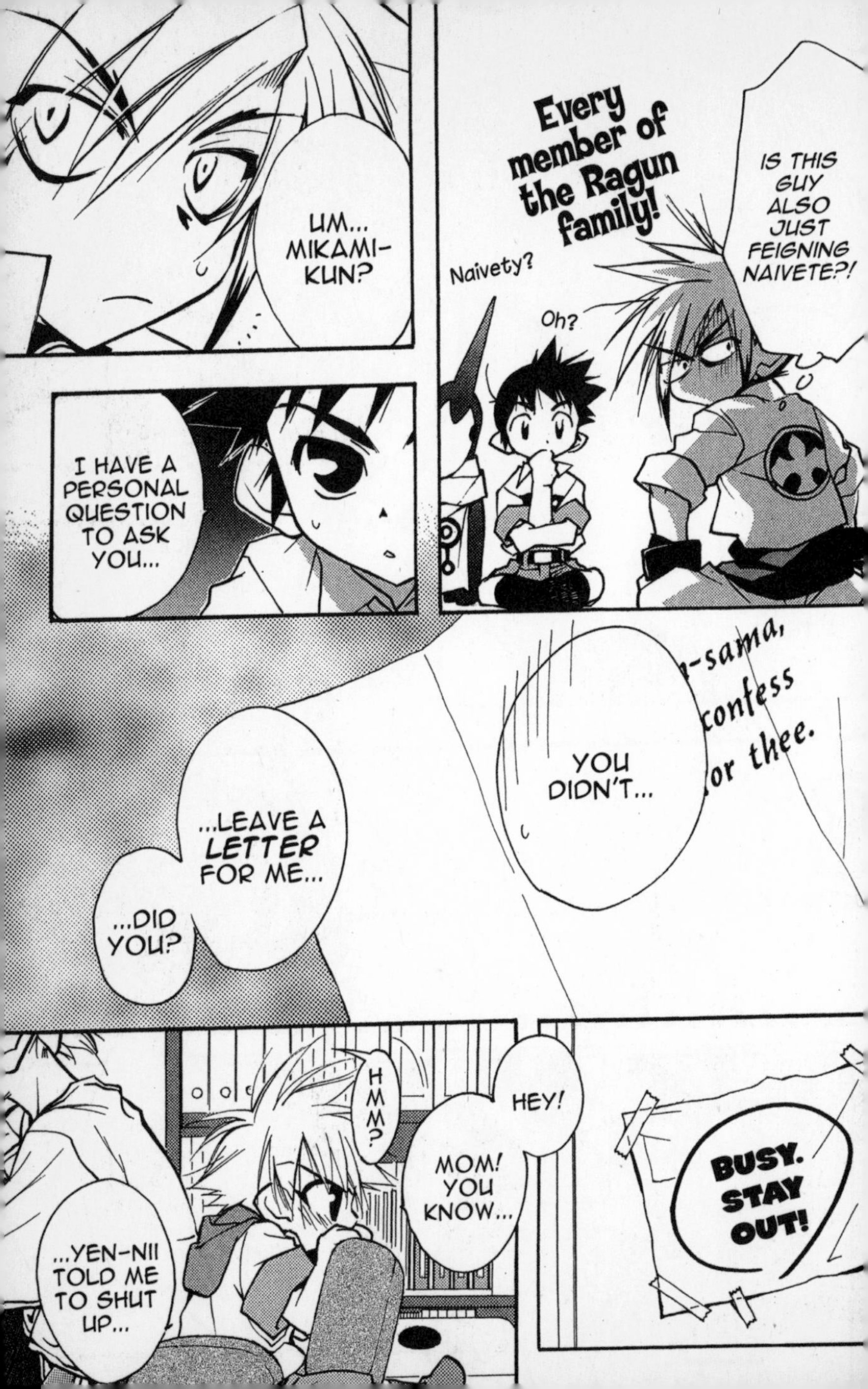
IS THIS GUY ALSO JUST FEIGNING NAIVETE?!
Every member of the Ragun family!
Naivety?
Oh?
UM... MIKAMI-KUN?
I HAVE A PERSONAL QUESTION TO ASK YOU...
-sama,
confess
or thee.
YOU DIDN'T...
...LEAVE A *LETTER* FOR ME...
...DID YOU?
BUSY. STAY OUT!
HEY!
HMMM?
MOM! YOU KNOW...
...YEN-NII TOLD ME TO SHUT UP...

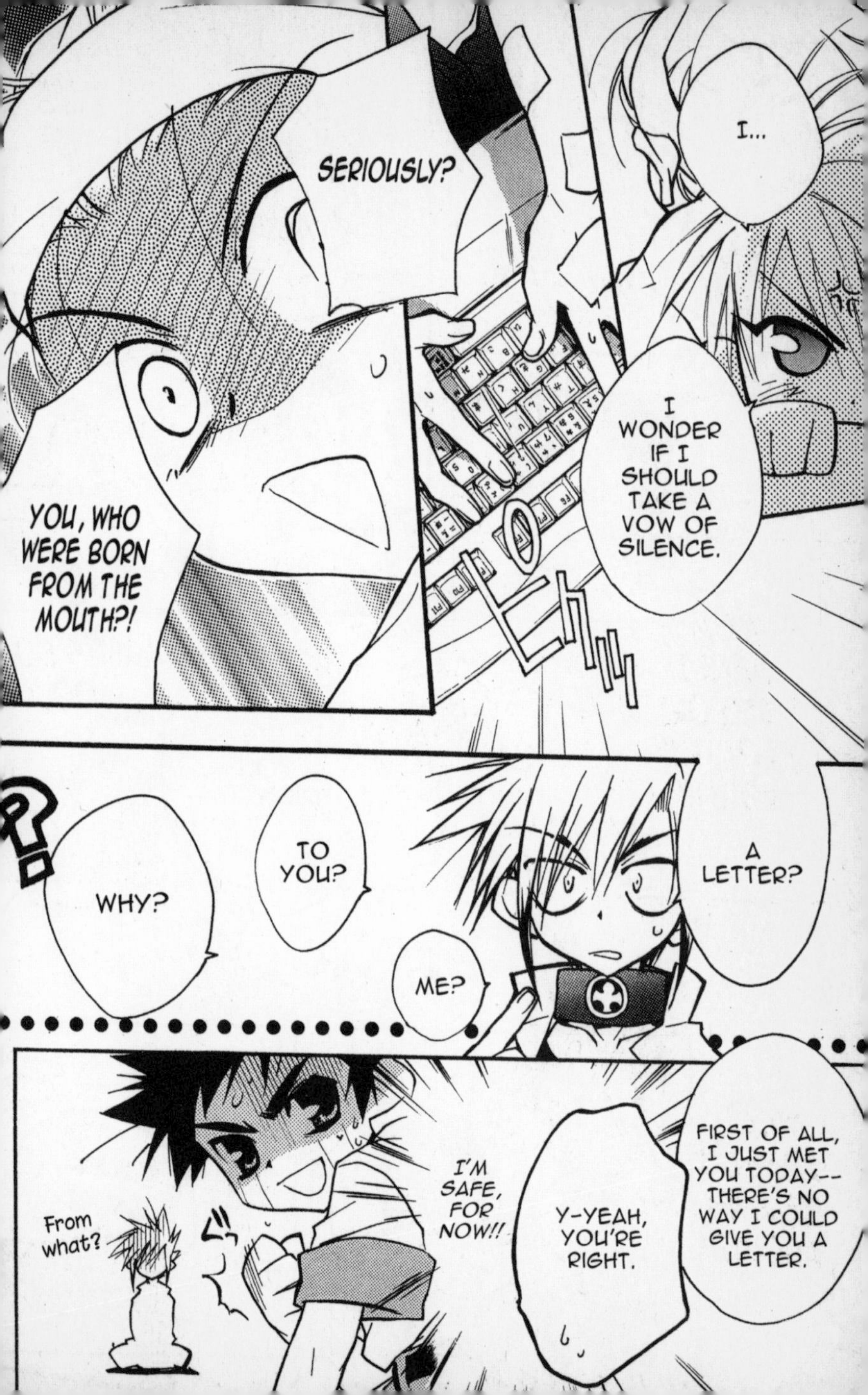
I...
I WONDER IF I SHOULD TAKE A VOW OF SILENCE.
SERIOUSLY?
YOU, WHO WERE BORN FROM THE MOUTH?!
A LETTER?
ME?
TO YOU?
WHY?
FIRST OF ALL, I JUST MET YOU TODAY-- THERE'S NO WAY I COULD GIVE YOU A LETTER.
Y-YEAH, YOU'RE RIGHT.
I'M SAFE, FOR NOW!!
From what?

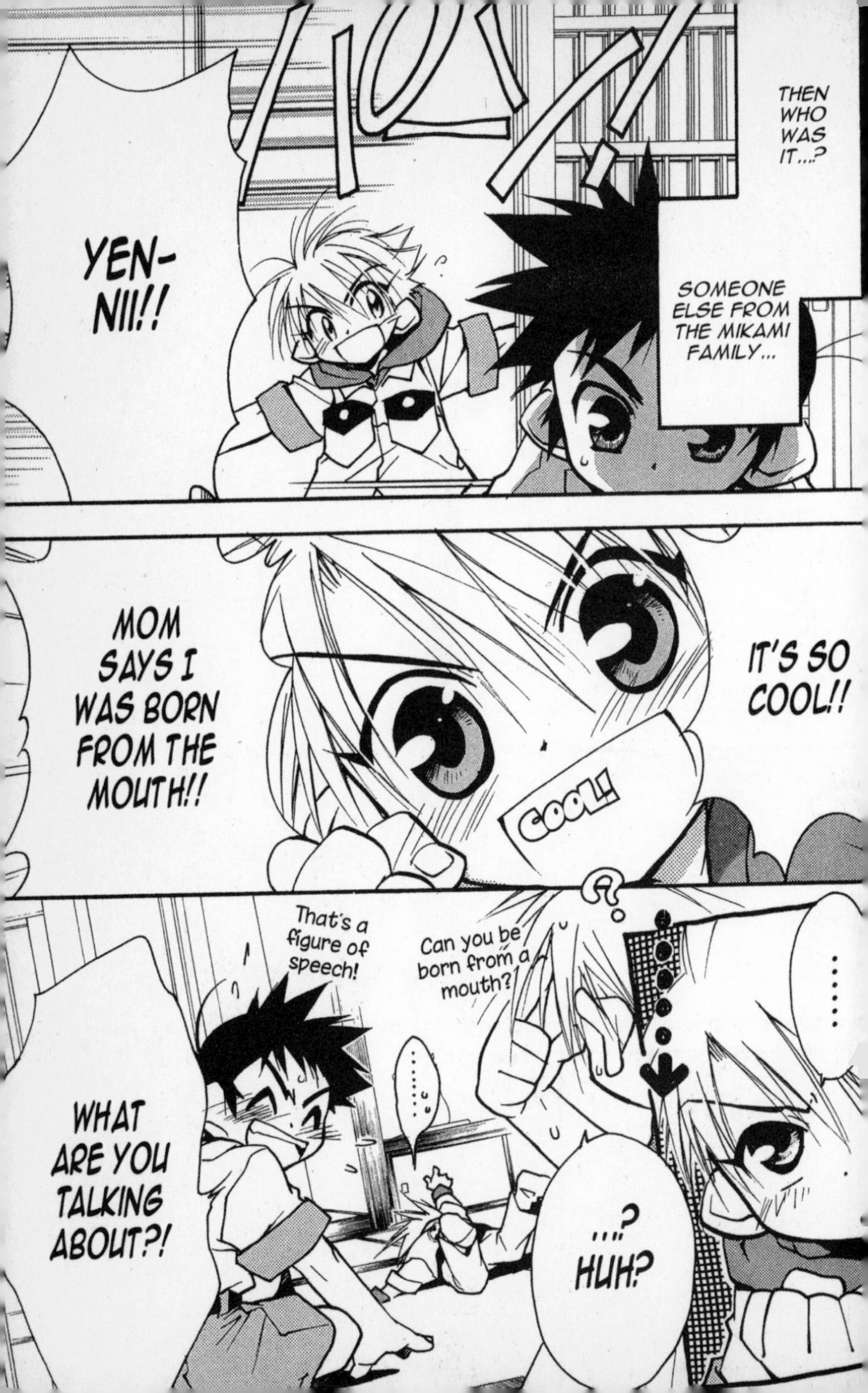
THEN WHO WAS IT...?
SOMEONE ELSE FROM THE MIKAMI FAMILY...
YEN-NII!!
IT'S SO COOL!!
COOL!
MOM SAYS I WAS BORN FROM THE MOUTH!!
......
Can you be born from a mouth?
...? HUH?
That's a figure of speech!
......
WHAT ARE YOU TALKING ABOUT?!

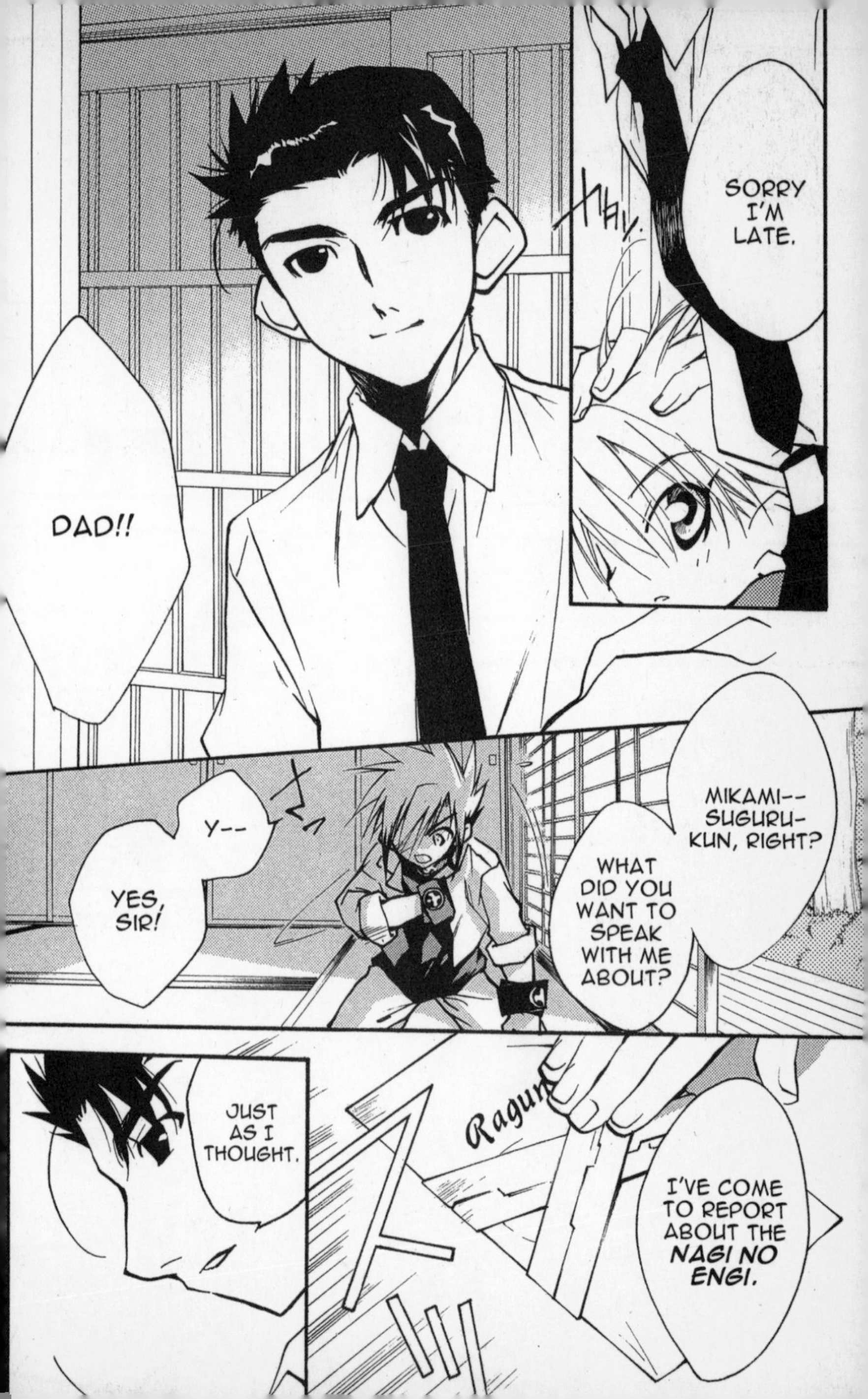
SORRY I'M LATE.
DAD!!
MIKAMI-- SUGURU-KUN, RIGHT?
WHAT DID YOU WANT TO SPEAK WITH ME ABOUT?
Y--
YES, SIR!
Ragun
I'VE COME TO REPORT ABOUT THE *NAGI NO ENGI*.
JUST AS I THOUGHT.

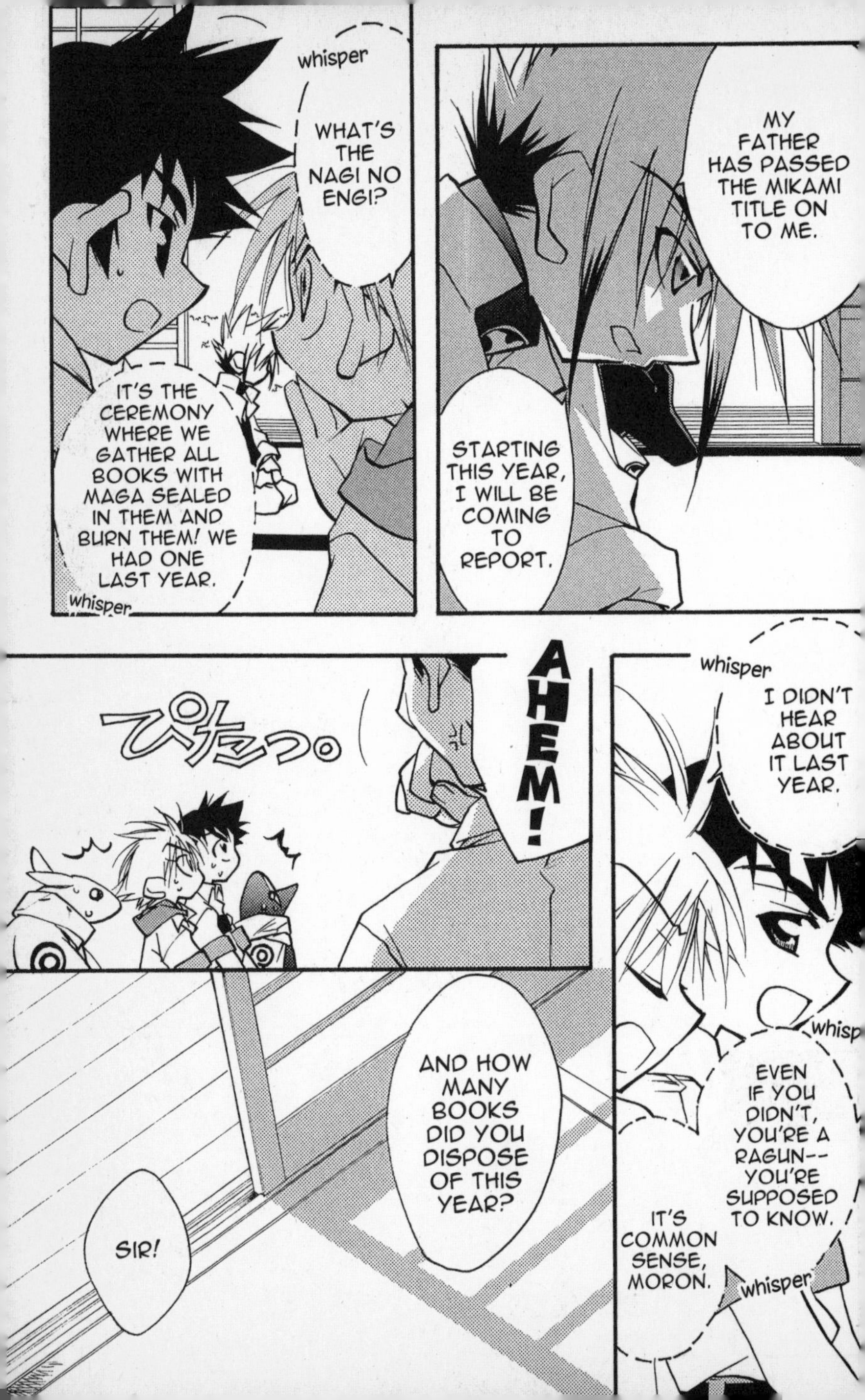
MY FATHER HAS PASSED THE MIKAMI TITLE ON TO ME.
STARTING THIS YEAR, I WILL BE COMING TO REPORT.
whisper
WHAT'S THE NAGI NO ENGI?
IT'S THE CEREMONY WHERE WE GATHER ALL BOOKS WITH MAGA SEALED IN THEM AND BURN THEM! WE HAD ONE LAST YEAR.
whisper
whisper
I DIDN'T HEAR ABOUT IT LAST YEAR.
whisp
EVEN IF YOU DIDN'T, YOU'RE A RAGUN-- YOU'RE SUPPOSED TO KNOW.
IT'S COMMON SENSE, MORON.
whisper
ぴたっ。
AHEM!
AND HOW MANY BOOKS DID YOU DISPOSE OF THIS YEAR?
SIR!

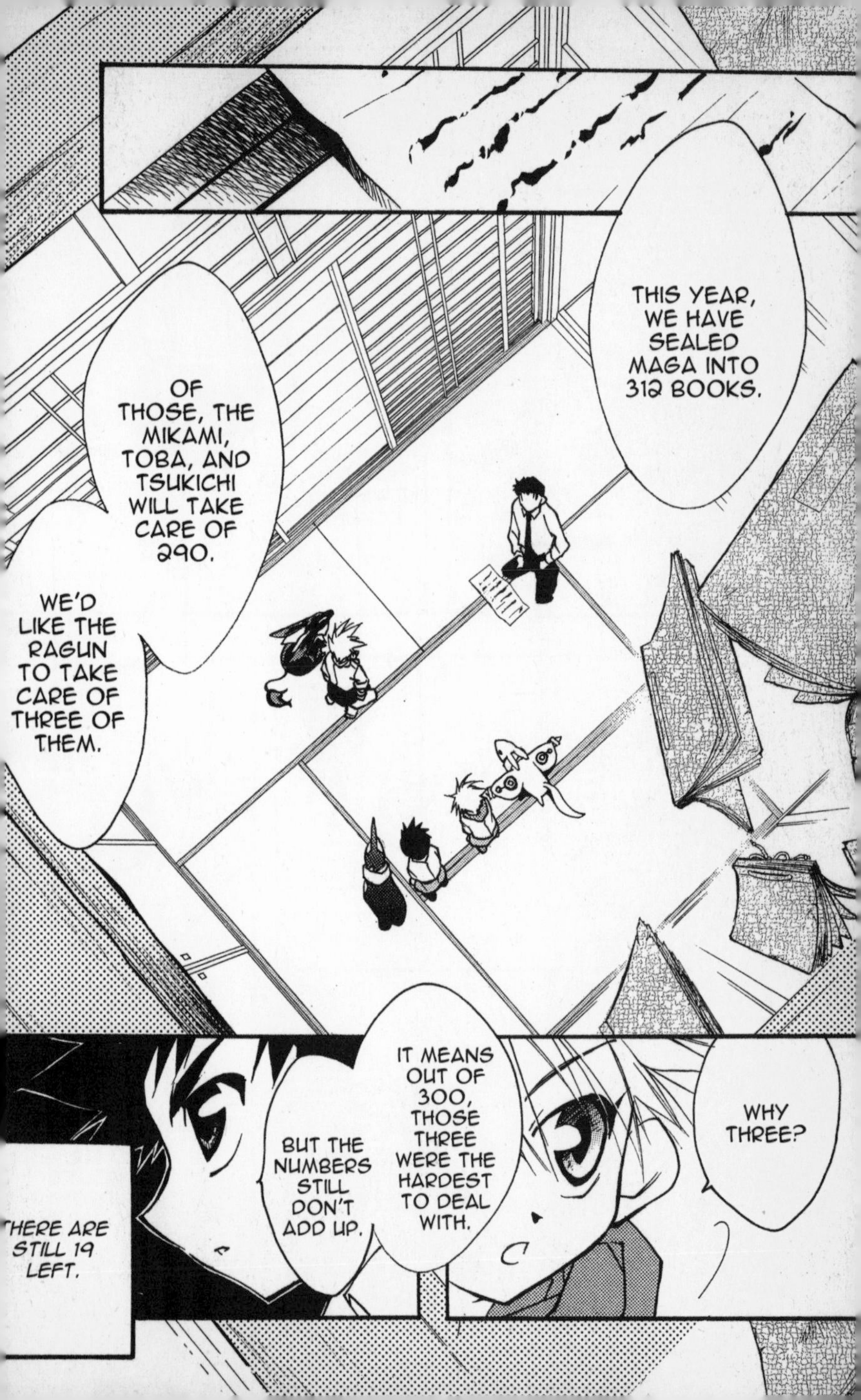
THIS YEAR, WE HAVE SEALED MAGA INTO 312 BOOKS.
OF THOSE, THE MIKAMI, TOBA, AND TSUKICHI WILL TAKE CARE OF 290.
WE'D LIKE THE RAGUN TO TAKE CARE OF THREE OF THEM.
WHY THREE?
IT MEANS OUT OF 300, THOSE THREE WERE THE HARDEST TO DEAL WITH.
BUT THE NUMBERS STILL DON'T ADD UP.
THERE ARE STILL 19 LEFT.

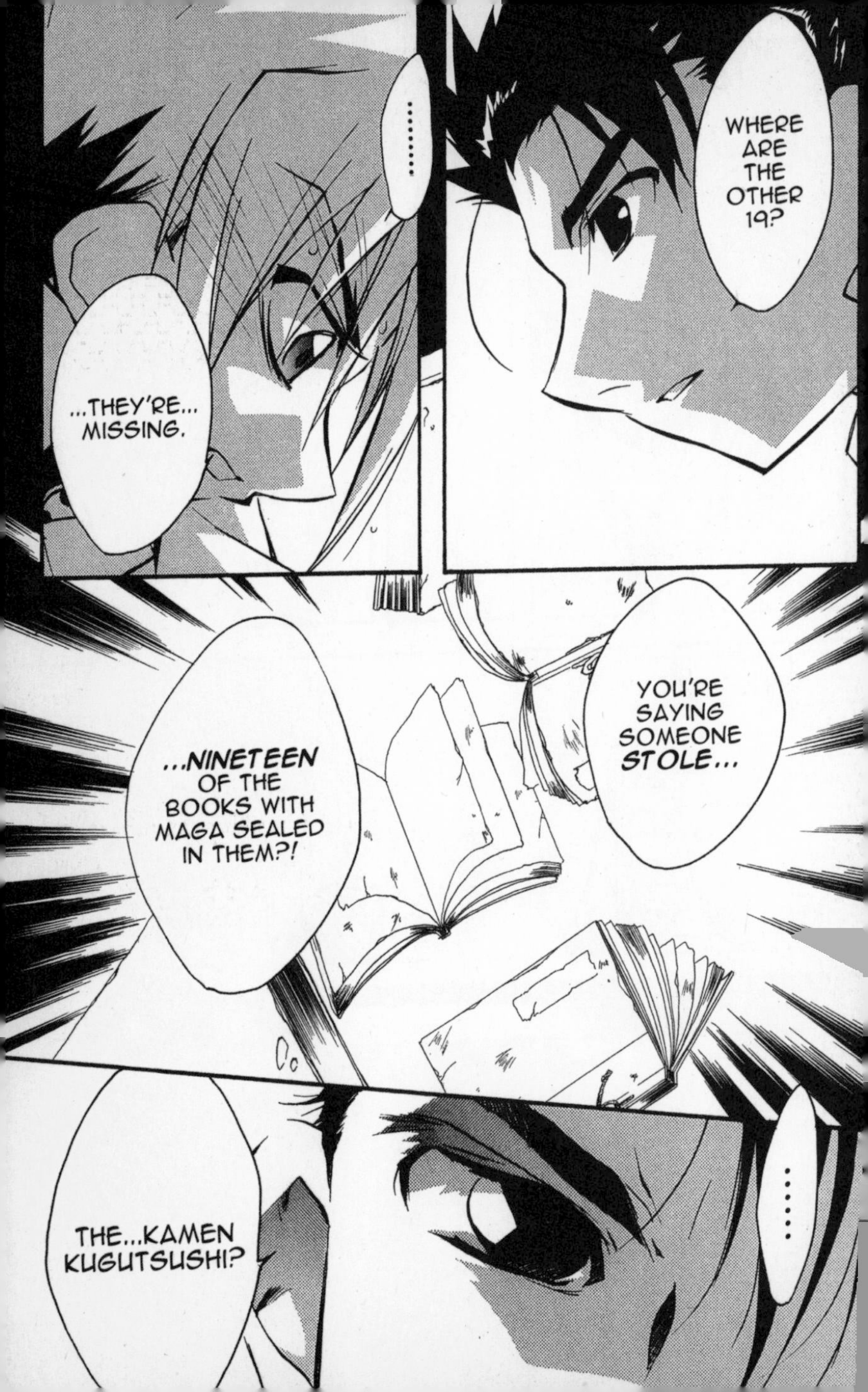
WHERE ARE THE OTHER 19?
......
...THEY'RE... MISSING.
YOU'RE SAYING SOMEONE STOLE...
...NINETEEN OF THE BOOKS WITH MAGA SEALED IN THEM?!
......
THE...KAMEN KUGUTSUSHI?

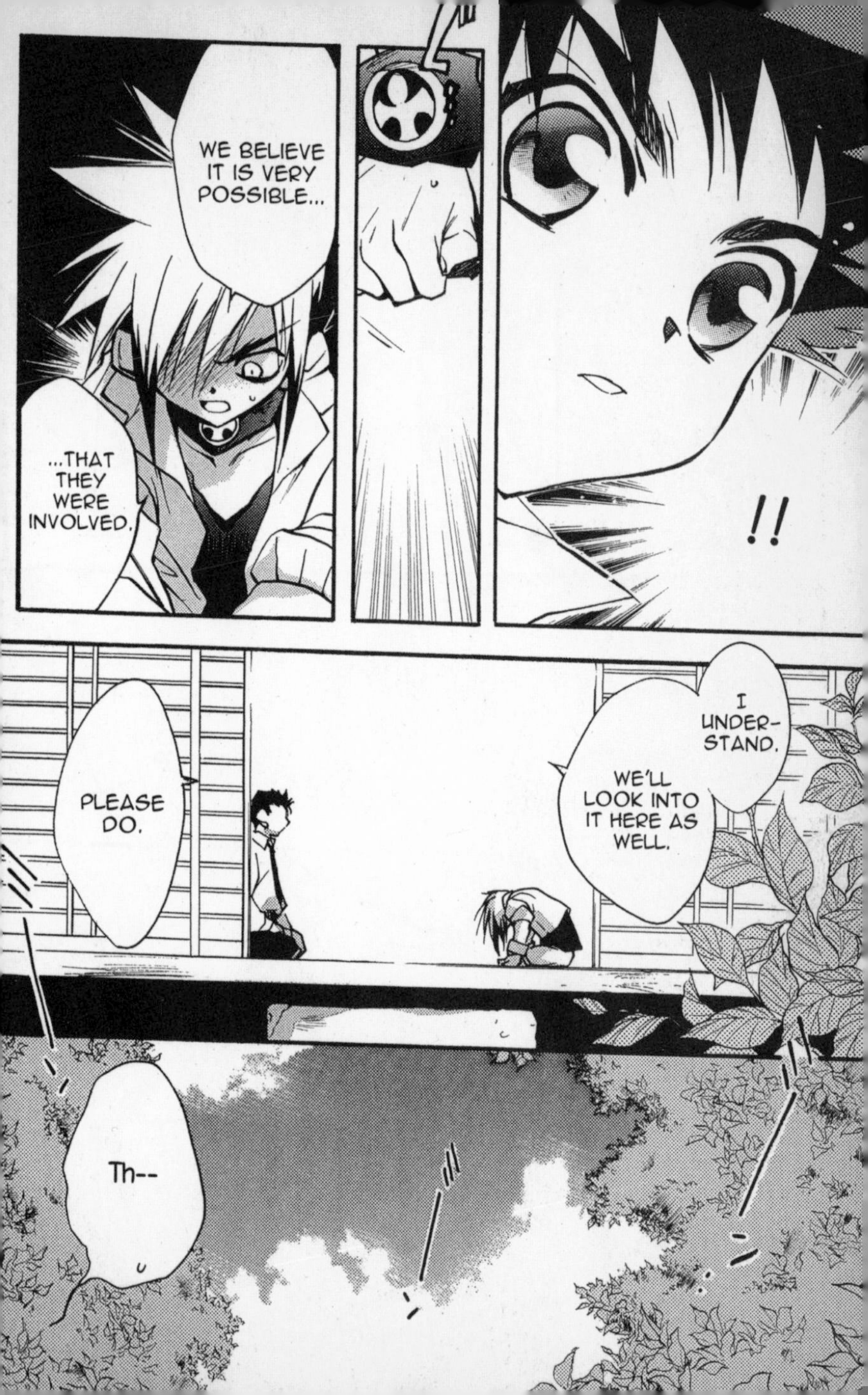
!!
WE BELIEVE IT IS VERY POSSIBLE...
...THAT THEY WERE INVOLVED.
I UNDER-STAND.
WE'LL LOOK INTO IT HERE AS WELL.
PLEASE DO.
Th--

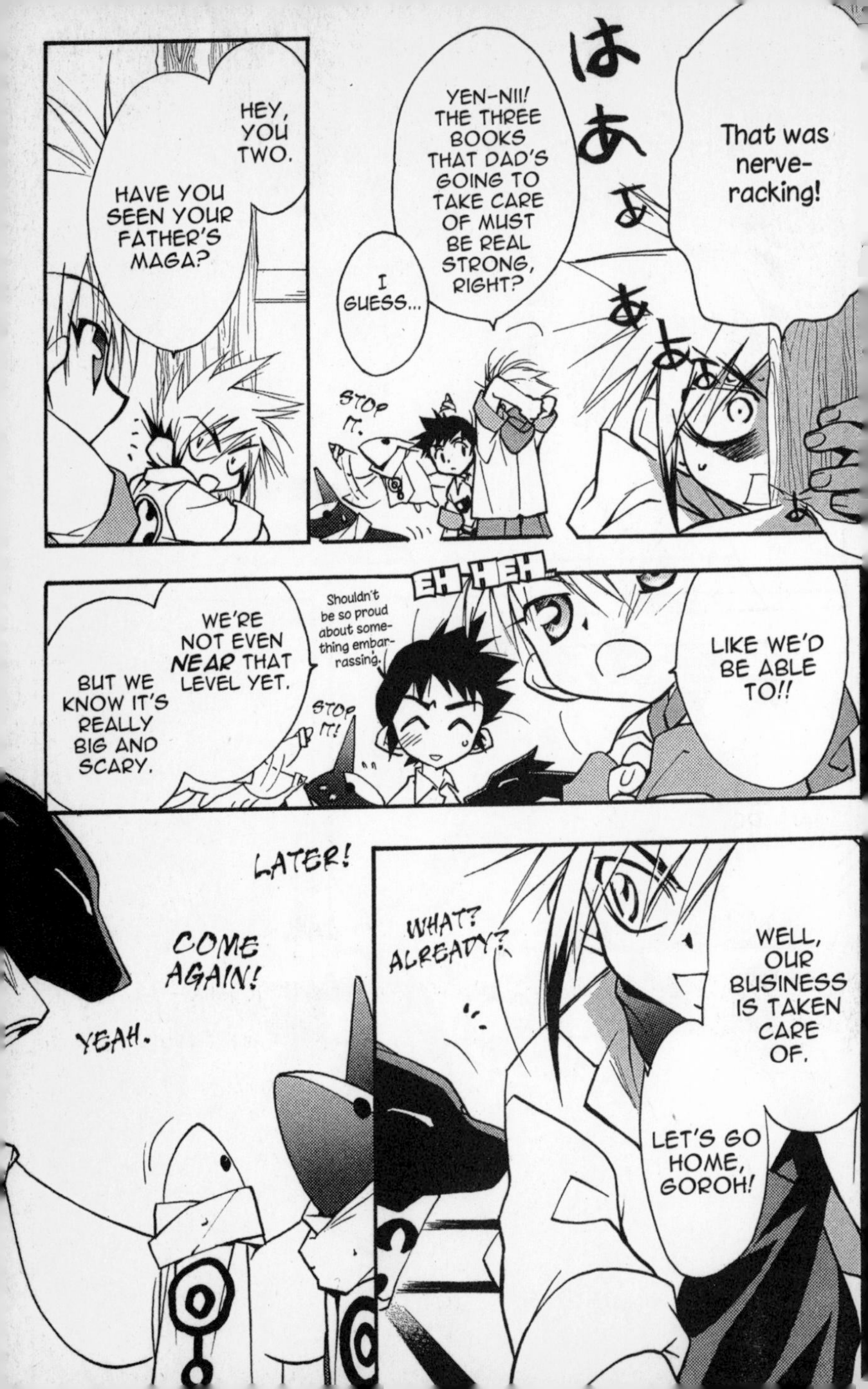
That was nerve-racking!
はあぁあぁぁぁ
YEN-NII! THE THREE BOOKS THAT DAD'S GOING TO TAKE CARE OF MUST BE REAL STRONG, RIGHT?
I GUESS...
STOP IT.
HEY, YOU TWO.
HAVE YOU SEEN YOUR FATHER'S MAGA?
EH HEH.
LIKE WE'D BE ABLE TO!!
Shouldn't be so proud about something embarrassing.
STOP IT!
WE'RE NOT EVEN *NEAR* THAT LEVEL YET.
BUT WE KNOW IT'S REALLY BIG AND SCARY.
WELL, OUR BUSINESS IS TAKEN CARE OF.
LET'S GO HOME, GOROH!
WHAT? ALREADY?
LATER!
COME AGAIN!
YEAH.

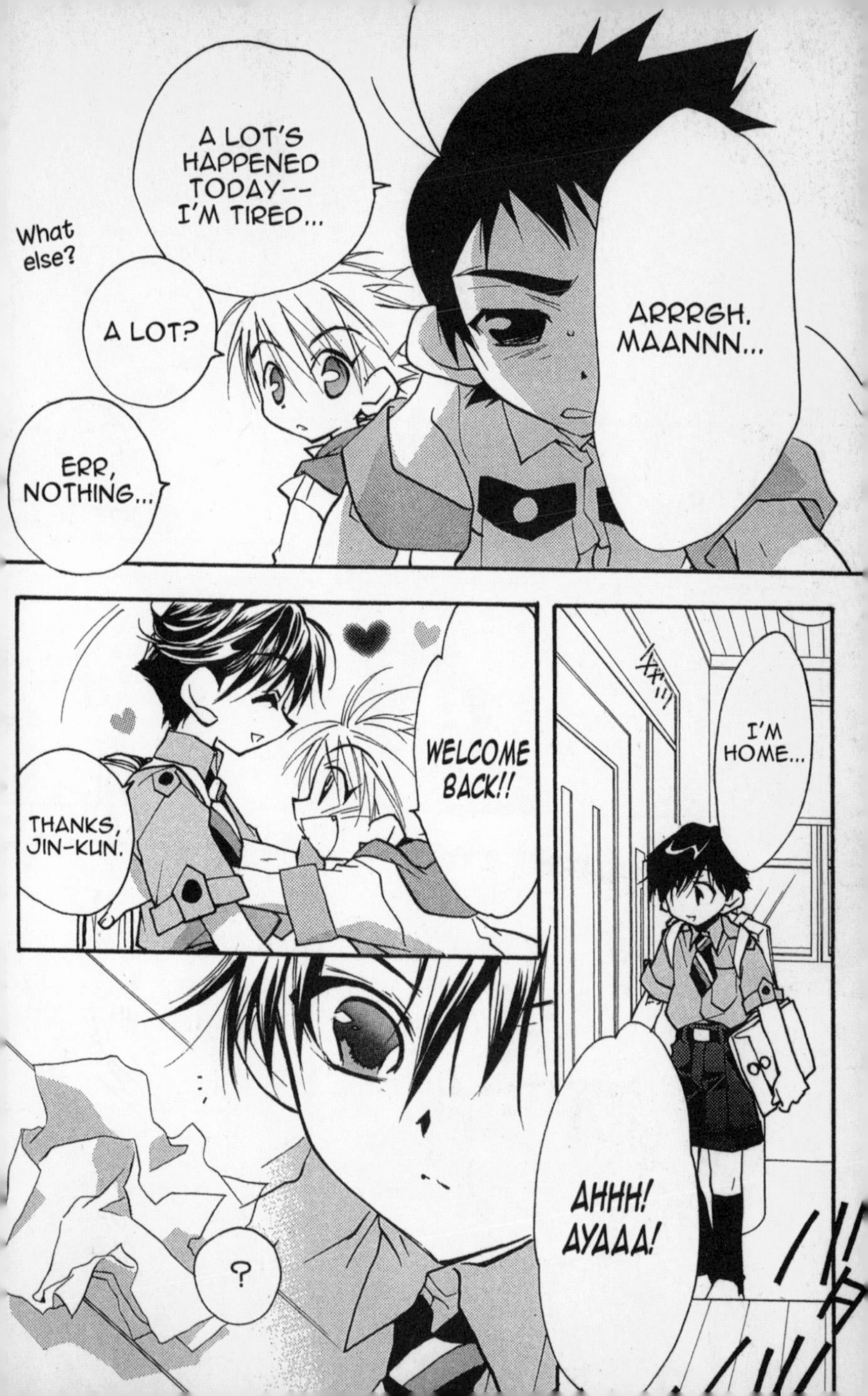
ARRRGH. MAANNN...
A LOT'S HAPPENED TODAY-- I'M TIRED...
A LOT?
What else?
ERR, NOTHING...
I'M HOME...
AHHH! AYAAA!
WELCOME BACK!!
THANKS, JIN-KUN.
?

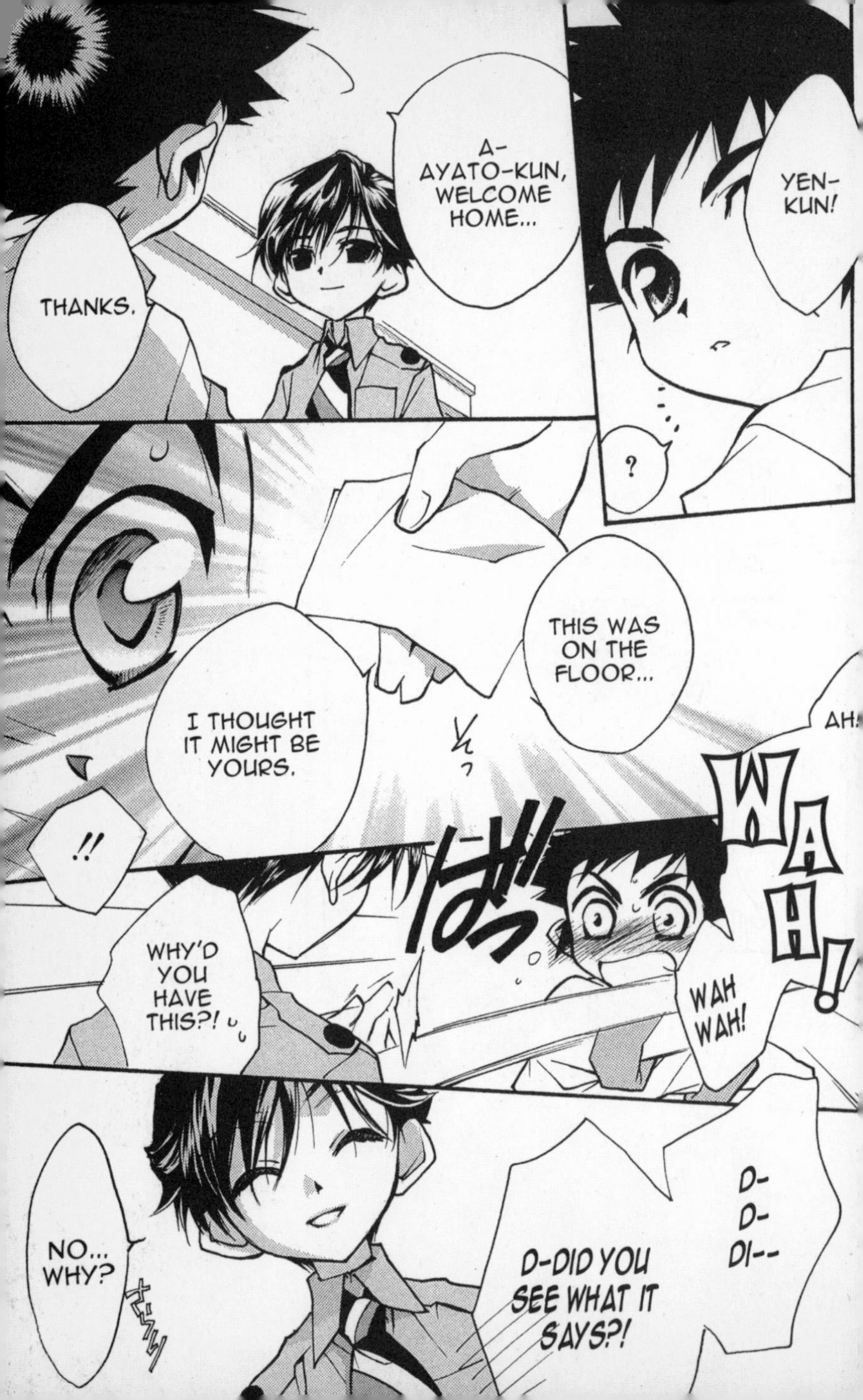

YEN-KUN!
?
A- AYATO-KUN, WELCOME HOME...
THANKS.
THIS WAS ON THE FLOOR...
I THOUGHT IT MIGHT BE YOURS.
!!
AH!
WAH!
ぱっ
WAH WAH!
WHY'D YOU HAVE THIS?!
D- D- DI--
D-DID YOU SEE WHAT IT SAYS?!
NO... WHY?

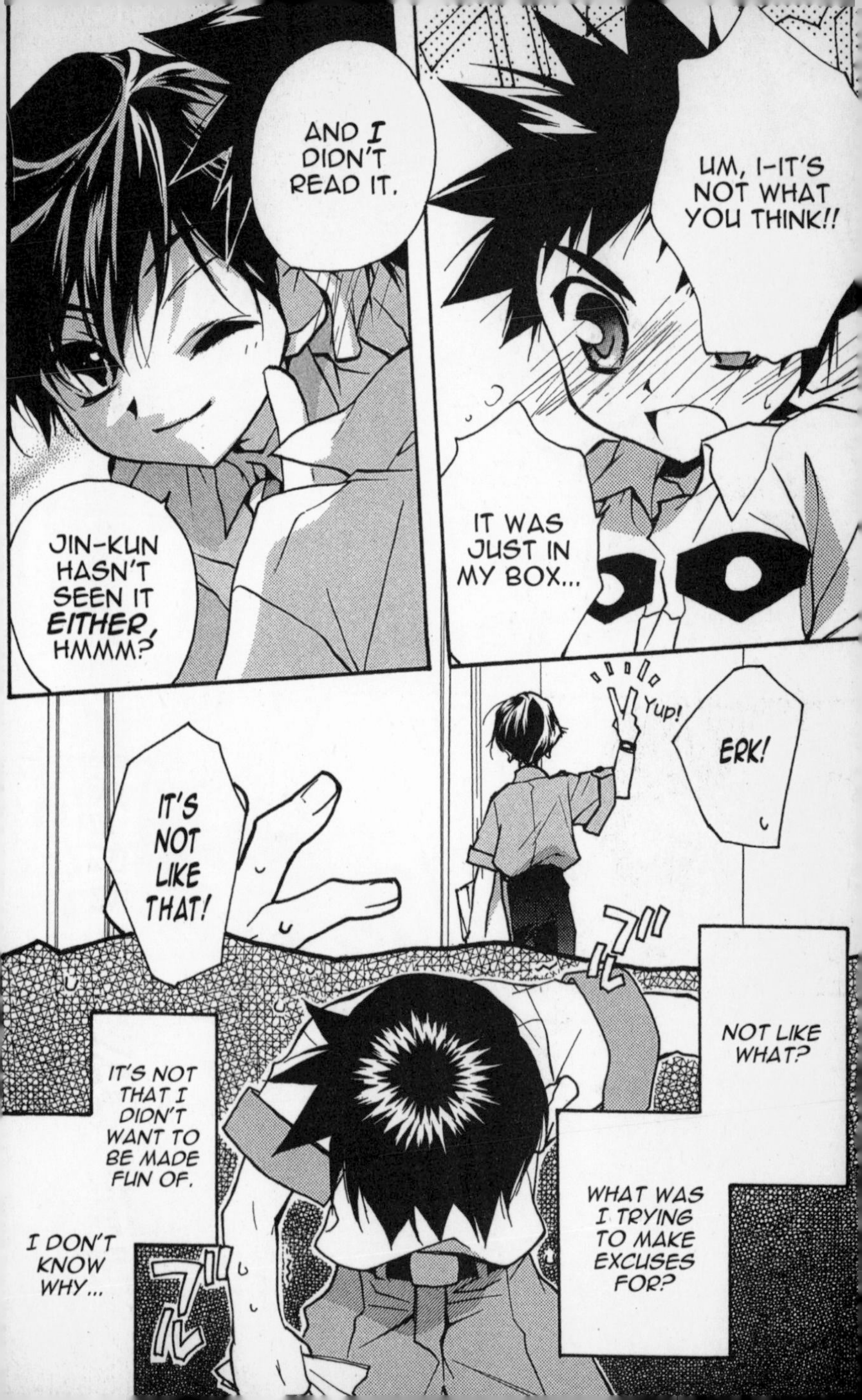
UM, I-IT'S NOT WHAT YOU THINK!!
IT WAS JUST IN MY BOX...
AND I DIDN'T READ IT.
JIN-KUN HASN'T SEEN IT EITHER, HMMM?
Yup!
ERK!
IT'S NOT LIKE THAT!
NOT LIKE WHAT?
WHAT WAS I TRYING TO MAKE EXCUSES FOR?
IT'S NOT THAT I DIDN'T WANT TO BE MADE FUN OF.
I DON'T KNOW WHY...

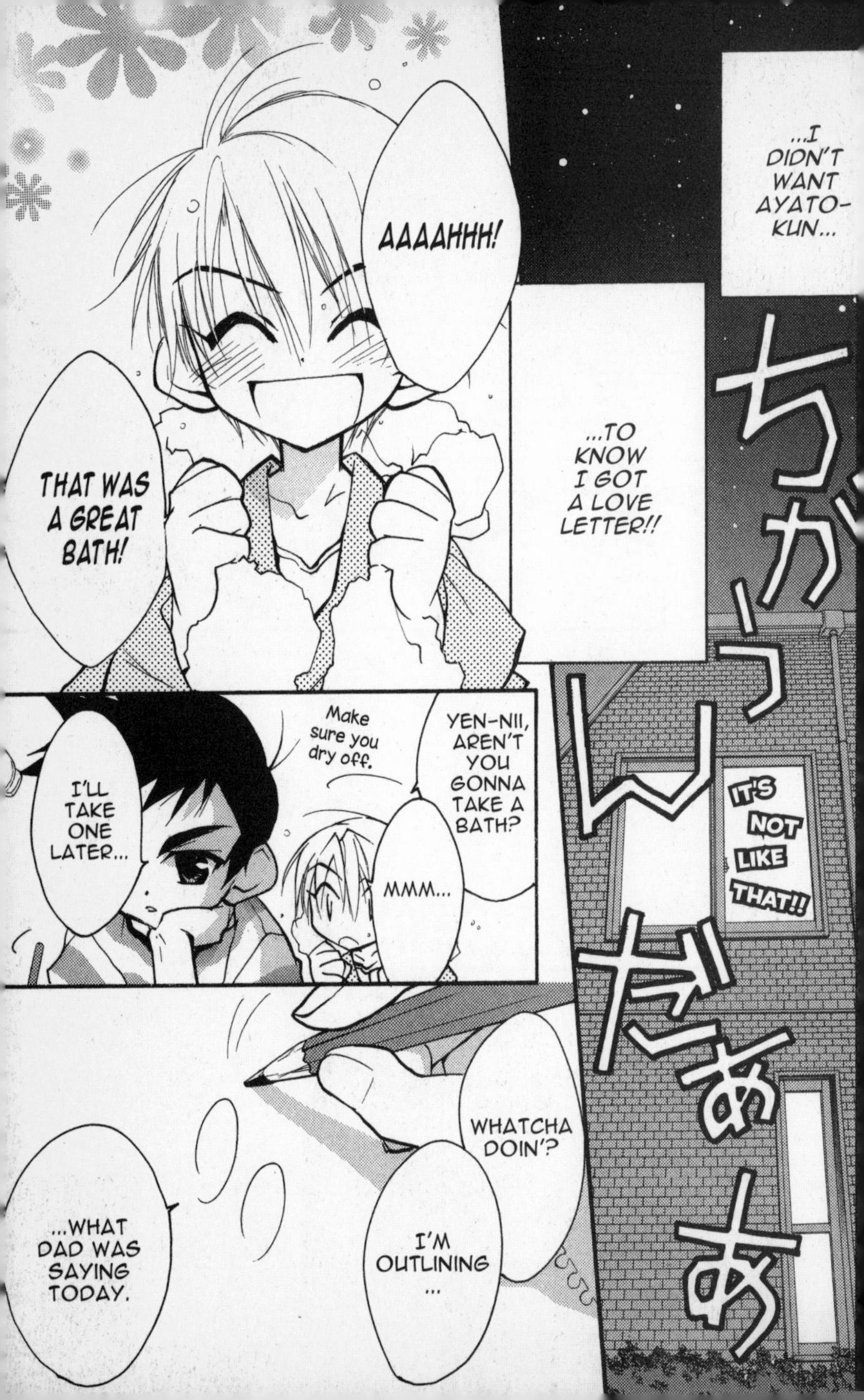
...I DIDN'T WANT AYATO-KUN...
ちがうんだぁあ
IT'S NOT LIKE THAT!!
...TO KNOW I GOT A LOVE LETTER!!
AAAAHHH!
THAT WAS A GREAT BATH!
YEN-NII, AREN'T YOU GONNA TAKE A BATH?
Make sure you dry off.
MMM...
I'LL TAKE ONE LATER...
WHATCHA DOIN'?
I'M OUTLINING...
...WHAT DAD WAS SAYING TODAY.

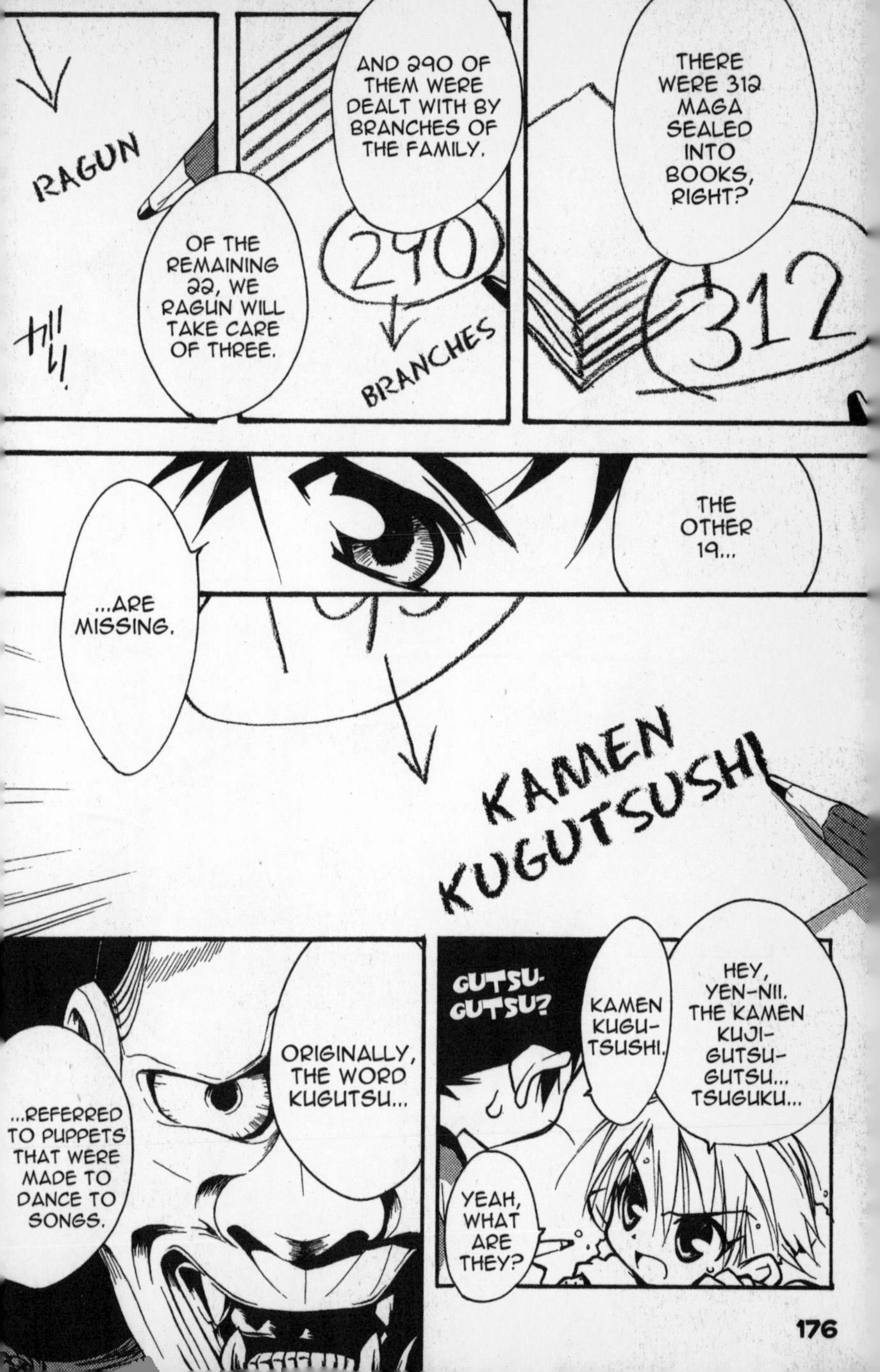
THERE WERE 312 MAGA SEALED INTO BOOKS, RIGHT?
312
AND 290 OF THEM WERE DEALT WITH BY BRANCHES OF THE FAMILY.
290
BRANCHES
RAGUN
OF THE REMAINING 22, WE RAGUN WILL TAKE CARE OF THREE.
THE OTHER 19...
...ARE MISSING.
KAMEN KUGUTSUSHI
HEY, YEN-NII. THE KAMEN KUJI-GUTSU-GUTSU... TSUGUKU...
KAMEN KUGU-TSUSHI.
GUTSU-GUTSU?
YEAH, WHAT ARE THEY?
ORIGINALLY, THE WORD KUGUTSU...
...REFERRED TO PUPPETS THAT WERE MADE TO DANCE TO SONGS.

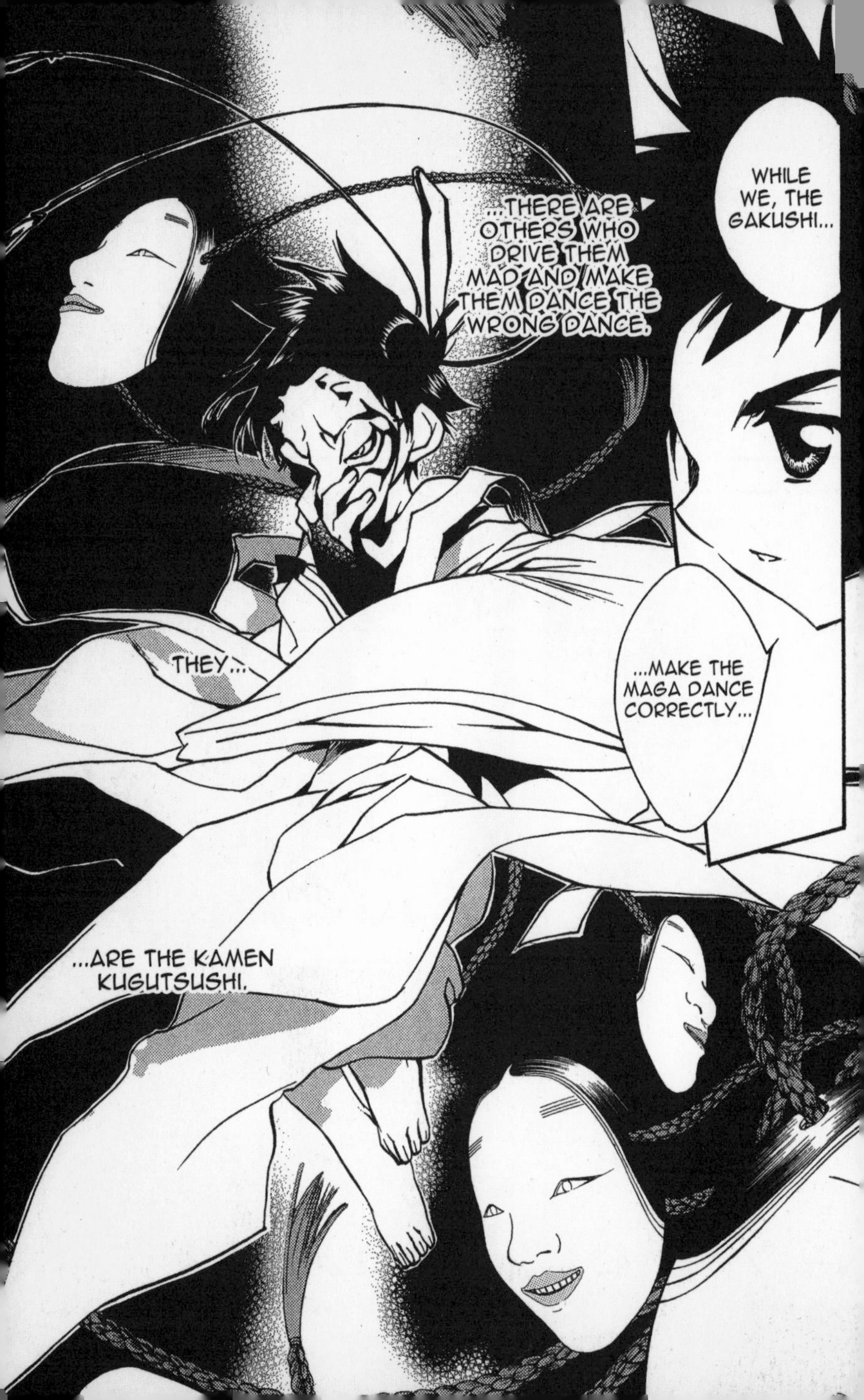
WHILE WE, THE GAKUSHI...
...MAKE THE MAGA DANCE CORRECTLY...
...THERE ARE OTHERS WHO DRIVE THEM MAD AND MAKE THEM DANCE THE WRONG DANCE.
THEY...
...ARE THE KAMEN KUGUTSUSHI.

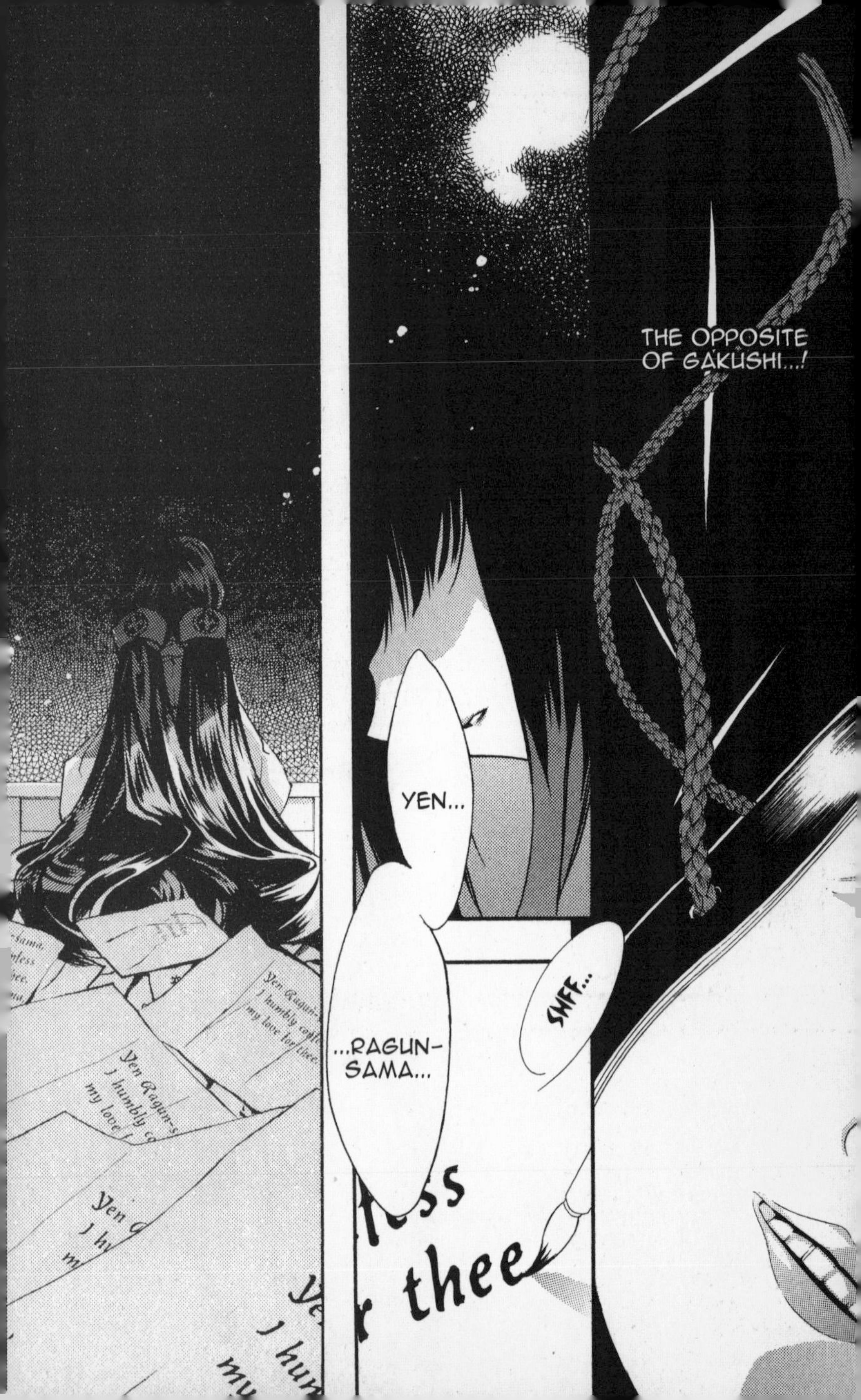
THE OPPOSITE OF GAKUSHI...!
SHFF...
YEN...
...RAGUN-SAMA...

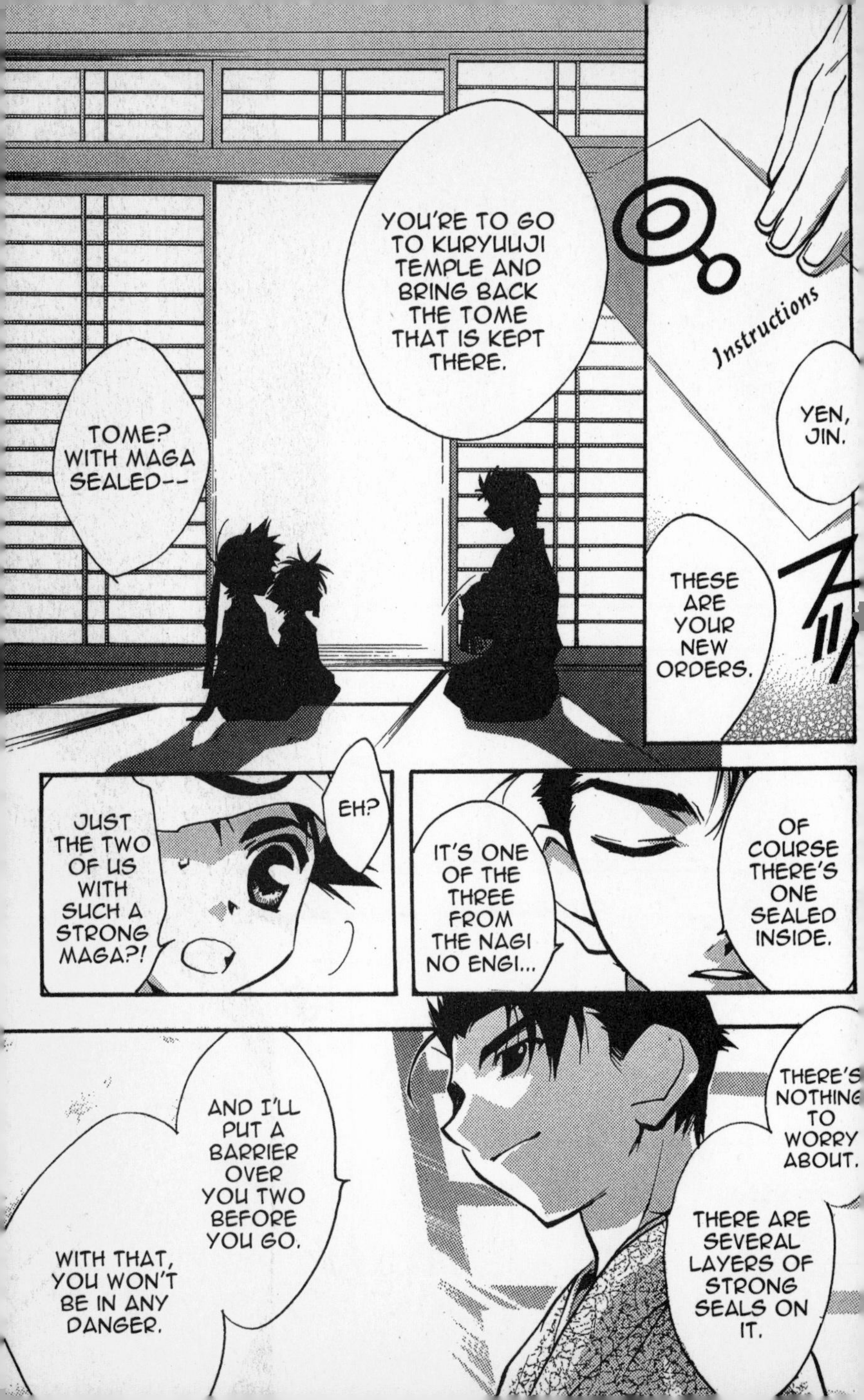
Instructions
YEN, JIN.
THESE ARE YOUR NEW ORDERS.
YOU'RE TO GO TO KURYUUJI TEMPLE AND BRING BACK THE TOME THAT IS KEPT THERE.
TOME? WITH MAGA SEALED--
OF COURSE THERE'S ONE SEALED INSIDE.
IT'S ONE OF THE THREE FROM THE NAGI NO ENGI...
EH?
JUST THE TWO OF US WITH SUCH A STRONG MAGA?!
THERE'S NOTHING TO WORRY ABOUT.
THERE ARE SEVERAL LAYERS OF STRONG SEALS ON IT.
AND I'LL PUT A BARRIER OVER YOU TWO BEFORE YOU GO.
WITH THAT, YOU WON'T BE IN ANY DANGER.

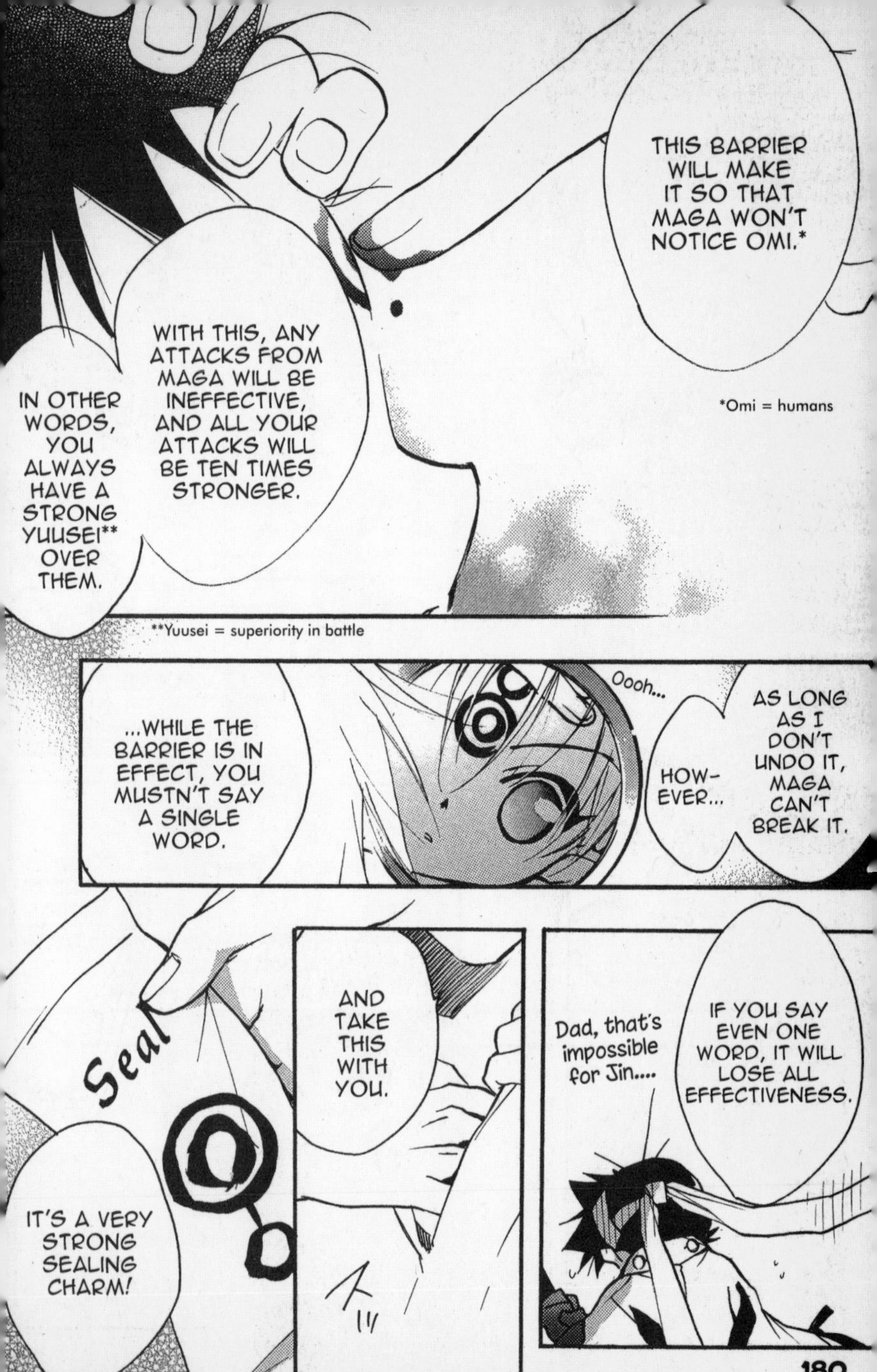
THIS BARRIER WILL MAKE IT SO THAT MAGA WON'T NOTICE OMI.*
WITH THIS, ANY ATTACKS FROM MAGA WILL BE INEFFECTIVE, AND ALL YOUR ATTACKS WILL BE TEN TIMES STRONGER.
IN OTHER WORDS, YOU ALWAYS HAVE A STRONG YUUSEI** OVER THEM.
*Omi = humans
**Yuusei = superiority in battle
AS LONG AS I DON'T UNDO IT, MAGA CAN'T BREAK IT.
Oooh...
HOW-EVER...
...WHILE THE BARRIER IS IN EFFECT, YOU MUSTN'T SAY A SINGLE WORD.
IF YOU SAY EVEN ONE WORD, IT WILL LOSE ALL EFFECTIVENESS.
Dad, that's impossible for Jin....
AND TAKE THIS WITH YOU.
Seal
IT'S A VERY STRONG SEALING CHARM!

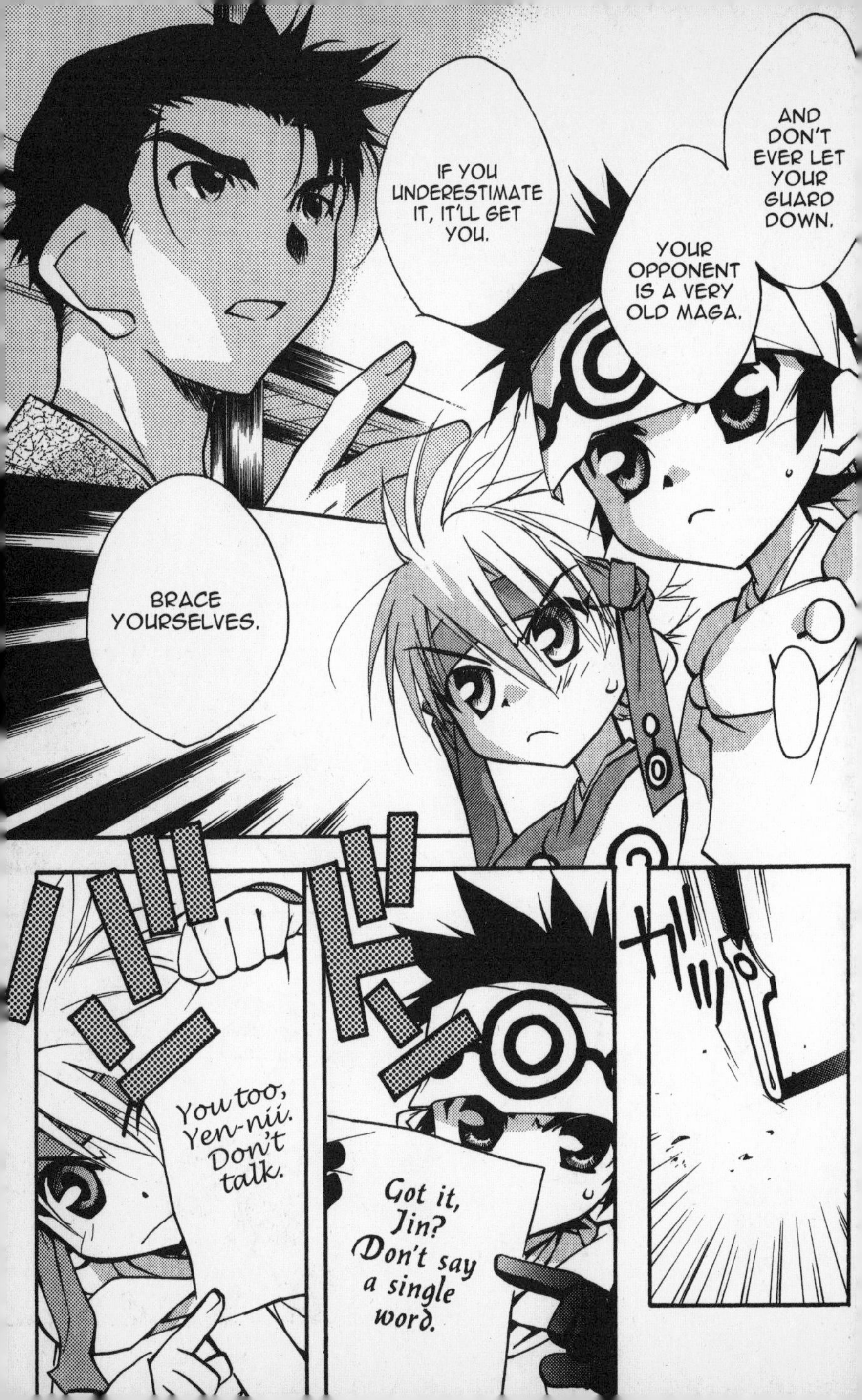
AND DON'T EVER LET YOUR GUARD DOWN.
YOUR OPPONENT IS A VERY OLD MAGA.
IF YOU UNDERESTIMATE IT, IT'LL GET YOU.
BRACE YOURSELVES.
Got it, Jin? Don't say a single word.
You too, Yen-nii. Don't talk.

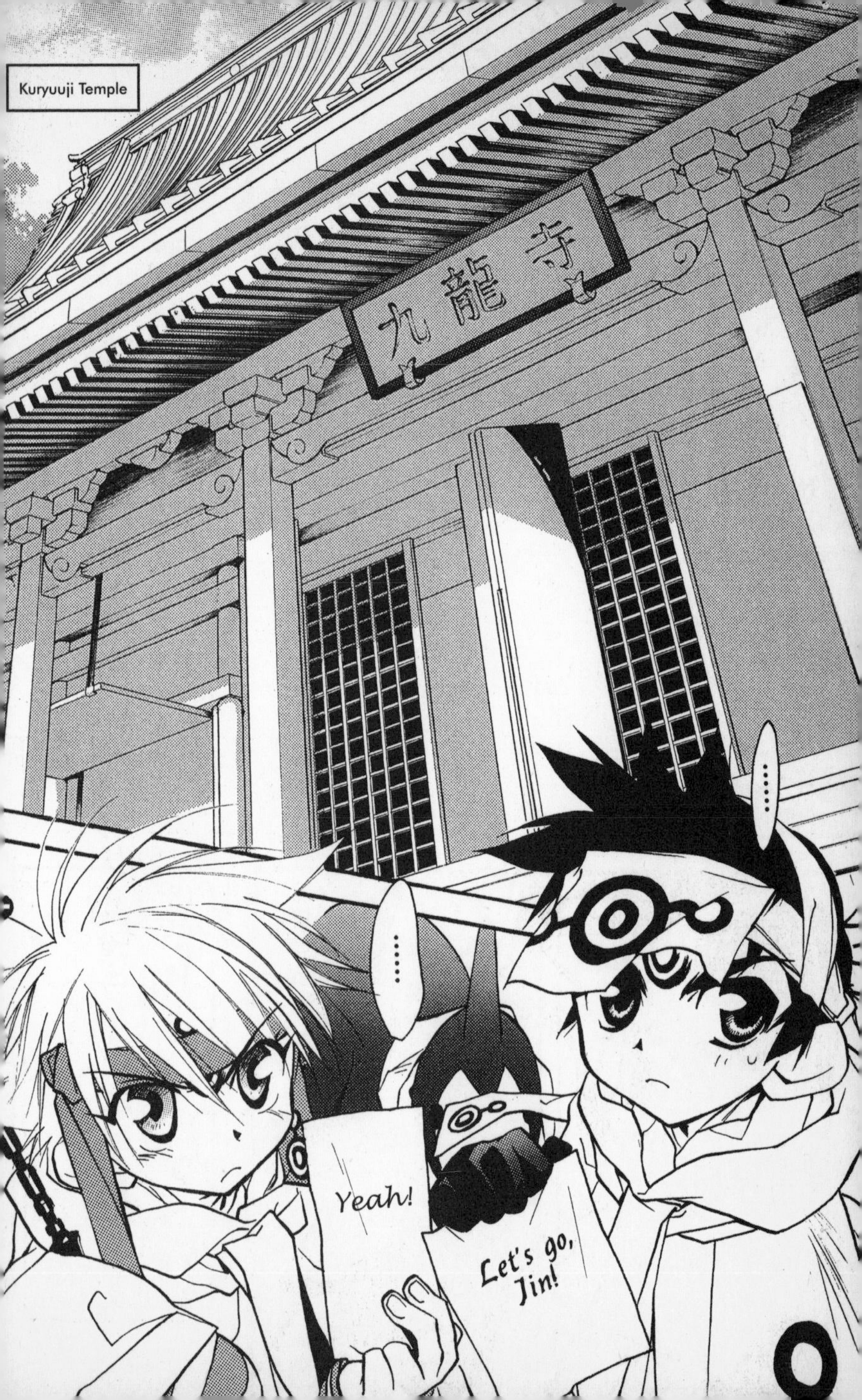
Kuryuuji Temple
九龍寺
......
......
Let's go, Jin!
Yeah!

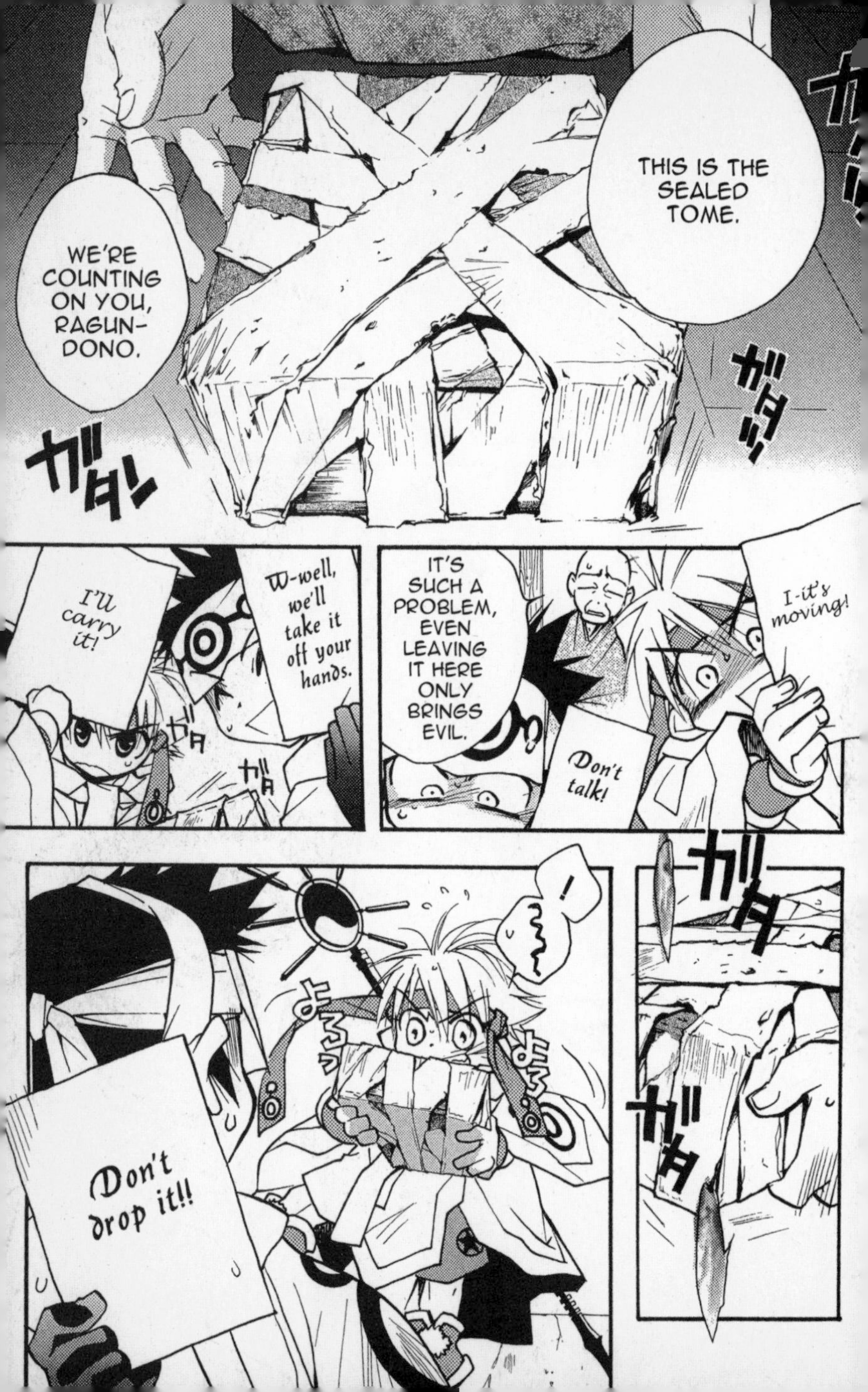
THIS IS THE SEALED TOME.
ガタッ
WE'RE COUNTING ON YOU, RAGUN-DONO.
ガタン
I-it's moving!
IT'S SUCH A PROBLEM, EVEN LEAVING IT HERE ONLY BRINGS EVIL.
Don't talk!
W-well, we'll take it off your hands.
I'll carry it!
ガタ
ガタ
ガタ
ガタ
!
よろっ
よろ
Don't drop it!!

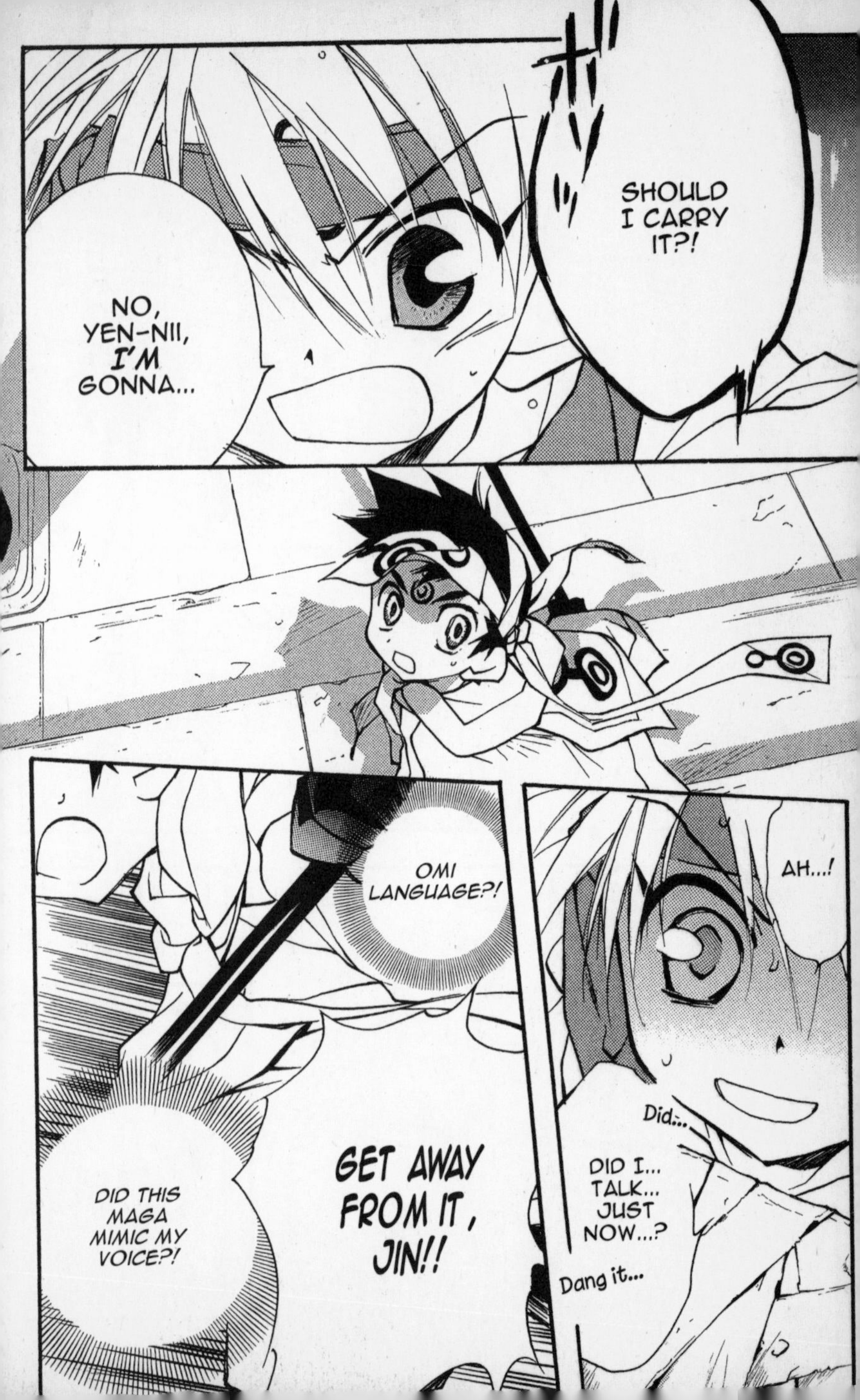
SHOULD I CARRY IT?!
NO, YEN-NII, I'M GONNA...
AH...!
Did...
DID I... TALK... JUST NOW...?
Dang it...
OMI LANGUAGE?!
GET AWAY FROM IT, JIN!!
DID THIS MAGA MIMIC MY VOICE?!

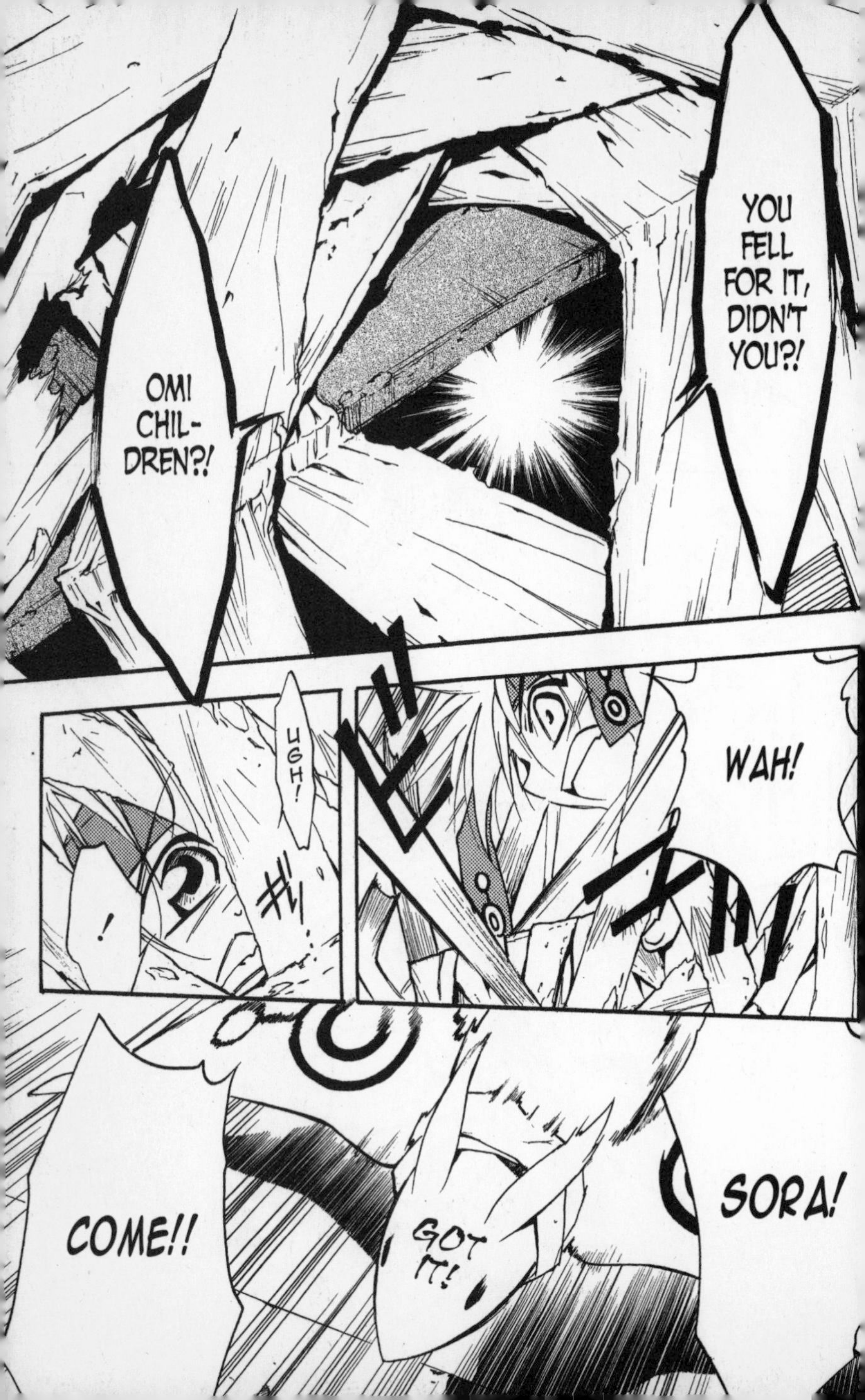
YOU FELL FOR IT, DIDN'T YOU?!
OMI CHILDREN?!
WAH!
UGH!
SORA!
GOT IT!
COME!!

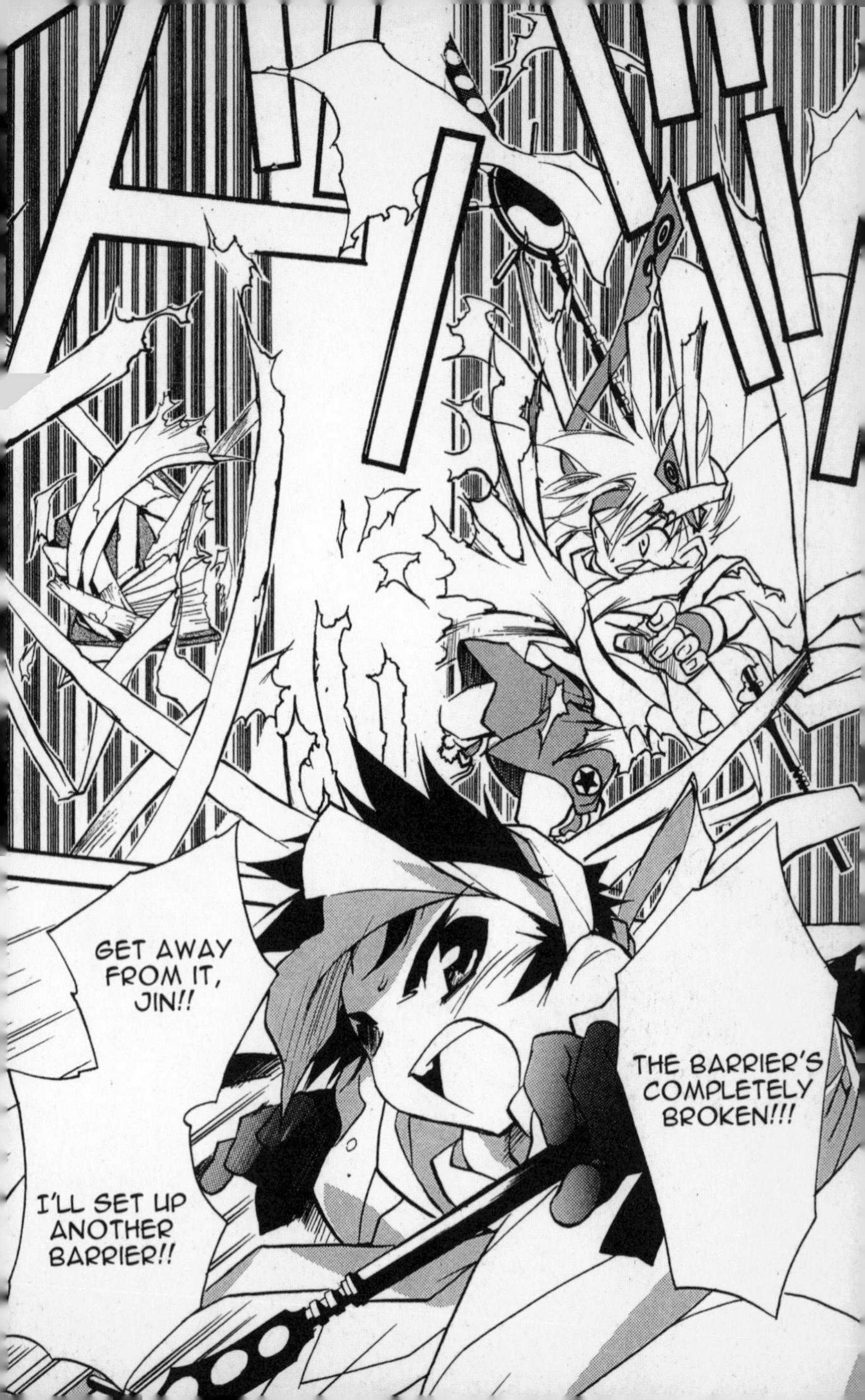
THE BARRIER'S COMPLETELY BROKEN!!!
GET AWAY FROM IT, JIN!!
I'LL SET UP ANOTHER BARRIER!!

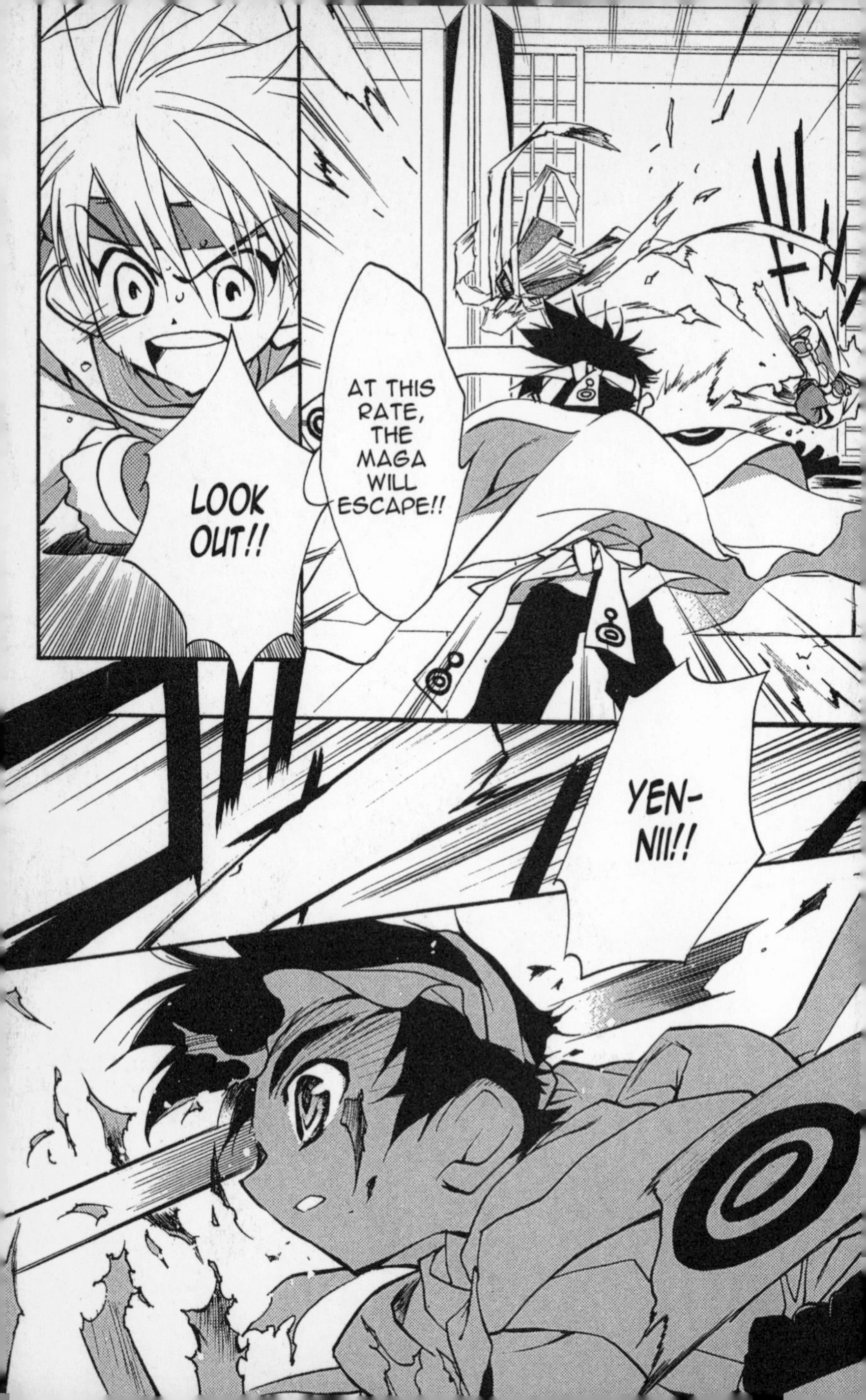
AT THIS RATE, THE MAGA WILL ESCAPE!!
LOOK OUT!!
YEN-NII!!

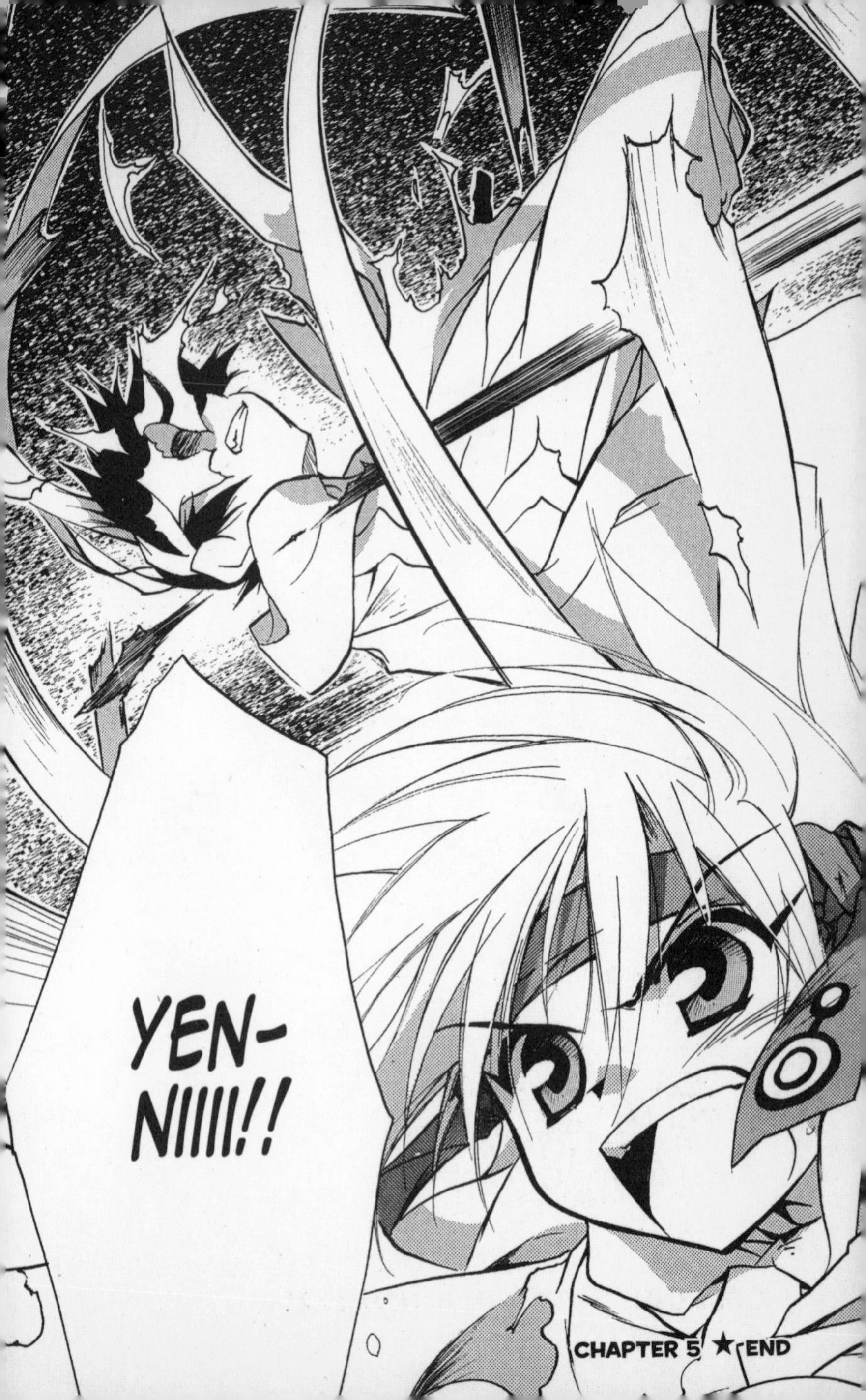
YEN-
NIIII!!
CHAPTER 5 ★ END

TO BE CONTINUED IN VOLUME 2!

LAGOON ENGINE
らぐ通
LAGOON ENGINE 2002 YUKIRU SUGISAKI ★ FANART COLLECTION

PRESENTING FANART FROM ALL THE READERS! ♥

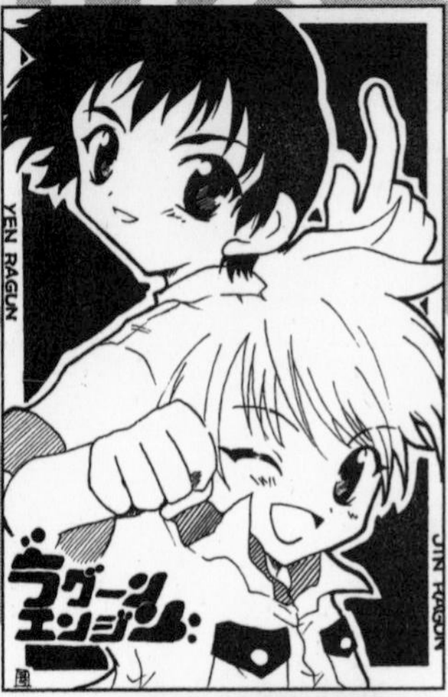
YEN RAGUN
JIN RAGUN
ラグーン
エンジン
AOMORI PREFECTURE, KOTONI-SAN

MIE PREFECTURE, RYUUKI-SAN
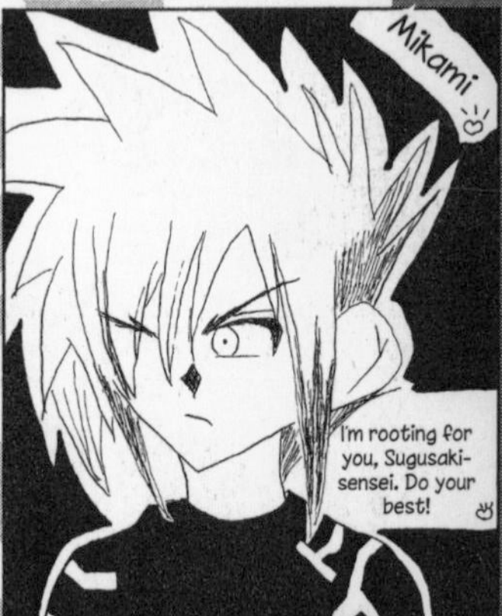
Mikami
I'm rooting for you, Sugusaki-sensei. Do your best!

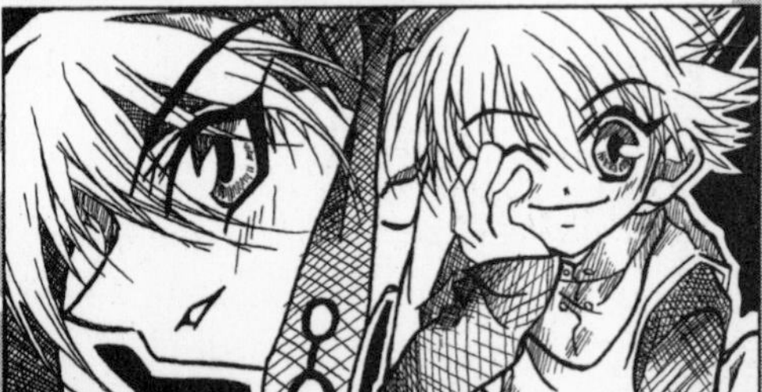
AICHI PREFECTURE, YUKARI-SAN

SHIZUOKA PREFECTURE, KRAD-SAN
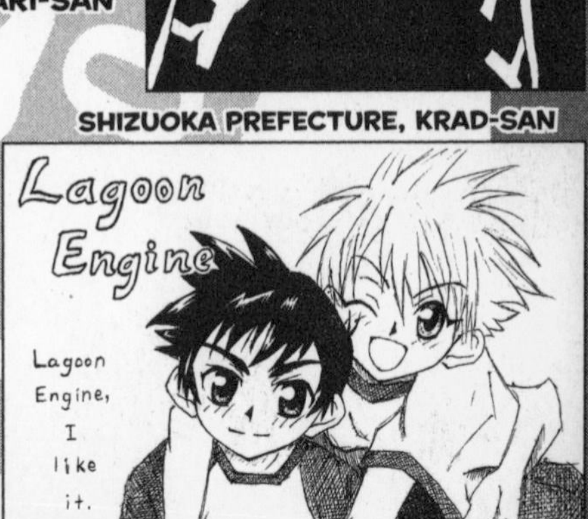
Lagoon Engine
Lagoon Engine, I like it.

OSAKA METROPOLITAN AREA, LION MODOKI-SAN
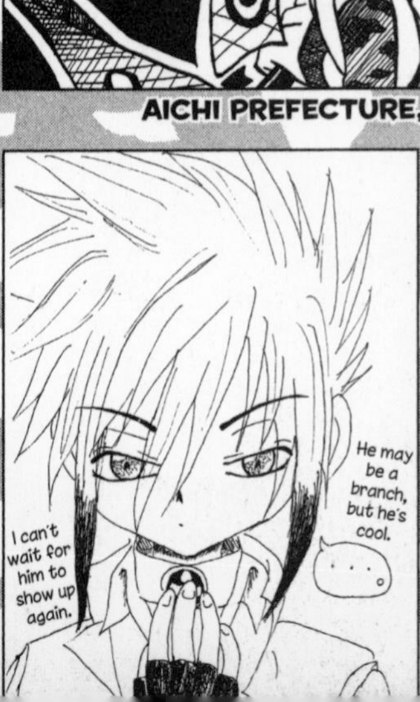
He may be a branch, but he's cool.
I can't wait for him to show up again.

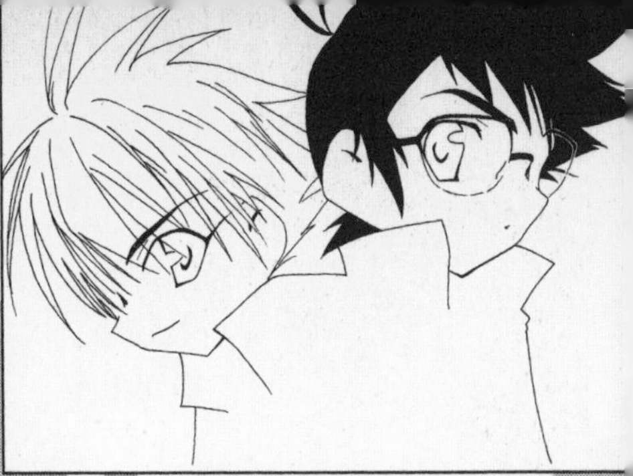

TOKYO CAPITAL, A.K.-SAN

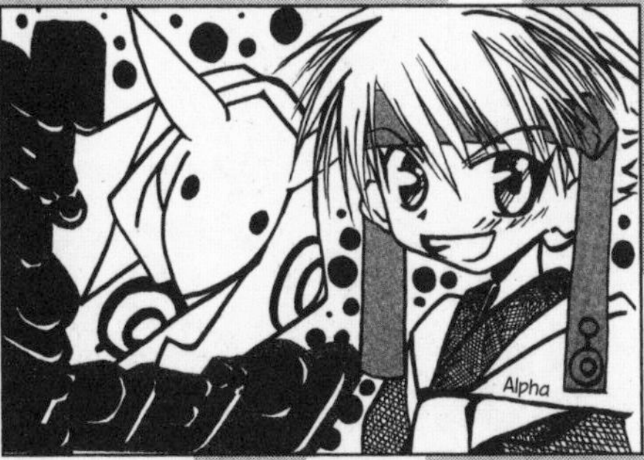
Alpha

IWATE PREFECTURE, ALPHA-SAN

KANAGAWA PREFECTURE, SHION-SAN

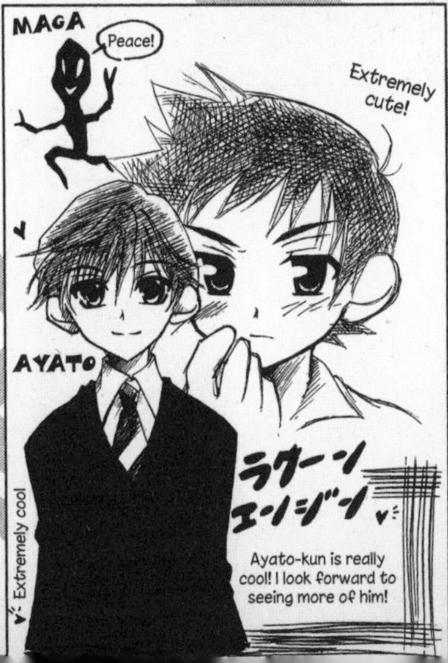
MAGA
Peace!
Extremely cute!
AYATO
ラグーンエンジン
Extremely cool
Ayato-kun is really cool! I look forward to seeing more of him!

SAITAMA PREFECTURE, HOKUTO-SAN

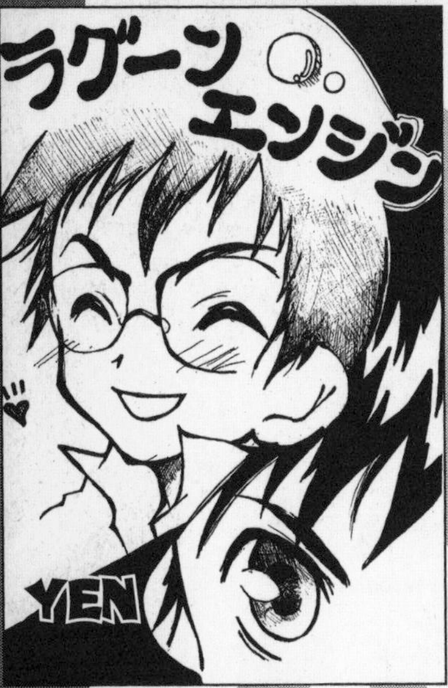
ラグーンエンジン
YEN

KAGOSHIMA PREFECTURE, HIROSHI-SAN

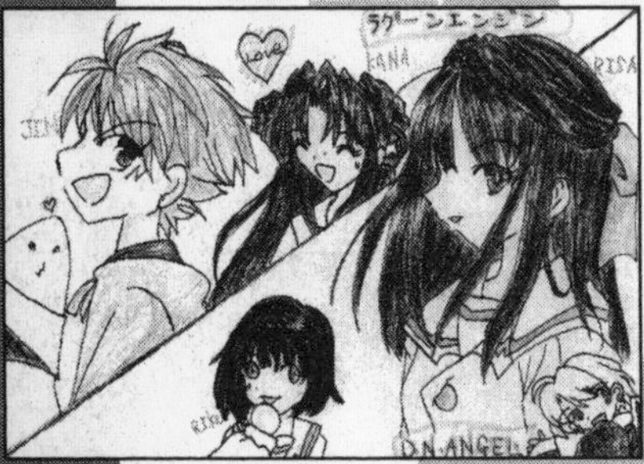
ラグーンエンジン
D.N.ANGEL

CHIBA PREFECTURE, KIRARA HATSUKI-SAN

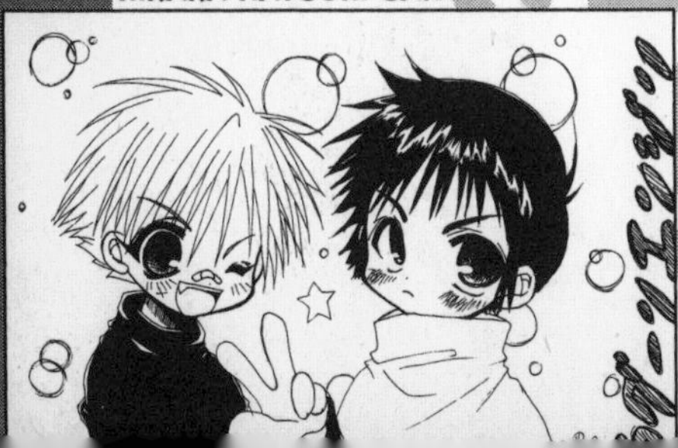

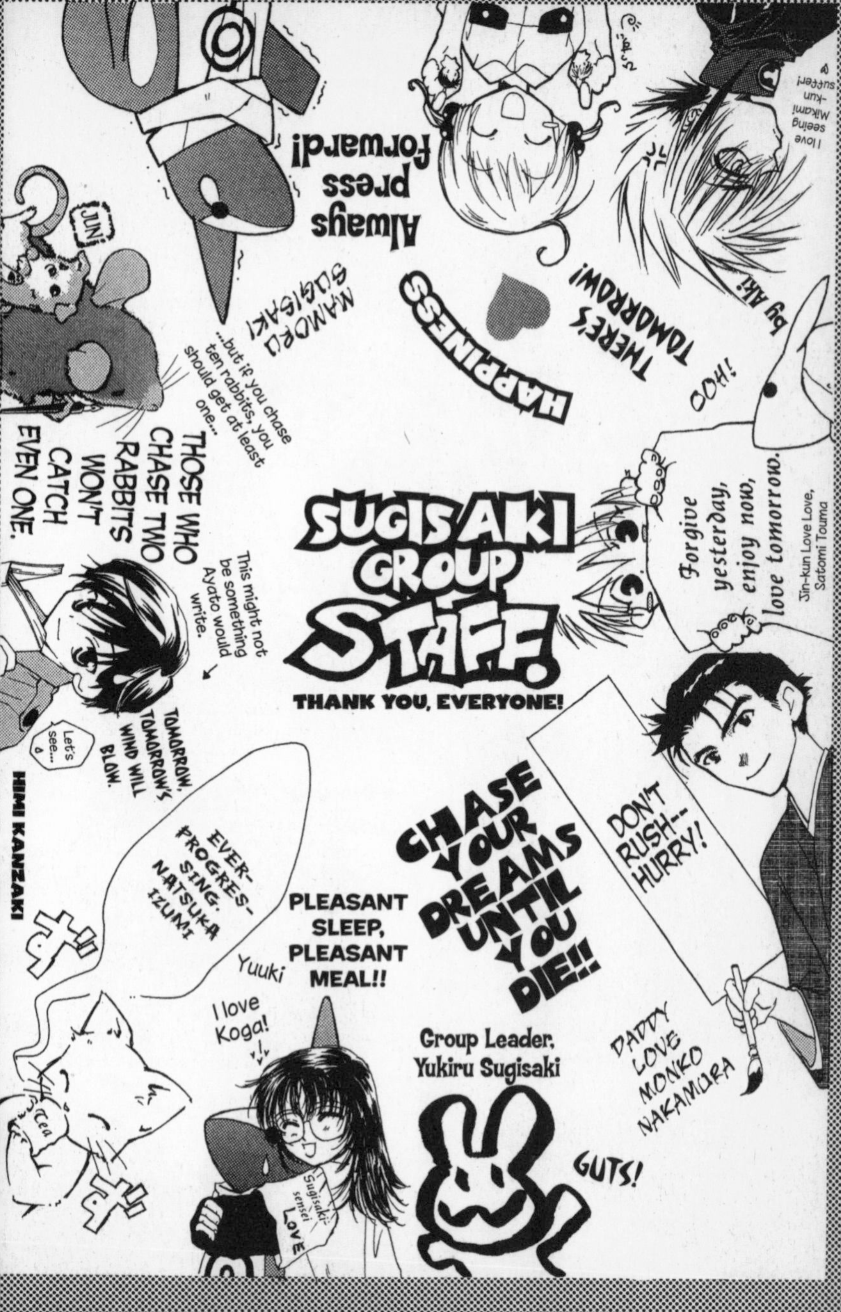
SUGISAKI GROUP STAFF!
THANK YOU, EVERYONE!
CHASE YOUR DREAMS UNTIL YOU DIE!!
DON'T RUSH--HURRY!
DADDY LOVE MONKO NAKAMURA
Group Leader, Yukiru Sugisaki
GUTS!
PLEASANT SLEEP, PLEASANT MEAL!!
Yuuki
I love Koga!
Sugisaki sensei LOVE
EVER-PROGRES-SING. NATSUKA IZUMI
HIMI KANZAKI
Let's see...
TOMORROW, TOMORROW'S WIND WILL BLOW.
This might not be something Ayato would write.
THOSE WHO CHASE TWO RABBITS WON'T CATCH EVEN ONE.
...but if you chase ten rabbits, you should get at least one...
MAMORU SUGISAKI
JUN
Always press forward!
HAPPINESS
THERE'S TOMORROW!
by Aki
I love seeing Mikami-kun suffer!
OOH!
Forgive yesterday, enjoy now, love tomorrow.
Jin-kun Love Love, Satomi Touma

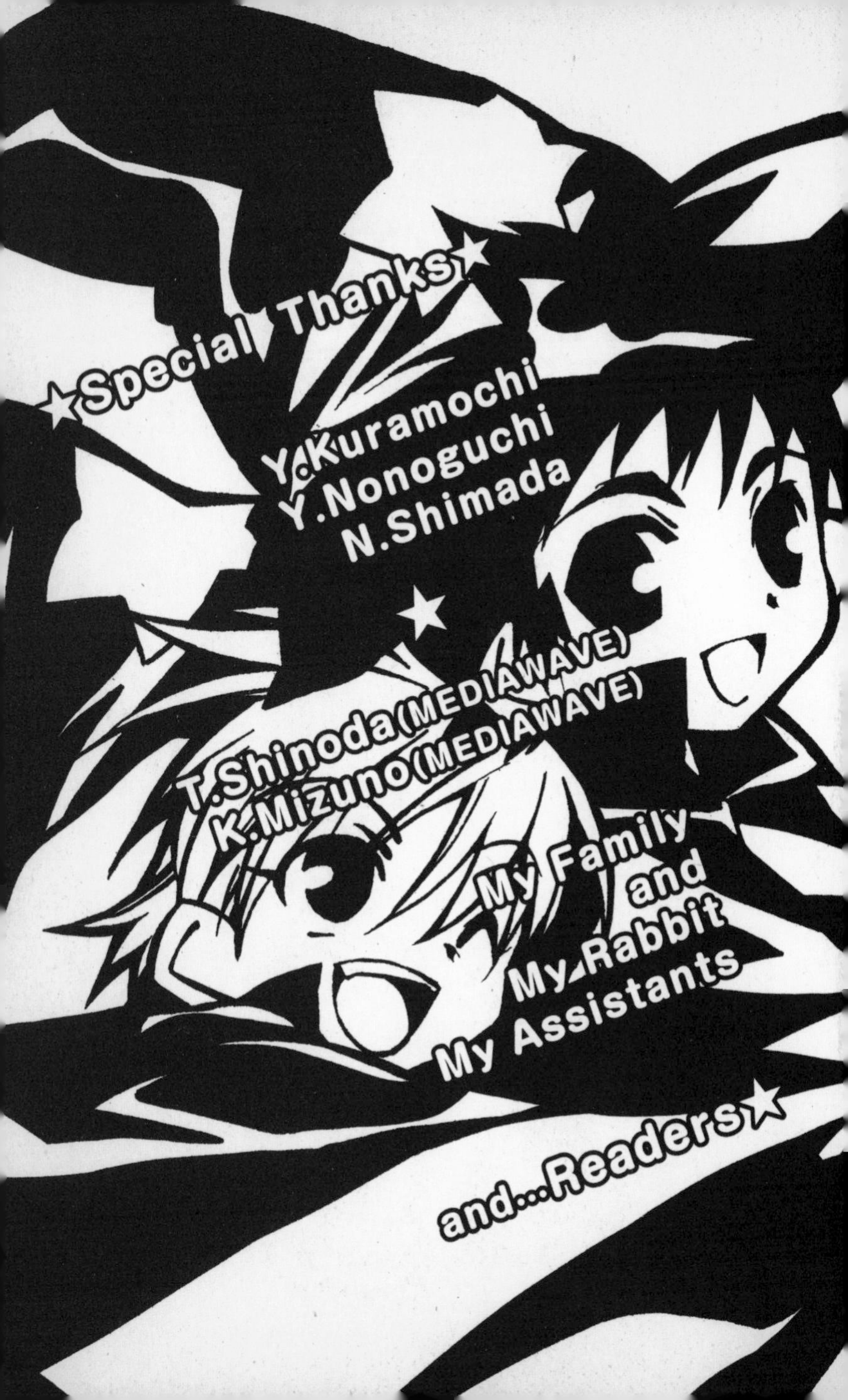
★Special Thanks★
Y.Kuramochi
Y.Nonoguchi
N.Shimada
★
T.Shinoda(MEDIAWAVE)
K.Mizuno(MEDIAWAVE)
My Family
and
My Rabbit
My Assistants
and...Readers★

IN THE NEXT VOLUME OF

ラグーンエンジン

LAGOON ENGINE

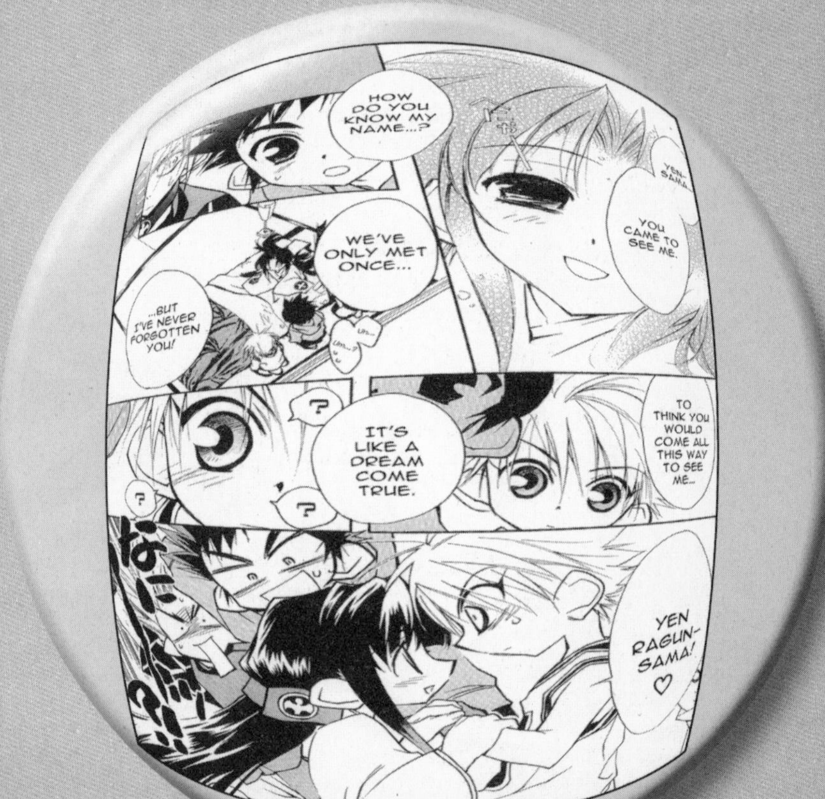
YEN-SAMA...
YOU CAME TO SEE ME.
HOW DO YOU KNOW MY NAME...?
WE'VE ONLY MET ONCE...
...BUT I'VE NEVER FORGOTTEN YOU!
TO THINK YOU WOULD COME ALL THIS WAY TO SEE ME...
IT'S LIKE A DREAM COME TRUE.
?
?
?
YEN RAGUN-SAMA! ♡

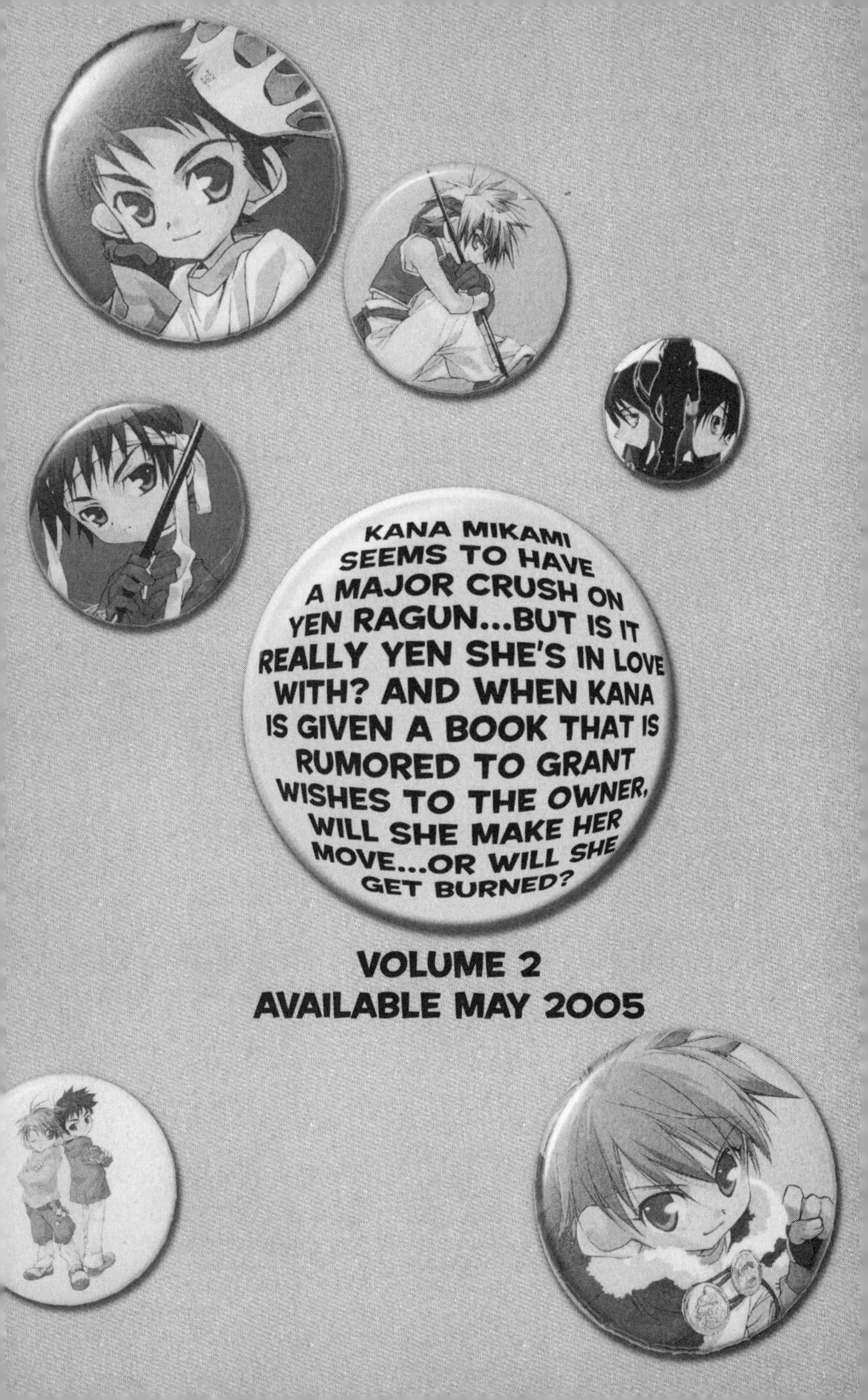
KANA MIKAMI SEEMS TO HAVE A MAJOR CRUSH ON YEN RAGUN...BUT IS IT REALLY YEN SHE'S IN LOVE WITH? AND WHEN KANA IS GIVEN A BOOK THAT IS RUMORED TO GRANT WISHES TO THE OWNER, WILL SHE MAKE HER MOVE...OR WILL SHE GET BURNED?
VOLUME 2
AVAILABLE MAY 2005

ALSO AVAILABLE FROM ☺TOKYOPOP®

PLANETES
PRESIDENT DAD
PRIEST
PRINCESS AI
PSYCHIC ACADEMY
QUEEN'S KNIGHT, THE
RAGNAROK
RAVE MASTER
REALITY CHECK
REBIRTH
REBOUND
REMOTE
RISING STARS OF MANGA
SABER MARIONETTE J
SAILOR MOON
SAINT TAIL
SAIYUKI
SAMURAI DEEPER KYO
SAMURAI GIRL REAL BOUT HIGH SCHOOL
SCRYED
SEIKAI TRILOGY, THE
SGT. FROG
SHAOLIN SISTERS
SHIRAHIME-SYO: SNOW GODDESS TALES
SHUTTERBOX
SKULL MAN, THE
SNOW DROP
SORCERER HUNTERS
STONE
SUIKODEN III
SUKI
TAROT CAFÉ, THE
THREADS OF TIME
TOKYO BABYLON
TOKYO MEW MEW
TOKYO TRIBES
TRAMPS LIKE US
UNDER THE GLASS MOON
VAMPIRE GAME
VISION OF ESCAFLOWNE, THE
WARCRAFT
WARRIORS OF TAO
WILD ACT
WISH
WORLD OF HARTZ
X-DAY
ZODIAC P.I.

NOVELS

CLAMP SCHOOL PARANORMAL INVESTIGATORS
SAILOR MOON
SLAYERS

ART BOOKS

ART OF CARDCAPTOR SAKURA
ART OF MAGIC KNIGHT RAYEARTH, THE
PEACH: MIWA UEDA ILLUSTRATIONS
CLAMP NORTHSIDE
CLAMP SOUTHSIDE

ANIME GUIDES

COWBOY BEBOP
GUNDAM TECHNICAL MANUALS
SAILOR MOON SCOUT GUIDES

TOKYOPOP KIDS

STRAY SHEEP

CINE-MANGA®

ALADDIN
CARDCAPTORS
DUEL MASTERS
FAIRLY ODDPARENTS, THE
FAMILY GUY
FINDING NEMO
G.I. JOE SPY TROOPS
GREATEST STARS OF THE NBA
JACKIE CHAN ADVENTURES
JIMMY NEUTRON: BOY GENIUS, THE ADVENTURES OF
KIM POSSIBLE
LILO & STITCH: THE SERIES
LIZZIE MCGUIRE
LIZZIE MCGUIRE MOVIE, THE
MALCOLM IN THE MIDDLE
POWER RANGERS: DINO THUNDER
POWER RANGERS: NINJA STORM
PRINCESS DIARIES 2, THE
RAVE MASTER
SHREK 2
SIMPLE LIFE, THE
SPONGEBOB SQUAREPANTS
SPY KIDS 2
SPY KIDS 3-D: GAME OVER
TEENAGE MUTANT NINJA TURTLES
THAT'S SO RAVEN
TOTALLY SPIES
TRANSFORMERS: ARMADA
TRANSFORMERS: ENERGON

You want it? We got it!
A full range of TOKYOPOP
products are available now at:
www.TOKYOPOP.com/shop

09.21.04T

ALSO AVAILABLE FROM TOKYOPOP®

MANGA

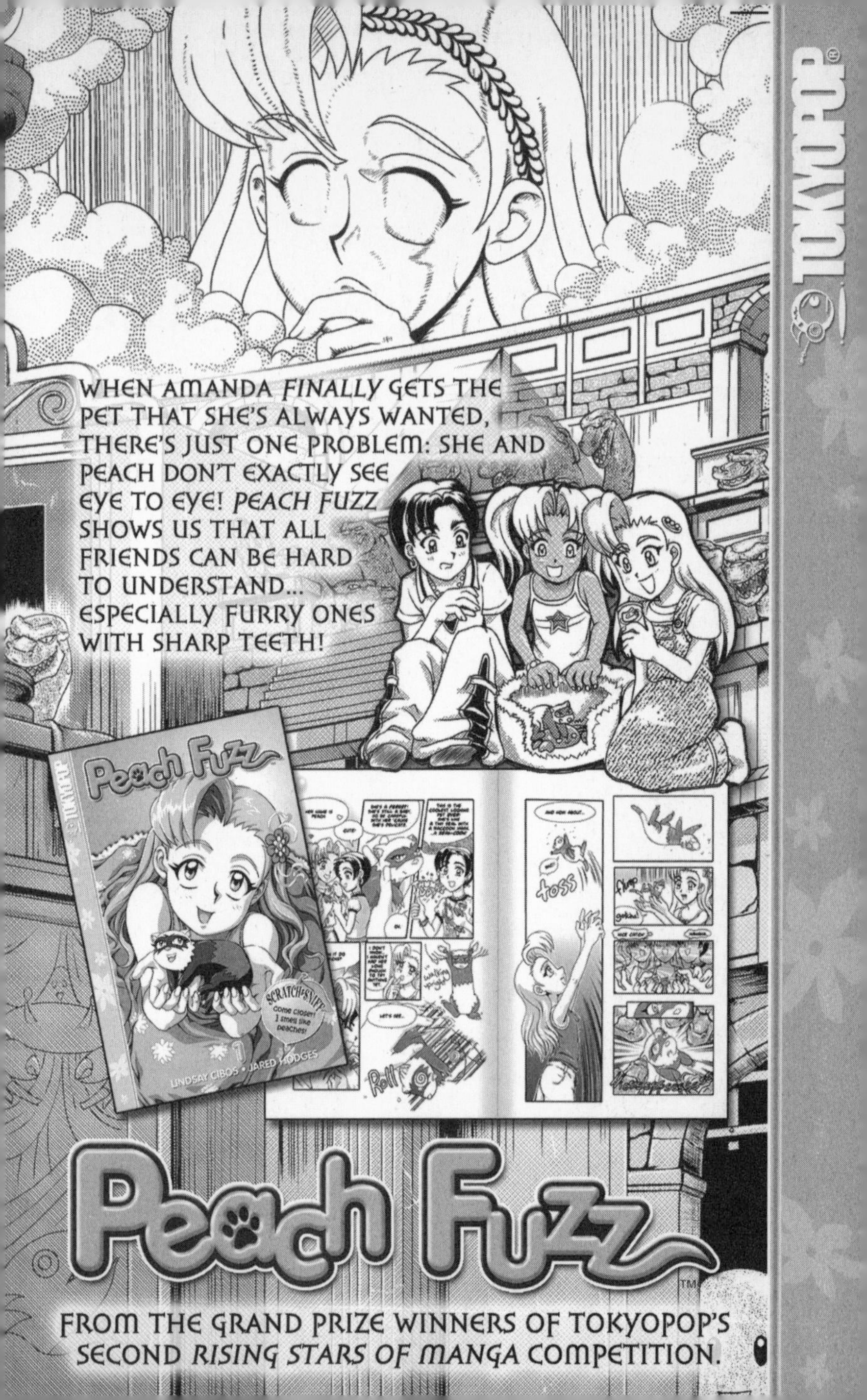
TOKYOPOP
WHEN AMANDA *FINALLY* GETS THE PET THAT SHE'S ALWAYS WANTED, THERE'S JUST ONE PROBLEM: SHE AND PEACH DON'T EXACTLY SEE EYE TO EYE! *PEACH FUZZ* SHOWS US THAT ALL FRIENDS CAN BE HARD TO UNDERSTAND... ESPECIALLY FURRY ONES WITH SHARP TEETH!
Peach Fuzz
SCRATCH+SNIFF! Come closer! I smell like peaches!
1
LINDSAY CIBOS • JARED HODGES
toss
Roll
Peach Fuzz™
FROM THE GRAND PRIZE WINNERS OF TOKYOPOP'S SECOND *RISING STARS OF MANGA* COMPETITION.